Inventing the Berbers

THE MIDDLE AGES SERIES

Ruth Mazo Karras, Series Editor

Edward Peters, Founding Editor

A complete list of books in the series is available from the publisher.

INVENTING THE BERBERS

History and Ideology in the Maghrib

RAMZI ROUIGHI

PENN

UNIVERSITY OF PENNSYLVANIA PRESS

PHILADELPHIA

Published by
University of Pennsylvania Press
Philadelphia, Pennsylvania 19104-4112
www.upenn.edu/pennpress

Printed in the United States of America on acid-free paper
1 3 5 7 9 10 8 6 4 2

Library of Congress Cataloging-in-Publication Data

Names: Rouighi, Ramzi, author.
Title: Inventing the Berbers: history and ideology in the Maghrib / Ramzi Rouighi.
Other titles: Middle Ages series.
Description: 1st edition. | Philadelphia: University of Pennsylvania Press, [2019] | Series: The Middle Ages series | Includes bibliographical references and index.
Identifiers: LCCN 2018051027 | ISBN 9780812251302 (hardcover)
Subjects: LCSH: Berbers—Historiography. | Berbers—History—Sources. | Berbers—Africa, North—History. | Africa, North—History—647-1517. | Berbers—Ethnic identity.
Classification: LCC DT193.5.B45 R68 2019 | DDC 961/.004933—dc23
LC record available at https://lccn.loc.gov/2018051027

Contents

Introduction

Berbers, Maghrib: the people, their country. Everybody knows that, and that is what everybody knows. But it has not always been the case. Before Muslim Arab conquerors began using the word بربر (*barbar*) to refer to people who lived in what they called "the West" (*al-maghrib*), both people and region were known by a host of other names. In fact, before Berber and Maghrib, no one thought that the inhabitants of northwest Africa belonged together or that the entire landmass represented a single unit. The first time anyone thought that was in Arabic. Trying to understand this shift from one set of names to another, one map to another, a historian faces a series of challenges that can be separated into two general kinds. First, there are challenges arising from the handling of the sources, which tend to be late and not written to address such a question. Second, there are hurdles pertaining to the assumptions of modern historians. These include deeply held notions about the relation between collective identity (nation), country, religion, and language; and a centuries-long history of interpreting medieval sources in a way that reinforces these assumptions.[1]

If this were not enough, as modern academics conferred on the Berbers characteristics of prenational groups like the Franks and the Goths, they also envisaged their reduced nationhood. For under French colonial domination, a modern Berber nation-state was simply not in the cards. After the Second World War, the reaction against the devastations of nationalism and racism did not extend to the category Berbers, which did not benefit from the critical energy of that reaction. Instead, the category remained mired in discussions of cultural heritage, victimized ethnic identity, and national aspirations. The national independence of Morocco and Algeria, but not Berberia, situated Berber identity both at the infranational level and as a counter nationalism but with a sense of Berber temporal precedence (native, original, etc.) and medieval Arabization and Islamization through a mixing with Arabs.[2] These processes are reflected in the predominant place that anthropology, together with linguistics, occupies in the study of Berbers. Unpacking the entanglements created by modern relations and forms of knowing helps identify defining modalities of what it means to be Berber.

Together, these issues have combined to produce a peculiar consensus: the Berbers are the indigenous inhabitants of the Maghrib, their homeland. The basic idea is that even if the categories shifted after the seventh century, the people still had the same ancestors. For many reasons, however, this is not an acceptable position. No one would equate, say, Roman and Italian or Hun and Hungarian. Doing so would banish what historians identify as the stuff of history, and replace it with the stuff of ideology. But that is exactly what the early Arabic authors did. They displaced the old categories by adding Berber to them, creating a de facto equivalency among all of them: the Hawwāra became Hawwāra Berbers; the Zanāta, Zanāta Berbers; and all became Berbers. They also projected all these categories back into a remote past. They did not think the Berbers were indigenous, as moderns do, but they made them the descendants of Noah or tied them to some other ancient story. But for the historian, the phenomenon is still the same: at a certain point in time, under conditions that need to be ascertained, the Arabs began to populate their Maghrib with Berbers. I call this process Berberization, and it is the subject of this book.

Berberization was slow, but it eventually made associating the Berbers with the Maghrib seem natural. Even today, stating that the Berbers came to be thought of as the indigenous inhabitants of North Africa under specific historical conditions elicits immediate puzzlement. Other than academic historians and a few historically minded others who would find the historicity of a social category banal, most people might consider that whether one calls them Berbers or something else, the people were the same. And since their ancestors lived in the area for the longest time, they were indigenous. In the words of an anthropologist of Morocco, scratch a Moroccan, find a Berber.[3] Perhaps, but thinking in this particular way is not natural, either. Instead, thinking historically about social categories—how they become ordinary, and how people use them to order their world—situates them in relation to both modern and premodern ideologies and scholarly crochets.

Defining Origins

Many studies on the Maghrib and its history begin with an attempt to define the Berbers as a way of introducing subject matter and cast of characters.[4] These introductions usually include a discussion of the etymology of the word, its ties to the word *barbarian* and perhaps to the memory of the collapse of the tower of Babel. While offering a few anecdotes on the subject may satisfy the requirements of an introduction, a proper definition requires a degree of accuracy and coherence that has usually led those historians who have tried to define the Berbers to consult experts in related fields, such as anthropology, archaeology, and linguistics.

For historical reasons, French has been the language of the most serious attempts to define the Berbers. The best available synthesis in English is the one co-authored by medievalist Michael Brett and archaeologist Elizabeth Fentress, which takes into account the most important statements in the field and gives an accurate representation of the state of the question.[5] As they endeavored to formulate a coherent definition of the Berbers, Brett and Fentress sought to clear a series of obstacles. Because of its quality, their definitional effort is a convenient way to introduce the subject to nonspecialists and give a sense of what this study intends to overcome.

Who are the Berbers and who counts as a Berber, according to Brett and Fentress?

> Just as the dialects are often mutually incomprehensible, so the people themselves are extremely heterogeneous: the existence of an ethnically unified "people" is no more demonstrable for the past than it is today. Indeed, there are a bewildering number of cultures, economies and physical characteristics. At best we can define Berbers as Mediterranean. In terms of their physical anthropology they are more closely related to Sicilians, Spaniards and Egyptians than to Nigerians, Saudi Arabians or Ethiopians: more precise characteristics are conspicuous by their absence, as a recent attempt at mapping a broad range of genetic traits has shown. We are thus immediately thrown into the problem of whom we are going to call a Berber and why.[6]

Immediately, Brett and Fentress encounter the problem of the ethnic heterogeneity of the Berbers, which appears as a problem only because they assume that the Berbers formed a unit of some sort. If not ethnographic unity, however, then perhaps physical anthropology—in other words, bodies and their appearance—could deliver a unity of "looks." It does not. After physical anthropology, Brett and Fentress make a foray into linguistics bringing into focus another basis for a definition of the Berbers: "The most common response [to the problem of whom one calls a Berber and why] is linguistic: Berbers are defined as people speaking Berber languages. . . . Indeed, one of the things that sets the Berbers apart is their language. . . . This was often commented on in the past, and a common myth links the odd-sounding language to the name 'Berber.' . . . The Berber dialects are part of the language group, the Afro-Asiatic, which comprises the Semitic languages and Ancient Egyptian."[7] Linguists use formal properties of living languages such as Sīwī and Arabic to classify them within language families like Berber and Semitic. The study of a number of related languages allows linguists to reconstruct the features of the parent language.[8] So, although proto-Berber and proto-Semitic are not extant or attested, it is still possible for linguists to know enough to distinguish between them, even if, in the case of these two families, they share a great many features because both split from the same parent language known as Afroasiatic. Understandably, dating the differentiation of undocumented languages and situating their bifurcation geographically is complicated and involves a lot of guessing. Yet, there is a great deal of good science behind it. When it comes to proto-Berber, the consensus is that it split from northern Afroasiatic somewhere in eastern Africa and then spread westward from there. There is less of a consensus about the date of that event, or events, but it varies from around 9,000 to only 3,000 years ago—a staggering range. Even as they work to reach more precise estimations, however, for linguists the question of the origins of Berber is largely settled. Like Arabic and Punic, Berber came from the East, just earlier than they did.

Brett and Fentress repeat a statement that is very important among specialists: "What sets the Berbers apart is their language." That is a good basis for deciding whether an individual or group is Berber:

> The ability to speak a Berber language gives us an objective basis for asserting that a given individual is Berber . . . but if we restrict ourselves to a linguistic definition of Berbers when discussing their history there will be few groups we can discuss with certainty. A cultural definition appears more promising, but when applied to the past becomes unsatisfactory. Unfortunately, this is a common procedure: perceptions of Berber culture derived from modern anthropology are often casually back-projected to antiquity. Worse, they are then used to justify a judgment that Berbers were culturally immobile.[9]

Brett and Fentress are correct: until the seventeenth century, sources in Berber languages are relatively rare, fragmented, and not evenly distributed.[10] They do not explain why they believe that the extremely heterogeneous Berbers and their bewildering number of cultures, economies, and physical characteristics have a single history. But they are right about the circularity involved in projecting modern representations into the distant past and then using them as evidence of cultural stasis. Surprisingly, the conclusion Brett and Fentress draw from this sensible observation takes them in an entirely different direction: "The least unsatisfactory solution seems to be to use the term 'Berber' in the broader sense of those groups who were perceived to be indigenous North Africans, both in antiquity and in the middle ages, as well as anyone who is still perceived that way today."[11] More significant than the lack of sources to shed light on what people might have perceived in the past, let alone whether they could even have perceived someone to be an indigenous North African, the notion of indigeneity allows Brett and Fentress to tag those human beings for whom there are only archaeological artifacts as Berber or proto-Berber—not to be confused with the proto-Berber of linguists.

The notion that all prehistoric human settlements found in North Africa are related to the Berbers is not universally accepted, however. In her excellent presentation of the state of archaeological knowledge on the subject, Malika Hachid argues that Capsian and Mechtoid civilizations combined to form proto-Berbers at a particular time, between 11,000 and 10,000 BP. This is how she explains it: "If we have somewhat insisted on Capsian portable art and then on parietal art from the Saharan Atlas it is because we consider Capsian Protomediterraneans to be the artisans of Berber identity and culture to which the Mechtoids contributed as they integrated.[12] When it comes to their language, if the Capsians brought with them the rudiments of the Berber language, they could not but absorb some aspects of the language of the Mechtoids."[13] For Hachid, the Capsians "brought with them" the foundations of the Berber language from the East, which makes it, but not them, not indigenous. By absorbing some of the language of the Mechtoids, the Capsian Protomediterraneans indigenized Berber—at least in part. The total absence of evidence of Mechtoid or Capsian languages is not critical because Hachid's Berberness (*Berberité*) is as it turns out tied to art. In spite of Hachid's timorous statements about the lack of "a perfect homology between human type and culture," she uses categories such as "robust negroid" and "fine negroid" to discuss the geographic, ethnic, but not racial, origins of people who might have combined to form the proto-Berbers.[14] More than how she arrived at her conclusion, however, the idea that proto-Berbers emerged only 10,000 years or so ago, or maybe only 7,000 years ago in the Sahara, leaves us with a very long time of non-Berber human presence in the area from the Atlantic to the Nile and from the Mediterranean to the Sahara. Likewise, without a linguistic definition, there is no reason why the proto-Berbers could not be proto-Algerians or proto-Maghribīs.

But obviously, as Brett and Fentress' definition illustrates, not everyone is willing to give up on the linguistic factor, "one of the things that set the Berbers apart."[15] Naturally, the appearance of proto-Berbers is not innocuous. It is tied to the question of indigeneity, which has not been the friend of historicizing, at least when it comes to preventing anachronism. In any case, from the point of view of indigeneity, the word Berber is problematic: "Of course, even the use of the name 'Berber' is somewhat arbitrary: it is of external origin, and certainly not a Berber word. . . . The word for Berber today is either '*Tamazight*' or '*Imazighen*', the first referring to their language, the second to the people who use it."[16] What is significant here, more than what category to use, is that Brett and Fentress deem the word Berber unsuitable, not because it lumps together a multitude of groups and occults the temporal specificity of documented collective categories and not because there is anything wrong with the linguistics behind it, but purely because it is an exonym.

They contrast the foreignness of the category with the indigeneity of the people. This too is critical. For behind the act of defining is the discourse on the indigenous origins of the Berbers. But since each discipline produces its own timeline for the "emergence of the Berbers," definitions that incorporate all these timelines have a hard time reconciling them. If there is a consensus among archaeologists, linguists, and biologists, however, it is for dating the origin of Berber long before "the term [was] first recorded in Arab authors."[17] What should stand out here is the reliance on philology (etymology), physical anthropology and archaeology, cultural anthropology, and linguistics—in short, everything but history—for a definition of the Berbers.

Since Brett and Fentress mention genetics and since that subfield of biology has been completely transformed following the sequencing of the human genome in 2000, it may be useful to highlight the contribution of biology to the Berberization of the remote past.[18] When it comes to biology, however, the word *origin* does not always refer to the same event. On the one hand, there are the origins of all life-forms on earth, which go back millions of years. As complex living organisms, the Berbers have their origins in early amino acids and other life-supporting molecules. The Berbers are also great apes and therefore share with all humans an original moment of distinction from other hominids. In this respect, the origins of the Berbers are the same as those of New Yorkers and Indonesians.

In another register, the question of origins refers back to biological differentiation between human populations in time. For this, specialists use a naturally occurring mutation that passes on to offspring to date the emergence of an ethnicity. In other words, the first bearer of the marker is the common forebear of an ethnos, a statistically defined population. As often happens, however, the mutation that best identifies an ethnic group through the male line (Y chromosome) does not quite match the chronological information carried by the female line (mtDNA), and the common male ancestor of a given group lived sometimes hundreds of years and thousands of miles apart from its common female ancestor.[19] For instance, the most common male marker among modern Berbers (E-M81) goes back 5,600 years, whereas some mtDNA lines go back 50,000 years—close to the time human language is thought to have first emerged.

Members of a population such as the Berbers carry a multiplicity of markers, some of which are much older than any evidence of modern human beings in northwest Africa. In other words, some of the ancestors of the Berbers must have come from somewhere else, something that hardly makes the Berbers special. Moreover, if one identifies the Berbers not with those markers prevalent among current populations, as is common practice, but rather with those mutations that took place exclusively in northwest Africa, only a fraction of today's Berbers would qualify. But when they collect data from contemporary speakers of Berber languages and use them to produce Berber ancestors who lived thousands of years ago, biologists contribute to populating that past with Berbers. Until they test ancient and even fossil DNA, Berber DNA remains tied to modern populations who speak any one of the many Berber languages. Once we have Numidian DNA, we will have a different kind of problem on our hands. Until then, it is fair to say that there is still a difference between being biologically related to someone and belonging to the same social group—as Americans know all too well.

Parallel to the effort to cast the Berbers as indigenous is the drive to show that they have a privileged relation with the land, their homeland (*Heimat*), and that they therefore have a more legitimate claim to it than anyone else did in the past or does in the present. But rather than try to set up indigeneity tests based on recent and even fossil DNA, attention to Berberization brings into focus the earliest time it was even possible to think that any group belonged in "North Africa." Unlike the formation of the protolanguage, the timing of a frequently occurring mutation, or the types of snails prehistoric groups seem to have really enjoyed, that is an event that historians can illuminate.

Historical Origins

No one was a Berber in northwest Africa before the seventh century, and that is when this study must begin. Then again, since the earliest extant Arabic sources are from a little more than a hundred years later, that starting point is somewhat truncated. To be more precise then, this study begins with the earliest references to Berbers in Arabic sources. What is striking about early Arabic usage is that the word Berber did not refer to anything like an ethnic group, not in the late antique Greek and Latin sense of what "ethnic" meant. In fact, it did not even mean anything like a "people," or at least not exclusively so. This means that more than a century after the first raids of the 640s, the transformation of various northwest African groups into Berbers, their Berberization, was incomplete. However, since the groups that came to be called Berber in Arabic had not formed a unified entity prior to the conquests, this is not very surprising. Had the Arabs found a single kingdom that ruled over what they called the Maghrib, they could have called its people Berbers and that would have been that. But that is simply not what happened. A little like the Indians of the Americas, most Berbers did not even know they were being Berberized, at least not for a while. Moreover, had the Arabs conquered only the region immediately west of Egypt, their Berbers might have been geographically limited to that area. They might have eventually called people in the western Maghrib Berbers too, but that is not necessary. The counterfactual highlights the importance of the conquests, an importance heightened by the circumstance that the earliest Arabic sources that mention the Berbers are narratives of these very conquests.

Not just chronologically, but also conceptually, Berberization begins with the conquests. The shift of perspective solves the problem of anachronism, while also making better sense of what took place. Imagining the conquests as triggering the Berberization of various groups allows us to resolve many of the apparent contradictions found in the sources and supports coherent historical explanations that connect events with their representation in the sources. The same approach can then be extended to later moments when the discourse on the Berbers was transformed, augmented, and adapted. Of course, treating the category as if it remained stable throughout the medieval period is also anachronistic. Methodologically, the study of the conquests can serve as a model of how to handle later instances of Berberization. In order to highlight this point, the book will describe multiple sites of Berberization and thus multiple historical origins. For without the reproduction of Berbers, they would have simply disappeared like the Numidians and the Getulians.

Framing the historical problem in these terms draws attention to the formation of an imperial knowledge in Arabic and to its circulation across a vast area. It also points to the eventual emergence of the Maghrib as the primary, if never lone, center of Berberization. In other words, our multiple sites were chronologically and geographically distinct. That, in turn, suggests that the historical record may not include all instances of Berberization since documentation on some of these sites may not exist. Yes, this poses a serious challenge to this attempt to understand Berberization, but historicizing begins with recognizing and accepting the limits of the knowable.

This book is not a history of the Berbers. The focus here is not on what happened to the Berbers, but rather on how it became possible to think that something happened to Berbers in the first place. The only claim this book makes is that the process was and remains historical. But as the discussion of how Berbers have been defined shows, a study of the making of Berbers faces multiple hurdles. By assuming the existence of Berbers in ancient times and by using the category as if what it signified remained unchanged over the entire medieval period, modern historians have engaged in a Berberization of their own. In fact, this modern Berberization has set the terms of historical research about a whole set of subjects, the conquests of the seventh century being only one. Berberization has even informed the prevailing periodization. These are not marginal considerations. And since the modern historiography of the medieval Maghrib has been entangled in the experience of French colonial domination and its aftermath, difficulties abound. Insisting on the historicity of social categories like Berber allows us to sidestep issues tied to the impact of colonialism and colonial historiography. However, just as it does not try to blame or shame medieval elites for exploiting their social subordinates or medieval intellectuals for representing the Berbers in ways that fit dominant ideologies, the book could not possibly fault modern intellectuals for doing the same. That is not the point here, even if it is conceivable that someone might misunderstand that.

The Mother of All Texts

At the heart of the functioning of Berberization in modern scholarship lies the Khaldunization of knowledge about the Maghrib, which began in the nineteenth century. Ibn Khaldūn's work is not just fundamental to the constitution of modern historical knowledge about the medieval Maghrib, but is part of the very matrix that has generated that knowledge itself. Without Ibn Khaldūn, there is simply no medieval Maghrib.[20] He stands at the end of the period and is, given his importance, the last medieval author. The Khaldunization of the field of knowledge has authorized, validated, and oriented scholarship, determined its questions, weighed on its explanations and interpretations, and even inspired its speculations.

The Ibn Khaldūn in question here is not the fourteenth-century author of the *Kitāb al-ʿibar* (Book of Examples) and its famous introduction (*al-Muqaddima*). Instead, he is the author of the *Histoire des Berbères* (1852–56), de Slane's French translation that gave language and structure to modern studies on the medieval Maghrib. Through repetition, duplication, and multiple variations on set themes, historians constituted a Khaldunian historical field, and as they did so, they established the textual basis for projecting the Berbers into the pre-Islamic past, which has precluded the identification, let alone study, of Berberization. On the one hand, the language of de Slane's translation made it harder to imagine that the Arabic category could have emerged in time or evolved over time. More importantly, the quality of Ibn Khaldūn's thinking and the breadth of his work conferred on the text an immediate authoritative character, especially because other medieval texts were either unknown or not easily accessible, and many of those who jumped on the Ibn Khaldūn bandwagon preferred French to the original Arabic. By the time the first serious historical studies on the medieval Maghrib began to appear, there was already consensus on the importance of Ibn Khaldūn. This explains why the framing of these studies, the questions they raised, and the periodization they established can all be attributed to this one text.

While it is critical to situate modern Ibn Khaldūn in modern Berberization, it is also necessary to remember that the work of the historian Ibn Khaldūn crystallized the extent of Berberization of discourse in the fourteenth century. Through Ibn Khaldūn, nevertheless, medieval Berberization comes to shed light on the constitution of a modern historical field and the specific conceptual entanglements it has created for historians, and—although not the focus of this book—for nonhistorians too.

Organization

This book is divided into three parts, each with two chapters. The first part, entitled "Medieval Origins," examines Arabic sources on the Berbers and relates them to political and other developments that illuminate them. Chapter 1 treats the question of origins as one about chronology and tries to ascertain the historical conditions that best illuminate the earliest references to the Berbers in Arabic. Since there was no preexisting people whom the Arabs simply called by a different name, the word Berber carried a range of meanings associated with specific social activities and institutions, chief among which was the military. The chapter contrasts the political situation in al-Andalus and the Maghrib to establish a shift in the usage of the category. Chapter 2 attempts to enshrine the historicity of the category by examining multiple sites of Berberization, from al-Andalus to the Maghrib and Egypt. The chapter demonstrates that the category did change, and that it was not the same everywhere.

In the second part of this book, the focus shifts to an analysis of the idea that the Berbers were a people and that the Maghrib was their homeland. Chapter 3 explores how medieval authors envisaged the Berbers by analyzing the functioning of genealogy (*'ilm al-nasab* or *'ilm al-ansāb*), paying close attention to their classificatory schemes and categories. But rather than consider the entire Arabic archive, the chapter examines a selection of documents that shed light on the organization and content of Ibn Khaldūn's work. Since Ibn Khaldūn's text comes to have such an immense place in modern historiography, the chapter serves also as an introduction to his medieval work. In the same fashion, Chapter 4 tests the idea that Arabic sources have always thought of the Maghrib as the country of the Berbers (*bilād al-barbar*). It too leads to Ibn Khaldūn and to his ideas on the subject. Looking to explain the circumstances that allowed medieval authors to conceive of the existence of the Berbers and the Maghrib in the remote past, these two chapters identify elements in the constitution of modern historical thinking on these same topics, with Ibn Khaldūn serving as the link between the two.

In Part III, modern Berberization comes into focus, through a consideration of select sites of modern Berberization. Given the importance of French colonial rule in Algeria, the chapters are concerned more narrowly with Algerian developments to identify critical elements in the modern making of the Berbers and to trace their evolution over time. Chapter 5 argues that the publication of de Slane's translation of Ibn Khaldūn was a major event in the formation of modern knowledge on the Berbers. Chapter 6 analyzes the historiography of the medieval Maghrib in the last century in order to explain why and how Berberization came to be hidden.

PART I

Medieval Origins

There is the prejudice of thinking the ancients better informed than ourselves about the times that lay nearer to them. The scholars of King Alfred's time [r. 871–99] knew much less about Anglo-Saxon origins than we do. Vico's warning against this prejudice is of great importance because, when developed on its positive side, it becomes the principle that the historian does not depend on an unbroken tradition for his knowledge but can reconstruct by scientific methods a picture of a past which he has not derived from any tradition whatever. This is the explicit denial that history depends on what Bacon called memory, or in other words the statements of authorities.

—R. G. Collingwood, *The Idea of History*

Chapter 1

Berberization and Its Origins

Starting with zero Berbers in northwest Africa, Arabic authors gradually populated the region they called the Maghrib with Berbers. They did not do so instantly or uniformly, but after a few centuries, there was no doubt that there had always been Berbers in the Maghrib. No one formed a plan to achieve the Berberization of the region and its peoples, and so early evidence comes in the form of fragmentary accounts and references. In early Arabic texts, and across a number of narrative genres and disciplines, we encounter different Berbers or rather different usages of the category Berber.[1] When we analyze these, the broad outlines of early Berberization become clear, although not without a serious effort on our part. The late date of extant sources, at least a century after the earliest raids west of Egypt, poses a serious challenge to the historian. The even later date of extant sources from the Maghrib poses another. Yet, taken together, early Arabic texts do allow us to reconstruct a chronology of political struggles and to use it to evaluate usage of the category Berber. Unfortunately, however, it is impossible to gauge the reaction of those the Arabs called Berbers—at least not for a while.

Before the West and Its Sources

Before the birth of the prophet Muḥammad (ca. 570), Arabians called Barbar (بربر) those who lived across the Red Sea in the area the ancient Greeks and Romans knew as Barbaria.[2] In so doing, they agreed with other ancient peoples.[3] Although late antique texts in Arabic are rare, one finds Barbaria and its Barbar in poems preserved and compiled in the eighth and ninth centuries. For example, a poem attributed to ʿUdayy b. Zayd (d. 587) mentions in the same line the people of Barbar (*āl barbar*) and al-Yaksūm (Axum), while another by the infinitely more famous Imru'u al-Qays (6th c.) has a passing reference to Barbar horses.[4] Without any doubt, Arabians were familiar with their neighbors to the west long before the first raids on northwest Africa in the 640s.[5] It is significant here that a certain fount of knowledge about these eastern Berbers, oral and written, existed in Arabia and in Arabic before the seventh century, because it explains why at least some references found in early Arabic sources do not refer to western Berbers. Not as significant, but still noteworthy, these early references had little to do with Berbers being barbarians—something that seems to distinguish Arabic sources from contemporary texts in other languages.

The ancient Barbaria of East Africa is well documented. It appears in the first-century *Periplus of the Erythrean Sea* and in the geography of Ptolemy (ca. 90–ca. 168).[6] The geographer Marcianus of Heraclea Pontica (fl. 400) refers to it in his *Periplus of the Outer Sea*.[7] Barbaria is again described as being across the Red Sea from Arabia in the famous sixth-century travelogue left by Cosmas Indicopleustes, and in the writings of his contemporary Stephanus of Byzantium.[8] In addition to geographical knowledge about the Red Sea coast and its peoples, Egyptians kept the knowledge of the existence of Barbaria to their south in the names of city gates and markets. In his chronicle of the conquest of Egypt, Ibn 'Abd al-Ḥakam (d. 871) mentions a Barbaria market (*sūq barbar*) in the city of Fusṭāṭ. While the inhabitants of Barbaria, barbarians, and Maghribī Berbers are all *barbar* (بربر) in Arabic, the absence of the definite article in *sūq barbar* means that the market was for merchandise from the region of Barbaria and thus is not a pre-Islamic reference to western Berbers.[9]

Early Arabic sources like conquest narratives (*futūḥ*) juxtaposed reports and traditions about eastern and western Berbers without trying to sort them out, leading to a degree of semantic instability.[10] In fact, it is not always clear whether the authors of these compilations believed the reports they wrote down pertained to eastern or western Berbers. For instance, in his description of raids conducted during the caliphate of 'Umar b. al-Khaṭṭāb (d. 644) against areas controlled by the Byzantine Romans, al-Wāqidī (d. 823) cited the presence of Berbers among other clearly East African groups: "In the Ṣa'īd, there were Nūba, Barbar (بربر), Daylam, Ṣaqāliba, Rūm, and Qibṭ; and the Rūm were dominant."[11] Elsewhere in the text, al-Wāqidī shares that "the king of Bujāwa and his ally the king of Nūba gathered those people around them from the land of the Nūba, the Bujāwa, and the Barbar (البربر) and they all came to Aswān."[12] In other instances, al-Wāqidī puts Berbers with Bujāwa, Nūba, and Fallāḥīn, and describes them with the Sūdān as people who use elephants in warfare.[13] While it is possible that the references here are to barbarians rather than Berbers, al-Wāqidī did not refer to any other barbarians and mentioned Berbers only in his reports about regions south of Egypt.

Similarly, East African Berbers appear in a tradition about the collection of the poll tax on non-Muslims (*jizya*). According to the historian al-Balādhurī (d. ca. 892), "[The prophet] Muḥammad took the *jizya* from the Zoroastrians of Hajar, [his caliph] 'Umar (d. 644) took it from the Zoroastrians of Fāris, and [the caliph] 'Uthmān (d. 656) took it from Barbar (*barbar*)."[14] In this report, both Hajar and Fāris are toponyms, and there is no reason to believe that Barbar refers to anything other than the region.

In a similar vein, when the great *literato* Ibn Quṭayba (d. ca. 889) gives a genealogy of the sons of the prophet Nūḥ (Noah) in his *Kitāb al-ma'ārif*, the inhabitants of Barbaria appear alongside other East Africans: "As for Kūsh and Kan'ān, various kinds (*ajnās*) of Sūdan [Blacks], the Nūba, the Zanj, the Qarān [Fazzān?], the Zaghāwa, the Ḥabasha, the Qibṭ, and Barbar are among their descendants."[15] In his section on the kings of Yemen, however, western Berbers enter the picture to remarkable effect: "Ifrīqis b. Abraha b. al-Rāyish raided in the direction of the West (*al-maghrib*) in the land of Barbar (*arḍ barbar*) until he reached Ṭanja [Tangier]. He transported the Berbers (*al-barbar*) from the land of Falasṭīn [Palestine], Miṣr [Egypt], and the Sāḥil [Red Sea coast but here Mediterranean?] until the areas where they live today. These Berbers belonged to those left over (*baqiya*) from those who killed Yūshu' b. Nūn. Ifrīqis is the one who built Ifrīqiyā, which was named after him. He ruled for a hundred and sixty four years."[16] There is nothing exceptional about a mythological king of Yemen going on campaign westward and reaching Barbaria (*arḍ barbar*). However, the next clause has him raiding all the way to Tangier, a land where Maghribī Berbers lived in the ninth century.[17] The oddity of the creature, or the collage, is even more striking as Ifrīqis takes Berbers from Palestine, Egypt, and Barbaria to the Maghrib with him—combining the story of Palestinian origins of the Maghribī Berbers with the existence of Berbers in East African Barbaria.[18] Luckily for us, Ibn Quṭayba and others did not always try to reconcile the information they culled from oral traditions and written records of varying origins. The narrative practices they subscribed to, especially those pertaining to faithfulness to the sources, account for the temporal, linguistic, and geographic heterogeneity of their reports, and thus of the presence of archaic or fossilized representations of the Berbers in relatively late texts.

The early medieval Arabic *barbar* (بربر) also conveyed the Greco-Latin understanding that barbarians spoke unintelligible languages. For example, al-Balādhurī recorded that "Ibn al-Kalbī [(d. ca. 819)] said: Ifrīqish b. Qays b. Sayfī al-Ḥimyarī conquered Ifrīqiyā in the pre-Islamic period (*jāhiliya*) and so it was named after him. He was the one who killed Jirjīr [Gregory] its king. He said about the Barābira: how predominant is the babble of these people. So, they were named Barābira."[19] It is in his work on the genealogies of southern Arabians that Ibn al-Kalbī mentioned this anecdote—or something close to it: "Ifrīqish b. Qays b. Ṣayfī is the one who conquered (*iftataḥa*) Ifrīqiyā, and it was named after him.[20] He also killed its king Jirjīr. And it is then that the Barbar received their name [because] he told them 'How plentiful is your babble!'"[21] Even if by the ninth century, Arabic authors tended to use this anecdote to refer to the Berbers of the Maghrib, it is improbable that the initial report or reports on which it is based originated in the Maghrib. On the one hand, one must acknowledge the relatively late date of Arabic texts emanating from the Maghrib compared to those from the East (Mashriq). On the other, since there is no evidence that pre-Islamic Arabians used the terms *barbarī/barbar* to describe non-Arabic speakers, it is likely that the earliest extant Arabic reports are translations or adaptations from languages like Greek. Yet, to express the idea of foreign speech and foreignness, Arabs had used *'ajam* and *'ajamī*, which pertained to Persians and their language. If one does not believe that the anecdotes are later adaptations of lore originating in lands where "barbarian" was the preferred term, one has to explain why Arabs preferred the loanword to their own. Moreover, since describing a Maghribī Berber language as *'ajamiyat al-barbar* became common without anyone noting that it was an odd, let alone pleonastic, construction, the idea that the Arabic word Berber is a simple loan from the Greek and Latin "barbarian" ignores the history of usage in Arabic.

Before the Arabs conquered their lands, Egyptians used the term "barbarian" to describe people who spoke languages unknown to them. In fact, it is possible that they used the term to refer to speakers of Berber languages living west of Egypt. In this case, Berber and "barbarian" would have applied to the same groups. Since Egypt was the point of departure of the earliest raids and military campaigns into northwest Africa, it is plausible that Arabs from Arabia did not really distinguish between Berber and barbarian but that Coptic and Greek speakers in Egypt did. With time, the distinction the latter made came to be represented in Arabic.

Learned or not, etymologies did not constitute the authoritative final word on how the Berbers received their name. Genealogy did. Even if etymologies were mostly entertaining, they do allow us to document the utilization of preexisting traditions about barbarians in the new imperial situation. At the same time, the military conquests gave the word Berber meanings that distinguished it from both "barbarian" and *ʿajam*. Most notably, in conquest narratives (*futūḥ*), Berber refers mostly to groups in northwest Africa. With time, this specialization in the usage became the most dominant one, though the memory of the Berbers of eastern Africa did not disappear.[22]

If the early Arabic category did not quite match the classical notion of barbarian, more scholars had to find a way of explaining how Berber came to refer to the peoples that inhabited the Maghrib. For Gabriel Camps, Berber became successful because it mapped onto a category that had broad usage and acceptance prior to the conquests. As he explained it, "The Berbers of the Arabs are the Moors of the Romans."[23] According to this understanding, instead of conquering the Berbers, the Arabs conquered the Moors (Lat. Mauri, sing. Maurus) and just called them by a "new" name. This new equation offers an elegant solution to the gap in the evidence, as Latin and Greek sources become scarce after the sixth century, and Arabic ones begin to appear only in the eighth.

In his excellent study of the Moors between the fourth century and the seventh, Yves Modéran thoroughly examined the use of the category in late antique sources. His goal was to determine the role of the populations named Moors, then Berbers, in the evolution of Roman Africa in the three centuries preceding the Arab conquest.[24] Noting the difficulties inherent in the use of "Berber" to analyze the pre-Islamic period, he commented on the scholarly practice of translating "Moor" as "Berber":

> [It] imposed itself immediately on the first historians of late antique Africa without any justification, and has remained unchanged until the present. In fact, as we shall see, if in the sixth century the Moor was still a native African (*autochtone*) whom the Romans considered to be "non-Romanized," he could possess a cultural complexity that is far from the "pure Berber" dear to nineteenth-century scholars.[25] In order to respect the sources, and avoid any anachronism and all ideological ambiguities

> [inherent] in the word "Berber," we will mostly speak here of "Moors." But as we will see, obvious stylistic reasons make it so that we could not avoid "Berber" in some sentences.[26]

Modéran is right to be distrustful of the anachronism at the heart of the equation. But it is sufficient here to point to the fact that for late antique authors the Moors were not barbarians and that they had nothing to do with East African Barbaria. Thus, Moor and Berber did not carry the exact same meanings—and this is so, even before analyzing the use of the category in Arabic after the conquests.

In any case, given the lack of contemporary evidence, it is impossible to know how the early conquerors conceived of the various groups they encountered during their protracted campaigns (640s–710s). The earliest uses of the category Berber in relation to Maghribīs emerged out of the confrontation of conquering armies with groups that exhibited distinct social, political, and cultural characteristics, an insight implicit in Gabriel Camps' equation. The analysis of the ways early narratives of the conquests deploy the category Berber requires an examination of the events they describe and of the factors influencing the recollections of Mashriqī writers of the ninth century.

How the West Was Made

Before the armies of the caliphs triggered a large-scale reordering of the political map in northwest Africa, three types of political arrangements had prevailed there. First, there were areas under direct Byzantine control, mostly in the East and centered on Carthage. Second, a number of tribes (*gentes*) were associated, more or less formally, with the Byzantines. Third, there were *gentes* and others that were politically autonomous. Parallel to these arrangements, a network of unevenly distributed Christian churches sustained an array of political relations and social distinctions that did not neatly map onto imperial ones. The Byzantines ruled coastal areas from the area west of Egypt they called Libya Inferior to Libya Superior (Cyrenaica), Tripolitania, and then all the way around the coast through Byzacena, Zeugitana (Africa Proconsularis), Numidia, and Mauretania. They also controlled a small area in the West, what they also called Mauretania, around Septem (Ceuta) and Tingis (Tangier). Given the role of their naval forces in securing control over those areas, Byzantine influence did not extend too far from the coasts, relying mostly on a network of strategically placed military outposts to secure their domination. In the broadest possible comparative terms, the Byzantines controlled no more than a third of the medieval Maghrib, if that. Though it is reasonable to believe with most historians that these were the most densely populated areas, we must note, also with most historians and archaeologists, that documentation is scarce for most areas of what became the Maghrib, and that we hardly know anything about vast expanses. Yet there is no doubt that in the less-known areas there were settled and nomadic peoples and that thinking of them in negative terms, as our sources often do, as either non-Byzantine barbarians or non-Christians pagans, says very little about them.

As for the Muslim conquests, it is worth insisting that they occurred in stages, took many forms, and spanned many decades.[27] The earliest raids into Cyrenaica and Tripolitania, which followed the conquest of Alexandria in 641, did not always lead to a settlement of Arabs or the establishment of lasting political ties. Instead, Arab generals based in Egypt led armies westward and went back to home base with loot. Over time, the successive waves of conquerors elicited vigorous resistance in northwest Africa and led to the gradual reorganization of the political map away from arrangements that had characterized the preconquests period. Whatever their makeup or ideological orientation, various groups in northwest Africa came to recognize the importance of new centers of power, especially as political struggles in the Mashriq had an immediate impact on the identity of the leaders, the course of action they took, and the composition of their armies.

Following the First Civil War (656–61) in Arabia and the imposition of Umayyad rule in Damascus (661–750), military expansion in the western territories received renewed impetus. Perhaps the most significant signal of the imperial designs of the Umayyads was the establishment of a garrison town (*qayrawān*) in Ifrīqiyā in 670. Under the leadership of ʿUqba b. Nāfiʿ, al-Qayrawān became the capital of Arab presence in the West. This did not mean, however, the immediate elimination of the Byzantines, who remained a political player for three more decades until 698. After the defeat of the Byzantines, the Umayyad masters of al-Qayrawān tried to expand their control beyond that small region.

As they raided, imposed tributes and taxes, and accumulated captives, the imperial armies came up against a number of polities, which had gained influence since the reordering of power begun in the 640s.[28] The ability of these groups to raise armies made them formidable opponents and useful allies. After a protracted series of battles, intrigues, alliances, victories, and reversals of fortune, some northwest Africans joined with the rulers of al-Qayrawān. Although their social background is not known, many of them became clients or *mawālī* (sing. *mawlā*) of Arab leaders, a status that gave them new political and legal standing. These clients fought alongside the Arabs and, as far as one can tell, came to espouse Mashriqī ideologies in vogue at the time. Northwest African clients became a vital military force especially because they were able to raise armies in the region, a feature that made them attractive to generals who would have had to wait for reinforcements from Egypt or from the Umayyad capital of Damascus in Syria (al-Shām). However, their contribution to the new order did not extend beyond this military role, since the administration remained tightly in the hands of the conquerors.

In the first decade of the eighth century, an Umayyad army reached the African *finis terra* on the Atlantic coast, their forays into the pre-Saharan and Saharan regions remaining rather limited. The spectacular capture of the Mediterranean cities of Sabta (Septem) and Tangier gave the governor of al-Qayrawān control over the major cities and routes of northwest Africa, and made him the most powerful man west of Egypt. With that, the conquest of the Maghrib was over—at least as far as the *futūḥ* narratives are concerned. The Umayyads (661–750) chose this juncture to make the Maghrib a single province (*wilāya*) ruled from its base in Ifrīqiyā.[29] This was the first time in recorded history that the entirety of northwest Africa became an administrative unit.[30] The creation of a province was the expression of the desire to bring taxation, military organization, and leadership in the hands of Mūsā b. Nuṣayr, the newly appointed governor. From then on, the Maghrib was also the Umayyad province whose capital was al-Qayrawān.

In 711, the new governor of Tangier, the *mawlā* Ṭāriq b. Ziyād, crossed the Mediterranean into Iberia with an army predominantly composed of northwest African supporters of the Umayyads.[31] A few months later, Mūsā b. Nuṣayr followed him there and took over command of the imperial armies. In a few years, the Umayyad troops accumulated victories and pushed their raids far into the northern regions. Al-Andalus was born. The Arab elite put in place a system of precedence that guaranteed them preferential treatment. It ensured that the prophet Muḥammad's kin and those whose ancestors were his companions received a greater share in the distribution of booty, tax revenues, and honors. In addition, tensions between northern and southern Arabs, which had been so critical to the character of Umayyad rule in the Mashriq, reached the Maghrib.[32] The military elite supporting the Umayyad dynasty fought hard to establish and maintain mechanisms that distinguished between Muslims. In general, Maghribīs, *mawālī* or not, were on the receiving end of these policies, even if they contributed troops to the conquest of Iberia and to the pacification of the Maghrib.

By the 730s, Umayyad rule came under attack in the Mashriq and the Maghrib. The grievances of opponents included the nepotism, rapaciousness, and arbitrary brutality of Umayyad officials. In this regard, the discontent of those who had reasons to expect something from the government of al-Qayrawān did not differ greatly from that of non-Arab and Arab Muslims in other regions. Imperial expansion had made winners of some and losers of many. In 739 and 740, rebellions spread from al-Qayrawān to Tangier, seriously threatening Umayyad rule in the Maghrib. Anti-Umayyad Arabs, some of whom had fled Umayyad police in the Mashriq, formed alliances with rebel groups. In al-Andalus, a similar rebellion in 741–72 showed that disunity among Arabs could seriously challenge the status quo. Inter-Arab strife was resolved by the arrival of an army of Syrians, which utilized an Umayyad-inflected Arabism to overcome the rivalries and jealousies between northern and southern Arabs, and between newcomers and "older" families.[33]

When the ʿAbbāsids and their supporters put an end to Umayyad rule in Damascus in 750, al-Qayrawān hailed the new rulers.[34] Al-Andalus took another route. The pro-Umayyad camp welcomed the arrival of the sole surviving member of the Umayyad dynasty and in 756, after routing a vigorous opposition, declared an independent Umayyad emirate in al-Andalus. When we begin to have sources in the late eighth century, the political situation in the Maghrib presents us with a few rival kingdoms that, other than the Aghlabids (800–909) in Ifrīqiyā, had clearly non-Mediterranean centers of power. Whether the Barghawāṭa on the Atlantic, the Idrīsids in Fez, the Midrārids in Sijilmāsa, or the Rustamids in Tāhart, the new capitals were at a safe distance from raids and large-scale invasions from the sea.[35] Ideologically, these Muslim kingdoms marked their autonomy from the ʿAbbāsids of Baghdad by favoring teachings marginalized in the Mashriq.

The Berbers and the Conquest of the Maghrib

As a literary genre, the narratives of the Islamic conquests (*futūḥ*) came after the biographies of the Prophet (*sīra*) and his companions, and the formation of the early community of believers. The stories compiled in them record the making of an empire, the names of those who participated in its campaigns, and the tales that circulated about them. Within a teleological frame tale and with presentist overtones, *futūḥ* authors recounted a series of stories of piety, martial prowess, and administrative genius, as well as their negative equivalents. At the same time, these accounts contain information about the conditions under which this or that area had first come under the rule of the caliph—by force or by treaty—an issue that had gained new significance after the ʿAbbāsids toppled the Umayyads and sought to consolidate their own power. Lodged at the heart of the succession of narrative units (or sections) is a multiplicity of intra-Muslim arguments with legal, theological, literary, and of course political implications.

Futūḥ authors such as al-Wāqidī, al-Balādhurī, and Ibn ʿAbd al-Ḥakam prided themselves on relaying their reports with the proper pedigree. Like *ḥadīth* specialists, they included a chain of transmission that referred back to a war veteran, an eyewitness, a known official written document, or the words of someone, preferably reliable and notable, who reported something relevant to their story. These reports did not always share the perspective or language of the *futūḥ* authors. In spite of the overall teleological frame, the language of the building blocks of these narratives, the individual narrative units (*akhbār*), was often archaic, or at least older, especially in its use of categories, and necessitated authorial intervention to bring it up to par with contemporary commonplaces and worldview.

There should be no doubt that prior to the Arab conquests, the political conditions that prevailed in northwest Africa militated against the idea that Romanized and non-Romanized "natives" (Moors, various *gentes*, and barbarians) formed a single people with a common ancestry and past and that the Arabs conquered their lands and won them to Islam. Yet, this is exactly the idea that frames the *futūḥ* narratives. In the tales of the conquest of the Maghrib, or its "opening" to or by Islam, the Berbers are an essential ingredient and a vital catalyst enabling and ordering the narration. But, and there should be no doubt about this as well, *futūḥ* authors never described a conquest of *the* Berbers, and only of raids (*ghazw*) on particular tribes that were Berber and cities that were inhabited by Berbers or surrounded by them.[36] This is the case even as their texts present the Berbers as a single people. In other words, there is no extant text entitled *The Conquest of the Berbers* and no section with that title within those that are available. For a number of reasons, the authors simply did not think like that.[37] Instead, they told the story of the making of the empire in the guise of the victory and spread of Islam.

The richest early source of information on the conquests of the Maghrib and al-Andalus, Ibn ʿAbd al-Ḥakam's *History of the Conquests of Egypt, North Africa, and Spain*, presents us with a variety of usages for the category Berbers, including the ones already discussed above. The Berbers first appear in an introductory section on the Copts, which precedes the narration of the conquest of Egypt.[38] As characters in the saga of conquest, the Berbers receive their own introduction, in the form of a genealogy inserted between the tale of the conquest of the Fayyūm and that of Barqa (Cyrenaica).[39]

> The Berbers were in Palestine. Their king was Jālūt [Goliath]. When the prophet Dāwūd [David] killed him, the Berbers left [Palestine] in direction of the Maghrib until they arrived in Lūbiya and Marāqiya both of which are two districts (*kūra*) in western Egypt (*miṣr al-gharbiya*) that were irrigated by rain and not the Nile river.[40] The Berbers separated there: The Zanāta and Maghīla advanced into the western areas (*maghrib*) and inhabited the mountains.[41] The Luwāta advanced and inhabited the land of Anṭābulus [Pentapolis], which is Barqa.[42] [The Berbers] separated in this Maghrib and spread in it until they reached the Sūs.[43] The Hawwāra settled in the city of Labda [Leptis] and the Nafūsa settled in the city of Sabrata leading those Romans who had lived there to emigrate. The Afāriqa who had accepted Roman domination remained there and paid tribute as they had done to all those who conquered their country.[44]

Other than the reference to their settlement in the Sūs, the Berbers seem to have been an eastern phenomenon, limited to the former Byzantine Zeugitana (Africa Proconsularis), Byzacena, Tripolitania, Cyrenaica (Libya Superior), and Libya (Inferior). While there is a notable gap in the information about the region between Numidia and Mauretania II (Tingis and Septem), this notice generally covers Byzantine-dominated areas. The Maghrib in question here is nothing but the Byzantine areas, and thus those taken over by the Umayyads. Even if there is no explicit reference to the Arabs, the very existence of the Afāriqa (Romans of the province of Africa) and their behavior toward conquerors assume the Muslim conquest of Ifrīqiyā and its seizure from the Byzantines. This early report, which lacks information about those who inhabited most of what will become the Maghrib, enables a crucial transformation of Moors and various *gentes* that had no particular sense of unity into Berbers.

Paradoxically perhaps, the act of insertion of the Berbers into the text is the most significant aspect of the tale of the conquest of the Maghrib, for it masks a patent lack of knowledge about the region and its inhabitants. Interestingly, after the formal introduction of the Berbers, the category is then absent from the narrative of the episodes that follow, including that of the conquest of Ifrīqiyā. Importantly, the insertion of the genealogy of the Berbers before the conquest of Barqa situates them geographically in the eastern Maghrib. The author has no use for the category until the tale of the death of ʿUqba b. Nāfiʿ at the hands of Kusayla b. Lamzam near Tahūdha (682), a full forty years after the first raids into Barqa. From the story of that battle, through the tale of the Berber queen al-Kāhina, and until the completion of the narrative of the conquest of the Maghrib, the word Berber appears ten times. When the author moves on to the conquest of al-Andalus, the word becomes more frequent. Since Ibn ʿAbd al-Ḥakam is often quoting from preexisting material, oral or written, it is worth noting that the reports he compiled about the conquest of the Maghrib have less use for the category than those relating to al-Andalus. As we shall see, this may not be accidental.

When the word Berber does appear in the tales of the deeds of Umayyad generals (ʿUqba b. Nāfiʿ, Ḥassān b. al-Nuʿmān, Zuhayr b. Qays, and Mūsā b. Nuṣayr), it identifies a vague enemy, without specific information about tribe, ethnicity, or geographical origin—the genealogy filling that knowledge gap: "ʿUqba b. Nāfiʿ arrived at Tahūdha with very few men. There, Kusayla b. Lamzam stood against him with a large number of Romans and Berbers, having already heard that ʿUqba had been deserted by a great number."[45] Ibn ʿAbd al-Ḥakam then gives a different account of the death of ʿUqba, which presents interesting features:

> ʿUqba advanced to the Sūs. He came up against [the army of] a man among the non-Arabs (*ʿajam*) with thirty thousand men. [With ʿUqba], there was ʿUmar b. ʿAlī and Zuhayr b. Qays who had six thousand men. God vanquished the man. Then the son of al-Kāhina the Berber (*ibn al-kāhina al-barbarī*)[46] followed ʿUqba and buried every water source he used until he arrived in the Sūs without realizing what the Berber had done. . . . When he left [the Sūs] to return [to Ifrīqiyā], the waters had been sullied, and the Berbers rallied against him . . . until ʿUqba . . . was killed.[47]

Here again "Berber" fills in for precise information, like the name of al-Kāhina's son and the identity of the enemy.[48]

In the last report about his death, 'Uqba first defeats the Berbers then dies at their hands: "He went with his army until he fought against the Berbers who were unbelievers and they were all killed. . . . Then he left [Ifrīqiyā] to battle the Berbers and had with him five thousand men from Egypt. . . . He and all those with him were killed. 'Uqba died in the year sixty-three."[49] Again, these reports establish the location of the battle, its date, and the names of those with 'Uqba when he died. What kind of Berbers were these? Who were their leaders? Such questions are unanswerable precisely because "Berber" is a tag for the antagonist in the story, the enemy.[50]

When the next imperial hero, Ḥassān b. al-Nu'mān, enters the scene he faces defeat at the hands of al-Kāhina, "who was at the time queen of the Berbers."[51] After a strange turn of events, Ḥassān appoints one of al-Kāhina's two sons as the head of a "group of Butr Berbers" (*jamā'a min al-barbar min al-butr*) in his own army, and then al-Kāhina is defeated and dies.[52] Nothing in the text even suggests that there was a single Berber kingdom and that its queen ruled over all the Berbers. At best, al-Kāhina was the queen of some Berbers—unless the term Berber applied only to her subjects. At the same time, it is not surprising to see a female antagonist raised to the rank of queen.[53] All non-Arab females who appear in these stories are queens and princesses. In this example, the fact that the Berbers have a queen raises the profile of Ḥassān's story.

Shortly after the introduction of the Butr, we learn that they constitute, with the Barānis, the two kinds of Berbers: "Ḥassān settled in al-Qayrawān, built its Friday mosque, organized the administration, and imposed the *kharāj* tax on the non-Arabs (*'ajam*) of Ifrīqiyā and on those who lived with them [believing] in Christianity from among the Berbers, the majority of whom were Barānis, the Butr being a small minority."[54] In this passage, *'ajam* does not seem to apply to Berbers, although the basis of the distinction between Berber non-Arabs and others is not clear. On the other hand, the distinction between Butr and Barānis Berbers seems promising. Unfortunately, information within the text about the various groups described as such does not allow us to discern a socioeconomic, cultural, or linguistic reality behind them.[55] These two categories do not correspond to any known groups of Africans before or even after the conquests; this text is the earliest record of the classification of the Berbers into two groups. In any case, Butr and Barānis appear only in the context of the tales of the conquests, though later authors who referred back to the tales also relay this distinction made in them. That is not to say that the distinction did not originally correspond to some political or social reality in the Maghrib or al-Andalus at the time of the conquests. But by the time the *futūḥ* narratives were compiled in the Mashriq, the memory of those specifics had faded and such details were subsumed under genealogical lineages. The disappearance of the distinction between the Butr and Barānis in all but antiquarian learned references suggests that it was a fossilized trace.

The last few references to the Berbers in the tales of the conquests of the Maghrib pertain to one of the most prevalent usages of the term in early Arabic texts—Berbers as slaves: "Al-Layth b. Sa'd recounted that when Mūsā b. Nuṣayr raided the Maghrib, he sent his son Marwān [raiding] with an army and the latter captured a hundred thousand [people]. He also sent his nephew with another army and he too captured a hundred thousand. When al-Layth b. Sa'd was asked who [these people] were, he said: 'the Berbers.'"[56] As a brand of slave, the term Berber superseded the social and political identity of individuals, something a slave did not have.[57] The clearest expression of this supersession, and therefore of the suppression of information about Maghribī social realities, is the absence of Berber communities in the Mashriq, in spite of the transfer of large numbers there. *Futūḥ* authors do not refer to Berber neighborhoods, Berber mosques, Berber markets, or leaders of the Berbers in the Mashriq.

Representations of Berbers in the earliest tales of the conquests of the Maghrib demonstrate both the usefulness of the category and its analytical poverty. However, with the so-called Berber revolts of the 740s, a new political reality emerged in which Berbers became a constitutive part. No longer unbelievers and enemy, Berbers came to play a critical role in the imposition of a new order. While they did not necessarily notice the linguistic shift, *futūḥ* authors like Ibn 'Abd al-Ḥakam recorded it.

The Conquest of al-Andalus and the Berber Revolt

If not caused by the completion of the *futūḥ* in the Maghrib, the conquest of Iberia in 711 definitely followed the assertion of Umayyad caliphal power over the entire Maghrib in the preceding few years (695–710).[58] At least this is how Arabic *futūḥ* authors, and many modern historians, present it. But in spite of the similarities in the methods and even personnel of this conquest and others, a significant degree of discontinuity appears in the administration of the conquered territories, as Iberia presented the conquerors with its own political realities. In Iberia, Umayyad generals found a Visigothic kingdom supported by a number of prominent Visigothic and Hispano-Roman families, bishoprics with various degrees of independence from the Visigoths, and areas, especially in the mountains, that were more or less autonomous.

Arab generals (*amīr*, pl. *umarā'*) sent from al-Qayrawān and Damascus dominated the political scene in the newly minted Umayyad Iberia—it is not clear when the designation al-Andalus became standard. Their exploits, which are only as spectacular as the collapse of the Visigothic order, led to a large transfer of wealth away from the old elites. At the same time, struggles among Umayyad generals who represented various constituencies in the empire were rife, as is clear from the high turnover of governors. Whatever its causes, the instability at the core of Umayyad presence in al-Andalus was exacerbated by the defeat of an important army at the hands of the Frankish Charles Martel in 732. With this defeat, Umayyad forces were largely confined to the Iberian Peninsula, where conflicts inherent in the establishment of a new ruling group came to the fore—not least among the conquerors themselves.

In an empire stretching thousands of miles, maintaining the privileges of the relatively small group around the Umayyads became difficult. With the end of the conquests, the Umayyad elite faced the expectations of those they had relied on to preserve their rule—their allies and clients among Maghribīs (*mawālī*) foremost among these. Rather than promote these new Muslims and make a place for them in the imperial system, the Umayyad elite chose to close ranks and maintain their monopoly on power and the financial privileges they derived from leading military activities. When paying for the Umayyad armies became a challenge, the governor of Egypt Ibn al-Ḥabḥāb looked for revenue by imposing a heavy tax on the lands (*kharāj*) of the Berbers in 740:

> In Ṭanja (Tangier), the Berbers rose up (*intafaḍat*) against 'Ubayd Allāh b. al-Ḥabḥāb and killed his representative (*'āmil*) 'Umar b. 'Abd Allāh al-Murādī. The person responsible for that was Maysara al-Faqīr al-Barbarī al-Midgharī who led the Berbers, claimed the title of caliph, and received their pledges of allegiance [as their caliph]. Maysara then appointed 'Abd al-A'lā b. Jurayj al-Ifrīqī, whose origins were Roman, and who was the *mawlā* of

> [the governor of Ifrīqiyā Mūsā] b. Nuṣayr, as leader over Ṭanja. Then, [Maysara] went to the Sūs, which was under the control of Ismā'īl b. 'Ubayd Allāh and killed him. That was the first rebellion of the Berbers in the lands of Ifrīqiyā.[59]

The Umayyads reacted by sending "prominent figures (*wujūh*) from among the [Meccan] Qurayshīs and the [Medinan] Anṣār," under the leadership of the Qurayshī Khālid b. Abī Ḥabīb al-Fihrī, against these Berbers.[60] All were killed in a battle remembered as the "battle of the nobles" (*ghazwat al-ashrāf*). Fearing that his rule in the Maghrib was in jeopardy, in 741, the Umayyad caliph Hishām b. 'Abd al-Malik (r. 724–43) dispatched a large army under the leadership of Kulthūm b. 'Iyāḍ:

> When Kulthūm arrived in Ifrīqiyā, he ordered its people to gather war machines and to go out with him on a campaign against the Berbers. He put [the Meccan] 'Abd al-Raḥmān b. 'Uqba al-Ghifārī in charge of al-Qayrawān and [the Meccan] Maslama b. Sawāda al-Qurashī as chief military commander. After Kulthūm left to fight the Berbers of Ṭanja, the Ṣufrī [Persian] 'Ukkāsha b. Ayyūb al-Fazārī rebelled against [al-Qayrawān] in the region of Qābis. ['Ukkāsha] sent a brother of his toward Sabrata where he gathered the Zanāta and laid siege on the people of the market of Sabrata, led by Ḥabīb b. Maymūn, in their mosque. When the news reached Ṣafwān b. Abī al-Malik, the emir of Ṭarablus, he went in that direction [with an army] and found al-Fazārī's brother [and the Zanāta] still besieging the people of Sabrata and fought against them. Al-Fazārī was defeated and his followers from among the Zanāta and others were killed, so he fled to his brother in Qābis.[61]

While the account of this rebellion continues, this excerpt shows that the category Berber is reserved for the revolt of Ṭanja, and that in Ifrīqiyā the fight was between Arab "nobility" and anti-Umayyad *mawālī* who espoused Ṣufrī ideas that called for the abolition of Arab privilege among Muslims. Even more striking is the appearance of the Zanāta as such, that is, not as Berbers, but as identifiable political players in intra-Muslim conflicts. Ibn 'Abd al-Ḥakam gives another unattributed version of the events in which Kulthūm and his nephew Balj b. Bishr fought against a coalition of Ṣufrī Zanāta. The haughtiness of Kulthūm and Balj and their mistreatment of one ʿAbd al-Raḥmān b. Ḥabīb led to their defeat, and the death of Kulthūm. Balj ran away to al-Andalus pursued by Abū Yūsuf al-Hawwārī, a Berber rebel (*ṭāghiya min ṭawāghī al-barbar*). The conflict between Balj and Ibn Ḥabīb was taken to al-Andalus, where it led to a serious political rift.

Narratives of the so-called Berber revolt (*fitna*) are included within the tales of the conquest of al-Andalus, and not, for instance, in those of the conquests of Ifrīqiyā or the Maghrib. Written from the point of view of Umayyad rule, they are critical of those Arab generals who behaved unjustly toward Arabs, as they did toward the *mawālī* and their Berber allies. Even more importantly, however, the narrative takes place in two geographical locations: Ifrīqiyā, the seat of Umayyad power, and al-Andalus, Ṭanja being fully part of Andalusī politics. In these reports, "Berbers" tends to refer to an enemy of imperial legitimacy. However, the narrator identifies the individual leaders of the Ṣufrī more fully, like ʿAbd al-Wāḥid b. Yazīd al-Hawwārī al-Madhamī and Khālid b. Ḥumayd al-Zanātī al-Hatwarī. This is notable because the narrator does not specify that either al-Zanātī or al-Hawwārī was Berber. In other words, being Ṣufrī was politically more significant in Ifrīqiyā. These are not the Berbers of the original conquests of the Maghrib, nor are they the Berbers of al-Andalus.[62]

Again, in the case of the struggles over Ṭarablus and its region, Berbers are nowhere to be found. Instead, there are Hawwāra and Zanāta, even when Arab rebels subscribe to anti-Umayyad ideas like the ones preached by the Ibāḍīs:

> When ʿAbd al-Raḥmān b. Ḥabīb sent his brother Ibn Ḥabīb to be his governor in Ṭarablus, [the latter] took [the Arab from Kinda] ʿAbd Allāh b. Masʿūd al-Tujībī who was the leader of the Ibāḍīs and killed him. [As a consequence,] the Ibāḍīs gathered in Ṭarablus [against him]. ʿAbd al-Raḥmān then dismissed his brother and appointed [the Syrian] Ḥamīd b. ʿAbd Allāh al-ʿAkkī. Among the Ibāḍīs, there was ʿAbd al-Jabbār b. Qays al-Murādī and al-Ḥārith b. Talīd al-Ḥaḍramī. Together, they besieged ʿAbd Allāh near Ṭarablus. . . . Then ʿAbd al-Jabbār took over Zanāta and its lands. So ʿAbd al-Raḥmān b. Ḥabīb designated Yazīd b. Ṣafwān al-Maʿāfirī as governor of Ṭarablus and sent Mujāhid b. Muslim al-Hawwārī to appease the people and prevent Hawwāra from joining ʿAbd al-Jabbār. Mujāhid remained months among

> the Hawwāra until they expelled him and he ran to Yazīd b. Ṣafwān in Ṭarablus.[63]

After this, Yazīd b. Ṣafwān dies in "a place in the land of Hawwāra," and 'Abd al-Raḥmān b. Ḥabīb defeats competitors in the "land of Zanāta." After these battles, "'Abd al-Jabbār and al-Ḥārith took control of all of Ṭarablus."

Unlike the tales of the early raids and the heroic feats of 'Uqba, Ḥassān, Kusayla, and al-Kāhina, these notices are replete with precise information about political struggles, ideological differences between the major players, and the names of the leaders. If references to the Zanāta suggest a single political force, those to the Berbers do not, and, understandably, the author has no use for the category.

That said, in the last unattributed report included in *The History of the Conquests*, a certain Ismā'īl b. Ziyād al-Nafūsī becomes leader of the Berbers. "Ismā'īl and his companions were killed and many Berbers captured" and transferred to Ṭarablus where they were killed.[64] Ibn 'Abd al-Ḥakam thus ends his conquest narrative with the Umayyad victory in Ṭarablus. It is unclear from the narrative whether "Ismā'īl and his companions" belong with "the Berbers" or whether the Berbers were their allies. In any case, their defeat allowed the Umayyad general to capture Berbers, whose execution was a strong signal to would-be enemies.

There is a great deal of difference between Mashriqī reports found in the narratives of the conquests of the Maghrib and those found in narratives of the conquest of al-Andalus and its aftermath. On the one hand, the reports have different sources, which, given the time that had elapsed since the events recounted, is not necessarily surprising. The attribution of various tales to particular sources becomes less regular after Ibn 'Abd al-Ḥakam ends his section on the military conquest of al-Andalus. The narrative on the succession of governors in Ifrīqiyā and al-Andalus holds together as a unit and presents us with a pro-Umayyad version of the Berber revolt and its aftermath. The perspective of the stories, their tone and language, demonstrate a high level of familiarity with Umayyad politics in Ifrīqiyā, even more so than in al-Andalus. However, because many Umayyad supporters fled Ifrīqiyā for al-Andalus after the demise of the dynasty in 750, it is possible that Ibn 'Abd al-Ḥakam collected his information from the likes of the Andalusī historian Ibn Ḥabīb (d. 852), who traveled to Egypt and studied there.

Unfortunately, *The History of the Conquests* provides no information about the tumultuous decade between 745 and 756, which saw the victory of the

Umayyad party in al-Andalus.[65] Based on this one source, it is unclear what made the so-called Berber revolt in Ifrīqiyā "Berber." Rather than a unified Berber party threatening the Umayyad order because of the unjust ways it treated all Berbers, the narrative suggests that constant infighting, personal jealousies, and factionalism within the ruling circles constituted the real threat. In Ifrīqiyā, where they are situated by Ibn 'Abd al-Ḥakam, these conflicts mobilized the *mawālī* as well as the Hawwāra and Zanāta. While in some instances, there may be a sense that the Berbers constituted a unified threat, more often than not this is lost in the denigration of anyone claiming leadership based on alternative Islamic ideals, especially those represented in the Maghrib. In these reports only the Umayyads and their Arab supporters are portrayed as legitimate.

The Maghrib After the Umayyads

In the early ninth century, the Maghrib looked nothing like it did in the 740s, where Ibn 'Abd al-Ḥakam's narrative left it. As early as 742, the Zanāta founded an independent Ṣufrī emirate in Tilimsān (742–89). In the Tamisna, along the Atlantic coast, the Barghawāṭa (744–1058) ruled. In 757, another group of Ṣufrīs founded an emirate in Sijilmāsa in the southern region of Tāfilalt in the western Maghrib. A few years later, Ibāḍīs took over al-Qayrawān and Ṭarablus, eliciting a reaction from pro-'Abbāsid forces. In 761, the Rustamid Ibāḍis (761–909) were successful in establishing their rule in Tāhart in the central Maghrib. If the political map were not complicated enough, a descendant of the Prophet through his grandson al-Ḥasan b. 'Alī founded an emirate near ancient Volubilis in 788/9. From their capital in Fez, the Idrīsids (788–959) maintained their influence over a reasonably large territory, while the pro-'Abbāsid Aghlabids established their rule in al-Qayrawān (800–909) after defeating Ibāḍīs in Ifrīqiyā.

Details on these dynasties are scarce and unevenly distributed.[66] Information is rare in the ninth century, but becomes better in the tenth, and is a lot better by the fourteenth century. Unfortunately, this poses a serious problem because it makes it difficult to measure the reach of the Berberization of discourse and its variation among those living under these competing polities. On the other hand, the little we do have is telling. The history of the Rustamids written by Ibn al-Ṣaghīr at the beginning of the tenth century, which is based mostly on oral reports collected from learned Ibāḍīs, illustrates this rather well. In order to give an account of the establishment and evolution of this Persian dynasty in the central Maghrib, Ibn al-Ṣaghīr identifies the major players as Arabs, *'ajam* (Persians), and a number of tribal groups, such as the Nafūsa and Hawwāra. Ibāḍī ideas had matured in the process of organizing an opposition to the Umayyads and then 'Abbāsids. The Ibāḍīs offered an overarching ideological cover for the rule of this dynasty. Under the Rustamids, Tāhart attracted intellectuals from around the Muslim world.[67] Doctrinal differences between constituted factions in the ninth century suggest that the original political pact (*ḥilf*) between Ibn Rustum and the Hawwāra (Zanāta) forces did not necessarily rest on the appeal of clearly articulated Ibāḍī ideals—although ultimately it is impossible to know for sure.

In this important early text, the word Berber only appears once:

> Some [learned] Ibāḍīs informed me that a group of people among whom the Hawwāra and other tribes were near the city of Tāhart and that the Hāwwāra had a leading group from among their chieftains (*ru'asā'*) who were known as the Aws—they were later known as the Banū Masāla.[68] Some Ibāḍīs told me that a leader of the Aws asked to marry the beautiful daughter of one of the leaders of the Berbers, from the Luwāta or another tribe. His proposal was accepted. Then someone who envied the Banū Aws from the Hawwāra sought [the Rustamid ruler] 'Abd al-Wahhāb [r.788–24] and told him: so-and-so had asked for the hand of the daughter of so-and-so for himself or his son. Knowing the man's standing among the leaders and the people, I could not trust that if he married his daughter to the man and there was fusion and then kinship, the two tribes would join and outnumber you. So you must ask for her hand.[69]

Perhaps Ibn al-Ṣaghīr had a particular reason not to use the word Berber more often. Even so, in this one instance, the word expresses a potential threat that the Berbers as a whole constituted to the rule of the Persian Rustamids. However, for Ibn al-Ṣaghīr's informants, whether the Hawwāra, Zanāta, and Luwāta were Berbers was not as significant as the actions they took as political players. Using the word Berber would only confuse matters by forcing a reduction of political specificity. This everyone seems to have understood very well. Since the Berbers did not act as a bloc and did not represent a single party, there was really no point in using the category to describe politics. However, when a "Berber" Hawwārī leader pointed out that the dynasty's existence depended on the frail balance of power between tribal forces, he was positioning himself vis-à-vis the Persian ruling family by raising the danger of Berbers coming together against the Rustamids.[70] Unlike the Zanāta, Hawwāra, and others, "the Berbers" never formed a dynasty that ruled anywhere in the Maghrib, let alone all of it.[71]

The conflict between Ibāḍī Tāhart and the pro-ʿAbbāsid Aghlabid rulers of Ifrīqiyā was not limited to skirmishing. Ibāḍīs had garnered support in the areas to the south and east of Ifrīqiyā, constituting a serious threat to Aghlabid power. As was explained, it was mostly against the Ibāḍīs that al-Aghlab and his son Ibrāhīm (r. 800–812) imposed the rule of the imperial elite and their allies in Ifrīqiyā. The victory of anti-Umayyad forces in the Mashriq did not mean the disappearance of the privileges of those who arrived in Ifrīqiyā as agents of that empire. The Aghlabids represented the ability of the erstwhile Umayyad elite to refashion itself to maintain its social domination. These political realities inform the writings of the Ibāḍī scholar Ibn Sallām (d. after 887). His *Kitāb* is the earliest extant Arabic text written by a Maghribī "Berber."[72] As an Ibāḍī scholar writing in Ifrīqiyā, Ibn Sallām offered an Ibāḍī perspective on Islamic tenets, legitimate rule, and Muslim learning that contrasted with what circulated in al-Qayrawān.[73] Prominent in his approach was the demonstration of the closeness of Ibāḍī ideas to the original prophetic message using a variety of textual and oral sources.

Interestingly, all references to Berbers occur in the oral reports Ibn Sallām gathered. Most of these references are found in only one of the twenty-one sections of the book. Looking at the earlier written material he selected, one notices that it did not mention the Berbers, suggesting a more recent currency of the term among Ibāḍīs. However, it is in this text that a mirror image of the negative lumping of the Berber as an unbelieving enemy unworthy of leading the community of Muslims finds its earliest expression.[74] For instance, Ibn Sallām includes a number of reports in praise of the Berbers, the most prominent among which is the one that has the angel Jibrīl informing the prophet Muḥammad that Islam would grow in the Maghrib and that the Berbers would be its standard-bearers.[75] In other words, the Berbers fight to establish the true faith in contrast to the Arabs (i.e. the Aghlabid elite), who fight only for money (*al-dīnār wa al-dirham*).[76] Ibn Sallām even calls into question the association between Berber and barbarian, offering a report that claims that the word Berber derives from the root "to multiply" (*tabarbarū ay kathurū*).[77]

Ibn Sallām's *Kitāb* depicts the Berbers as devout Muslims. They are one of the many non-Arab peoples who constitute the community of Muslims with the Arabs. They are a "people" in the same sense that the Arabs are a people. Yet, this version is not necessarily consistent with the Ibāḍī message. In fact, Ibn Sallām gives the more identifiably Ibāḍī position in a report on the early Ibāḍī leader Abū al-Khaṭṭāb. According to the report, the Ibāḍīs were readying to confront the Umayyad general Ibn al-Ash'ath when one of them called on "the people of Hawwāra" (*āl Hawwāra*) to ready for battle. When he heard that, Abū al-Khaṭṭāb ordered that the man be flogged and that the call be made to all good Muslims instead.[78] For the Ibāḍī leader, Islam transcended tribal affiliation, associated for him with the pre-Islamic period (*jāhiliya*)—and, of course, the politics of the Umayyads. But, of course, and as both Ibn al-Ṣaghīr and Ibn Sallām show, the Ibāḍīs did not put an end to tribal politics, or at least the Rustamids did not.

For Ibn Sallām, the category Berber functions in the exact same way as the category Arab does. This explains why he appends it to Hawwāra, Zanāta, Nafūsa, and other "Berber" tribes. This move tells us that his imagined interlocutors were not the Berbers.[79] However, by embracing this gesture common among non-Berber Arabic authors, Ibn Sallām participated in the Berberization of Ibāḍī discourse. His pre-Berber stance led him to the propagation of an exonym imposed on people who did not necessarily identify as such.

Furthermore, on more than one occasion, Ibn Sallām translates Arabic reports into *barbariya*, the language of the Berbers, which he obviously knows. Since the category Berber functions to efface specific information, it is not clear which of the Berber languages he refers to. Again, for someone steeped in Arabic learned culture as he was to use the language of the Arab elite to describe his own language is not particularly surprising—unless he considered his Berber language as the only Berber language, which is unlikely. As they broadened their knowledge beyond Ibāḍī texts, members of the Ibāḍī elite seem to have absorbed the categories of the non-Ibāḍī imperial Arab elite, old and new, far and near.[80]

Two centuries after the end of the conquest of the Maghrib, Berbers became Berbers in dominant representations. This is significant since some Maghribī intellectuals began to use the category to refer to themselves. In the Maghrib of the close of the ninth century, Berbers existed only in the minds of Arabs and among those Maghribīs who thought like them. At the same time, and given the east-to-west character of the conquests and their rather slow pace, from the 640s to the 700s, it is understandable that easterners in Ifrīqiyā developed relations with the empire earlier than westerners did. This is why the practice of representing various groups as "Berber" is more likely to be an "eastern" phenomenon. Add to that the Arab-centric politics that developed in al-Qayrawān (Ifrīqiyā) and the Ifrīqiyan origins of the earliest Arabic sources from the Maghrib, and the "eastern" origins of the Berbers become even more pronounced. Yet, in spite of this, the settler-dominated organization of the society and its inability to impose its domination beyond Ifrīqiyā after the 740s greatly circumscribed the reach of Arab-centric imperialism in the Maghrib. Although an Andalus-like situation in 800 resulted in the victory of the Aghlabids, this occurred decades after the establishment of an Andalusī Umayyad emirate in 756.

Making an Umayyad Andalus

Much changed in al-Andalus after the large army led by Balj b. Bishr landed there—after failing to put an end to the Berber revolt in the Maghrib. The arrival of the new Syrian army reset the balance of power that had prevailed until then. Importantly, the Syrians were clearly intent on keeping power in Arab hands, though not necessarily in the hands of those Arabs who had settled there after the original conquest (*baladiyūn*). After the ʿAbbāsids put an end to Umayyad rule in Damascus, the Syrians saw an opportunity to impose their rule in al-Andalus. But between the internecine struggles and the opposition of those that the new army had slighted since its arrival, Syrians proved incapable of imposing their rule alone. With allies among both Arabs and Berbers, old (*baladiyūn*) and newly arrived, the Umayyad ʿAbd al-Raḥmān proved a formidable operator against anti-Umayyads of all stripes. Although his ascension to the throne in Cordoba was a major event, his ability to impose his rule beyond the city's immediate surroundings took years of both warfare and diplomacy. Significantly, when the earliest Arabic sources describe the events that led to the victory of ʿAbd al-Raḥmān in 756, they do so long after usage of the category Berber had become naturalized.

In the political order that gradually emerged in al-Andalus, the Berbers, as such, became a constitutive component of a society dominated by the

Umayyads. Just as the designation Arab gained new significance when imperial tribesmen settled outside the peninsula among non-Arabs, so too did the term Berber come to define a distinct component of the new Iberian political scene.[81] Arriving in al-Andalus as Hawwāra, Zanāta, *mawālī*, or something else, the new non-Arab settlers gradually became Berbers tout court—not because this was a natural outcome or because it was their original or authentic identity, but because of the politics that led to the triumph of the Umayyads. It is in this narrow sense that al-Andalus was the first home of the Berbers.[82]

Before the establishment of the Umayyad emirate in al-Andalus in 756, Umayyad governors had succeeded one another, sent there from Ifrīqiyā to administer territories conquered mostly during the early years. After defeating the Visigoths, the new conquerors took control of cities, rich agricultural lands, and even the less fertile areas in the highlands. Had the Berbers been restricted to the poorer areas and the Arabs to the richer ones, it would be easier to depict the first three decades as having established a hierarchical system based on ancestry. Unfortunately, the evidence is not clear on this subject, in particular about whether a major redistribution of lands followed the landing of the large Syrian army in 741. And even if toponymic evidence can be interpreted as showing that Berbers settled in mountainous areas more than elsewhere, it clearly does not show that they did so as Berbers, but rather as Zanāta (Ceneta, Gineta, Azenanet), Nafzāwa (Nifzies), Maghīla (Maguila), Awrāba (Orba), and other specific groups. However, whether they settled there right after the original conquest or later, no Barbaria came to be in al-Andalus, even if some areas were known to have been settled primarily by Berbers.[83]

Extant early chronicles, biographical dictionaries, and geographical works do not give a clear picture of the economic situation in the early years of al-Andalus, beyond the tales, sometimes fantastic, of the immense treasures amassed during the conquests. It is therefore difficult to relate the political struggles recounted in the chronicles to the evolution of agricultural production, labor relations, or commerce, for instance. Yet, the constitution of prominent wealthy families (*buyutāt*) from among those who had an active role in politics suggests that, at least when it comes to the elite, power and wealth went hand in hand. In any case, the chronicles tend to reduce the struggles that led to Umayyad victory to the ambitions of individuals and confer on their actions an "ethnic" or "sectarian" motivation, when it is not simply personal revenge. When one looks at the matter a little more closely, however, it seems that the Umayyads challenged the very idea that anyone but they could have *mawālī*. More than anything else the Umayyads did, their monopolization of this form of social and political organization (*walā'*) set the period after the foundation of the Umayyad emirate apart from the period that preceded it—even if it took the Umayyads decades to actually achieve these goals. Again, in the absence of contemporary evidence it is difficult to call it an official policy, but thinking in these terms helps account for the representation of Berbers in the sources as individuals (*mawālī*) attached to the Umayyads and as tribal chiefs. In other words, not all Berbers were Berber in the same way, and the word Berber did not have the same signification. In the next century or so, there was a difference between those Berbers who maintained their tribal organization and settled, by choice or by force, in poorer areas, and the very few individuals who occupied prominent positions in the Umayyad government and passed down their wealth and influence to their families. These two "types" of Berbers figure prominently in the sources, mostly because of the perspective of the early authors. However, it is worth insisting that "Berber" did not refer to a socially homogeneous group, and not just because various tribes migrated to al-Andalus from different parts of Africa. The imposition of a modified Arab domination by the Umayyads, their active participation in maintaining the privilege of powerful Arab families at the expense of all other sectors of society, meant that early authors had an empirical basis for associating "Berber" and something like "socially subordinate Muslim"—with all that entails in terms of representation.

Evidence that the Berbers of al-Andalus truly became a cardinal category in the dominant discourse comes oddly enough not in Arabic but in Latin. In the so-called *Chronicle of 754*, the anonymous author equated the Arabic Berber and the Latin Moor (Maurus), which was a common way of describing people across the sea in Latin.[84] Yet, in spite of this usage, the chronicle offers the earliest evidence of the emergence of the "Berbers of al-Andalus" as an entity distinguishable from the Berbers of the Maghrib.[85]

The Moors of Spain as Berbers

The *Chronicle of 754* spans the period between 661, when the Visigoths still ruled, and the politically charged period that preceded the foundation of the first Muslim dynasty in al-Andalus. Two years after the presumed date of composition of the chronicle, the sole surviving son of the Umayyad dynasty, which had ruled from Damascus between 661 and 750, found his way to the eastern Maghrib, his Nafzawī mother's homeland, and from there to al-Andalus, where the Umayyad party brought him to power in Cordoba. As this Latin chronicle utilizes both Latin and Arabic texts as sources, it combines a certain understanding of "Moor" with a notion of "Berber" that is otherwise previously unattested.

In a passage about the period preceding Umayyad victory, the author of the *Chronicle of 754* describes the material benefits that the Berbers and Arabs in al-Andalus enjoyed, and at the expense of whom: "In the era 763 (725), in almost the sixth year of the emperor Leo and the one hundred seventh of the Arabs, a Saracen by the name of Yahya succeeded at once by orders of the princes. He was a cruel and terrible despot who raged for almost three years. With bitter deceit, he stirred up the Saracens and Moors of Spain by confiscating property that they were holding for the sake of peace and restoring many things to the Christians."[86]

The Moors of Spain are not simply Moors and are not the same as the Moors of Africa (Libya): "Although he was preeminent in courage and fame, a Moor named Munnuza, hearing that his people were being oppressed by the harsh temerity of the judges in the territory of Libya, quickly made peace with the Franks and organized a revolt against the Saracens of Spain [in 731]."[87] There seems to be a contradiction, or at least a tension, in the author's usage. On the one hand, "Moors of Spain" represent one group in Spain, act as such, and deserve to be treated as such in the author's mind. On the other, when it comes to their motivations, they seem to be moved by Pan-Moor solidarity, and thus in reaction to events taking place in Libya rather than Spain. Munnuza clearly betrayed the Saracens and broke the oath that tied him to them, an act that would typically bring him dishonor and disrepute. However, and as the author explains, Munnuza "was preeminent in courage and fame," and these character traits made him a valuable ally of the Franks. The idea that he would react to the abuse of Moors in northwest Africa against his Saracen coreligionists is consistent with the Arabic narratives' depiction of a Berber threat. Yet, Munnuza's rebellion preceded the Berber revolt, and the author seems to have projected sentiments closer to the time of his composition of the chronicle rather than those of the 720s and 730s. He is acutely aware of the special character of the anti-Umayyad revolts that took place across the empire: "All that vast desert, from which the Arab multitudes had arisen, was full of unrest, unable to tolerate the injustice of the judges."[88] Interestingly, the judges are to blame for the broad anti-Umayyad revolt, not the Saracens in general. Yet, when it comes to the Maghrib, the Arab yoke comes into play:

> In the western region, which extends to the southern zone and which is occupied more than any of the others by the Moors, the inhabitants openly shook their necks from the Arab yoke, unanimous and determined in their wrath.[89] When [the Umayyad ruler of Damascus] Hisham [r. 724–43] realized the scale of the rebellion, he immediately sent powerful reinforcements of 100,000 soldiers to the African governor. . . . The whole army found itself divided into three groups: one part was held captive in the hands of the victors [i.e., the Moors]; another, like vagabonds, turned and fled, trying to return home. A third part, confused and not knowing where to go, headed for Spain—oh the pain!—with Balj, a man of good lineage and an expert in military matters, as their leader.[90]

Whereas the Moors of Spain act defiantly against the Saracens because of feelings they have toward their brethren on the African continent, the Moors of Libya do not seem to have shared those sentiments, since they did not cross the sea to come to their rescue.[91] Nothing in the sources suggests that the Moors actually sought to form a universal alliance, let alone have anti-Umayyad forces land in al-Andalus from Africa. The specter of this alliance, however, illuminates the ultimate coming together of Yemeni and Syrian factions, which constituted the actual Arabs of Spain. In other words, the vagueness that characterizes the politics of the Moors is the other side of the pact that ultimately brought the Umayyads to power in 756. The fear of Pan-Berber actions lends validity and a rationale to a coming together of Arabs.[92]

The "Moors of Spain" were critical to the making of Umayyad peace in al-Andalus. The victory of the Umayyads did not lead to the disappearance of all Berbers from the scene. Since 'Abd al-Raḥmān relied on African supporters that made the journey with him to al-Andalus and helped him seize power, that would have been difficult to achieve. At the same time, he relied on both Syrians and Yemenis and, in spite of imposing Umayyad dynastic rule, which limited some of their privileges, retained the predominance of "Arabs" notably by granting powerful Arab families a near monopoly on all official positions. After they lost to the alliance of "Arabs," the Berbers became a subordinate "Muslim" group with privileges not available to non-Muslims (*ahl al-dhimma*). In this sense, "Islam" was the ideological umbrella that expressed the actual coming together of Arabs and Berbers in al-Andalus under Umayyad rule. Being "Arab," or claiming Arab descent, became a standard, the lack of which legitimated and rationalized the disenfranchisement and subordination of fellow Muslims.

The dynasties that came to rule in northwest Africa faced political situations that were markedly different from that of al-Andalus and, in fact, varied widely among themselves. One should simply remember that different groups supported these dynasties, that they espoused different ideologies, and that they engaged in armed conflict against one another, at least in some cases. However, as far as we can tell from the extant sources, compared to its central place in the articulation of political discourse in al-Andalus, the category Berber was marginal in the Maghrib.

A consequence of the importance of the distinction between Arabs and Berbers in al-Andalus was that authors made preexisting categories fit the new circumstances. While some of those who settled in Iberia from northwest Africa were known as Zanāta, for example, they became "Zanāta Berbers" after the victory of the Umayyads. This was achieved even if prior to the Umayyads they may not have felt that they belonged to the same community or people as other northwest African groups. Identifying the Zanāta as Berbers was a result of the ideology associated with a dominant social group, which judged groups in terms of their ancestry (genealogy) and date of conversion to Islam. This specific context, with a particular configuration of "Arab" and "Muslim," accounts for categories such as "Arabized" (Ar. Mustaʿrab, Sp. Mozárab) to describe "Christians" living under "Muslim" rule. While this may seem all too obvious to some readers, it is worth mentioning here that being "Arabized" did not gain currency at that time in the Maghrib or in the Mashriq. Similarly, the category *muwallad*, which referred to the offspring of a Berber slave and a free Arab, reflected politics in al-Andalus (and Mashriq) but not the Maghrib.[93]

Early Berbers and Beyond

The earliest references to Berbers in Arabic are to East Africans who lived across the Red Sea from the Arabian Peninsula. Egyptians knew about these East African Berbers (*Barbar*) and used the word "barbarian" (*barbar*) to refer to a number of groups living outside the full control of the imperial cities. Beginning in the 640s, raids into northwest Africa led to the appearance of Berber slaves in eastern markets. The imperial elite prized these slaves, and within a couple of generations, the mothers of prominent individuals were Berber slaves. In the Mashriq, Berber became a brand of slave. In the Maghrib, Berber was a category used to describe the peoples conquerors encountered, first in Cyrenaica and then gradually moving westward as far as Tangier. The Berberization of various groups followed from the practice of the Arab conquerors of applying the same category to all those who resisted them. In the years following the conquest of Iberia, two differentiated groups, Arabs and Berbers, emerged in the process of securing the Umayyad imperial order in al-Andalus. Rebellions against the Umayyads brought about the 'Abbāsids in Ifrīqiyā. In al-Andalus, an Umayyad ruler emerged victorious and reestablished the dynasty there, with Arabs and Berbers as a constitutive political unit. In the Maghrib, a number of dynasties emerged and had to contend not with all Berbers but only those that mattered politically. The designation Berber thus had a particularly Andalusī coloration.

The fact that medieval authors did not think in historicizing terms explains their systematic fusion of these usages. Once they integrated the body of learned knowledge, which circulated over long distances, characterizations, anecdotes, and narratives lost connection to the contexts from which they emerged. The prevalence of cutting-and-pasting and paraphrasing among the literati ensured a thorough Berberization of knowledge in Arabic by the ninth century. The unique political situation in al-Andalus and the late date of Maghribī sources illuminate the pervasiveness of Andalusī usage, even though the "Made in al-Andalus" tag is not always visible. With time, other sites of Berberization developed that took Berbers for granted. Analyzing the ways in which intellectuals deployed the category illuminates the conditions that shaped the evolution of Berberization over time, as the next chapter will demonstrate.

Chapter 2

Making Berbers

A historically new category, Berber came to describe a wide range of groups and individuals who did not imagine belonging together. There are reasons for this. In spite of what the new conquerors believed, the social, political, and cultural conditions in northwest Africa did not facilitate the lumping of all non-Romans from western Egypt to the Atlantic Ocean under a single heading. Even the category Moor, which had the greatest chance of mapping onto Berber, did not quite match the conquerors' understanding. In fact, those who imposed imperial rule in the Maghrib (640s–710s), and after them those who led its political reordering (740s–800), did not seek to foster the formation of a single Berber entity. They did not do so inadvertently either. Basic divide-and-rule wisdom stood against anything of the sort. In fact, as both preconquest polities and the dynasties that emerged after the 740s attest, northwest Africans kept their politics from covering anything like a single "Berber world."

When Andalusī usage entered the Maghrib, it shaped Berberization there too, although one must always check this influence against the social relations of power that prevailed in the Maghrib—and for centuries, those remained doggedly small in scale. This was not because Berbers were particularly reluctant to form a single society but rather because the conditions that would put such a project in motion were never there. If anything, the very idea of such a society, a united Berber Maghrib, is a result of later Berberization. It is a projection. Whether it came from a negative sentiment toward Berbers stemming from the fears of the Arab elite, or a positive one, actual conditions remained stubbornly uncooperative. In some basic sense, the category's semantic richness and instability, as well as its ghostly hollowness, correspond to the political, economic, and cultural diversity found in the Maghrib. These attributes did not necessarily constitute an impediment to further Berberization, but they did shape its character.

The category Berber was like a ghost haunting the lives of people in the Maghrib. For a long time, most of them did not even realize it. They had other ghosts to worry about. Then the hard work of convincing them of a reality in which that particular ghost played a role began to pay off. It was hard work because their worlds made enough sense with the ghosts they knew. Over time, however, they came to recognize the new ghost's name and even acknowledge its presence in their lives. What they did with the category once they appropriated it depended a great deal on how they organized their societies and on their priorities. And so naturally, Berberization of the social world in the Maghrib brought about the creation of a multitude of ghosts, all bearing the same name but each with particular features and qualities. Although this fact complicates the work of the historian who has to take into consideration a great number of sites of Berberization, it corresponds more accurately to the phenomenon itself. The idea of a single Berber world was only one of the products of Berberization, and could not possibly constitute evidence of the independent existence of that world. In other words, the universal Berber was produced locally and was therefore not the same everywhere. This is particularly worth insisting on here because of the influence that the modern "universal Berber" has had on historiography.

Sources, Methods, and Berber Specters

Historians work with the sources they have. In this case, the sources emanate from centers of power and the social groups related to them. There is of course nothing spectacular about this fact or that our approach must address it. Given the proximity of the sources to centers of power, an analysis of the elites' specific contribution to Berberization is required. However, such an analysis is not the equivalent of a complete or even adequate account of the evolution of the category over time. Rather, it ties changes to the category Berber to specific historical circumstances. Even if our sources imagine politics to be coextensive with struggles between social elites, and thus tend to minimize the involvement of the greater part of their societies, they still offer a record of the difficulties elites encountered in imposing and maintaining their domination. Attacks on the ideological claims of opponents bring into focus the hard work of ideologues in representing the rule of their favorite party as seamless and natural. Even if the sources do not allow us to form a full picture of social relations and of the mechanisms of imposing and maintaining social inequalities each and every time, they do show that in these predominantly agricultural societies, control of land, labor, and the mechanisms that secured the transfer of wealth was of vital political significance. As Berberization makes sense only in relation to actual social relations of power, it is therefore worth insisting on what would otherwise seem obvious. The sources do not allow us to know just how much it mattered to the farmhand, the slave, or the shepherd, who lived at or near subsistence level, whether the king was Berber or only Ṣanhāja. They do record, however, large-scale famines, devastating epidemics, droughts, and crop failures, as well as the heartless burning of harvests by warring elites. It is up to us to consider whether any such events came to shape the process of Berberization.

Once references to Berbers became commonplace, new significations tended to augment previous ones, and modify them, but not always displace or even compete with them. This is why a diachronic approach to Berberization can be beneficial. Instead of a study of the representation of Berbers in Arabic literature across time, which runs the risk of lumping all "Berbers" into a single "Berber," a diachronic approach enables us to differentiate between dominant and other representations and to link them to changing social relations of power. Even if in most cases it is possible only to guess what those relations were, because the sources are quiet or inexistent, doing so grounds Berberization and safeguards its historicity.

When modern historians began to imagine a single Berber past, they posited the idea of "Berber permanence" to help them organize their studies. Thanks to a critique of the underlying logic and the untenable assumptions at its core, the transhistorical Berbers are a monument to the errors of the past. However, if the idea of changeless Berbers rightly offended their conscience, historians still think of one history for all Berbers. For example, in *The Berbers*, Michael Brett and Elizabeth Fentress articulated their project in terms of positioning the Berbers as "protagonists in their own [single] history," which, they argue, had been silenced by Pan-Islamic sentiments, French colonial policies, and the political Left's tendency to "suppress ethnic differences":[1] "We are moving towards a specifically Berber history and anthropology, as opposed to an ethnography coloured by European preconceptions, tailored to duality—the ability to assimilate the hegemonic culture without suppressing the traditional culture—which has permitted

Berber scholars this double view, the meta-level without which it is impossible to study oneself. We ourselves can hardly offer a 'Berber view,' but we have tried to use material written by Berbers as much as possible."[2] Fine. Or not fine, actually, because historians work with the sources they have. All of them. Besides, what is a Berber view? Traditional culture? In the last few decades, concerted efforts to "help" the Berbers against those who have conspired to leave them out of history, their history, have produced a number of exemplars. Medievalist Maya Shatzmiller offers eerily similar diagnosis and treatment:

> It is easy to see why a Berber contribution to the Islamic legacy was not recognized, even rejected. Since the Berbers had no written language, it was assumed that if they made any contribution at all, it was not as Berbers, but within an Arab and Islamic cultural framework, or that they were absorbed into Arab society and culture, and participated in high culture. Yet, historians are willing to recognize that the heretical movements which appeared in medieval North Africa represented a form or resistance to Islamic and Arabic acculturation, even though they were using symbols taken from this culture to express it. More importantly, there is a reasonable amount of evidence to challenge the view that no independent Berber intellectual or literary activity existed, and to substantiate expressions of self awareness in the Arab chronicles. They provide us with numerous manifestations of "unofficial" Berber creativity, if only we care to read them correctly. Together these might have been only a few types of response, but they are the ones we can document.[3]

Whatever else can be said about the assumptions behind such an analysis, a focus on Berberization eschews some of the most obvious difficulties: the existence of a timeless Berber self-awareness and of a "Berber" entity being suppressed by an Arab-Islamic cultural framework.[4] Interestingly, such a perspective makes it difficult to properly situate statements made by medieval writers, like the ones made by the anonymous fourteenth-century author whose book formed the basis of many of Shatzmiller's insights: "Non-Berber kings ruled the Maghrib [and that includes] the Fāṭimids, the Umayyads, the Idrīsids, and the Almohads—some consider the latter to be originally

Muḍar [Arabs]."[5] Rather than an oppressive Islamic state, the anonymous author delivers a deliberate and forceful inscription of his Berber pride within an Islamic logic.[6] Interestingly, and unlike modern nationalists, for instance, the author does not refer to any pre-Islamic states as having ruled over Berbers in the Maghrib. Kingship was a site of production of honor, and so, naturally, the author looks for the points of pride of the Berbers around kings. Doing so, he also explains why his book does not focus on those dynasties. Does he think that non-Berber kings victimized Berbers or that Berber kings brought an end of history?

In a related register, when modern historians suggest or imply that the lives of Berbers were somehow better when they were ruled by fellow Berbers, they invite misunderstanding of both past and present. Taking sides with kings, whether they fashioned themselves as Berber or were so represented by others, remains as problematic as expressing a preference for one party or form of rule. The way this has been achieved in modern historiography is through a periodization that sets up a period of "Berber dynasties." It is not that these dynasties were not Berber in some sense, but rather that the fact that they were "Berber" should explain and even order historical change: "The [Almoravid and Almohad] Berber empires, fired by religious fervor, forged a legacy of unification that continues to inspire contemporary Maghribis. After the disintegration of the Almohad empire in the thirteenth century, three other Berber dynasties—the Ḥafṣids, Zayyanids, and Marinids—took over and reconfigured another Maghribi trilateralism."[7] Perhaps they did. But from the foundation of the Almoravid dynasty in the 1060s to the demise of the Ḥafṣids in the 1570s, there are five "Berber" centuries that lead, conveniently enough, to the three modern states of Tunisia, Algeria, and Morocco. Even if it were not teleological, this perspective enshrines and naturalizes both the ideological perspectives of the sources and the state-centric nationalist ideology of the moderns, all without explanation. When historians deploy medieval and modern ideologies to tell stories of the emergence of the modern state, political history is no longer a history of politics but a history that is political. Describing contemporary Maghribīs as heirs to medieval Berber empires and Berber dynasties is itself an artifact of this historiographic act.[8]

These historiographic issues highlight the benefits of focusing on Berber production as a separate phenomenon. While the previous chapter approached the question with the goal of establishing a chronology of early

Berberization, it should be clear that once the category came into use it did not acquire a stable and unchanging meaning. The sources leave no doubt about that. Thus, the analysis of Berberization entails an examination of these changes over time. Limiting ourselves to a few of these sites or moments underlines their multiplicity and thus the multiple origins of the making and remaking of Berbers. In spite of its obvious challenges and limitations, the discussion of a few elements of the complicated political histories of various regions and kingdoms brings forth the most salient features of particular forms of Berberization. While a review of political events gives us a sense of the groups inflecting Berberization, it is less informative about the relation between dynastic politics and the daily lives of commoners (*al-ʿāmma*). In this regard, analyzing a few legal cases in which Berber customs come into play is a convenient way to explore the ways Berberization operated. Even if they constitute too small and unrepresentative a sample of the mass of documented legal cases, they demonstrate that Berberization was naturalized by individuals and institutions trying to address practical problems of daily life.

Umayyad Berber Politics in al-Andalus (756–912)

The military role of the Berbers in al-Andalus shaped the form and content of Berberization there. While the large numbers of northwest Africans that landed in Iberia in 711 following Ṭāriq b. Ziyād had benefited materially from that conquest, their luck changed under the Arab emirs, changing dramatically with the coming of Balj b. Bishr and his policies of dispossession and relocation.[9] In spite of this, however, and owing to the success of their rebellions of the 740s, many Berbers kept control of lands around the peninsula. Circumstances were to change dramatically again with the foundation of the Umayyad emirate in 756. The young Umayyad prince ʿAbd al-Raḥmān had fled the ʿAbbāsid takeover of Damascus in 750 and had run to the Maghrib, where his mother was from.[10] There, he was able to elude ʿAbd al-Raḥmān b. Ḥabīb al-Fihrī, the governor of Ifrīqiyā, thanks to the protection he found among the Maghīla. Three years or so later, he left for al-Andalus in the company of both Berber and Arab supporters.[11] Upon his arrival in al-Andalus, ʿAbd al-Raḥmān encountered the former governor of Ifrīqiyā, whom the Arabs of al-Andalus had chosen as their leader.[12] After he built a broad coalition of Berbers and Arabs (mostly Yemenis), the Umayyad emir defeated the Arabs (mostly Muḍar), and those among the Berbers who had supported them.

Once he declared the foundation of an Umayyad emirate in Cordoba, ʿAbd al-Raḥmān enlisted the help of Berbers to secure his rule. Many of these Berbers crossed the sea to be part of his army. This new wave of immigrants allowed the Umayyads to prevail over the constant rebelling of the Arabs. In addition to them, the Umayyads utilized non-Muslim slaves (*mamālīk*): "[He] bought slaves from every region. Between Berbers and slaves, there were forty thousand men on his payroll (*diwān*). . . . With [their help] he took control of al-Andalus [in 773,] and broke the Arabs and imposed Umayyad rule over them."[13] ʿAbd al-Raḥmān I (r. 756–88) used Berbers primarily in the military, both to check "internal" threats and to defend the northern border areas. Overall, and in spite of passing references to a "Berber army" or to "the Berbers of such-and-such a place" in al-Andalus, the magnitude of these migrations, the location of their settlements, and their place of origin in the Maghrib remain difficult to know.[14] One thing is certain, however: when Balj's army landed in al-Andalus it was the last time a large number of Arabs did so. In fact, other than the soldiers who followed each governor, the armies of Mūsa b. Nuṣayr and Balj constituted the bulk of Arab settlement in al-Andalus. While one may question the accuracy of the statement about 40,000 soldiers "between Berbers and slaves," its flipside is that whatever it was, the number of Arab soldiers could not be larger than that; when we have numbers at all, the armies that fought at various battles seems to have been much smaller.

Small numbers or not, the military potential of the Arabs had to be dealt with. ʿAbd al-Raḥmān I maintained the privileges of the Syrians, who received land grants (*iqṭāʿ*) and an exemption from the *ʿushr* tax in exchange for their services. Neither the Berbers nor the "old Andalusī families" (*baladiyūn*) were as lucky, having to pay that tax in addition to their service requirements.[15] In general, land grants to tribal leaders reproduced social hierarchies among Berbers. This helps explain why "Berbers" retained their tribal names, evidenced in both toponymy and literary sources.[16] Especially with the land grants (*tasjīl*) of the second half of the ninth century and the tenth, Berbers like the Banū Dhī al-Nūn, Banū Zarwāl, and Banū Razīn controlled large areas around fortified towns. They had the right to pass them onto their children and to administer them as they pleased, provided of course that they participated in defeating the dynasty's enemies.

The Berbers' lack of mastery of Arabic, which was the language of administration and law, legitimated their near-total absence from official positions and their military "specialization." However, a focus on the linguistic aptitudes of Berbers would underestimate the Arab elite's sense of entitlement to government positions and their vehement attacks against those Berber individuals who were appointed to high positions like that of *ḥājib* or *wazīr*. Moreover, since the constitution of a corpus of authoritative texts took place mostly in the course of the ninth century, it is prudent to take descriptions of the failure of Berbers to master Arabic texts with a grain of salt. This is especially true because prominent Berber courtiers attest to their mastery of the language throughout the period. In fact, once it became a matter of technical skill, rather than birth, Berbers held a number of official positions like judgeships. Those among the Berbers who wanted their children to compete for government jobs took steps to remedy what the Arabs saw as a rationale for excluding them. But these families did not represent the majority of Berbers in al-Andalus, at least not in the eighth and ninth centuries.

This broad outline sheds light on the absence of Berbers among the earliest Arabic authors in al-Andalus and on the reasons behind the political and military nature of early references to Berbers. It also illuminates the negative portrayals of Berbers in early Andalusī sources. Since their authors believed politics to be an elite activity focused on the character, intentions, and actions of prominent individuals, they were not particularly interested in subordinate social groups, unless something about them illuminated the actions of the powerful.

Slave Branding

> Sicilian judges were asked about the purchase of a slave on whose body is found the mark of cauterization (*kayyu nārin*). The experts (*ahl al-maʿrifa*) believed [the slave] was cauterized to cure a disease.
>
> Answer: If he is a Berber slave, their expertise can be ignored because the Berbers are known to cauterize even when there are no illnesses. The same does not apply to the Byzantines (Rūm) who only do so to cure a disease. In that case, it is a hidden defect because the illness might re-appear.[17]

Apparently, branding healthy slaves was a Berber tradition. From the judge's statement, it seems that Berber slave owners customarily branded their Berber slaves. Although it was a Berber tradition, it is doubtful that Berber slaves were as desirous to uphold it as their owners were. We do not have their express opinion on this, but it is a safe assumption. By the time the Aghlabids conquered Sicily in the 820s, and thus before this Sicilian judge was writing, Berbers had become Muslims and could not legally be enslaved. Logically, then, this case could not possibly pertain to a Berber slave but only to a slave owned by a Berber master who practiced the Berber tradition of branding. In this sense, the word Berber refers to a slave owner, a meaning that early conquest narratives do not record. As was shown in the previous chapter, *futūḥ* authors described thousands of Berber slaves taken to the Mashriq by force but no Berber slave merchants selling their fellow Berbers. Historians have pointed out that the claims that Berbers had reneged on their conversion may have come from slavers who saw their profitable trade threatened. Likewise, it seems that the slave trade may have been behind the formation of polities in southern Ifrīqiyā. But Ibāḍis who engaged in the trade did not use the word Berber in their sources. Is this because they limited its use to those northwest Africans they enslaved? It is simply difficult to say. But even if they did not, a Berber slave in an Aghlabid-Ifrīqiyan sense could be a slave purchased from Ibāḍī Berbers. All of this is to say that the reference to Berber slave-branding raises more questions than it answers.

The body of Berber customs (*ʿurf* or *ʿāda*) that experts (*ahl al-maʿrifa*) introduced into Islamic law may demonstrate the great variation in local practices in the Maghrib, and thus differences between Berbers. While it is not always possible to gauge the relations behind these customary practices, the selection of socially prominent individuals as experts guaranteed that judges would side with the beneficiaries of the status quo. Examples that pertain to slavery leave no doubt about this.

In another case, a judge opined on the case of a slave owner who put shackles on a slave who had made repeated attempts to run away. For the judge, the decision was reasonable because "the master had treated that slave so kindly."[18] When an ingrate slave ran away in spite of the kindness of his master, the Berber tradition of shackling offered an acceptable remedy.[19] If we do not question the judges and the judicial traditions they established, we might overlook the slaves' opposition to Berber slavers and their traditions and thus silence those other Berber traditions that compelled those in shackles to prefer freedom to bondage. Not only would we be taking the side of slavers and judges against slaves, but our sense of social realities would be distorted and lacking. When some Berbers enslaved other Berbers, it is difficult to know whose perspective Brett and Fentress would have found more Berber.

Between Fāṭimid and Umayyad Caliphates (10th Century)

The Aghlabids (800–909) ruled in Ifrīqiyā with the blessing of the ʿAbbāsids (750–1258) and largely maintained the privileges of a martial Arab minority over everyone else, a fact that translated into their control of the most productive lands and those who worked them.[20] Unlike the Umayyads of al-Andalus, the Aghlabids did not mobilize Berber armies against their enemies. Since they rose to power in the process of subduing those associated with the Berber revolts, especially those who had found in Ibāḍī ideas a way of dissociating being Muslim from being Arab, doing so would have been contrary to their interests. That is why in Aghlabid Ifrīqiyā "Berber" tended to refer to Ibāḍī Rustamids and their supporters, the threat that surrounded the Aghlabids from Tripoli to the Zāb. In practice, however, instead of Berbers, the Aghlabids had to contend with the Hawwāra, Kutāma, Nafzāwa, and the Zanāta, and even had some success convincing the latter to rally them.

Among all those who opposed the ʿAbbāsids in the Mashriq in the second half of the ninth century, the Ismāʿīlīs garnered a great deal of attention.[21] Incapable of defeating the ʿAbbāsids militarily, they organized an underground opposition, focusing their energies on sharpening their arguments against the injustices of the ruling dynasty in support of their Shīʿī alternative. The formation of "Islamic learning" owes a great deal to the debates, controversies, and attacks they elicited. Unsurprisingly, anti-ʿAbbāsid ideas attracted those Maghribīs who were on the receiving end of Aghlabid domination. Among these were the Kutāma, who controlled areas to the south and west of Ifrīqiyā. In the early years of the tenth century, the Kutāma put an end to both the Rustamids and the Aghlabids and in 909 brought to power someone who claimed to be a descendant of the prophet Muḥammad.

The Fāṭimids were not the first descendants of the Prophet who ruled in the Maghrib; they were preceded by the Idrīsids (788–974).[22] Yet, paradoxically, it is with the coming of the (Arab) Fāṭimids that the domination of the Arab elite in Ifrīqiyā ended; the Kutāma and their Ṣanhāja allies made sure of that. The impressive scale of the transfer of property that followed the waves of expropriation and land grants changed the social balance of power in Ifrīqiyā—and with it the discourse on Berbers. In the Maghrib, the Fāṭimid takeover introduced a political difference between those Berbers who supported the Fāṭimid Imām and those who did not. Fāṭimid expansionism in the regions immediately across the Strait of Gibraltar threatened the Andalusī Umayyads' influence there. Mobilizing Berber forces against the Fāṭimids, the Umayyads landed armies on the African continent, funded Fāṭimid opponents, and engaged in a fierce ideological struggle against them. The most spectacular gesture in this regard was certainly the declaration of an Umayyad caliphate in 929, soon after the Umayyad 'Abd al-Raḥmān III (r. 912–61) defeated Ibn Ḥafṣūn's very serious rebellion in al-Andalus. In the course of securing their power, the Umayyads relied on Berber troops from al-Andalus and the Maghrib, with the Zanāta playing a prominent role.[23]

In spite of their successes, however, the Fāṭimids could never fully impose their power on the entire Maghrib, especially after some Kutāma rebelled against them when they executed the original leader of the Shī'ī "missionary effort" (*da'wa*) in 911. Two decades later, an even more serious rebellion threatened their survival as rulers of Ifrīqiya. After taking al-Qayrawān, Ibāḍī rebels surrounded al-Mahdiya, the Fāṭimid capital, and threatened to put an end to the dynasty. At the last moment, an army led by the Ṣanhāja Zīrī b. Manād came to their rescue and routed the rebels (946). A little more than two decades later, the victory of Fāṭimid armies in Egypt led the entire dynasty to relocate there, leaving Ifrīqiyā to Zīrī b. Manād.

The confluence of Fāṭimid expansion and intra-Iberian politics was a fertile ground for the migration of Berbers to al-Andalus. Some, like the Banū Ṣāliḥ of Nākūr, who had resisted the Fāṭimids, ended up fleeing to Malaga, where 'Abd al-Raḥmān III allowed them to settle. The Umayyad caliph tried to attract a great number of Berber cavalrymen to his capital. In addition to the Banū Ṣāliḥ, 'Abd al-Raḥmān III succeeded in attracting a number of Izdāja after they were attacked by the Fātimid governor and leader of the Banū Yafran who took control of Tāhart. The ousted ruler of Tāhart gathered a number of Jarāwa and left for al-Andalus. 'Abd al-Raḥmān III revived his grandfather's policy of importing Berbers to serve in his military, fully aware of the political danger such a force could constitute. Umayyad suspicions and fears were not unwarranted, as some Berbers allied with the Idrīsids of Fez dealt them serious blows in the 970s. The challenge was obviously to balance the threat an elite corps posed with the benefits of having it on one's side. In his successful war against the Idrīsids, the Umayyad al-Ḥakam II (r. 961–76) relied on an army constituted of Andalusī Berbers, Berbers from the Maghrib, and a mix of other Andalusīs, making sure to be very generous to the leading Berber cavalrymen.[24] Many of these Berbers had fled to al-Andalus because of the Fāṭimids and the Idrīsids. For our purposes, the Berberization of the Umayyad armies had a tremendous effect on politics, especially given the role these Berbers came to play in the demise of the Umayyad dynasty.

After a Kutāma army helped conquer Egypt and install the Fāṭimids as caliphs there, the Ṣanhāja Zīrids they left in charge in Ifrīqiyā gradually began to claim power. Retaining their ideological ties with the Fāṭimids for a while, the Zīrids eventually broke away from them (ca. 1047) and, in the early twelfth century, ruled in their own name. For historians, their reign heralded the era of Berber kingdoms. While "Berbers" had constituted the effective power behind most "important" dynasties that ruled in the Maghrib, it was the first time in history that "Berber" came to be the main adjective for a Maghribī kingdom. However, even if the Zīrids were Berbers, their kingdom was not a kingdom of or for all Berbers.

Buying a Horse

> [The judge Ibn Abī Zayd (d. 996) of al-Qayrawān] was asked about two Berber tribes who having fought, one of them wanted to appeal to another for help against its rival. A member of the rebel tribe bought a horse for the chief of the sought-after tribe. The seller demanded money for the horse from the buyer, who said that the sale was made on behalf of the entire tribe. The seller insisted he sold it to only the one individual. The custom among them (*al-ʿurf ʿindahum*) is that gifts made to gain someone's support of the tribe (*rashwa*) are made on behalf of the entire tribe. His answer was: If their custom is truly such that the purchase was made on behalf of the collective, the buyer is responsible for only his share of the total. If not, he is responsible for the entire sum.[25]

The custom in question here is that a tribal chief acts like a broker on behalf of his fellow tribesmen and arranges battles for them so that they can improve their lot. Custom also regulated the chief's ability to commit young men during the agricultural season and the ability of the young to refuse. What this case points to is the Berber business of war, which was not limited to wars between Berber tribes. In other words, the militarization of Berber tribes was not a natural phenomenon; it worked itself out through tribal organization and led to a formalization of practices recognized here as custom. Through this system of *rashwa*, dynasties purchased the service of tribal leaders, who delivered soldiers. The biographies of a number of men who rose to prominent functions in urban courts suggest that their careers began as one of these Berber soldiers-for-hire. For the successful ones, participating in battles and tax raids proved more profitable than tilling, planting, herding, and harvesting. For those who did not come from the leading families in their villages, soldiering offered an opportunity to accumulate capital at a much higher rate than by doing agriculture, and thus an opportunity to improve their relative social position in the village—if they returned. We can also speculate about the amount of the "broker" fee that chiefs received in these "Berber" customary cases. In our case, one may wonder how the chief handled dividing the horse, but we can guess that, in general, chiefs fared better than their kinsmen, to say nothing of their kinswomen. For that too was the custom among them (*al-ʿurf indahum*).

Fāṭimid Berbers in Egypt

The prominent role of the Kutāma in the conquest of Egypt and in the Fāṭimid army contributed to the process of Berberization there and is thus worth examining more closely.[26] After the foundation of Cairo in 969 and the emigration of the Fāṭimid caliph al-Muʿizz (r. 953–75) from Ifrīqiyā in 974, Egyptians became acquainted with the Kutāma in a particular way. Even if their number was large enough to maintain the power of a foreign dynasty, the Kutāma soldiers were as representative of their Berber societies as soldiers usually are of theirs. Their military function remained the most defining aspect of their social existence in Egypt, although unlike other foreign contingents they seem to have settled among the local population—eventually disappearing as a distinct group. In the early decades of Fāṭimid rule in Egypt, the Fāṭimid historian al-Qāḍī al-Nuʿmān (d. 974) praised the Kutāma, recording their special place in official discourse as early supporters (*ṣanāʾiʿ* and *awliyāʾ*) of the Fāṭimid dynasty. For him, as for the rulers, the

Kutāma deserved the fiscal and political privileges they received. The way the category Berber appears in his history confirms this general assessment.[27] It also shows how some Maghribī notions found themselves in Egypt—part of the official self-representation of the dynasty. For instance, it is with the Fāṭimids that the old Aghlabid discourse on Berbers landed in Egypt, although it was adjusted to the political role the Kutāma played in Egypt.

Al-Qāḍī al-Nuʿmān was born in al-Qayrawān in the early tenth century. As an educated, youthful supporter of the Ismāʿīlī Fāṭimids, he joined the new government and rose in the ranks to occupy the highest judicial office. His writings, which first articulated Ismāʿīlī legal doctrine, gained him the favor of the dynasty. His familiarity with the Ismāʿīlī missions (*daʿwa*), the political machinations, and battles that preceded the emergence of a Fāṭimid caliphate in Ifrīqiyā makes his history particularly informative. As the official story of a small group of militants who took over power from established dynasties, his *Iftitāḥ al-daʿwa* (The Beginning of the Mission) is full of the sort of score settling that the victorious tend to inscribe in such narratives, and its handling of the category Berber is neither radical nor particularly noteworthy, except that it shows the marginality of the category in official Fāṭimid discourse.

Al-Qāḍī al-Nuʿmān used the category Berber only a dozen or so times in his *Iftitāḥ al-daʿwa*. Instead, the historian preferred categories such as Kutāma, Hawwāra, and Zanāta, which were far more helpful in narrating the making of the Fāṭimid order. For him, as for those who lived in Aghlabid Ifrīqiyā, Berber was an epithet that lumped groups together, and was mostly reserved for groups of unknown identity—or for those whose identity was not worth knowing.[28] Berbers lived far from urban centers, were either rebellious or refractory, and were mostly an unpleasant bunch.

In a passage that illustrates well the functioning of the category, the author places the Berbers outside his region: "He instructed them to go beyond Ifrīqiyā to the frontiers of the Berbers (*ḥudūd al-barbar*), and then each one to proceed separately to a [different] region."[29] Such a statement appears to suggest that there were no Berbers in Ifrīqiyā. In the dominant discourse of the Umayyads, Aghlabids, and Fāṭimids, Berbers were groups outside of Arab Ifrīqiyā, somewhere all the way out there—perhaps around the Ibāḍī communities in the south. Even if the political realities had changed since the Aghlabids, the idea was still pervasive.

Likewise, it was natural for al-Qāḍī al-Nuʿmān to use the category Berber to disparage opponents: "Then [Sahl] said, 'O Abū Tamīm! You are our chief, our commander, and son of our commander, and our in-law. Would you then accept for your sisters that the Berbers, that is the Mazāta, take them into captivity, and that your brothers and cousins be slain at their hands?'"[30] Many of the supporters of the Fāṭimids were Berbers as well, and yet al-Qāḍī al-Nu'mān did not think this use of the category would slight them, as they would not identify as Berbers but rather as Kutāma, Hawwāra, or some other tribal group. When the historian depicted Fāṭimid supporters as Berbers, it was in the context of narrating a ruse to put pressure on a chief. The word Berber appears again when a chief explains his supporters' inability to understand the fine points of Fāṭimid teachings, and by implication those that would require them to perform certain services: "He is a man from the people of the East who, as you know, are devils. Our *'ulamā'* are Berbers (*barābir*), a people who do not have that intelligence. If they were to debate, he would win the argument against them, and they will find no argument against him."[31] Not unlike the Andalusī Berbers, these Berbers lacked intellectual savoir-faire. On the other hand, the same al-Qāḍī al-Nu'mān praised the Kutāma and other Berbers who brought the Mahdī 'Ubayd Allāh to power in 909. In a language full of allusion, the historian related a story about the link that the leader Abū 'Abd Allāh al-Shī'ī made between the Kutāma and the Ismā'īlī belief in the power of the coming of the Mahdī. Apparently, the role of the Kutāma was foretold, their name being a sign for the secrecy surrounding their mission (*da'wa*) to elude the agents of the unjust caliph: "By God, this ravine has only been named after you, for it has been reported in the traditions that the Mahdī will emigrate far away from his fatherland, at a time of vicissitudes and troubles, during which his defenders will be the best of men whose name will derive from *kitmān* (concealment), and you Kutāma are the ones referred to, because you originate from this ravine which is called Fajj al-Akhyār (the Ravine of the Righteous)."[32] After his victory over the Aghlabids, the Fāṭimid Mahdī did not go after those who had been pillars of the Aghlabid order. Instead, he welcomed them and maintained them in their property and privileges. He also brought his Kutāma supporters into the Aghlabid capital of Raqqāda and settled them there. They settled there as Kutāma and not as Berbers, and everyone seems to have understood that.

In Egypt, each army within the Fāṭimid military specialized in a particular weaponry or fighting style, according to its own "traditional" ways: "The blacks served as heavy infantry, the Daylams as light infantry employing bows and javelins, the Turks as mounted archers, and the Berbers as cavalry employing lances."[33] The Berbers in question here are the Kutāma cavalrymen and not the Ṣanhāja foot soldiers who also followed the Fāṭimids to Egypt. Unlike the Kutāma, however, the poorly remunerated Ṣanhāja were near the bottom of the military hierarchy—some even returned to the Maghrib. Those who remained did not receive land grants nor did their salaries allow them to afford a great deal, though it is unclear whether they would have fared any better had they simply stayed home.[34]

The privileges of the Kutāma eroded with time as the Fāṭimids recruited more mercenaries from central Asia and purchased slave soldiers from eastern Africa and from Europe to confront new enemies. The Kutāma remained an important component of the Fāṭimid system, but the policies enacted under al-ʿAzīz (r. 975–96) and al-Ḥākim (r. 996–1021) made for a more diversified military. While this strategy allowed the Fāṭimids to win a number of significant wars, especially in Syria, it created the conditions for a conflict between these groups. As they responded to crises, real and perceived, Fāṭimid rulers often rescinded the privileges bestowed on individuals and groups by their predecessors, and thus fueled discontent among a class of politically active groups. At the same time, land grants tied military privilege to agricultural production, which, given the ecology, varied greatly and was sensitive to disruptions like the rebellions that plagued the country in the first half of the eleventh century.

Even if general and broad, this brief outline of Fāṭimid politics shows that the terms of the Berberization of discourse in Egypt and Syria were distinct, tied as they were to the realities of rule in those regions. The adaptation of ideas that originated in the Maghrib to local circumstances took time and was shaped by political developments in the Mashriq. This is what makes Fāṭimid Berberization noteworthy.

Andalusī Berberism

After the death of the second Umayyad caliph, his underage son was proclaimed caliph, but the actual power was held by Muḥammad b. ʿĀmir (d. 1002), a general renowned for leading the expansion of Umayyad territory by fighting Christians.[35] That policy led to increasing reliance on foreign troops, mostly Ṣaqāliba (Slavs) and Berbers.[36] The new Berbers were mercenaries from the Maghrib, with no special ties to al-Andalus other than their employer. After the death of the powerful *ḥājib* Ibn ʿĀmir, his generals and the enemies he had made along the way saw an opportunity to make political claims of their own.[37] In the following three decades, the Umayyad territory was gradually parceled into small entities led by various factions (*ṭawā'if*, sing. *ṭā'ifa*) whose political agendas ranged from Umayyad restoration to different versions of Arab, Slav, and Berber rule, and coalitions made of permutations of any of these—and which, for good measure, often included Castilians and others.

The new Berbers, like the Zīrids, found themselves in jeopardy after the death of Ibn 'Āmir. Their opposition to those "Arabs" who resented their influence took the form of "Berberism," an idea that fused the political aspirations of a number of powerful Andalusīs of Maghribī origin. The fact that a Zīrid dynasty ruled in Ifrīqiyā must have emboldened them. That said, and given their diverse composition in reality, the alliances that led to the formation of independent Berber dynasties did not quite live up to the strictest Berberism. Rather, the alliances that supported "Berber" dynasties were actually comparable to those that helped propel rival dynasties with anti-Berber agendas. Collectively, the new dynasties that replaced the Umayyad order were known as *mulūk al-ṭawā'if*, the Party Kings (1013–86).[38]

The establishment of Berber emirates was the culmination of the process of political polarization of the Andalusī elites begun in the last few decades of Umayyad rule. In fact, and this is hardly controversial, the emergence of the Taifa kings accounts for the particularly militant discourse on identity and difference at the time. In the contentious ideological competition between dynasties, Berberism conferred on the category Berber a new layer of signification. Berber solidarity and anti-Berber sentiment were two sides of the Janus-faced coin of dynasty formation and identity reformulation. Unsurprisingly, it became natural for Andalusī intellectuals to identify individuals in terms of their ancestry—something modern historians used as evidence to support their own discourses on identity.

Andalusī Berber dynasties, which competed for power and honor, elicited intellectual and artistic products of a particular coloration. The struggles between Arab and Berber emirates fostered sentiments of pride in one's own group and antipathy toward others. These two expressions of the victory of a new form of elite identity-politics envisioned "Berber" and "Arab" as alternative ideological articulations of dynastic domination. That is why the two categories end up looking even closer to each other than ever before. Since the two shared in a general political and cultural imaginary, which paralleled their socioeconomic and institutional similarities, they expressed their pride and rivalry in the same general framework. The same is true of the search for prestigious lineages that generated many treatises on genealogy and, of course, many more genealogies. In this regard, the relationship between al-Andalus and both the Mashriq and Arabia (where Arabs came from) and the Maghrib (where Berbers came from) was reimagined and recreated.

New Bedouin Arabs in the Maghrib

The Fāṭimids claimed that they were behind the migrations of the Banū Hilāl and Banū Sulaym to the Maghrib, presenting them as retribution for the Zīrids' betrayal. There are, however, many reasons historians have doubted the ability of the then-embattled Fāṭimids to achieve such a grand feat. The arrival of thousands of Bedouin Arabs in the Maghrib and the wars they fought against city-based Berber dynasties created conditions for a particular brand of learned catastrophism, which has had an extraordinarily long and rich life. The Arab Bedouins challenged Ṣanhāja domination in the eastern Maghrib and inflected the struggle between the Zīrids (1015/1057–1148) and their Ḥammādid (1015–1152) cousins.

Zīrids and Hammādids were "Berber," although in a particularly "Andalusī" sense—otherwise they were both Ṣanhāja. Because we do not have sources from the Banū Hilāl and Banū Sulaym dating from this period, it is difficult to gauge how they framed the politics in which they entered headfirst. Their epic poems recorded much later about these heroic times identify the Zanāta and other Berbers by name—but one needs to situate that discourse in its own context. In any case, these new Arab Bedouins arrived at a time when Berberism was the rage among Berber dynasties of al-Andalus. But unlike in al-Andalus, the Arabs that mattered politically in the Maghrib were not urbanites with prestigious aristocratic pedigrees who thought they were better than parvenu Berbers. The Arabs of the Maghrib were Bedouins who showed no interest in *parvenir.* The fact that these two versions, Andalusī and Maghribī, were not quite the same is pertinent because the majority of extant chronicles that inform us about earlier periods date back to this period, or later. Although their authors made extensive use of earlier texts, they express interpretative schemes in vogue at the time of their composition. Regardless of the position of the individual author vis-à-vis this or that dynasty, Berber or not, the assumption that tagging an individual or group as Berber was sufficient to explain all sorts of phenomena seemed obvious to all.

Taifa Berberization Again

The fall of Cordoba in 1031 put an end to the political fortunes of the Umayyad dynasty. The entitled expectations of elite Arabs took the form of independent city-based emirates whose sense of self far outmatched their military power. Likewise, self-esteem was not lacking among the Berber Taifas (*tawā'if*), even if they belonged to "old" families like the Dhū al-Nūn, who had settled in al-Andalus centuries before "new" families like the Zīrids. While the Slavs also formed independent kingdoms, thus explaining the fixation on ancestry among intellectuals, the Berbers alone were on the receiving end of the blame game, held responsible for the end of the caliphate and the negation of its cultural accomplishments, and for weakening the power of Islam and Muslims in al-Andalus.[39] Although the Berbers were not alone in rebelling against the Umayyads, historians remembered the period as the time of the Berber rebellion (*fitnat al-barbar* or *al-fitna al-barbariya*). Animus against the Berbers' destructiveness found renewed strength after the Almoravids (1040–1147) of Marrakesh sent armies to al-Andalus in 1085 to end intra-Muslim conflicts and save Islam from Christian advances.

The Almoravid conquest of al-Andalus and the centralization of power in their hands led to a realignment of power relations in the peninsula following the elimination of Taifa kingdoms. Among other effects, this led to new employment opportunities for erstwhile pro-Taifa Andalusīs, who became Almoravid officials and courtiers. Mālikī jurisprudence, which had thrived under the Umayyads, came to constitute the link between the Almoravid dynasty and Andalusī urbanites. While opposition to the Almoravids was rife among Taifa elites who had been defeated and stripped of their privileges, those urban families that had been more measured or simply opportunistic found favor with the new masters. Many of these families had produced judges and continued to perform those functions in al-Andalus and now also in the Maghrib.[40]

The Almoravids were Ṣanhāja. They were thus Berbers who unseated, among others, numerous Berber Taifas, thus adding another layer of identity politics to the historical record. Their triumph in al-Andalus meant that Berbers of varying origins constituted urban dynasties that generated honor and prestige. Rather than being Berbers in general or Berbers in the abstract, these were specific Berber groups that became kings, the way the Zīrids and Ḥammādids had been in the Maghrib.[41] As the Ṣanhāja were Bedouin Berbers who had only recently settled in cities, members of the defeated old Arab elite found much in their behavior to lament and ridicule. When the Maṣmūda Almohads conquered al-Andalus in the twelfth century, yet another tribe of Berbers had invaded, eliciting another wave of winners and losers, realignments, and proclamations about Berbers and their character. This conquest also reaffirmed the place of genealogy and genealogists as a source of essential knowledge.

As Maghribī rulers became patrons and employers of Andalusī intellectuals during the rule of the Almoravids (1040–1147) and Almohads (1121–1269) in al-Andalus, Maghribīs occupied important functions in the administration, such as judgeships, while Andalusīs performed similar functions in the Maghrib. The formation of a class of intellectuals that straddled both sides of the strait added an Andalusī Taifa note to Maghribī Berberization.

A New Home for Poor Berbers

> [Judge] Ibn Rushd [d. 1126] was asked by some of the Berbers (*barābir*) from across the strait (*al-ʿudwa*) who had arrived in Cordoba as a contingent (*jumūʿ*) in 515 AH [1121/2] about a man and a woman who had committed fornication (*zaniyā*) without taking appropriate precautions (*bi-ghayri istibrāʾ min al-māʾ al-fāsid*) and had (multiple) children. They then separated by announcing their divorce, reconciled, divorced a second time, reconciled, and then divorced a third time. They then accused each other of being the cause of the situation and denied having done any of what was stated above. When they consulted the muftis (*ahl al-fatwā*), they were told that all their contracts were invalid (*fāsid*) and that their children were not considered legitimate. While their affairs were being sorted out, the husband of the woman died. Their children did not inherit from him, and his property was distributed to the poor.[42]

After her husband died, the widow and her children probably sought the help of her husband's companions, who referred her case to the authorities.

Ibn Rushd does not represent the Berber soldiers who had arrived recently as members of specific tribes but as *barābir*; this commonly used plural form may have carried a hint of deprecation, depending on context.[43] Of course, the soldiers knew what tribe they belonged to; it just did not matter to Ibn Rushd. At the same time, the couple does not seem to have belonged to a tribe either—at least not in al-Andalus.[44] It is unlikely that they could have behaved like this had they been living among their kin, as they would have in their village back in the Maghrib. In fact, we do not know that they were from the same tribe or even region—*barābir* took care of that. This is not to say that Berbers did not divorce, remarry, or have children out of wedlock, just that it would have been harder to live in sin in front of relatives and even harder to disperse an adult male's wealth in a village setting. Customs and young men working to enforce them would have made it very difficult for the problem to arise in the first place, the cost of such a trespass being very high and known to all. The stories of runaways, elopers, and other émigrés are not simply about the pursuit of happiness. In a sense, this couple's story is about the freedoms and disadvantages that come with leaving one's home.

The inability of the soldiers to resolve the matter themselves suggests that their incorporation into an army of Berbers in al-Andalus disabled the tribal mechanisms they knew could resolve such a case. For one thing, the fact that they had come from tribes with different customs might have made it practically difficult. Who knows? However, as soon as they joined the army, the rules that applied to their lives were those of the ruler, who decided where they lived, how they were paid, and when they fought. These rules, backed by the judicial system, were their ticket to a better life in al-Andalus. The threat that such an affair posed to their reputations matches the judge's tone: ah, low-class Berbers and their crazy stories . . .

Almohads and Others

The twelfth century saw the making of a large empire led by the Maṣmūda followers of the Mahdī Ibn Tūmart (d. 1130).[45] After they put an end to the rule of the Almoravids in Marrakesh (1147), the Almohads (1121/1147–1269) expanded their dominion under ʿAbd al-Muʾmin (r. 1130–63) and his successors. At its peak, the Almohad empire stretched from the western borders of Egypt to the Atlantic and then north into al-Andalus. The largest medieval empire in the Maghrib, and the only political entity that encompassed the entire Maghrib, the Almohads set the historical stage for an unprecedented degree of unity and integration—even if actual circumstances were a little less grandiose. In spite of their incontrovertible military successes, however, the Almohads faced a good deal of fierce opposition, which weakened their reach, especially in the eastern regions that were far from Marrakesh, their capital. As far as rebellions go, however, no other threat to Almohad rule was as serious as that of the Banū Ghāniya, the branch of the Almoravids who ruled over the Balearic Islands and sought to reclaim their dynasty's rule in the Maghrib.

In their struggle against the Almohads, which lasted throughout Almohad rule, the Banū Ghāniya made alliances with anyone who rejected the Almohads, including foreign armies like the one that invaded the eastern Maghrib from Ayyūbid Egypt.[46] Between the Almohad policy of responding militarily to threats like these and their other policy of giving defeated foes the chance to join them, Almohad political history reads like an uninterrupted stream of military campaigns against ever-changing permutations of a large cast of characters. The Almohads' broad use of mercenaries, Christians and not, prioritized political considerations and gave them precedence over ideological purity, even as Almohad propaganda insisted on it.[47] The vagaries of politics apart, however, the long Almohad century saw the deepening of intellectual and cultural ties between the Maghrib and al-Andalus—in spite of the complaints of many in al-Andalus—and the appearance of Berber-language texts as an integral part of the functioning of Almohad government.[48]

The Almohad empire's expansion over the entire Maghrib and al-Andalus, its policy of writing the spoken language of the Maṣmūda, attracting Andalusī intellectual superstars, and seeking to develop an aesthetic brand for itself created the conditions for an adaptation of Andalusī ideas about Berbers to the new situation.[49] Andalusīs such as Ibn al-Ṭufayl (1105–85) and Ibn Rushd (1126–84) both lived and worked in Marrakesh, while others, like the Sufi Abū Madyan (d. 1197) and Ibn Sab'īn (d. 1270), had stellar careers in the Maghrib.[50] In many ways, these intellectuals deemphasized the importance of "being Berber" while appealing to "Berber religiosity." Whether they articulated ideas about the universal application of religious commandments like the jurists or the limited number of those who could really understand them, as the Sufis did, these intellectuals did not emphasize ancestry. At the same time, the organization of the Almohad government itself instituted a tribal logic. While scholars have examined a great many facets of

Almohadism, it is worth acknowledging the multifaceted and contradictory tendencies it engendered, especially in reference to the deployment of the category Berber.

Andalusīs in the Post-Almohad Maghrib

The Almohads had their hands full between the Banū Ghāniya rebellions in the Maghrib, the aggressive campaigning of the Castilians and their Aragonese, Navarran, and Portuguese allies in Iberia, and the resistance of Andalusī elites who jockeyed for Taifa kingdoms of their own. In the early decades of the thirteenth century, maintaining their outstretched empire became a serious challenge for the Almohads. After a large Almohad army was routed in al-Andalus (1212), the dynasty began a retreat from al-Andalus and then from other regions, until it found itself defending areas closer and closer to Marrakesh. When the Almohads left, the kingdoms that emerged in al-Andalus had no reasonable expectation of reclaiming the territory once ruled by the Umayyads. If anything, their modus operandi was close to that of the first Taifa kingdoms, which had precipitated the arrival of the Almoravids and then the Almohads in the first place. After the fall of the Almohads, the three dynasties that took over in the Maghrib, the Marīnids (1244–1465), the ʿAbd al-Wādids (1235–1556), and the Ḥafsids (1229–1574), had a hard time rallying the sort of military force that would have allowed them to emulate their predecessors in more than just their slogans.[51] Al-Andalus had to fend for itself, and from the thirteenth century on, it did so irregularly and not very well, although it did take two centuries to put an end to the last Muslim kingdom in the peninsula.

The fall of important Andalusī cities led to the migration of members of the Andalusī urban elites to the Maghrib in unprecedented numbers. Elite Andalusīs found a place at the courts of Maghribī rulers, rising to very prominent positions thanks to their expertise in administration and various sciences—although their expertise had failed to protect them from losing their cities. For many reasons, Andalusīs ended up constituting distinct "communities" (sing. *jamāʿa*) in the Maghrib, usually with their own living quarters and representatives. As an Andalusī identity gradually emerged in the Maghrib, the old intra-Andalusī regional and urban jealousies gradually lost most of their political importance, becoming part of the points of pride of families who claimed old and prestigious pedigrees. These families bore the memory of al-Andalus in their stories and in the customs they treasured and which set them apart from the locals.

Many of the elite Andalusī immigrants were Andalusī Arabs, and for a variety of reasons, "Andalusī" came to be almost synonymous with "Arab" in the Maghrib. Andalusī intellectuals and experts created a need for their services by building up al-Andalus as the land of intellectual and technical superiority, while using the very real threat against all "Muslims"—that is, Arabs and Berbers—to elicit support or at least a feeling of solidarity. In other words, the integration of elite Andalusīs into the elites of the Maghrib accounts for the rearticulation of Andalusī cultural superiority.

The Arabness of the Andalusīs contrasted with the Berberness of their employers. There was nothing necessarily wrong with the Berber ancestry of the Marīnids, ʿAbd al-Wādids, or Ḥafṣids, just that, relatively speaking, they were not as "old" as the old Arab families whose ancestors participated in the Muslim conquest of al-Andalus (*futūḥ*)—of course, the Andalusīs just happened to have ancient ties to Islam and to the golden age of al-Andalus. In their writings, they insisted that their Berber masters had prestigious lineages and great ancestors and, in their own way, deserved the honors and prestige they claimed. This much the fourteenth-century author of the *Mafākhir al-babar* agreed with—with his book offering evidence of the many Berber accomplishments.[52] In their daily lives, however, elite Andalusī houses (*buyūtāt*, sing. *bayt*) kept to themselves and did not feel it was necessary to marry into these Berber families, satisfied with being the privileged heirs to their lost Eden. Synthesizing these ideas, Ibn Khaldūn (1332–1406) configured the history of the Maghrib as the history of those among the Arabs and Berbers who founded dynasties, rather than an Arab period when Arabs ruled followed by a period of Berber dynasties. His scheme allows for the contemporaneous existence of great dynasties with Arab and Berber genealogies. This was a major step in the Berberization of the Maghrib and its past.[53]

Berber Customs Again

In the last decades of the fourteenth century, the Ḥafṣids (1229–1574), who claimed the mantle of Almohad legitimacy, struggled to project their domination beyond the main urban centers of Ifrīqiyā. In the mountains, the locals enjoyed a great deal of autonomy from a dynasty that claimed to rule over them. Not only did they not pay taxes, or only on those occasions when soldiers went on tax raids into the country; they followed many customs that had no basis in the law of the cities' jurists. These customs encompassed inheritance rules, marriage, the organization of production (agriculture and transhumance), and the resolution of conflicts. Urban jurists recognized these customs as "systems" and the territories they covered as "lands where tribal law prevailed" (*arḍ al-qānūn*). And it seems that adults living under each legal regime had a general sense of the advantages and disadvantages of both. Villagers had some familiarity with the towns they visited on occasion for business. They had connections there, sometimes relatives who had settled there. Those who understood these differences best were those who took advantage of them, such as merchants and criminals. Thus it would be a mistake to imagine two completely separated worlds, one urban and dynastic and the other rural and tribal.

Tribal law was not the same in every tribe, of course, and tribesmen were very aware of this basic fact, especially when conflicts with neighbors brought this to the fore. If Islamic jurisprudence, which was associated with imperial and dynastic power, tended to envisage a broad homogenization of practices, tribal law responded to experiences on a far smaller scale. In this narrow sense, Pan-Berber sentiments did not correspond to the daily lives and horizons of Berber villagers. On the contrary, they may have run counter them. In the cities, of course, matters were different. But to the extent that some of the ideas that circulated in cities about Berbers pertained to Berbers "out there," it might be useful to examine an example of the relations between city and mountain Berbers, if only to refine our understanding of the sites of Berberization. The example comes from a legal case brought to the grand judge Ibn ʿArafa al-Warghammī (d. 1401) of Tunis, and pertains to a phenomenon that was common enough to necessitate clarification from the highest legal authority in Ifrīqiyā:

> [The grand judge of Tunis Ibn ʿArafa] was asked about this case: Jabal Waslāt is about two mail stations away from al-Qayrawān and the road to there is sometimes safe and sometimes unsafe. A woman who had run away from that mountain [i.e., Jabal Waslāt] arrived in the city to complain about her husband who had caused her harm. She desired to sue him and was afraid for her life if she were made to go back to him, having left him. The woman made multiple pleas to the ruler (*al-ḥākim*) [or his local representative]

who wrote to someone to prod the concerned husband to come from that mountain to the city. Sometimes the concerned [husbands] would come to the city, but in the majority of cases they do not. Then, a letter in unknown handwriting and confusing language arrived [presumably] from the person responsible for prodding the husband. It stated that the husband had become upset or ran way and that it was hoped that the husband would be convinced and that he might come. In fact, getting such letters in return occurs only in some cases; in others, the woman would just stay in the city in that [legal] state. If a long time passes [without her case finding resolution], the woman may seek a divorce based on the husband's failure to provide for her. She may prepare documents to the effect that her husband declined to face his responsibilities by staying in the mountains and refusing to present himself to court, and proceed to establish [legally] that the husband had failed to fulfill the stipulations regarding provision. [The question is,] Is [the wife] able to make a valid case against the husband even if she is the one who ran away after she had lived with him in the mountains, claiming that she feared for her life because he had harmed her? What if the woman insisted that her husband had intended to harm her? There is also the case of the destitute woman who arrives from the mountains seeking to be married [in the city], but her legal guardian is in the mountains. Should the ruler act as her guardian and marry her off if she is shown not to be married and it is difficult to contact her legal guardian in the mountains?

[Ibn 'Arafa] answered:

. . . [There is disagreement between jurists about the issue of fear.] But what I ascertained when I resided in al-Qayrawān about the surrounding villages was that they were outside the reach of the law. I see that the runaway woman cannot obtain [justice] in Jabal Waslāt or Jabal Hawwāra. Something like this occurred when another woman ran away from the Banū Ḥarīr, a village in the region of al-Qayrawān, distant nine miles [from the city]. Judge Ibn Qīdār returned the woman to her husband and a relative of hers after he told them to fear God's Judgment and His Punishment. They took her and killed her on the road back home. The same took place this year.[54]

Ibn ʿArafa's opinion continues, but this excerpt is long enough to allow us to say a few things. First, the word Berber does not occur at all, which, given our discussion, is not at all surprising—the fact that Ibn ʿArafa was himself Berber does not seem to have affected his response. He approached the question with the knowledge that even if correct, his judicial opinion would be unenforceable, and the lament that runs through his decision captures this sentiment. Second, at least in this legal opinion (*fatwā*), Ibn ʿArafa did not envisage a civilizing process to teach mountain Berbers not to beat or kill their wives and sisters. To the extent that his opinion was a call for action, it was limited to the legal duty of "enjoining good and forbidding wrong," already discharged by a predecessor, and to the need to find a suitable legal status for the runaway woman. The Berbers had their ancestral ways, and it was pointless to try to convince them to change them. Third, Ibn ʿArafa does not express moral superiority vis-à-vis "the Berbers"—and not just because he does not use the category. Presiding over various courts in Ifrīqiyā over the years, he was certainly aware that wife beating and killing were not restricted to villagers in the mountains or to Berbers. For him, the details of the case were "accidents," and the law did address them in their specificity. Yet, because of its logic, the law did not imagine Pan-Berber qualities and characteristics but only a series of specifics framed in relation to a universalizing discourse, the law. In the eyes of the jurists, Berbers were Muslims first; their customs were relevant to the pragmatic need to finding optimal outcomes and were thus of secondary relevance. That is a particular way of making the word Berber matter.

New Berbers for a New Maghrib

Between the defeat of the Almohads in al-Andalus and the fall of Naṣrid Granada in 1492, Islam became the primary rallying call for the remaining Muslims, paralleling the Christianization of political discourse in neighboring kingdoms, notably Portugal and Castile. Berbers did not completely disappear, and could still be blamed for the disasters that befell al-Andalus, but perhaps because of elite Andalusīs' need for Maghribī rulers in the lands to which they migrated, Muslim solidarity gradually overlaid anti-Berber rhetoric. As piracy and the trade in captives became increasingly lucrative, the ideological importance of religious categorizations rose, even before the Inquisition, the Wars of Religion, and the Ottoman-Spanish wars made them de rigueur.

Overall, the rise of Sharīfī politics in the western Maghrib, which emphasized the genealogical ties between the ruling elite and the prophet Muḥammad, and Ottoman rule combined to deemphasize the political significance of the category Berber. In the western Maghrib, and in spite of its many attempts, the Sa'dī dynasty (1554–1659) experienced serious difficulties imposing its rule on Andalusīs, 'Alawīs, and Ottomans, to say nothing of the lands controlled by various Berber groups. In the central and eastern Maghrib, the ruling Ottomans distinguished themselves from the locals in language, customs, and even legal school. The association of political and economic power with the Ottoman Empire made Berber a "local" phenomenon, something that the local representatives of the empire dealt with, as they did with the particularities of other regions under their rule. Although many Berbers and Arabs rebelled against the Ottomans, "the Arabs" and "the Berbers" as such did not rise up against the Ottomans. In any case, Turks or not, the Ottomans fought the Christians and that was good enough for those Maghribī elites whose privileges they protected. At the same time, because the Ottomans ruled in the Maghrib from the sea, their penetration into the country depended heavily on the collaboration of local elites. Beyond the area of hundred or so miles that they controlled, their influence diminished dramatically. Even within that Mediterranean band, the Ottomans struggled to subdue mountainous areas, ruling mostly from cities, where they established garrisons and from which they set out into "rebel" areas to collect taxes. The organization of the country into armed Sufi (not Berber) orders was only one of the features of this new imperial situation.[55]

Our Sister Should Marry One of Us!

> The jurist Abū Muhammad 'Abd Allāh al-'Abdūsī [d. 1466] was asked about a merchant of good moral standing and averred skill. [The man] made a living from trade, [and was] not known to be late [in paying his debts] or to take that which did not belong to him [rightly]. [The man] was of Qaysī background, an ancestry known to him and his forebears. He asked the hand of a woman from the Awrāba, a Berber tribe (*min qabā'il al-barābir*), but her family comes from a good line of preachers who had practiced in Tāza, her father having the [relatively low religious] position of *ṭālib*. Their family is among the old families of Tāza. Her brother

> who is her legal guardian married her off to the said man with her consent, and set the amount of the dowry (*mahr*) at the level of someone of her rank or higher. Some of her brothers who are not her legal guardians rose up after her guardian had agreed to the terms of the marriage contract, [claiming] that the man was not of a sufficient status to marry [their sister] and produced a deed (*rasm*) to that effect with the goal of annulling the marriage contract.
>
> He answered: If it is averred that the husband has the mentioned qualities, she is of equivalent status, the criteria for equivalency being, according to Ibn al-Qāsim, state (*ḥāl*) and wealth (*māl*). . . . There is no doubt that if we consider ancestry (*nasab*), he is from Qays and Qays are Arabs and she is from Awrāba who are Berbers, and the Arabs are better than the Berbers [when it comes to genealogy], so he is at least equivalent to her in genealogy. If we consider wealth, he is better than she is, as you have described.[56]

In the Fez of the fifteenth century, an Arab was not just good, he was good enough for an Awrāba girl from Tāza.[57] Without underestimating the importance of the judge's statement about the Arabs being better than the Berbers, one can appreciate its wickedness. The brothers who claimed honor based on their family's demonstrated piety were being reminded of the Arab origins of the prophet Muḥammad. Yes, not all Arabs were Qurayshīs, but Qaysīs were ʿAdnānīs like the Prophet. They may not have known that, but the judge certainly implied that they ran the risk of finding out. That said, the pride of the Awrāba brothers signals the importance of the discourse on genealogy among those who would eventually bring the Sharīfs to power.

Even if they did not think of themselves primarily as Berbers but rather as members of particular tribes, Berbers appealed to genealogical knowledge to achieve goals of their own. Did the girl's guardian truly believe that the Arabs were better than the Berbers? Or did he believe that getting the judge to support his decision over the objections of his brothers was more important? And did the brothers truly believe the merchant was an inappropriate party because he was an Arab, or did they have other reasons? Whatever may be the case, genealogical knowledge was obviously not an inert body of stories fabricated to make the powerful look good. While royal courts mobilized it to articulate their legitimacy claims, the science of *nasab* and its discourse on Arabs and Berbers "trickled down." It became available for manipulation by anyone with the slightest education and interest.

Berberization and Its Many Sites

The closer one comes to centers of dynastic power, the more Berbers one finds. The learned disciplines that developed systematic approaches to all Berbers and to Berbers-in-general were associated either with ruling dynasties or with those among the elites who opposed them but were no less dynastic in mindset. The Berberization of the knowledge of the dynasties and their supporters was the primary source of the Berberization of everyone else's. Yet, although they give us a sense of the success of this effort to Berberize, after nearly a thousand years, the sources still recorded Berbers failing to find any use for the category. In the absence of institutional mechanisms to impose a uniform Berberization on everyone in the Maghrib, "Berber" remained a primarily ideological notion, a specter, even when it was integral to the dominant political ideologies.

The instrumentalization of "Berbers" by successive dynasties conferred on the category a consistently martial character. Without it, the term Berber could have continued to be associated with slavery or acquired other connotations. The martial character of the Berbers is tied to the martial function of the elite, Berber and non-Berber, and to the closeness of the historical sources to centers of power. This too belongs in the column of historical origins, even if dominant dynastic knowledge imagined Berber origins in primarily genealogical terms. If dynastic power was the engine behind Berber production, genealogy was one of its primary modalities. By the time genealogists integrated the Berbers into their map of the world's known peoples, it had become unthinkable that there was a time when Berbers did not exist. But what exactly does it mean for Berbers to have been conceived of in genealogical terms? What does it mean for them to be a people? The next chapter will examine these questions more closely.

PART II

Genealogy and Homeland

A quelque activité humaine que l'étude s'attache, la même erreur guette les chercheurs d'origine: de confondre une filiation avec une explication.

—Marc Bloch, *Apologie pour l'histoire, ou, Métier d'historien*

Chapter 3

The Berber People

The notion of people, and those of nation, ethnos, tribe, and race, are constitutive of the modern world, and express modern social relations of power, institutions, and ideologies. Woven into both popular and academic forms of knowledge, these notions have helped make the Berbers a people for modern times. These modern Berbers, the by-product of modern Berberization, have found their way into the medieval period and concealed much more than the anachronism of moderns. In fact, modern Berberization has hurt our ability to historicize medieval notions and thus to understand how medieval writers occulted their own anachronism. However, the making of a people in modern times is not only a technical problem that professional historians face. Its ideological character explains some of the fuel behind modern Berberization and points to a particular site of hurdle-production for medievalists.

Whether as a people, a nation, an ethnos, or a race, modern Berbers have had a tremendous impact on the work of medievalists, especially in enabling anachronistic and ideological interpretations and explanations. Focusing as they do on understanding their sources, medievalists have failed to recognize the effects of modern Berberization on their work—although some have rightly cautioned against anachronism and the uncritical application of modern categories. In the case of the Berbers, these considerations have not been visibly at the forefront of the medievalists' concerns. Consequently, medievalists have tended to think of the Berbers as a people (or nation, race, ethnos, etc.) in a modern sense. Insisting as I do here on something as evident as the difference between medieval and modern conceptions brings into focus the work of translation as a critical site of Berberization, a question that will be examined in Part III.

What the historian Ibn Khaldūn (1332–1406) contributed to Berberization is a systematic organization of the past in genealogical terms, which, for the Maghrib, meant a history of the Arabs and Berbers who founded notable dynasties. Unlike other historians, however, Ibn Khaldūn presented the historical events he recounted as exemplifying and supporting his theoretically couched vision of historical change, an aspect of his work that has made him particularly attractive to moderns. The main purpose of this chapter is to make clear that late medieval Berberization represented by Ibn Khaldūn's *Kitāb al-ʿibar* is markedly different from modern Berberization. Part III will then show that the modern racialization, nationalization, and ethnicization of the medieval history of the Maghrib relied heavily and primarily on Ibn Khaldūn in spite of this otherwise obvious difference.

As they proceeded to bring about the gradual and ongoing Berberization of learned discourse, medieval Arabic authors did so with the linguistic and conceptual tools available to them. Even when they departed from common usage, they did so within social and cultural horizons specific to them. An examination of the medieval Arabic discourse on "peoples" is therefore a good place to begin. However, while an analysis of the ways medieval authors conceived of the Berbers and peoples more generally would help determine whether the handling of Berber stood out from that of similar categories, notably the category Arab, the goal here is slightly different. Because of the place that Ibn Khaldūn occupies in the field, his *Kitāb al-ʿibar* will receive special attention. In fact, the works discussed here will all "lead" to his. This deliberately narrow utilization of the body of pertinent texts does not claim to be a systematic and exhaustive study of the question—even if the texts considered here are far from being marginal in any sense.[1] At the same time, the works analyzed below point to issues that one encounters when trying to assess the specific contribution of the science of genealogy (*ʿilm al-nasab*) to historical writing, and through it to the Berberization of the past.

The One and the Many

Have modern scholars really neglected these issues? No, they have not. But they have tended to approach them in ways that have occulted the operations of modern Berberization, leading to a number of inconsistencies. Perhaps a concrete example will explain what I mean by this. Consider the very basic question of whether the Berbers represent a single people or a number of distinct peoples. The scholarly consensus, if there is one, is nebulous. For some experts, the Berbers are a single people. For others, they are many peoples. Still others maintain that the Berbers are not technically a people but rather a group best understood in nonethnic terms. This situation would be rather banal, however, if specialists did not also hold two or more of these apparently mutually exclusive propositions to be true at the same time.

In their contribution to Blackwell's Peoples of Africa series, historian Michael Brett and archaeologist Elizabeth Fentress offer a good example of both the difficulty of unpacking scholarly usage and the necessity to do so. The epigraph that begins their book is a famous passage from Ibn Khaldūn:[2] "[The Berbers] belong to a powerful, formidable, brave and numerous people; a true people like so many others the world has seen—like the Arabs, the Persians, the Greeks, and the Romans. The men who belong to this family of peoples have inhabited the Maghreb since the beginning."[3] For Ibn Khaldūn, the Berbers are a single, if numerous, people but also a family of distinct peoples. Brett and Fentress tend to echo his position: "The Berber peoples did not develop in a vacuum, and their history must be put into its North African context. . . . The role of the Berbers as protagonists in their own history has been lost in the process."[4]

On the one hand, the Berbers are a plurality of peoples; on the other, they have a single history. But not everyone agrees. For H. T. Norris, "Berber has a linguistic but not an ethnic reality."[5] Gabriel Camps seems to agree: "At no point in their long history do the Berbers seem to have had an awareness of an ethnic or linguistic unity."[6] However, both of these important contributors to our understanding of the Berbers state this fact only to deny it in effect. For instance, for Norris, "pagan survivals are everywhere in the [one] Berber world."[7] In a critical sense, the Berbers represent a single reality in spite of the absence of ethnic or linguistic unity, criteria for declaring the unity of other peoples. Brett and Fentress proposed a creative way out of this conundrum: "The problems inherent in discussing the Berbers become compounded when we turn to their material culture and ethnography. Here, it is harder to avoid generalities; generalities which will certainly be false in some of the patchwork of Berber peoples. . . . Yet, striking unities do exist and are worth *bringing out*."[8] Unfortunately, the authors did not expound on what these plural unities amount to and how they relate to the notion of multiplicity. Doing so may have marked the action of "bringing out" itself as an object of historical inquiry, thus opening the door to identifying the workings of Berberization. As it stands, however, the Berbers are a people, many peoples, and a people with no ethnic or linguistic unity. Perhaps it is in this logically complex sense that Brett and Fentress, following Ibn Khaldūn, see them as belonging among the nations, unfortunately again without specifying whether they do so as a single nation, multiple nations, or embodiments of some identifiable national unities: "The final adoption of the language as a means of expression in all modern media of communication is the culmination of four thousand years of history. While we cannot be sure it will not follow the Berber sermons of Ibn Tūmart into disuse, for the moment it has placed the Berbers themselves back among the nations of the world, where Ibn Khaldūn located them. It is a final justification for tracing their evolution under the title of *The Berbers*."[9]

Whether the Berbers are a people today is a question. Whether they have always been a people is another one. What it means for modern historians to use medieval texts as evidence to support modern arguments about the existence of people(s) is an altogether different problem. The perspective of this book is that the Berbers began to be a people in Arabic, and that in Arabic works they started becoming a people that has "always" existed. With this in mind, it is not at all necessary for the word Berber to have immediately and exclusively referred to a people in the singular or to a plurality of peoples. For instance, although it faded over time, the semantic association of the category Berber with slavery checks the tendency prevalent among medieval Arabic writers to take for granted genealogical knowledge and to present it as natural.

Berber as a Brand of Slave

The Berbers entered Arabic writings at the time intellectuals were forging the new disciplines and genres usually associated with the ʿAbbāsids (750–1258) and the so-called golden age of Islamic civilization. Within this imperial edifice, the literati pursued their desire for knowledge about the world and the peoples that inhabited it, gathering information, and compiling it in impressive tomes. By then, the Berbers were a known entity, and some Berber individuals were actually very famous. Everyone knew, for instance, that the mother of ʿAbd al-Raḥmān I (731–88), the first Umayyad ruler of Cordoba, was Berber, and so too was the mother of the ʿAbbāsid caliph al-Manṣūr (754–75). For the new imperial elite, slavery was a natural institution, and all great ruling classes, ancient and contemporary, took advantage of it. Naturally, domestic slaves formed a sizable component of ʿAbbāsid society.[10]

Slavery was central to the functioning of the military conquests (*futūḥ*) and to the workings of the empire, first under the Umayyads (661–750) and then under the ʿAbbāsids. It was a salient feature of the conquests of northwest Africa, from the early raids of the 640s to the establishment of the garrison town of al-Qayrawān (670) and the extension of imperial rule to the western regions at the beginning of the eighth century. Naturally, *futūḥ* narratives are replete with references to captives and slaves.[11] The trade in humans did not particularly bother the conscience of early *futūḥ* writers, who repeated the exaggerated reports lionizing imperial generals who shipped off captives by the thousands from the Maghrib. An excerpt from the earliest extant *futūḥ* work on the Maghrib leaves no doubt: "Al-Layth b. Saʿd recounted that when Mūsā b. Nuṣayr raided the Maghrib, he sent his son Marwān with an army and the latter captured a hundred thousand [people]. He also sent his nephew with another army and he too captured a hundred thousand. When al-Layth b. Saʿd was asked who they were, he said: 'the Berbers.'"[12] Berber slaves were simply a known and appreciated commodity in the slave markets of the empire, especially in Egypt, where they made the fortunes of many.[13] Muslim legal thinkers and jurists dealt with disputes that involved the trade in slaves by approaching them as they did other commercial enterprises. Whether they were themselves slavers or not, they naturally reproduced the language of those whose cases they considered. In the first half of the ninth century, the man credited with introducing Mālikī jurisprudence to the Maghrib wrote about the Berbers in a way his teacher and colleagues understood. Saḥnūn b. Saʿīd al-Tanūkhī (d. 854) believed that the Berbers formed a single entity, but not quite a people, as one might think. For him, the Berbers were a *jins*; and the usage of this term is worth examining, even if only briefly.

The term *jins* occurs in a number of cases pertaining to the trade in Berbers, but since Saḥnūn quoted from the opinions of his Madīnan master, Mālik b. Anas (d. 795), the usage in question harks back at least to the second half of the eighth century. In case after case, "Berber" appears to be nothing more than the brand that slaves from the Maghrib had. "Berber" was a type of slave, with particular specifications and qualities. This much is clear from the case in which Mālik judged that it was necessary for the buyer to restitute a slave he purchased with the understanding that he was Berber, only to find out he was only Khorasānian. Pointing to the "difference in quality" between the two, Mālik thought that restitution and reimbursement would render the sale void. In another case, Mālik thought that if a female slave were Berber or Khorasānian and the seller presented her as being "Slav, Iberian, or Hispanic," the seller had the choice of either returning her or not. He thought that because, as he explained, the *jins* of the Berber and the Khorasānian slave was superior (*afḍal* and *arfaʿ*) to that of the others.[14]

It may be that when they referred to Berbers in these terms, all these jurists meant was that they had a particular ethnic or regional origin. But there are other passages where Saḥnūn's language suggests that Berbers were, like all slaves, to be compared to objects and animals, rather than to other peoples like the Arabs:

> Consider the case of someone who borrows wood logs with the intention of returning logs that are similar [but not exactly the same]. Would doing so be acceptable according to Mālik? [Saḥnūn] answered: It is not permissible to lend a single log and then receive two logs of the same type (*ṣanf*) or of a different type unless their form is clearly different (*ikhtilāf bayyin*). In this [latter] case, there is no [legal] issue. [Mālik's opinion is understandable] because it is possible for someone to borrow logs from a palm tree of a certain diameter and length and then return palm tree logs that are smaller. If they are different in this way, there is no problem because these two types of wood, [the big and the small,] are different [in what they can be used for?] even if they both belong to the [category] of wood. Are you not able to see that there is no [legal] issue in the case of the Berber slave who trades in Spaniards who are not merchants or in the Sicilian who trades in Nubians who are not merchants even if they are all sons of Adam? The same [principle applies in the case of] the Berber merchant and scribe (*kātib*)[15] who speaks Arabic and who trades in Nubians who do not speak Arabic and [the case of] horses that may be lent [and exchanged] the ones for the others when the types and pedigree (*nujār*) are different even if they are all horses etc. The same applies to logs and clothes.[16]

Clearly, slavers used the word Berber the way one would a brand or a type of merchandise. Their practice of grouping all slaves from the Maghrib in this particular way makes the Berbers appear to be a single entity and thus one *jins*. However, not all writers agreed with this usage of *jins*. For instance, in his *Meadows of Gold* (*Murūj al-dhahab*) the historian and geographer al-Masʿūdī (d. 956) reported that "Goliath marched from Palestine accompanied by *ajnās* (sing. *jins*) of Berbers."[17] In this example, there was not a single *jins* of Berbers but many, al-Masʿūdī capturing the social and political (tribal) differentiation between Berbers. On the other hand, unlike al-Masʿūdī, slavers saw Berbers as a commodity. His understanding of differences between free Berbers was irrelevant to them because what defined a slave for them was precisely the lack of social and political autonomy that comes with freedom. In other words, for slavers, a slave does not belong to a tribe, and Saḥnūn relays this particular sense—the use of *jins* in both cases notwithstanding. For him, "Berber" is simply a marker of provenance. It does not reflect or even imply the sort of historical unity that characterizes a people.[18]

Whatever else can be said about early Berberization, the association of the term Berber with slavery ought not to be forgotten, especially as it left a remarkable imprint on the historical record. Limiting the scope of the analysis to the sole question of whether and how the Arabs considered the Berbers to be a people tends to ignore this evidence.[19] On the other hand, paying attention to terms like *jins* invites us to consider the linguistic tools with which Arabic authors conceived of the Berbers. If the Berbers were a people, what did that actually entail? Were they a nation? What words did Arabic authors use for the Berbers?

Many Words for People

Categories pertaining to tribes, peoples, and clans offer concrete examples of popular and learned notions. If the Berbers were a people in Arabic sources, they could be so only in relation to the system or systems of classification prevalent in that language. Of course, the development of a nomenclature pertaining to kinship relations in Arabic preceded its appearance in extant sources, the most extensive early source being the Qur'ān. Conveniently, the holy book was the object of serious and thorough study, as exegetes (*mufassirūn*) parsed and commented on kinship categories the way they did every word in the Qur'ān, thus giving us a concrete sense of the workings of genealogical knowledge, and the various classification scheme(s) it envisaged.

A suitable place to begin examining how these schemes worked is the usage of *shaʿb* and *qabīla*, words that are usually translated as "people" or "nation" and "tribe." The Qur'ān offers a good example in a widely known passage traditionally read at weddings: "We created you of a male and a female, and have made you *shu'ūb* (sing. *sha'b*) and *qabā'il* (sing. *qabīla*) so that you may know one another."[20] Early exegetes had no problem explaining this verse, as they were very familiar with the circumstances it meant to illuminate. The great historian and exegete al-Ṭabarī (d. 923) gives examples of usage to support his interpretation of this verse: "If one asks an Arab what people (*sha'b*) he is from, he will say: 'I am from Muḍar' or 'I am from Rabī'a.' When it comes to tribes (*qabā'il*), which represent a closer relationship, they are, for example, Tamīm which is part of Muḍar and Bikr of Rabī'a."[21] Further explaining his interpretation, al-Ṭabarī offers other definitions and commentaries on these two terms. As he reports it, the early exegete Ibn 'Abbās (d. 687) explained that "peoples" (*shu'ūb*) meant "great collectivities" or "groups" (*jummā'*) and that "tribes" (*qabā'il*) referred to "clans" (*buṭūn*). Others were of the opinion that *sha'b* referred to a "great tribe like the Banū Tamīm" and reflected a more distant kinship (*nasab ba'īd*), whereas "tribe" implied a closer circle of kin (*afkhādh*).[22] For Muqātil b. Sulaymān (d. 767), "by *shu'ūb* God means the 'heads' of tribes (*ru'ūs al-qabā'il*) which are the Rabī'a, Muḍar, Banū Tamīm, and Azd and by *qabā'il* he means the tribes (*afkhadh*) like the Banū Sa'd, Banū 'Āmir, Banū Qays etc."[23]

As tensions rose in the empire between Arabs and mostly Persian non-Arabs (*'ajam*), the so-called *shu'ubiya*, the exact meaning of such terms had tremendous implications. Historian Roy Mottahedeh commented on the political significance of these definitional differences. For him, "dispute over the nature of *shu'ūb* constituted one of the most fundamental issues dividing the shu'ūbīs and their opponents, an issue that has somehow gone unnoticed by modern historians."[24] Given the literary genres in vogue and the configuration of learned disciplines, the *shu'ubiya* controversy failed to resolve the deceptively simple matter of ascertaining the meaning of categories through which people imagined their social world, and their political and symbolic place in it. Fixing the meaning of these two terms did not get any easier with the passing of time. In the fifteenth century, exegetes still grappled with the passage and offered their own definitions: "*Shu'ūb* is the plural of *sha'b*, which is the highest level of kin. *Qabā'il* (sing. *qabīla*) is lower than *shu'ūb*. Then there is *'amā'ir* (sing. *'imāra*) then *buṭūn* (sing. *baṭn*) then *afkhādh* then finally *faṣā'il*. For example, Khuzayma is a *sha'b*, Kināna a *qabīla*, Quraysh a *'imāra*, Qusay a *baṭn*, Hāshim a *fakhdh*, and finally, al-'Abbās a *faṣīla*."[25]

Whether the terminology of kinship posed such a challenge because of the archaism of learned discourse in a time of linguistic change, or the question is rather the incorporation into an evolving standard language of a multiplicity of dialects and registers, the fact remains that the meaning of these categories was not set in stone. Their translation into modern English illustrates well the reason conscientious translators came to think of their work as one of interpretation:

> Pickthall (1875–1936): "We have created you male and female, and have made you nations and tribes that ye may know one another."[26]
>
> Yusuf Ali (1872–1953): "We created you from a single (pair) of a male and a female, and made you into nations and tribes, that ye may know each other (not that ye may despise (each other))."[27]
>
> Arberry (1905–69): "We have created you male and female, and appointed you races and tribes, that you may know one another."[28]

In spite of their complexity and the difficulty of translating them into modern English, both *sha'b* and *qabīla* represent kinship relations that assume a shared ancestry. This is not as obvious for the notion of *umma*, which is also commonly translated as "nation," but also as "people" and "community." As Frederick Denny noted, the Qur'ān suggests a broader semantic field:

> The word occurs some 62 times in the Kur'ān in the sense of religious community, as well as instances where it means "fixed term" and communities of animals like unto human groups. *Umma* also refers to the Patriarch Abraham as a model of righteousness. The Kur'ān teaches that each *umma,* perhaps in the sense of a generation of contemporaries sharing a common belief and value system, has an appointed term decreed by God. . . . In both Meccan and Medinan passages, *umma* may refer to the archetypal or potential unity of mankind and prophetic religion, using the phrase *umma wāḥida*. . . . There is in passages like this a foreshadowing of the full message of Islam as a restorer of the archetypal spiritual and moral unity of humans.[29]

The word *umma* acquired special political signification in the document known as the Constitution of Medina, which describes Jews as part of the same *umma* as the Believers.[30] This early political sense lost currency beginning in the early eighth century with the emergence of a new imperial ideology. In addition to its multiple other meanings, medieval authors used *umma* (pl. *umam*) to refer to kinship groups with a common genealogy. In his *Tabaqāt al-umam*, the historian, astronomer, and judge Ṣāʿid al-Andalusī (d. 1070) set up a distinction between those nations that valued philosophy and those that did not: "We have determined that in spite of the great number of their subdivisions and the differences between their religious practices, nations are divided into two categories (or classes) (*ṭabaqatayn*): one category cultivated the sciences and produced great works in the arts of knowledge (*funūn al-maʿārif*), the other did not contribute enough to the sciences to deserve being included alongside the other. [The second category] left little philosophy or useful knowledge."[31] Ṣāʿid al-Andalusī recognized the Indians, the Greeks, the Jews, the Persians, the Chaldeans, the Romans (Byzantines), and the Arabs for valuing philosophy.[32] Others, like the Chinese, had some qualities but lacked philosophy, his primary concern. And still others were very far from deserving any honor: "As for the Galicians, the Berbers, and the surrounding inhabitants of the Maghrib that belong to this category [of nonscientific nations, these] are nations that God has distinguished with despotism, ignorance, hostility, and violence."[33] In spite of their baseness, however, both Galicians and Berbers were distinct *umam*. While it may be correct to translate Ibn Ṣāʿid's *umma* as "nation," it is necessary not to lose sight of what universe of meaning his usage envisaged. In addition to such considerations, categories such as *umma* present us with a semantic richness, which some would see as inconsistency and incoherence because of the specialized usage they had in various disciplines. What I mean here is that in the hands of genealogists, the Chinese were the descendants of a common ancestor, whereas the geographers saw them as the inhabitants of a region whose borders they specified. Jurists followed a legal logic, while exegetes envisioned God's message to apply to humanity in its entirety. To each science its *umma*, but then most of our authors were polymaths who were not always mindful of their slippages.

Imperial Stories

Ibn Khaldūn uses genealogy as the organizing principle for his history. His is a history of the Arabs and Berbers, understood genealogically, and those among their contemporaries, also genealogically defined, who formed great dynasties. Dynastic history, which was the subject of history for him, was the expression of dynamics within and between kinship groups. At the time Ibn Khaldūn conceived his history, genealogy was a mature science that had deep roots in the imperial knowledge of the ninth and tenth centuries. As far as the genealogy of the Berbers is concerned, two moments stand out: the genealogies compiled after the imperial expansion and those composed in the midst of the political crises of the eleventh century. Together with the events that shaped his own life, these moments illuminate Ibn Khaldūn's artful articulation of a confluence between politics and genealogy. Although this perspective took centuries to crystallize, one of its lasting effects is that it consolidated the formal rapprochement between Berbers and Arabs.[34]

Among the early Arabic genealogists, Ibn al-Kalbī (d. 819/820) stands out as the greatest compiler of the genealogies of the Arabs, his *Jamharat al-nasab* being exemplary. In another compilation of his in which he focuses on the genealogies of northern Arabs (Ma'add) and Yemenis (Qaḥṭān), he mentions interesting facts about the Ṣanhāja and the Kutāma, who were, according to him, descendants of Yemenis from Ḥimyar who settled among the Berbers: "From Ḥimyar, Ṣanhāja and Kutāma settled among the Berbers. They were the descendants of al-Sūr b. Sa'īd b. Jābir b. Sa'īd b. Qays b. Sayfī and remain there until today."[35] The Arabian origin of at least some Berber groups seemed plausible at the end of the eighth century.[36] Beyond its legendary or invented character, this genealogy exemplifies the process by which knowledge of the Maghrib integrated imperial knowledge. In this way, Yemeni settlers in the Maghrib made room for themselves in the local and imperial collective memory. In the absence of sources, it is impossible to know what Ṣanhāja and Kutāma chiefs and their genealogists thought of such representations. Clearly, however, these genealogies contributed to the discourse on the similarity between Arabs (Syrians and Yemenis) and Berbers. They also introduced the idea that at least some of those who considered themselves Berbers may not have had Berber ancestors.

The resemblance between those groups who migrated from Arabia and the "locals," their similar modes of social organization and livelihoods, and their integration into the same imperial system made genealogies compelling. The imperial court's interest in knowledge about the provinces supported the development of works of "routes and kingdoms" (*masālik wa mamālik*) and "countries" (*buldān*) and delivered a plethora of "locales" that had to be accounted for, politically and ideologically. It is not a surprise, therefore, to find authors of geographical works drawing on genealogy to ground their narratives and give them vividness and relevance. This is why modern scholars have tended to think of them as ethno-geographical works.[37]

In his world geography, al-Yaʿqūbī (d. 897/8) relies on the language of kinship to describe Barqa (Cyrenaica) and those who inhabited it. Presented in the familiar language of genealogists, the Berbers of "ethno-geography" and those of conquest narratives came to populate the learned imagination: "The second mountain of Barqa is known as 'the western [mountain].' It is inhabited by a group (*qawm*) from Ghassān, a group from Judhām, Azd, and Tujīb and other Arab clans (*buṭūn*), and towns (*qurā*) [belonging to] Berber clans (*buṭūn*) from among the Lawāta, Zakūda, Wamfarṭa, and Waznāra."[38] With all the limitations and challenges to its power in the Maghrib, the ʿAbbāsid empire emerged as the primary agent for the production of knowledge about the Berbers.[39] What is striking about extant narratives is that the Berbers are never the principal focus. They appear as figurants in the genealogies of Arabs and in the imperial mapping of the world: known and familiar but still on the margins. And while presenting a catalog of Berber genealogies plucked from a variety of texts would give a sense of the variety of versions that circulated, highlighting their presence in nongenealogical works demonstrates the standing of genealogical science in the learned apparatus as a whole.

If imperial geographers celebrated the greatness and expansiveness of the empire by counting its cities, towns, mountains, rivers, and very diverse populations, chroniclers of the conquests established narratives memorializing the making of the empire. The epic tales of a fast-expanding empire, *futūḥ* narratives are told, however, in terms of the expansion of Islam and its message—a notable shift in meaning. *Futūḥ* writers drew on genealogical knowledge very naturally, as it allowed them to establish a common ground with their audiences. Reading the genealogy of a group like the Berbers allowed the audiences to situate tribal names they had never heard of and to draw on what they already knew to imagine a past distant from them—although we may sometimes forget that ninth-century readers thought of the seventh century as being remote.

The earliest extant *futūḥ* work that chronicles the conquest of the Maghrib actually centers on Egypt. Ibn ʿAbd al-Ḥakam's *Futūḥ miṣr wa akhbāruha* begins by establishing Egypt as the main subject with a discussion of the land's positive attributes and then known tales from legendary ancient times. The introduction mentions how the Copts settled Egypt after the flood and what the prophet Muḥammad said about the good treatment they should receive. Ibn ʿAbd al-Ḥakam (d. 871) then moves on to the *futūḥ* and weaves a narrative around memorable events and great feats of individuals, focusing on battles and raids, intrigues and conspiracies. Further anchoring the centrality of Egypt, his own home, the author expands the narrative beyond the conquest of Egypt. He includes the victories achieved by the heroic conquerors of Egypt, its outstanding generals, and governors who greatly expanded Islam's reach. In the early years of the conquests, Egypt was the imperial base and capital of the military effort in Africa. Egypt was also the base for the collection of information about the conquests, the conquerors, and the conquered regions. The tales of veterans and the various literary traditions from which the author gathered his information had a clearly Egyptian stamp on them—at least when the Maghrib is concerned.

The Berbers first appear in the *Futuḥ miṣr* in the introduction, in the section about the migration of the Copts into Egypt. As Ibn ʿAbd al-Ḥakam retells the well-known curse of Cham and his offspring, we learn that the Berbers and the Copts are cousins: "The eldest of Ḥām's sons is Kanʿān. . . . He is the father of all the Sūdān and the Abyssinians. His second son is Kūsh who is the father of the Sind and Hind. His third son is Fūṭ who fathered the Berbers, and his youngest and fourth son is Bayṣar who is the father of all the Copts."[40] Whether the Berbers in question here are the inhabitants of Barbaria in East Africa, as I believe, or those of the west is arguable. But there is no doubt that the Berbers' closest cousins are darker-skinned Africans (Sūdān). In the second genealogy found in the *Futūḥ miṣr*, however, the Berbers have a completely different origin. This genealogy precedes the conquest of Barqa (Cyrenaica):

> [Ibn ʿAbd al-Ḥakam] reported: The Berbers were in Palestine. Their king was Jālūt. When the prophet Dāwūd killed him, the Berbers left [Palestine] in direction of the Maghrib until they arrived in Lūbiya and Marāqiya both of which are two districts (*kūra*) in western Egypt (*miṣr al-gharbiya*) that were irrigated by rain and not by the Nile river.[41] The Berbers separated there: The Zanāta and Maghīla advanced into the western areas (*maghrib*) and inhabited the mountains. The Luwāta advanced and inhabited the land of Anṭābulus, which is Barqa.[42] In the Maghrib, [the Berbers] separated and spread in until they reached the Sūs.[43] The Hawwāra settled in the city of Labda and the Nafūsa settled in the city of Sabrata leading those Romans who had lived there to

> emigrate. The Afāriq who had accepted Roman domination remained there and paid tribute as they had done to all those who conquered their country.[44]

This introduction of the Berbers as a character in the saga that was to follow fit the format of genealogy, even if it is a very unusual one. The Berbers were not the descendants of Goliath, as would usually be the case, but only his subjects. In spite of its clear legendary character, this genealogy refers back to a political or historical relation, not a biological one. The Berbers may be related to one another but only as subjects of the same king. Although it is difficult to prove, this genealogy seems to adapt ancient material—perhaps pertaining to the East African Berbers or to populations that migrated "west" following an event like the Sasanian conquest of Egypt (618–21)—to the relatively recent emergence of Berbers in the Maghrib. A less speculative reading could combine this genealogy with the preceding one to constitute the Berbers as a group that existed in ancient times, one, like the Abyssinians and the Copts, that settled in Africa after the Flood. And like the Arabs, the Persians, and others still, the Berbers belonged in the grand narrative of the making of the same empire, understood as an opening of the lands to Islam (*fatḥ*).

Whatever its provenance, the idea that the Berbers had a single ruler in the person of Jālūt, and that they thus represented a single political bloc, comes again in the story of al-Kāhina. In an often-quoted passage, Ibn ʿAbd al-Ḥakam mentions that the enigmatic figure was "at the time, queen of the Berbers" (*wa hiya idh dhāk malikat al-barbar*).[45] The conflict between al-Kāhina and Ḥassān b. al-Nuʿmān takes for granted that all the Berbers were under her unified command—even if it was only the eastern regions of the Maghrib that were involved in these heroic struggles. In fact, many of those whose children would eventually become Berbers are outside the purview of Ibn ʿAbd al-Ḥakam's narrative. Given the author's own inclinations, the information available to him, and the lack of sources from those called Berbers, it is difficult to say what the Berbers thought of themselves and whether "Berber" meant anything to any of them.[46]

Ibn al-Kalbī and other imperial genealogists conferred on the Berbers a pre-Islamic past. They also enabled the narration of the conquest of the Maghrib by *futuḥ* authors like Ibn ʿAbd al-Ḥakam. The lack of consensus among Arabic genealogists about the ancestors of the Berbers as a whole and about the ancestors of this or that Berber tribe or people indicates both a demand for knowledge and a multiplicity of suppliers and interests. There was, however, an absolute agreement in favor of associating northwest Africa and its inhabitants with the Berbers, as well as some attempts to foster genealogical links between some Arabs and Berbers in the Maghrib. When they tried to make sense of this early material, later authors did not conceive of a Berberization of northwest Africa and its peoples. Instead, they saw the material as a collection of statements of varying reliability that needed sorting out.

Ibn Ḥazm: Arabs, Berbers, and Other Andalusīs

As prolific, innovative, and controversial polymaths go, Ibn Ḥazm (d.1064) is an extraordinary case, as he was also an autodidact. So says Ibn Khaldūn for whom he was an exception to the rule that learning is best acquired from a teacher.[47] In addition to a poignant autobiographical recollection of and commentary on his unhappy experience with love as a youth (*Ṭawq al-ḥamāma*), Ibn Ḥazm wrote around four hundred works ranging in form from relatively short epistles and specialized treatises to multivolume titles on topics ranging from history, theology, and law to genealogy, logic, and theological polemics.[48] As an intellectual, Ibn Ḥazm showed a consistent preference for independence of thought and a pronounced penchant for argument, not to say quarrel, often at the cost of his livelihood, personal security, and legacy, at least in the sense that having the circulation of his works limited by the ruler hampered their transmission, even if, thankfully, not completely. When it comes to the subject of the Berbers, two of his works stand out for their significance. The first is Ibn Ḥazm's massive compilation, *Genealogy of the Arabs* (*Jamharat ansāb al-ʿarab*), which is second only to the one written by Ibn al-Kalbī more than two centuries earlier. The second is his epistle *Merits of al-Andalus* (*faḍā'il al-andalus*), a short but clear expression of Ibn Ḥazm's thoughts on the standing of al-Andalus, especially in relation to the Maghrib. These two texts offer indications of Ibn Khaldūn's debt to Ibn Ḥazm.[49]

Ibn Ḥazm did not leave a clear statement of his intentions and aims in compiling the *Jamhara*. Consequently, specialists have had to infer his purpose based on what is known about him, his works, and his context. For the renowned Orientalist Évariste Levi-Provençal, Ibn Ḥazm had personal and social reasons for publicizing his own genealogy.[50] Also according to Levi-Provençal, genealogies had particular significance and popularity in al-Andalus because they were central to the legitimization of the rule of a minority and the competition between various families for prominence. In spite of the range of their interpretations, specialists have tended to agree with Levi-Provençal in attributing to Ibn Ḥazm a combination of personal, intellectual, and political motivations. While this may not be astounding, it is most likely true.

Ibn Ḥazm's earliest known ancestor seems to have been a Persian client (*mawlā*) of the Umayyads (661–750); a branch of his family had moved to al-Andalus when the Umayyads took power there. The Banū Ḥazm were fervent supporters of the Umayyads and occupied various prominent positions at the court. The Umayyads prided themselves on their Qurayshī origins and positioned themselves as arbitrators of the conflicts and competition between Syrian and Yemeni components of the Arab contingent in al-Andalus. The political history of the peninsula thus bears out the interest in genealogy in general and Arab genealogy in particular.

Ibn Ḥazm was a supporter of the pro-Umayyad camp that was defeated by the Berber party—he was even imprisoned by the latter.[51] Notably, his *Jamhara* is a genealogy of the Arabs (*ansāb al-ʿarab*) with the genealogies of non-Arabs included in an accompanying coda (*dhayl*)—the primacy of the Prophet, his family, and companions being his argument for focusing on the Arabs first.[52]

The *Jamhara* begins with this invocation: "Praise be to God, the Extinguisher of all Ages (*mubīd kull al-qurūn*), the First (*al-awwal*), the Ender of Dynasties (*mudīl al-duwal*), Creator of the World, the Sender of Muḥammad, peace be upon him, with the true faith."[53] Through these words, Ibn Ḥazm foregrounds the disappearance of ages, literally centuries, and the fall of dynasties. Rather than expressing a dark or fatalistic view of the world, he presents the distant past as an object of desire, the Prophet's background being the most legitimate subject of all. A more sustained examination of the invocation draws attention to Ibn Ḥazm's recalling of the end of the Umayyad era, and God's will, and to his first defense of genealogy, the actual aim of his introductory paragraphs.

Beginning with the Qur'ānic verse "We created you in tribes and peoples so that you may know each other," Ibn Ḥazm constructs a multilayered argument in support of the science that specializes in knowing the world's peoples: genealogy (*ʿilm al-nasab*). In addition to God's plan for peoples to know each other, Ibn Ḥazm mentions knowledge of the Prophet, his family, and his companions as a duty Muslims need to attend to. He then gives historically relevant material from the early conquests, particularly the peace treaties with certain non-Muslim tribes that specify fiscal arrangements, making knowledge of just who belonged to these tribes, that is, genealogy, legally relevant. Likewise, the examples he gives of the status of some tribes as free or servile had legal implications. Ibn Ḥazm broaches the sensitive subject of political leadership after the death of the Prophet, which led to the so-called civil wars that ended with the victory of the Umayyad dynasty and to the dissent of a number of groups. Prominent arguments for legitimacy hinged on the kinship of the leader with the Prophet and his tribe. As a science, genealogy had serious real-life relevance and utility.[54]

Ibn Ḥazm's genealogy of the Arabs begins with the three patriarchs ʿAdnān, Qaḥṭān, and Quḍāʿa. Ibn Ḥazm organizes his book as a series of concentric circles around these three figures, beginning with ʿAdnān, who counts the prophet Muḥammad among his descendants. Citing a number of reasons why the genealogies that come from the ancient past are difficult to ascertain, beyond those that are found in unquestionable sources like the Qur'ān, the Prophet, or someone close to him, Ibn Ḥazm notes the difficulty in evaluating the veracity of reports by Muslims and non-Muslims alike. For him, the information becomes more reliable with the availability of authoritative Arabic sources such as Ibn Isḥāq and Ibn al-Kalbī. Interestingly, because he proceeds outwardly from the circle closest to the Prophet, he covers the ʿAbbāsids (750–1258) before the Umayyads I (661–750) and the Andalusī Umayyads II (756–1031).[55]

The material found in the *Jamhara* is not exclusively genealogical, however. The author adds biographical information on individuals known to have been rulers or governors or to have led or participated in wars and battles. The entries on "descendants of X" often include references to the prominent positions held by some of them, major written works, or a noteworthy anecdote. In other words, Ibn al-Ḥazm made ample use of information he found in works of *ḥadīth*, biographical dictionaries, and chronicles, among other genres with which he was familiar. However, given the richness of the material on al-Andalus, the *Jamhara* reads also like a work of history, with great men, and some women, great dynasties, prominent families or houses, and outstanding poets, jurists, and courtiers. Because of its sources, the book focuses mainly on Arabia, the Fertile Crescent, and al-Andalus. Other regions where Arabs settled are mentioned but far less often and not in as much detail.

Information about al-Andalus and the Arabs that settled there is found throughout the *Jamhara*. In addition, Ibn Ḥazm takes great care in giving the family trees of prominent Andalusī families. For instance, he gives the family tree of the Banū Khaldūn of Seville:

> We mention now the Banū Khaldūn of Seville. It is said that they are the sons of 'Abd al-Jabbār b. 'Alqama b. Wā'il who was mentioned above. Among their great men was Abū Hāni' Kurayb, Abū 'Uthmān Khālid, the leaders (*al-qā'imān*) of Seville who were assassinated by Ibrāhīm b. Hajjāj al-Lakhmī. They are the sons of 'Uthmān b. Bakr b. Khālid b. Bakr b. Khālid known as Khaldūn, the one who first immigrated from the East (Mashriq). [Khaldūn] was the son of 'Uthmān b. Hāni' b. al-Khaṭṭāb b. Kurayb b. Ma'dī Karib b. al-Ḥārith b. Wā'il b. Ḥujr who was mentioned above. Among his sons are: Abū al-'Āṣī 'Amr b. Muḥammad b. Khālid b. 'Amr b. Khālid Abī 'Uthmān the aforementioned who was assassinated. None of his sons remain except for Muḥammad, Aḥmad, and 'Abd Allāh, the sons of the Abū al-'Āṣī mentioned above. [Among their great men is also] the aforementioned famous philosopher Abū Muslim 'Umar b. Muḥammad b. Baqiy b. 'Abd Allāh b. Bakr b. Khālid b. 'Uthmān b. Khālid who entered [al-Andalus] who is [known as] Khaldūn. . . . There are remaining [relatives of the Banū Khaldūn] in Seville known as the Banū 'Uṣfūr, which is a name that belongs to them.[56]

Although a bit long, this passage from the *Jamhara* gives a concrete sense of how the material from al-Andalus differs from the genealogies of prophets and those of the companions of the prophet Muḥammad. The association between a city and a great "family" presents itself as an objective reality that imposes itself on the organization of the *Jamhara*. Ibn Ḥazm naturalizes this development and frames it within a genealogical logic that parallels the political struggles that led to the demise of the Umayyads and the rise of the Taifas: the ruling families of Seville were Arab—in other words, not Berber or Slav (Ṣaqāliba).

One of the most distinctive features of the *Jamhara* is that it collapses the category Arab. Although this might not be immediately clear to all, it is useful to remember that the category Arabs exists in relation to non-Arabs (*'ajam*). In al-Andalus, the *'ajam* are mostly Berbers, whereas in the Mashriq, they are Persians.[57] There is thus a shift in what "Arab" means. This shift is obscured by the naturalization of Andalusī social and political distinctions.

"An Arab is an Arab is an Arab" enables Andalusī Arabs to claim the honors of their ancestors in Arabia. Also, and by implication, the Berbers populated the "land of the Berbers" (*bilād al-barbar*). But in the *Jamhara* this land of the Berbers is not the entire Maghrib. Ibn Ḥazm limits the geographic scope of the land of the Berbers to the areas controlled by Berbers in al-Andalus and those lands immediately opposite al-Andalus on the African side—a choice that matches well with Umayyad policies in al-Andalus and the western Maghrib.[58]

As I have already mentioned, Andalusī politics shed light on Ibn Ḥazm's inclusion of a series of afterthoughts on pertinent topics, such as the competition between Qaḥṭān and ʿAdnān, an ancient Arabian phenomenon, attested in older texts, but which gained special significance in al-Andalus. In the eighth century, the Arabs of al-Andalus fought along those lines (Syrians vs. Yemenis), and in the eleventh century, Arabs who articulated their politics in genealogical terms rediscovered this ancient rivalry, at least ideologically.

In the *Jamhara*, the Arabs do not exist alone. They exist within two frames: an ancient one, along with Persians and Israelites—the genealogies of both are included in summary form in the additional sections, and in a contemporary frame, alongside the Berbers and the *muwallads*, who were the descendants of the inhabitants of Iberia before it became al-Andalus. Ibn Ḥazm includes the genealogies of Berbers, although he is mostly interested in the prominent Andalusī families among them: "Miknāsa: From them came the Banū Wansūs, the clan of the vizier Sulaymān b. Wansūs. Zanāta: From them came the Banū al-Kharrūbī whose origins are from Laqant and the Banū al-Layth from Shanta Fīla. . . . From the Zanāta also [came] the Banū ʿAzzūn the rulers of Shanta Bariya. The emir ʿAbd al-Raḥmān b. ʿAzzūn informed me that they are the sons of Saʿīd after whom is named the Faḥṣ Saʿīd near Shūdhar who killed Thābit b. ʿĀmir al-Madyūnī."[59] Ibn Ḥazm's summary of the genealogy of the Berbers presupposes the development of Berber genealogical knowledge in the Andalus of his time. The Andalusī geographer Abū ʿUbayd Allāh al-Bakrī (d. 1094) collected a number of genealogies that originated in al-Andalus and the Maghrib. He famously wrote to a renowned historian in Marrakesh who told him that the most accurate (*aṣaḥ*) genealogies were compiled in Ifrīqiyā.[60] However, for Ibn Ḥazm, what matters about particular Berbers is their family trees in al-Andalus, not the Maghrib, and in spite of the aura that stems from its authoritative tone, his genealogy of the Berbers is largely Andalusī. It is Andalusī because it is a representation of what is known about the Berbers in al-Andalus, and for its organization of the information around prominent Berber houses (*buyūtāt*) tied to Andalusī cities or areas—exactly like the genealogies of Arabs and *muwallads*.

These few aspects of the *Jamhara* gain further significance in relation to Ibn Ḥazm's epistle *Merits of al-Andalus* (*Faḍā'il al-andalus*). As a genre, the discourse on the merits of a city or region emerged in the ninth century—before then biographers had focused on the merits of individuals.[61] A book in this genre commonly begins with a selection of statements extolling the city, usually by the prophet Muḥammad and his companions. The narrative then moves to the early contribution of the city to religious knowledge: *hadīth*, jurisprudence, and exegesis. A city's merits also included its mosques, people, markets, and even climate, but the biographies of intellectuals occupied a prominent place in these texts.

Although Ibn Ḥazm's *Merits of al-Andalus* falls well within these general parameters, it is unusual because it is a relatively short letter. And unlike those authors compelled by their love of tribe or country (*'aṣabiya*) to compose a record of its outstanding features, Ibn Ḥazm was responding to a query from a scholar in al-Qayrawān about the reasons behind the lack of books about great Andalusīs. That is Ibn Ḥazm's pretext for writing his epistle, although the Qayrawānī Ibn al-Rabīb al-Tamīmī had addressed the letter not to him personally but to a deceased cousin of his.

Without knowing more about the relation between Ibn al-Rabīb and Abū al-Mughīra 'Abd al-Wahhāb b. Aḥmad b. Ḥazm (d. 1046), it is difficult to make sense of Ibn al-Rabīb's statement about the lack of books on the merits of Andalusīs in Ifrīqiyā, especially that, as he says, there was constant back-and-forth of merchants and scholars between the region and al-Andalus. Travel between the two regions was so extensive that Ibn al-Rabīb commented: "If there came out from your country any new volume, it would have reached those in tombs in our country, to say nothing of those in houses and palaces."[62] Ibn al-Rabīb's invitation to discourse did not rest on a serious catalog of Andalusī works in Ifrīqiyā but rather on the desire to understand why in his *'Iqd al-farīd*, Ibn 'Abd Rabbih (d. 940) chose to focus so much on Baghdad rather than al-Andalus.[63]

Instead of focusing on Ibn 'Abd Rabbih and his choices, Ibn Ḥazm demurred at the notion that there were no books that highlighted the merits of his Andalus. His epistle responds by listing a vast number of works that compare favorably with the most famous and authoritative ones known at the time, never failing to take a jab at Baghdad—noting in passing that the best book about Ifrīqiyā and its merits was written by an Andalusī:[64]

> When it comes to the great monuments (*ma'āthir*) of our country, the historian Aḥmad b. Muḥammad al-Rāzī [887–955] authored a great many works [on the subject], among them a massive book in which he mentioned the roads of al-Andalus and its ports, its largest cities (*ummahāt al-mudun*) and the areas settled by the six Arab contingents (*ajnād*, sing. *jund*), and the particularities of each region (*balad*) and what is exclusively in it. It is a comforting wonderful book. If our Andalus could not pride itself on what the prophet is said to have said about our ancestors . . . this book would bring us sufficient honor.[65]

Ibn Ḥazm returns to al-Rāzī after reviewing only the most prominent works in the recognized fields of knowledge.[66] In his section on history, a genre that specializes in recording great feats, political and intellectual, Ibn Ḥazm mentions again his fellow Cordovan's works, notably his history of the rulers of al-Andalus and his *Description of Cordoba and Its Great Families*. Al-Rāzī (d. 925) authored a variety of other histories, and Ibn Ḥazm mentions those he had seen personally: a history of al-Andalus' greatest anti-Umayyad rebel, Ibn Ḥafṣūn (d. 917), and another on the Banū Qays, the Tujībīs, and the Banū al-Ṭawīl in the frontier areas (*al-thaghr*). Ibn Ḥazm also lists a number of city histories and biographical dictionaries, notably of the judges and jurists of Cordoba.[67]

In light of my discussion of the *Jambara* as a work of history, Ibn Ḥazm includes in the section "works of history" al-Rāzī's compilation *Genealogies of Famous Andalusīs*, describing it as "among the best genealogy books and its largest." He goes on to describe a *Genealogy* by Qāsim Ibn Aṣbagh as extremely good, its author having also compiled an excellent book on the merits of the Umayyads.[68] After another list of great histories, including *Genealogy of Andalusīs*, Ibn Ḥazm singles out the ten-volume history by his contemporary Abū Marwān b. Ḥayyān (987–1075) as being among the best ever written in this field.[69] There should be no doubt, therefore, that Ibn Ḥazm saw his own *Jambara* as a history and that he imagined history as the record of prophets, dynasties, and prominent families.

Ibn Ḥazm does not use the word Berber in his epistle, not even once, and nothing in the text suggests that the Berbers contributed to the greatness of al-Andalus. It is hard to see this omission as an accident, the author having expressed antipathy toward the Berbers in his other writings.[70] However, this exclusion validates a vision of al-Andalus in which there were Andalusīs and Berbers, the latter being excluded from the former.[71] The omission of Berbers from Ibn Ḥazm's *Merits* also points to a logic in which excellence in culture (civilization) and genealogy (ethnicity) are linked, the form of their interaction depending on incidents like geographical location. Although Ibn Ḥazm's passage about Cordoba's natural surroundings fits a long-standing discourse in Arabic, which was itself inherited from the ancients, one of its implications here is that Andalusī Berbers settled in areas that were not propitious for the development of what Ibn Khaldūn would call civilization. Yes, this is only implied, but it is exactly what stands out in an analysis of the *Jamhara*'s information on the location of Berber clans. More pertinent here than whether the Berbers had anything to be proud of is the notion that genealogically defined groups were bearers of not just honor but also the very elements that constitute works of history: politics and great works. Since the contributions of dynasties included urban infrastructure like walls, aqueducts, and mosques, one can see how the structure Ibn Khaldūn gave his own theorizing extends Ibn Ḥazm's thinking—his stance vis-à-vis the Berbers is not as relevant here as the form of his presentation.

My argument here is that Ibn Khaldūn's sources on genealogy, notably Ibn Ḥazm, emerged out of a specific historical context—the demise of the Umayyad caliphate and the emergence of the Taifas (*mulūk al-ṭawā'if*)—in which political ideologies put a premium on kinship, Arab and Berber in particular. The appearance of Berber genealogies at the end of Ibn Ḥazm's compendium on the genealogies of the Arabs (*Jamharat ansāb al-ʿarab*) expresses a certain politics within al-Andalus. To the extent that Ibn Khaldūn echoes that politics, his work invites further examination.

Genealogy and the Structure of History

In the first pages of his *Kitāb al-ʿibar*, Ibn Khaldūn describes the organization of the work and its division into an introduction and three books. While it is only the third book that focuses specifically on the Berbers, an awareness of the overall organization situates that book within his overall project:[72]

> The Introduction deals with the great merit of historiography, (offers) an appreciation of its various methods, and cites errors of the historians.
>
> The First Book deals with civilization and its essential characteristics, namely, royal authority, government, gainful occupations, ways of making a living, crafts, and sciences, as well as with the causes and reasons thereof.
>
> The Second Book deals with the history, generations [*ajyāl*], and dynasties of the Arabs, from the beginning of creation down to this time. This will include references to such famous nations and dynasties contemporaneous with them, as the Nabataeans, the Syrians, the Persians, the Israelites, the Copts, the Greeks, the Byzantines, and the Turks.
>
> The Third Book deals with the history of the Berbers and of the Zanāta who are part of them; with their *ancestors and generations*; and, in particular, with the royal authority and dynasties in the Maghrib.[73]

Actually, "ancestors and generations" refers to genealogical information, which serves the critical function of extending the temporal scope of Ibn Khaldūn's book back to the beginning of time. When there are no dynasties or when the ancestors of known dynasties left no record of their deeds and feats, genealogy steps in to fill the gap. The blending of tribal (genealogical) and dynastic (historical) information feeds into Ibn Khaldūn's broader argument for the move from Bedouin to urban civilization. At the same time, Ibn Khaldūn's approach endorses, validates, and exemplifies a configuration of knowledge in which genealogy is a recognized science. In fact, when he sides against those who claimed an Arab origin for the Zanāta, Ibn Khaldūn presents his work as offering critical assessment of not only historians (Introduction) but also genealogists. Naturally, just how he arrived at such a conclusion is worth examining.

The methodological sleight of hand at the heart of Ibn Khaldūn's work, the replacement of ignorance about the past with a discourse on genealogy, allows him to make a claim for exhaustiveness and the universal applicability of his new science:

> Thus, (this work) contains an exhaustive history of the world. It forces stubborn stray wisdom to return to the fold. . . . The work

> contains the history of the Arabs and the Berbers, both the sedentary groups and the nomads. It also contains references to the great dynasties that were contemporary with them, and, moreover, clearly indicates memorable lessons to be learned from early conditions and from subsequent history. Therefore, I called the work "Book of Lessons and Archive of Early and Subsequent History, Dealing with the Political Events Concerning the Arabs, Non-Arabs, and Berbers, and the Supreme Rulers who Were Contemporary with Them."[74]

In his own description of his work, Ibn Khaldūn insists on signaling exhaustiveness (Arabs and Berbers, sedentary groups and nomads, tribes and dynasties) and, through it, the applicability of his system to the history of all nations. In this light, Ibn Khaldūn's interest in genealogy and his reliance on genealogists may have expressed more than a respect for Bedouins and the Bedouin origins of his own dynastic employers in the Maghrib. A genealogical notion of the past is constitutive of his vision and, this is worth emphasizing, extends to the organization of the historical sections, the history of dynasties.

Ibn Khaldūn did not let his dependence on genealogists be open to facile dismissal, offering a defense reminiscent of Ibn Ḥazm's: "As for what has been reported about genealogy being a form of useless knowledge and harmless ignorance, leading experts (*a'imma*) such as ['Alī b. 'Abd al-'Azīz] al-Jurjānī [d. 1002] and Abū Muḥammad b. Ḥazm [d. 1064] and Abū 'Umar b. 'Abd al-Barr [al-Qurṭubī] [d. 1071] have weakened [the reports'] attribution to the prophet."[75] Beyond a rather commonplace subscription to a critical attitude toward genealogical information, a position he shares with many of his predecessors and contemporaries, Ibn Khaldūn applied this critical stance to a sizable, but ultimately finite, body of works. Because of the nature of genealogical information, it is not always clear why Ibn Khaldūn, or anyone for that matter, would express a preference for one version in particular, although there are guiding principles and overriding concerns that offer some orientation. For instance, he rejects the Arab origins of the Zanāta but accepts the 'Ālid claims of the Fāṭimids (909–1171) and the Idrīsids (789–985), both of whose dynasties rose in the Maghrib.[76] His rationale for this is interesting: "People are to be believed with regard to the descent they claim for themselves, but there is a difference between what is known and what is mere guess, between what is certain and what is merely conceded as possibly true."[77] All these considerations may seem abstract, and Ibn Khaldūn's position on the claims of early Maghribī dynasties unclear. However, as genealogy is constitutive of political ideologies and the claims made by the great dynasties that, for him, make history, taking a stand on the claims of one early dynasty has implications for one's position regarding later ones. For Ibn Khaldūn, the claims made about the descent of the Almohad Mahdī Ibn Tūmart (d. 1130) from the prophet Muḥammad mattered to the Ḥafṣid dynasty, which claimed the mantle of his leadership. In other words, in such cases, Ibn Khaldūn tends to be similar to those ʿAbbāsid intellectuals whom he chastised for going along with the ruling dynasty: "The ([pro-Almoravid] jurists') disavowal of (al-Mahdī's) descent from Muḥammad's family is not backed up by any proof. Were it established that he himself claimed such descent, his claim could not be disproved, because people are to be believed regarding the descent they claim for themselves."[78] But Ibn Khaldūn claims for his system a status greater than that of mere histories that present the past in an entertaining narrative that serves the ruling dynasty. His move to establish a new science, the science of civilization, is an argument for distinguishing his book from those of previous historians. After he establishes the conceptual basis for his new science, Ibn Khaldūn moves on to present the historical parts that support and illustrate his systematic interpretation of their hidden deeper meaning: "The Second Book includes the history of the Arabs, their generations/strata (*ajyāl*, sing. *jīl*), and their dynasties (*duwal*, sing. *dawla*), from the beginning of creation to this era. The book includes references to and a summary of the events of the dynasties of famous contemporary nations (*umam*, sing. *umma*) such as the Syrians (al-Siryāniyūn), the Nabataeans, the Chaldaeans (al-Kaldāniyūn), the Persians, the Copts, the Banū Isrāʾīl (Israelites), Banū Yūnān (Greeks), and the Romans."[79] Before launching into the histories proper, however, Ibn Khaldūn adds two prefatory introductions (*muqaddima*) explaining the logic of his organization of the material in the second and third books. In the first introduction, he accounts for the genealogy and the differences between the nations of the world that follow from it, linguistic and religious differences occurring in preexisting genealogically defined nations. The point of departure is the creation of man and God's plan, which works through distinctions among nations. Ibn Khaldūn handles the existence of a multiplicity of written genealogical traditions, notably biblical and Persian, by recognizing the homology between genealogical traditions and by accepting a set of equivalencies between the Muslim and biblical patriarchs and Persian ones.[80]

In the second introduction, Ibn Khaldūn explains the role genealogy plays in his book. Maintaining that a picture is worth a thousand words, Ibn Khaldūn finds the genealogical tree helpful in anchoring his conception of the past as proceeding from patriarchs to nations and then to dynasties. Interestingly, although his preferred category for expressing distinctions within a nation has been the word *jīl* (pl. *ajyāl*), Ibn Khaldūn uses the word *tabaqāt* (sing. *tabaqa*) to organize his history of the Arabs. For the Arab nation, Ibn Khaldūn counts four generations, three of which were pre-Islamic, based on a typology that imagines an ideal, original, or ur-Arabness and then a departure or distancing from it, in time and place. Paying attention to Ibn Khaldūn's nomenclature is important, especially in light of the modern translation of the work and the effects it has had on modern Berberization. In any case, Ibn Khaldūn describes the Arabs as an *umma* (nation), as having *ajyāl* and *tabaqāt*. Each of these occurs at different times as instances of the others; in other words, the Arabs are said to include *umam* (sing. *umma*), *ajyāl*, and *tabaqāt*, but the most ancient *umma* among the Arabs belongs to the first *tabaqa*.[81] The Berbers are an *umma* too and so, "the [Atlas] is inhabited by innumerable Berber nations (*umam*)."[82]

An example of Ibn Khaldūn's switching between one category and another will illustrate the instability of these categories, although not of the schema itself:

> From the beginning of the world until today, there have been four successive *ajyāl* of the Arabs. Each *tabaqa* of these has political ages (*'uṣūr*), *ajyāl*, dynasties (*duwal*), and tribes (*aḥyā'*) which have been attended to instead of other nations (*umam*) because of the great number of their *ajyāl* and the vast expanse of their royal authority. We will relate for each *tabaqa* the state of its *jīl*, some of its famous battles and dynasties, and those contemporary kings, nations (*umam*), and dynasties so that the ranks of *ajyāl* of the world and their succession can become known.[83]

More than a comment on Ibn Khaldūn's failure to impose a systematic usage, this passage illustrates the multiplicity of usages available to him in works he considered to be authoritative. It points to a genealogy of a literary kind, harking back to the origins of historical writing in Arabic, from the early biographies of the Prophet (*siyar*) and biographical dictionaries (*kutub al-ṭabaqāt*) to the conquest (*futūḥ*) narratives, and annals. In Ibn Khaldūn's scheme, books on various religions and sects (*milal* and *niḥal*) deliver information of a primarily political or historical character, although they sometimes offer Ibn Khaldūn fodder for his thesis about religious ideas strengthening tribal solidarity.[84]

Ibn Khaldūn's language brings into focus his sources and an effect on his "system" that he did not address by developing a reasoned terminology of his own. Of course, he was aware of the limitations of earlier texts, especially when it comes to the various sources of error. Yet, his criticism of the reliability of the information found in them did not extend to a critique of the categories that structure his work in such a fundamental way. At the same time, he did not simply copy and paste from earlier texts but rather conveyed a particular understanding of their aim and meaning. Ibn Khaldūn uses those terms interchangeably, although with certain tendencies and preferences.

Again, the goal here is not to suggest that Ibn Khaldūn or Ibn Ḥazm invented kinship or the significance of knowledge of genealogy but merely to highlight the critical place genealogy has in the organization of Ibn Khaldūn's work in order to characterize his reliance on Ibn Ḥazm, an authoritative source on Berber genealogies. The notion that one could write the history of the world as the history of the Arabs (Second Book) and the Berbers (Third Book), with other nations' histories coming in when they are contemporary with a particular Arab or Berber stratum, is Ibn Khaldūn's own. The intellectual genealogy of his representation of the history of the Maghrib as the history of these two nations is what is ultimately at stake.

A Home for the People

In spite of the semantic difficulties, it is still fair to say that by the fourteenth century, the Berbers were as much a people as the Arabs and the Persians were. Theirs was a way of being a people associated with a particular configuration of politics and ideology but without a political structure like a single Berber state. Even among the dynasties that represented themselves as Berber, there was no discernible Pan-Berber agenda, even if genealogists limited the number of Berber patriarchs to a few. On the other hand, Taifa politics and their aftermath, notably Almoravid (1062–1147) and then Almohad (1130–1269) rule, maintained the relevance of Arab/Berber dualism. And even as the Almohads legitimized the use of their own regional dialect in state affairs, they did not do so because they believed in the existence of a single Berber people, or with the goal of creating one. The actions of the Almohads and those of the Maghribī dynasties that succeeded them, and whom Ibn Khaldūn served, did not lead him to a radical departure from how his contemporaries imagined the Berbers. Yet, this is not the same as saying that his history of the Maghrib as the history of those Arabs and Berbers who founded ruling families there was inconsequential. After all, it was a rarefied example of dynastic history that focused its gaze on the few and delivered an ornate narrative that chronicled their actions. Whether those outside of his history imagined a single Berber people or many is only guessable based on the references to them found in works of Ibn Khaldūn and other learned men. Still, Ibn Khaldūn's history is partial in both senses of the term.

Moreover, as Ibn Khaldūn conceived of the history of the Maghrib as the history of those among the Berbers and Arabs who founded dynasties there, he set a temporal limit on the presence of the Arabs in the Maghrib, which, in turn, made the Berbers the people who inhabited the Maghrib the longest. For him, that made the Maghrib their home, the way Arabia was the home of the Arabs: "Our main concern is with the Maghrib, the home [*waṭan*] of the Berbers, and the Arab home countries [*awṭān*] in the East."[85] Of course, he believed that the Berbers settled in the Maghrib after the Flood, but for him that was a long time ago. Closer to his time, he noted the influx of new Arabs, the Banū Hilāl and Banū Sulaym, who had migrated to the Maghrib from the east: "At the present time—that is at the end of the eighth [fourteenth] century—the situation in the Maghrib, as we can observe, has taken a turn and changed entirely. The Berbers, the original population of the Maghrib, have been replaced by an influx of Arabs, (that began in) the fifth [eleventh] century. The Arabs outnumbered and overpowered the Berbers, stripped them of most of their lands, and (also) obtained a share of those that remained in their possession."[86] As Rosenthal's translation makes clear, the Berbers were the original population of the Maghrib. But is this an accurate representation of Ibn Khaldūn's understanding of the "home" of the Berbers? Furthermore, and with Berberization of discourse in mind, one wonders when and under what circumstances the Maghrib became the home of the Berbers, and when they became its original inhabitants. The next chapter seeks to offer elements for a historical answer.

Chapter 4

The Maghrib and the Land of the Berbers

First, there was a Maghrib. Then, in that Maghrib, there came to be a country (or land or home) of the Berbers (*bilād al-barbar*). The idea that the two have always been equivalent is one of the effects of Berberization. Before the conquest of northwest Africa, Arabic writers did not particularly associate the west (*al-maghrib*) with the Berbers. There were the inhabitants of Barbara (Barbaria) in East Africa, who were to the west of the Arabian Peninsula, and were thus technically "Berbers in the west." However, Arabic sources did not identify them with the west in a way that they eventually did their counterparts in the Maghrib. Before the military raids of the 640s, as far as the Arabians were concerned, northwest Africa was a number of faraway provinces and lands to the west of Egypt. Unlike Egypt, Byzantium, and Persia, northwest Africa is not mentioned in the Qur'ān or in any other pre-Islamic document in Arabic. It was at the margins of the lives of Arabians and of their conception of the world. On the other hand, there is every reason to believe that informed Egyptians had some knowledge of the Byzantine provinces of the west.[1] When it comes to what informed literate Arabs knew of the western African regions and, more importantly, the terms of that knowledge, we have to wait for the earliest extant Arabic sources. In these sources, however, the Maghrib and the *bilād al-barbar* were not synonymous, at least not immediately. Eventually, the Maghrib did become associated with the Berbers but in ways that do not fully match its modern representation as the exclusive homeland of the Berbers.

An examination of usage of the categories of Maghrib and *bilād al-barbar* in medieval Arabic sources shows a general lack of consistency. Furthermore, it shows that no one really believed the two categories to be equivalent. Although these findings support this book's overall argument about the gradual character of Berberization, focusing solely on Arabic works tends to leave aside evidence in Latin and Romance languages. In fact, European sources, especially commercial ones, suggest that the activities of traders around the Mediterranean left their mark on how the coast of Africa was represented, including perhaps in medieval Arabic. European sources, along with the unavoidable French translation of Ibn Khaldūn's *Kitāb al-ʿibar*, played an important role in naturalizing the equation of the Maghrib and the *bilād al-barbar* in modern scholarship. That is why this chapter, like Chapter 3, will pay special attention to Ibn Khaldūn and his contribution to Berberization.

The Maghrib as Land of Berbers

The idea that the Maghrib has always been the land of the Berbers is a cornerstone of modern historical thinking. A vital component of the functioning of modern Berberization, the idea has enabled and validated the conception of northwest Africa as a geographic unit or "region." The institution of the Maghrib as the transhistorical land of the Berbers has tended to occult the historical circumstances of the emergence of the idea and its evolution over time, let alone its relation to a historically specific process such as Berberization. In fact, the notions that the Maghrib constitutes a coherent geographic unit and the Berbers are its original inhabitants are two sides of a single modern coin. Although this was not always true, it is essential to emphasize that, at least in the last century or so, these two notions have been conjoined and that they have been necessary to the implementation of modern Berberization.

Just to be clear, before Arabic authors eventually did so, no writer ever conceived of northwest Africa as a unit, let alone as the home of a single people called the Berbers. This is true even if, reading modern scholarship, it is almost impossible to know that. The question is therefore not simply why modern historians have tended to think otherwise, but how their doing so was part of modern ideological developments that have stood in the way of historicizing the process of Berberization. After more than a century of anachronistic projection, the idea that the Arabs conquered the Berbers and their land, North Africa, is very widely accepted. As H. T. Norris put it, "When the Arab Conquests began the whole of North Africa was Berber country."[2] Half a century earlier, Maurice Vonderheyden had made this equally explicit statement:

> North Africa is the country of the Berbers. Perhaps it is not useless to recall one more time the vitality of this people, who, though many times subjected to diverse conquerors after fierce resistance, knew to maintain its language and customs. However, it is necessary to distinguish between two parts of this country. The first, to the west of Bougie, has always been particularly reticent to accept any influence from outside. Until a very recent era, the [western] Maghreb remained purely Berber. In contrast, the eastern part of *Berbérie*, which we call, with the Arabs, Ifrīqiyā, has always been more open to invasions. Its population has always been more mixed.[3]

Before the "Arab conquests," there were no Berbers, no North Africa, let alone North-Africa-as-Berber-country. As for Vonderheyden's reference to "pure" and "mixed" Berbers, they do recall essentialist conceptions associated with modern discourses on identity. However, the issue here is not "semantic" in the sense that one should feel comfortable sweeping it under the rug. Rather, it is that such malformed ahistorical constructions undermine the ability of modern scholarship to historicize, notably by obfuscating the work of Berberization. For although modern experts have not always seen the Berbers as a nation, the relation they have imagined between them and the Maghrib, their country (or homeland), has largely mirrored the connectedness that Europeans have imagined exists between European nations and their own homelands—not everyone, not always, but still . . . Whatever can be said about them, medieval Arabic writers simply did not think in these terms.

Modern historians transformed the Maghrib into the land of the Berbers in the process of establishing a particular set of questions, lines of inquiry, and modes of interpretation. Notably, they did so not by engaging in theoretical discussions on the validity of specific assumptions and presuppositions, but rather in the process of constructing historical arguments about unquestionable phenomena such as the Romanization of the Berbers, their conversion to Christianity, and, for medievalists, their conversion to Islam and their Arabization.[4] The conception of the Maghrib as the original homeland of the Berbers was a by-product of these arguments, which both relied on it and, through a tautological shadow play, enshrined it as a fundamental, self-evident, if ahistorical, truth.

The modern French notion Berbérie encapsulates the historiographic practice at the heart of the momentous transformation of the Maghrib into the land of the Berbers. Mostly by declaring Maghrib and Berbérie to be synonyms, colonial historians established the latter not because it was accurate but, unlike the Arabic Maghrib, it was also neutral or somehow more "authentic" and "true." The French did not invent the category Berbérie after they conquered Algiers, however. But they did transform it into one of the pillars of colonial knowledge, pointing to the critical shift of conceptualization under colonial rule that accompanied the marginalization of native knowledge. Here is an early colonial definition of the Maghrib and its inhabitants:

> The northern part of Africa received from the Arabs the name *Magreb*. This word, which means "Sunset," is justified by the western situation of the African coast relative to Egypt and the other countries where the power and civilization of the Arabs first resided. However, its geographic meaning has varied greatly. . . . The Arabs designated more particularly in the Middle Ages under the name *Magreb* the large portion of the African continent, the only part known to the ancients, which faces Europe and which includes the entire Mediterranean coast from Tripoli to Morocco. Christian sailors and merchants gave the country its true name, *Berbérie*, in other words, "country of the Berbers," its first natives (*indigènes*). In modern times, the political regime established there by the Turks justifiably made [the name] *Barbarie* prevalent; these inhospitable lands became for civilized Europe the Barbary Coasts (*Côtes de Barbarie*) or the Barbary States (*États Barbaresques*).[5]

The other French colonial nickname for the Maghrib was of course North Africa (*Afrique du nord*, *Afrique septentrionale*), short for French North Africa. Although it presented itself as a primarily geographic notion, the designation North Africa did not apply to all the northern regions of the continent of Africa but mainly to those to the west of Tripoli, which were under French rule. Without belaboring the point here, French North Africa was not the same as the medieval Maghrib, which included al-Andalus, nor was it equivalent to ancient Greek and Roman ways of referring to the area west of Egypt.[6] With time, North Africa, Berbérie, and North-Africa-as-Berbérie prevailed over the name Maghrib (Maghreb), which became the term preferred by native intellectuals and European connoisseurs. In fact, and although after the independence of Morocco, Tunisia, and Algeria, the name

Maghrib made its reappearance, it was effectively a translation of the colonial Berbérie: the "land of the Berbers," its original inhabitants. This understanding of the term persists even though in the 1980s these independent nation-states, plus Libya and Mauritania, declared their desire to build an Arab Maghrib.

Reacting to what he saw as methodological insouciance, the historian Abdallah Laroui pointed out some of the difficulties that arise when examining the history of the Maghrib as a whole and the need to develop a critical awareness of the historical specificity of categories of analysis. "The ideal," he notes, "would be to start with a history of historiography; to trace the genesis of the concept of the Maghrib and discover how it ultimately took on an objective definition."[7] While historical writings alone could not account for the objectivity of the category Maghrib, and thus a history of historiography would be at best one of the components of a much broader project, Laroui's insight represents a critical shift toward greater attention to the categories that support our thinking, the Maghrib being a most obvious one.

The surprisingly short entry on the Maghrib in the second edition of the *Encyclopaedia of Islam* is a convenient starting point for a discussion of the challenges facing a project like Laroui's:[8]

> Al-Maghrib: The name given by Arab writers to the part of Africa which Europeans have called Barbary or Africa Minor and then North Africa, and which includes Tripolitania, Tunisia, Algeria and Morocco. The word Maghrib means the west, the setting sun, in opposition to the *mashriḳ*, the east, the rising sun (Levant), but as Ibn Khaldūn remarks, the general denomination was applied to a particular region. The extent of this region, moreover, varies according to different authors.[9]

Giving a number of examples of these differences, Georges Yver sides with Ibn Khaldūn and identifies the southern boundaries "as far as the barrier of moving sands separating the country of the Berbers from the land of the Negroes." Yver relies on Ibn Khaldūn again to refute other medieval authors and to exclude some areas from the Maghrib:

> Ibn Khaldūn does not accept this delimitation [made by Abū al-Fidā' (1273–1331)], because, he says, the inhabitants of the Maghrib do not consider Egypt and Barḳa as forming part of their

> country. The latter commences only at the province of Tripoli and encloses the districts of which *the country of the Berbers* was composed in former times. Ibn Saʿīd [(1213–1286)] and later Maghribī writers limit themselves to reproducing with a few variations in detail, the information of Ibn Khaldūn [(1332–1406)].[10]

While the significance of Yver's treatment of Ibn Khaldūn as a privileged source will be discussed in greater length in the next chapters, Ibn Khaldūn's idea that the Maghrib "encloses the districts of which the country of the Berbers was composed in former times" requires some unpacking. Did Ibn Khaldūn define the Maghrib based on an ancient map? At the same time, did the Maghrib not encompass districts that did not belong in the country of the Berbers? It is enough to note that Yver's reading of Ibn Khaldūn takes for granted the idea that "in former times" all the Maghrib was Berberland.

The Berbers, the *Balad*, the *Bilād*, and the *Buldān*

The idea that the Maghrib and the land of the Berbers were synonymous was not an instantaneous development. Before the conquests, the only land of Berbers the Arabs wrote about was the Barbar in East Africa. They thus had to discover the Maghrib, an imperfect process that took many decades. At the same time, they had to engage in the Berberization of the inhabitants of northwest Africa and transform existing groups into Berbers. That too took a lot of time, although everybody in the Mashriq came to know rather quickly that there were Berbers living in the Maghrib, because Berber slaves flooded the markets. The challenge was that the various groups the Arabs called Berbers had not thought of themselves and each other as such, nor had they had the habit of using their imputed common ancestry as a principle to organize their societies.

In spite of this early Berberization, however, individuals in the Maghrib did not come to be known as so-and-so the Berber. Only slaves or *mawālī* who had lost their original kinship affiliation came to have the *nisba* al-Barbarī, the Berber, added to their name.[11] As a sign of the provenance of a commodity and as a social marker of subordinate status, current or past, the *nisba* "al-Barbarī" implied the existence of Berbers and of a land of Berbers (*bilād al-barbar*) in the most general and unspecific sense. It did so, however, only in the East, among the slave-owning elites. In the West, where kinship groups that gradually began to think of themselves as Berbers kept their old names, or embraced new ones, the epithet al-Barbarī was largely unknown. There were also no cities, no rivers, no mountain ranges, and no deserts described as al-Barbarī in the Maghrib. To the extent that it existed at all, the *bilād al-barbar* was a vague umbrella category, but as soon as one looks for it to indicate anything other than the act of imposition itself, it shows no analytical pertinence.

In addition to the difficulties caused by such considerations, there is another, which stems from the richness and suppleness of the Arabic language. The word *bilād*, and thus our notion of what the *bilād al-barbar* could have meant, presents us with rather complicated usage. In his *Arabic-English Lexicon*, E.W. Lane gives a sense of the challenge:

> ***Balad*** (which is masc. and fem.) and ***balda*** both signify the same; namely, [a country, land, region, province, district, or territory: and a city, town, or village: or] any portion of the earth, or of land, comprehended within certain limits . . . cultivated, or inhabited, or uncultivated, or uninhabited: or the former signifies any place of this description; and the latter any portion thereof: or the former is a generic name of a place [or country, or region, or province] such as El-ʻIrāḳ and Syria; and the latter signifies a particular portion thereof such as [the city or town of] El-Baṣrah and Damascus; or these are post-classical applications: or the former a tract of land, or district, which is an abode, or a place of resort, of animals, or genii, even if containing no building . . . and the latter, a land, country, or territory, [belonging to, or inhabited by, a people,] syn. *arḍ*: [a meaning assigned in the Qāmūs to *balad*; but this appears to be a mistake occasioned by the accidental omission of the word *al-balda*.[12]

Although Lane's choice of punctuation takes some getting used to, the entry is rather clear in conveying that the word *balad* is capacious, and, importantly for us, it includes notions like country, district, and territory, which today have narrower and more specialized meanings. Moreover, even if we are able to ascertain what it means in the singular, we have to contend with what the plural form adds:

> The pl. (of the former) is *buldān* (and of the same, or of the latter) *bilād* [which latter, regarded as pl. of *balda* in a more limited sense

> than *balad*, is often used as meaning provinces collectively; i.e. a country:] *buldān* is syn. with *kuwar* [which signifies districts or tracts of country; quarters, or regions; and also cities, towns, or villages].[13]

Clearly, the difference between the singular and the plural is not very clear, and, unsurprisingly, various authors commonly used *balad*, *bilād*, and *buldān* to describe the very same place. Yet, for the Maghrib to be the (original or exclusive) homeland of the Berbers in a modern sense, the messy reality of medieval usage must be forgotten. After reading Lane, it seems almost as if, whether they wanted it or not, medieval writers could not have made a simple use of any of these terms. In fact, other than the authors of dictionaries who recorded the intricacies involved, most learned writers used the terms as they commonly would and not in a technically precise way.

If an examination of the term *bilād* does not seem illuminating with regard to *bilād al-barbar* being the equivalent of an entity like the Maghrib, usage of the word *manzil* (pl. *manāzil*), which connotes a temporary settling of nomads and from there a "home," tends to go in the same direction. In his *Kitāb al-buldān*, al-Ya'qūbī (d. 897) describes multiple homes of the Berbers: "Al-Ramāda is first among the homes (*manāzil*) of the Berbers, inhabited by people from Mazāta and others belonging to ancient non-Arabs (*'ajam*). There is also a group of Arabs belonging to the Baliy, Jahīna, Banū Madlaj, and a mix of others (*akhlāṭ*)."[14] All one has to do is believe that a *bilād* is a collection of *manāzil*, but, as Lane explained, that is not always a correct interpretation. In any case, let us just assume for the sake of argument that *bilād al-barbar* was a straightforward, stable, and uncomplicated notion and that all medieval authors agreed. Doing so turns our attention to the category Maghrib, which, as was mentioned above, first referred to the West.

The Maghrib in Question

The word *maghrib* refers to the West. The term is old and is attested in the Qur'ān.

> To Allah belongs the East (*al-mashriq*) and the West (*al-maghrib*).[15]

The term also means "the setting sun" and by extension "the lands where the sun sets." References to this West usually contrast it with the East, without further distinction and without any sense that it constituted an administrative province, a region, or a unit of any kind. This is clearly the sense that al-Wāqidī (d. 823) gives it when he tells the story of the encounter between the envoys of the prophet Muḥammad (d. 632) and the Roman emperor Heraclius (d. 641).

> It is necessary for [Muḥammad's] religion to expand until it fills the East (*al-mashriq*) and the West (*al-maghrib*).[16]

The chronicler al-ʿUṣfurī (d. 854) thought that both Sicily and Sardinia belonged in the "country of the *maghrib*."[17] In a similar vein, the tenth-century geographer al-Iṣṭakhrī (d. 957) evaluated the size of China in these terms: "Regarding the kingdom of China, it extends [over an area equal to the distance traveled in] four months by [one traveled in] three months. . . . If you crossed it from the east to its western border (*al-maghrib*) in the land of Tibet, it extends four months."[18] Geographers could obviously not do without one of the cardinal directions. Naturally, this meaning is widely attested and occurs often; it indicates a general western direction rather than a direction toward the Maghrib of northwest Africa.

Some evidence suggests that Egypt may have preceded northwest Africa as a Maghrib. For instance, in his *futūḥ al-buldān*, al-Balādhurī (d. 892) reports a statement made by the Umayyad caliph ʿUmar b. ʿAbd al-ʿAzīz (r. 717–20) about the conquest of the Maghrib, a fact full of legal implications for the inhabitants and the government's coffers: "The only towns we conquered through a peace treaty in the Maghrib were three: Alexandria, Kafr Ṭīs, and Salṭīs."[19] All these cities were in Egypt. Although al-Balādhurī begins his narrative of the conquest of the Maghrib "proper" well west of Alexandria, his text still includes an early report in which Egypt had been the Maghrib, or maybe just west. Of course, Egypt was to the west of Arabia, the Levant, Iraq, and territories farther east from whence came many geographers, travelers, and compilers of entertaining *mirabilia* about the world and its peoples. Egypt was a very important point of reference in eastern written and oral traditions.

South of Egypt, the *bilād al-sūdān* was also in the West (*maghrib*). For an easterner writer such as al-Istakhrī that seemed natural: "We did not mention the *bilād al-sūdān* in the West (*maghrib*), the Buja, the Zanj, and those other nations (*umam*) around them."[20] The reason that this *maghrib* is to the south of Egypt is that the Buja and the Zanj are East Africans. In a related sense, the Egyptian Ibn 'Abd al-Ḥakam (d. 871) describes the great Umayyad general Ibn Abī Sarḥ as "leaving for the *maghrib* to conquer Ifrīqiyā."[21] Since the Umayyads had not yet conquered what came to be "the Maghrib," this formulation does not necessarily imply that Ifrīqiyā was a part of the *maghrib* in anything more than the general sense that it was in the West. Yet, and this is due to the anachronism of these authors, Ibn 'Abd al-Ḥakam and others wrote about this early Maghrib and Ifrīqiyā as if they had always been distinct provinces or regions. Perhaps a related example will help make this point crystal clear. Both Ibn 'Abd al-Ḥakam and his Andalusī contemporary Ibn Ḥabīb (d. 852/3) believed that Ṭariq b. Ziyād had crossed into a preexisting "Andalus." For them, al-Andalus was just the Arabic name of a land that existed before the Umayyad troops conquered it. Ibn Ḥabīb can thus write about pre-Islamic Hispania as al-Andalus: "Ludhrīq belonged to Asbahān. In al-Andalus Asbahān are called Ishbān who are the Goths, the kings of the non-Arabs (*'ajam*) of al-Andalus."[22] This brand of blatant anachronism covers up a more subtle one when it comes to the Maghrib. Because the Umayyad armies did not conquer "what came to be known as the Maghrib" instantly, the Maghrib existed as an unstable notion for at least seven decades.

After the foundation of al-Qayrawān in 670, the Umayyad caliphs sent commanders (*wālī* or *amīr*), often described as governors in the literature, though the sources have the tendency to give an exaggerated sense of the political situation. In fact, it is difficult to think of the city as the capital of the entire Maghrib prior to 710, the date at which chroniclers claim the Umayyads had finished conquering it. Of course, the political history matters here, and it is critical to remember that al-Qayrawān was taken over by Kharijite rebels in the 740s and that by the time the pro-'Abbāsid Aghlabids took over in 800 the Maghrib was already divided into a number of competing polities. Since our sources were all written after that date, it is not surprising that at least some of them would portray al-Qayrawān as having always been the capital of the entire Maghrib: "Al-Qayrawān is the most prominent city in the land of the Maghrib after Cordoba in al-Andalus, which is larger. It is the city where the governors (*wulāt*) of the West/Maghrib reside."[23] Although he is seemingly describing an innocuous fact, al-Istakhrī is well aware that the staunchly anti-'Abbāsid Fāṭimids overthrew the Aghlabids in 909 and that they ruled the Maghrib, or at least claimed to do so, from their new capital in Mahdiya. As he writes, "Barqa used to have governors (*'āmil*) [appointed] from Egypt until came the Mahdī 'Ubayd Allāh the ruler of the Maghrib who conquered it and eliminated the governors appointed from Egypt."[24] Recalling the Aghlabids (800–909), however, al-Istakhrī makes their influence extend well beyond the boundaries of Ifrīqiyā—something they never achieved. Since the Aghlabids were, at least nominally, ruling with 'Abbāsid sanction, his rhetorical move extends 'Abbāsid claims westward. Seeing Ifrīqiyā stand for the entire Maghrib becomes less of a surprise.[25]

Ninth-century *futūḥ* writers were not indifferent to these political gestures, which oftentimes touched them personally. For instance, the idea that control over Ifrīqiyā meant rule of the entire Maghrib mapped rather well onto the early conquest, especially the old Umayyad claims that they conquered the Maghrib from their base in al-Qayrawān. The added benefit of conceiving of Islamic, rather than Umayyad, conquests, was that it dispensed with the 'Abbāsids' enemies. For both Ibn 'Abd al-Ḥakam and al-Balādhurī, the ruler of Ifrīqiyā controlled the area between Ṭarablus (Tripoli) and Ṭanja (Tangier).[26] Again, while this agrees with our understanding of the areas under Byzantine domination, these descriptions make Ifrīqiyā encompass the entire Maghrib. The seemingly idiosyncratic pronouncements of individual writers make better sense in relation to the political claims of various dynasties.

Even without a discussion of the terms by which the Maghrib was imagined, which would raise the question of their equivalence with the *bilād* of the *bilād al-barbar*, it is clear that the Maghrib did not emerge as a fully formed entity with three distinct subregions (al-Maghrib al-Aqṣā, al-Maghrib al-Awsaṭ, and Ifrīqiyā), as Georges Yver and others suggest. Conceiving of a gradual reification of the category Maghrib enables us to return to the question of its relation to the Berbers and their *bilād* with a degree of critical distance that allows us to ask again whether the evidence agrees with H. T. Norris' characterization of "the whole of North Africa" as "Berber country" before the Arab conquests.

The Maghrib and the *Bilād al-Barbar*

Futūḥ authors did not describe a conquest of the Berbers but rather a *fatḥ* or *futūḥ* of the Maghrib. As Fred Donner has shown, the difference between the victory of Islam and the military conquest and domination over various groups was important to these authors and to our understanding of the events. However, the fact that the sources do not describe the conquest of the Berbers by the Arabs (or even Muslims) does not in itself prove that they did not think the Maghrib to be the land of the Berbers. Had they described a conquest of the Berbers in the Maghrib, it would surely have helped. They did not, and so we have to find out whether the early Arabic sources describe the Maghrib as having been first settled by Berbers.

As it happens, the idea that Berbers settled in areas of the Maghrib that were already inhabited was actually most common and finds countless echoes in the genealogies found in *futūḥ* literature. Ibn ʿAbd al-Ḥakam cites this version of the Goliath story:

> The Berbers were in Palestine and their king was Goliath. When David killed him, the Berbers left in direction of the Maghrib until they reached Lūbiya and Marāqiya, which are two districts (*kūra*) of western Egypt that obtain their water from rain and do not receive any from the Nile. There the Berbers separated. Zanāta and Maghīla advanced to the Maghrib and settled in the mountains. Luwāta moved to Anṭabulus, which is Barqa, and from there they separated and spread throughout the Maghrib until they reached the Sūs. Hawwāra settled in the city of Labda. Nafūsa moved into the city of Sabrata, which led the Romans to migrate but the Afariq, who were the servants of the Romans, remained and [paid tribute] as they did to anyone who conquered their country.[27]

In a different version, Ibn Khordadbeh (d. 912) describes the Berbers' migration from Palestine and their settlement in the Maghrib:

> When the Berbers took Tripoli, which means three cities, from the Romans and settled there, the Romans migrated to the Mediterranean island of Sicily. Then, the Berbers migrated to the Sūs al-Adnā, which is after Tangier . . . after which the Afāriq and the Romans returned to their cities after making peace with the Berbers. [The Afāriq and the Romans] made the Berbers abhor the cities and [prefer] the mountains and the deserts. That is how the cities returned to being Roman until the Muslims conquered them.[28]

Not only were the Berbers not originally in the Maghrib; there were Romans and Afāriq there when they arrived.[29] In these genealogies, there is no reason whatsoever to think of the Maghrib as the original home of the Berbers but only that some *bilād al-barbar* was/were in the Maghrib.

The Isfahānī geographer Ibn Rosteh (d. early 10th c.) expresses an even starker distinction between Maghrib and *bilād al-barbar*: "The second clime . . . goes onto the land of the Maghrib (*arḍ al-maghrib*) through the middle of the land of Ifrīqiyā (*bilād Ifrīqiyā*) then it goes through the land of the Berbers (*bilād al-barbar*) and ends at the Western Ocean (*baḥr al-maghrib*)."[30] Likewise, in addition to the presence of Romanized Afāriq, al-Yaʿqūbī reported that the "true" people (*ahl*) of a Maghribī city like Berenice were not Berbers: "The inhabitants of the [city of Barnīq] include the descendants of ancient Rūm [Greeks] who were its people (*ahl*) and a group of Berbers from the Taḥlāla, Siwa, Masūsa, Maghāgha, Wahla, and Wajdāna."[31] Moreover, and in addition to the presence of non-Berbers in the ancient Maghrib, and thus of the existence of non-Berber *bilād* in the Maghrib, there were a few cases of *bilād al-barbar* outside northwest Africa. There was the one in East Africa and another, more interestingly, in al-Andalus.[32] For the prolific Cordoba native Ibn Ḥazm (d. 1064), the Berbers were a political nuisance, and the great Umayyad ʿAbd al-Raḥmān III (r. 912–61) deserves credit for bringing the areas they controlled under his rule: "Then was born ʿAbd al-Raḥmān b. Muḥammad son of the emir ʿAbd Allah. Unlike all those who preceded him among his [Umayyad] ancestors, he bore the title of caliph and *amīr al-muʾminīn* and took on the [caliphal] name of al-Nāṣir li-dīn Allah. He ruled for fifty years and six months [during which] he ruled over al-Andalus and a great part of the land of the Berbers (*bilād al-barbar*) in a way that none of his predecessors in al-Andalus had."[33] This *bilād al-barbar* and Ibn Ḥazm's reference to "some Berber areas" (*baʿḍ nawāḥī al-barbar*) not only allow for lands of Berbers to be outside the Maghrib of Africa; they assume that the Maghrib is the land where most but not all Berbers live.[34]

If the Maghrib had been widely held to be the land of the Berbers, that fact would definitely have found its way into the geographic encyclopedia written by Yāqūt al-Ḥamawī (d. 1229) six centuries after the first raids into Barqa (Cyrenaica). Yāqūt collected many reports, written and oral, on the Maghrib and the Berbers, some unattested anywhere else, and it would be natural for him to describe the inhabitants of the Maghrib as primarily Berbers, at least in the pre-Islamic period. He did not. In fact, his entry on the Maghrib does not even mention the Berbers:

> The Maghrib: Opposite of the Mashriq: large lands (*bilād*) and vast expanse: some reported that its limits are from the city of Milyāna, which is the farthest border of Ifrīqiyā, to the farthest mountains of the Sūs, after which [there is] the Ocean. The island of al-Andalus is part of [the Maghrib] even if it is closer to the North. The length of this [Maghrib] is, on foot, two months long. I have previously mentioned its borders in the definition of Asia, those interested in looking at that will find it there.[35]

For Yāqūt, the Maghrib was a purely geographic notion with no indication that it corresponded, or not, to administrative realities, currently or in the past. The *bilād al-barbar* appears, however, in the entry on the Berbers:

> The Berbers: It is a name that encompasses many tribes (*qabā'il*) in the mountains of the Maghrib the first of which is Barqa. [The mountains extend] to the end of the Maghrib and the Ocean and south to the Land of the Blacks (*bilād al-sūdān*). [The Berbers] are innumerable nations (*umam*) and tribes (*qabā'il*) and each place is named after the tribe that inhabits it (*tanziluhu*). The sum of their lands (*bilād*) is known as the land of the Berbers (*bilād al-barbar*). There are disagreements about their origins (*ukhtulifa fī aṣli nasabihim*) and the majority of the Berbers claim that they are descended from the Arabs but these are fabrications and lies.[36]

As a good compiler, Yāqūt gives a number of genealogies of the Berbers, the names of famous Berber tribes, and a number of anecdotes gathered from illustrious authors like the geographer and traveler Ibn Ḥawqal (d. after 978) who visited the Maghrib in the mid-tenth century. What distinguishes Yāqūt al-Ḥamawī's definition is, of course, its reliance on the recognized forms of knowledge (sciences) of the time, from genealogy and geography to *ḥadīth* and *adab*.[37] Yāqūt's dictionary (*mu'jam*) is a reasoned compilation based on authoritative sources the author believed to be reliable and others he used to illustrate the errors that he found in the record of learned references. As his definition makes clear, Yāqūt thought the Berbers inhabited the mountains of the Maghrib, which were the lands of the Berbers. In spite of the towering presence of the Atlas Mountains, however, the Maghrib is no Tibet, and among those known Berber tribes he mentioned, some inhabited pre-Saharan areas and other low-lying plains that were far from being mountainous. Yet, the appearance of mountains in the definition suggests a particular usage of the word. As it happens, in many texts before his, authors had occasion to draw a contrast between urban dwellers and a number of mountain peoples. Often times, the distinction had political undertones and expressed both fear and ignorance—sentiments that Yāqūt relayed even if they contradicted his knowledge of the world. Beyond these considerations, however, Yāqūt enunciates the most cogent articulation of what the land of the Berbers meant: the sum of all the areas where Berbers settled (*tanzilu*). Not the entire Maghrib, just those areas inhabited by Berbers. Not always and forever either, just when they did.[38]

Home of Coastal Berbers?

Andalusīs and Maghribīs call the other side of the Strait of Gibraltar their *ʿudwa*, the side across the sea from them. But owing to other circumstances, not all of which are clearly discernible, Andalusīs took to calling what is the northern part of Morocco today the *bilād al-barbar*. As the geographer al-Bakrī (d. 1094) notes, "The mountain of Albīra can be seen from across the sea in the *bilād al-barbar*."[39] Andalusīs had already been used to thinking of Berbers as a component of their society, and of non-Arab Maghribīs as Berbers. This sentiment was reinforced when Berber soldiers recruited by the Umayyads landed in al-Andalus to help the dynasty achieve its own goals. Dissatisfied parties resented these newcomers, including "old" Berbers, who had settled in al-Andalus long before then. With the particularly "Arab" coloring of Umayyad ideology, anti-Berber resentment was also politically expedient, as it kept the Berbers in check. This much and the imperial policies of the Umayyads on the African continent reinforced Andalusī usage.

Less visible, if relatively well documented, were the activities of Andalusī merchants who took their wares to a number of small African ports and set up relations with "Berbers." For authors like al-Bakrī, Andalusī merchants were responsible for the foundation of market towns on the African coast, their presence being attested prior to the expansion of cities like Tannas, Wahrān, Bijāya, and Būna.[40] While these merchants knew which Berbers they were dealing with, from Andalusī authors like al-Bakrī we gather that they used the phrase *bilād al-barbar* to refer to the areas inland from the ports where they were settled or had business. This nuance in meaning is usually difficult to discern, especially because it competed with the existence of other areas also known as *bilād al-barbar* and with the overriding assumption that it was just another name for the Maghrib.

In the *Nuzhat al-mushtāq*, the geographical work written for King Roger II of Sicily, the Sabta native and great geographer al-Idrīsī (d. 1065/6) offers a few clues about this secondary usage. When he describes al-Marsā al-Kabīr near the city of Wahrān, al-Idrīsī notes that "[al-Marsā al-Kabīr] has no equivalent among the ports [situated] on the coast of *bilād al-barbar*."[41] A century before al-Idrīsī, Ibn al-Qūṭiya (d. 977) described a "coast of the Berbers" (*sāḥil al-barbar*).[42] Al-Idrīsī, al-Bakrī, and others conceived of a plurality of *bilād al-barbar*; the coast of Africa was only one of them. Without the activities of merchants, and the political discourse in al-Andalus, it could easily have been the coast of the Maghrib. Al-Bakrī gives another example of this more specific meaning: "The fourth clime [includes] Egypt Ifrīqiyā *al-barbar* and al-Andalus. It has Gemini (*al-jawzā'*) and Mercury (*'uṭārid*)."[43] Because the latitude includes al-Andalus but not the Sūdān, it is reasonable to infer that *al-barbar* is either an error or short for the northern "Mediterranean" *bilād al-barbar*. It is perhaps the same part of the Maghrib that Andalusī rebels fled to after being defeated when, according to the great Andalusī litterateur Ibn al-Abbār (d. 1260), "their supporters fled to Toledo where the locals rejected [Umayyad] rule while others sought refuge on the coasts of the *bilād al-barbar*."[44] While it is hard to be definitive on the basis of statements like these, my sense is that from the eleventh century on, this novel Andalusī usage was copied from authors like Ibn al-Qūṭiya and al-Idrīsī and found its way into Maghribī and non-Maghribī texts. However, it is also my argument that unlike the other *bilād al-barbar*, this particular Mediterranean one had a rich life in contemporary Latin and Romance sources.

Barbaria, Barberia, Berberia

In the early years of the nineteenth century, before the French had conquered Algiers, no one doubted that Barbary was the name of the southern Mediterranean shores.[45] Everyone had used that name for ages, and although the Spaniards, the French, and the Italians pronounced it differently, everyone realized that it was the same name. In fact, the name had been in use so long that no one really knew where it came from. Those who scoured the known Arabic sources could only offer the explanations they found in them, which were tentative, inconsistent, and ultimately not compelling. These were ideal conditions for conjecture, speculation, and lucubration, and the European cognoscenti delivered. The Milanese author of the encyclopedic *Ancient and Modern Costumes* offered his own musings:

> Writers have expressed many opinions about the etymology of Barbaria. Some claimed that after they conquered the country, the Romans named it thus following the custom that the fathers of the Republic had of calling barbarian all foreign nations. [Leo Africanus] derives this word more reasonably from the Arabic language saying that the Arabs gave the country this name because its inhabitants had a coarse language similar to a confused murmur that in Arabic was called Barbar. This writer suggests that the word came from the word Bar, which means desert, repeated twice. They say that the Arabs were followed by enemies one time and, not knowing where to hide, screamed: to the desert, to the desert.[46]

In spite of being defective, the etymology offered by the Milanese Giulio Ferrario (1767–1847) presumed some knowledge of Arabic. In another attempt, a less philological but more "Catholic" approach gave an equally plausible origin: "Berberia, named thus after they had the barbarity of leaving the Faith of Christ, and Roman laws, to embrace that of the Arabs, and the cursed faith of Muḥammad (Mahoma)."[47] Whatever else can be said about these two etymologies, and the hundreds like them published after the sixteenth century, they seem to be utterly immaterial to whether the Maghrib and *bilād al-barbar* referred to the same entity. However, they do point to a literate tradition with its own distinctiveness. For northern Mediterranean authors writing in Latin, and later in Romance languages, the Saracens took over Christian territories and, as a result, the Moors left the church in droves. The names of ancient provinces and bishoprics remained in use long after they had ceased to have any sense in actuality. But as they grappled with the new political situation, northerners simply continued to use the categories they knew, and which were recorded in their books, and used by their ancestors. That Barbaria should be the name of northwest Africa was simply not there, at least not in the seventh and eighth centuries. Five centuries later, however, Barbaria was ubiquitous. In this northern "Berberization," first came Barbaria, then came the Berbers—Moors and Saracens remaining the preferred names for the people(s). For centuries, therefore, Barbaria simply had no Berbers.

For the most part, Africa, Numidia, and the Mauretanias were the provinces that later Latin authors remembered. After the defeat of the Byzantines, the polities that emerged in the Maghrib did not keep to late antique boundaries. New capitals, new kingdoms, and novel formulations appeared, not always where the old ones had been, putting a strain on the old categories. In a 1076 letter to the Ḥammadid ruler al-Nāṣir (r. 1062–88), Pope Gregory VII (d. 1085) acknowledged al-Nāṣir's rule over the central Maghrib in these terms: "Anzir, regi Mauritaniae Sitiphensis provinciae, in Africa."[48] While the Ḥammādids (1015–1152) may indeed have ruled over the area covered a few centuries earlier by the province of Mauretania Sitifensis, describing it as being in Africa was a stretch. The papal chancery applied the name of the ancient province of Africa to a much broader territory—much like some early Arabic writers and possibly some at the Ḥammādid court who hoped to take away Ifrīqiyā from the hands of their Zīrid (1015–1148) cousins. This same Africa is found two centuries later in the letter that Innocent IV (d. 1254) sent the Christians of the regions of Africa (*universis Christianis in Africanis partibus constitutis*) announcing the appointment of the new bishop of Morocco (*episcopo Marrochitano*), itself a deformation of Mauretania.[49] Even when the chancery retained the old categories, it gave them new meanings. It is thus not as simple as saying that the church was conservative.

In any case, this expansive notion of Africa was not the only version of Africa. The cities and kings that signed peace and commerce treaties with Maghribīs were mindful of the political situation and its many changes. Unsurprisingly, their "Affrica" mirrored these changes. For example, the treaty signed between Pisa and the Ḥafṣid Abū Zakariyā Yaḥyā (r. 1229–49) identifies the domain under the latter's control as being over all of Africa and the territory of Bijāya (*in totam Affricam et in totam terram de Bucea*).[50] This corresponded well to the recent Ḥafṣid conquests and their control of Bijāya, a city that had not always been attached to Ifrīqiyā. In fact, under the Ḥammādids, Bijāya had been the capital of the central Maghrib.[51]

Peace treaties record the claims made by rulers, often in exhaustive detail. In the Pisan version of the peace treaty he signed with the Pisans, the Marinid Abū 'Inān Fāris (r. 1348–58) is described as "King of Fessa, Michinese, Sale, and Moroccho, the lands (*terre*) of Sus and Segelmese, the lands of the center (Mezzo), Teze, and Tremizen and al Gier and Bugiea, and Ghostantina, and the lands of Buona, Beschera, and the lands of the Zeb, and the lands of Africa and Capisi, and the lands of Biledel Gerid, and Tripoli, and Tangia, and Gibeltari, and Ronda, and all other lands that belong to them, and the West and the East, and Ispagnia."[52] Although the document's date maybe problematic, its description of Abū 'Inān's recent conquests in the Maghrib agrees with Marīnid propaganda. For instance, its listing of all of the Marīnid ruler's possessions could have easily been dispensed with by a reference to a category like "Maghrib" or "Africa." Although doing so would have undercut some of the flattery the Pisans may have wanted to shower on their new associate, something they had done in the past, it would have also been an incorrect description of Marīnid self-representation, which insisted on listing all of the possessions of the ruler. In fact, given how close it is to the latter, it is almost certain that the Pisan document was a translation of an Arabic one. Although it is difficult to be certain, *terre* appears to be a translation of *arḍ* rather than *bilād*. The Bilād al-Jarīd (Biledel Gerid) was recognized as a unit by the Marīnid and Ḥafsid courts; the *bilād* was thus part of a proper name and in no need of translation. The absence of the *bilād al-barbar* suggests that the category did not emerge from or match the official maps of royal courts in the Maghrib. Again, when the political situation in the Maghrib was not very clear and when there was no expectation that Maghribīs would read a document, "Saracen lands" was often sufficient.[53]

In any case, in the fourteenth century, the Pisan chancery did not hesitate to describe the Ḥafṣid Abū Fāris (r. 1394–1434) as the ruler of Tunis, the East, the West, and all of Barbaria (*regis Tunisi, Sarchi, Garbi et totius Barbariae*).[54] In the Italian version of the same document, we find "Barberia," a spelling used by others.[55] Around the same time, a commercial document in French prefers "Barbarie" without further indication as to its location, though it is reasonable to infer that what is meant is the coast of Africa, given the sort of access these merchants had at the time.[56] Frequent commercial runs to the African coast made the phrase "voyage to Barbarie" so commonplace that it came to be preceded by the definite article: it had become "a thing."[57]

Seen from the northern Mediterranean, the coast of Africa was a privileged destination for sailors, merchants, missionaries, mercenaries, pirates, and various officials.[58] While they definitely ventured inland too, their primary mode of entering the country was through the sea. Since the Almohads and their successors controlled the coasts for centuries, there was a sense to seeing the coast as a unit. Given that the ideological framing in post-Umayyad al-Andalus (and post-Zīrid Maghrib) included a distinction between Arab and Berber dynasties, and since all the dynasties that controlled the coast were, in this particular sense, Berber, Barbaria fits in this sense as well. Whether it is because of the importance of Andalusī merchants at a particular point in time, their overwhelming presence as privileged commercial brokers at the courts of the Maghrib, or the influence of Catalan merchants with whom they were conversant, northerners responded by thinking of the entire southern shore of the Mediterranean as Barbaria/Barbarie/Barberia.[59]

Moreover, the "voyage to Barbarie" corresponded to the actuality of commercial enterprise across the Mediterranean. The major commodities exported by Africans, such as wool and leather, left from a number of ports, access to which depended heavily on turbulent political circumstances. In this context, "Barbary wool" (*lana barbaresca*) and "Barbary leather" (*pelliccerie di Barberia*) make good sense as brand names.[60] Furthermore, Barbaria corresponded to the actual practices of sea captains who only rarely made a single stop on the African coast. Their trips to Barbaria appealed to a pool of investors interested in conducting business in a host of African ports. Naturally, the ships that were headed "for Barbaria" usually hugged the coast and made multiple stops before heading back home. The emergence of pirates, many of whom chose to hide in smaller ports not usually open to foreigners, reinforced the currency of Barbaria.

Noting the existence of two cities named Tripoli around the Mediterranean, Arabic writers usually distinguished between the Tripoli of the East (al-Shām) and that of the West (al-Gharb). For Latin and Romance writers, the western Tripoli became Tripoli or Tripol de Barbaria; the Barbaria in question being the Ifrīqiyā of the Ḥafṣids, not the entire coast of Africa.[61] Yet, with the currency Barbaria/Barberia gained, it is not clear that anyone remembered that the two were originally distinct. There is quite a bit of irony in the fact that Barbaria came to translate the Arabic Ifrīqiyā, which, from the earliest sources, had the distinction of not being either Maghrib or *bilād al-barbar.*

In any case, even when Barbaria encompassed the entire Maghrib, it was a Maghrib of Moors and Saracens, not Berbers. For instance, the sixteenth-century geographer Leo Africanus was not Berber. In the words of his English translator, he was a "More."[62] Leo himself struggled with translation: "Our writers say that Africa is divided into four parts: Barbaria, Numidia, Libya, and the land of Blacks. Barbaria begins at the mountain called Meies, which is the farthest point of the Atlas Mountains, distant three hundred miles from Alexandria. . . . It is the noblest region of all Africa; its inhabitants have a brown color, are rational, and live according to good laws."[63] Africa stood for the Maghrib and Barbaria for Africa (Ifrīqiyā) and the Maghrib or only its coastal areas (*bilād al-barbar*). The instability at the heart of his attempt to combine ancient and current categories in Latin and vernacular with changing Arabic ones is a perfect illustration of the semantic effects the introduction of Barbaria had on existing categories. The extraordinary explosion of writings about the peoples of a world being discovered eventually transformed the Moors into Berbers. But as late as the sixteenth century, that was not yet the case.

Ibn Khaldūn and the *Bilād al-Barbar*

Did Ibn Khaldūn think that the Maghrib was coextensive with the land of the Berbers? Did he think that the Maghrib was the original home of the Berbers? The answer to both these questions may be negative, but it is still useful to review the appearance of the *bilād al-barbar* in the *Kitāb al-ʿibar* if only to highlight the synthetic character of Ibn Khaldūn's new science. Doing so also shows how his understanding of the relation between the Berbers and the Maghrib lends itself to the particular adaptations made of it by moderns.

Ibn Khaldūn's clearest enunciation of the Maghrib as *bilād al-barbar* comes in his description of his book: "Our main concern [in the book] is with the Maghrib, which is the home (*waṭan*) of the Berbers, and with the lands (*awṭān*, sing. *waṭan*) controlled by the Arabs in the Mashriq."[64] The Maghrib may not be the *bilād al-barbar*, but it is still the home (*waṭan*) of the Berbers—although Ibn Khaldūn did not use these terms in a technical sense.[65] That said, it is legitimate to wonder whether beyond the choices of categories, Ibn Khaldūn thought anything close to the Maghrib was the homeland of the Berbers: "There are few cities and towns in Ifrīqiyā and the Maghrib. The reason for this is that these regions belonged to the Berbers for thousands of years before Islam. All (their) civilization was a Bedouin (civilization)."[66] But from "thousands of years before Islam" to the modern "original," "native," "indigenous," and "autochthonous" there are a few hurried steps, and perhaps even a leap:

> I built the book around the history of the nations (*umam*) that populate the Maghrib these days and inhabit its various regions and cities, and on those who formed dynasties, both long- and

> short-lived, including the rulers and allies they had in the past. These two peoples (*jīlān*, sing. *jīl*) are the Arabs and the Berbers. They are the two peoples that have resided in the Maghrib for such a long time that one can hardly imagine anyone else resided (*ma'wā*) there but them and the people of the Maghrib know of no other humans (*ajyāl al-ādamiyīn*) inhabiting [the Maghrib] but these two.[67]

Like his contemporaries and predecessors, Ibn Khaldūn believed that the Berbers settled in the region after the Flood. For him, the long period of their residence in the Maghrib makes it their home.

In his attempt to establish a new science, the science of civilization, Ibn Khaldūn developed a critical but also pragmatic stance that allowed him to revisit the works of predecessors and select from them what he agreed with and what substantiated his claims. He also, and famously, criticized to the point of ridiculing those writers, especially historians, who failed to use their rational faculties, contenting themselves with relaying information without judging its plausibility, let alone its truth. Although his ideas on history may not have been unique to him, they were definitely more critical than those of most. But when it comes to his stance vis-à-vis the faculties of geographers, he seems to be a great deal more lenient. Based on his use of information and direct quotations from geographers like al-Idrīsī and al-Bakrī, it is fair to say that Ibn Khaldūn subscribed to their general assumptions about the world.[68] Notably, when he expressed geographic ideas, he used the language of geographers, which, as we have seen, represents the *bilād al-barbar* in a particular way: "This is the description of the Mediterranean Sea, which constitutes the northern border of the Maghrib. As for [the Maghrib's] eastern and southern borders, there are moving sands that form a barrier between the *bilād al-barbar* and the land of the Blacks (*bilād al-sūdān*). [This barrier] is known among the nomadic Arabs as the 'Arq. This 'Arq fences off the Maghrib from the south."[69] This *bilād al-barbar* is similar to that of Yāqūt al-Ḥamawī, and not a synonym for the Maghrib. Another description of the same area supports this interpretation: "The [Veiled Ṣanhāja] came from near the countryside of the Abyssinians (*nazalū min rīf al-ḥabasha jiwāran*) and settled between the *bilād al-barbar* and Bilād al-Sūdān, forming a barrier [between the two].[70] These Veiled [Ṣanhāja] and their tribes have to this day occupied the areas near the Blacks (*al-sawād*) as a barrier between them and the sands which border the *bilād al-barbar* of the two Maghribs and Ifrīqiyā."[71]

Clearly, the *bilād al-barbar* is not the same as the Maghrib—although it is a bit surprising to see that the Ṣanhāja are distinguished from other Berbers. This was not the only time Ibn Khaldūn set a Berber *umma* like the Ṣanhāja apart from other Berbers: "There is a great difference in this respect between the Arabs and Berbers (on the one hand), and the Veiled [Ṣanhāja] (Berbers) and the inhabitants of the hills (on the other)."[72] Before attributing the dissonance of such statements to an inconsistency in Ibn Khaldūn's thinking, a closer examination shows that they tend to occur when he is thinking as a geographer about the relation between nature and human societies or as a geographer trying to situate a particular group, like the Ṣanhāja, on a medieval map. Of course, if we allow for some Berbers not living in the land of the Berbers but in a frontier area between Berbers and Blacks, it becomes difficult to imagine the Maghrib as the *bilād al-barbar*.[73]

In other instances, Ibn Khaldūn seems to subscribe to the "northern" or "coastal" location of the *bilād al-barbar*: "The rank (of admiral) is restricted to the realm of Ifrīqiyah and the Maghrib, because both Ifrīqiyah and the Maghrib are on the southern shore of the Mediterranean. Along its southern shore the lands of the Berbers extend from Ceuta to Alexandria and on to Syria.[74] Going east, [the fourth clime] passes through the *bilād al-barbar* of the Maghrib al-Aqṣā and the Maghrib al-Awsaṭ, Ifrīqiyā, Alexandria, Arḍ al-Tīh (Sinai), Palestine, and al-Shām."[75] Sometimes, it is as if Ibn Khaldūn locates the *bilād al-barbar* exclusively in the Mediterranean areas of the Maghrib: "The Berber countries are in the contrary position. Their fields are fine and their soil is good. Therefore, they did not have to procure anything (from outside) in order to be able to cultivate agriculture, which is widely and generally practiced there. This is the reason for the cheapness of foodstuffs in their country."[76] If such statements make it difficult to hold that Ibn Khaldūn believed the Maghrib and the land of the Berbers to be coextensive and synonymous, whether his use of the *bilād al-barbar* expressed an Andalusī perspective still requires an argument, even if his debt to Andalusī intellectuals is beyond question. Unsurprisingly, however, the idea that the *bilād al-barbar* was the part of Africa opposite al-Andalus appears logically in the *Kitāb al-ʿibar*: "Then ʿUqba b. Nāfiʿ went to Ṭanja where Lulyān the ruler of Ghumāra and Ṭanja obeyed him, gave him gifts, and other offerings. [Lulyān] directed him to the *bilād al-barbar* which was behind him in the Maghrib, like Walīlī which belonged to the Zarhūn, the land of the Maṣmūda (*bilād al-maṣāmida*), and the Sūs (*bilād al-sūs*), that were "Zoroastrians" (*al-majūsiya*) and not Christians."[77] In another example of his debt to

Andalusīs, Ibn Khaldūn twice repeats the quote by Ibn Ḥazm refuting the Ḥimyarite genealogy of the Zanāta.[78] Elsewhere, it is as if the Zanāta were not Berbers at all: "The beginning of the *jīl* of the [Zanāta] in Ifrīqiyā and the Maghrib is the same as the beginning of the Berbers ages ago. No one truly knows its beginning but God."[79] Perhaps he means that the Zanāta are as old as the Berbers themselves. But that would not be true, since the Berbers appear in Arabic sources before the Zanāta. But technicalities aside, this statement refers us back to a time when Ifrīqiyā and the Maghrib were separate, and neither of them was defined primarily as *bilād al-barbar.*

The Maghrib and the Indigenous Berbers

If the argument were that there is enough evidence to reassess fundamental scholarly assumptions about the Maghrib and the Berbers, the work would be done. No historian could possibly believe with H. T. Norris and others that before the Arab conquests the whole of North Africa was Berber country and that it is so even if medieval Arabic authors, including Ibn Khaldūn, did not believe that to be the case. But trying to convince historians of that is not the goal here. Rather, it is to show how Berberization functions to deny the category Berber its historicity.

An examination of the ways medieval Arabic authors conceived of the Maghrib and the land of the Berbers demonstrates that they did not imagine categories such as those to emerge in time or to evolve with changing circumstances. They did not think such categories to be historical. Unsurprisingly, they had no qualms projecting them into a remote mythological past. Their institutions, social relations of power, and their organization of knowledge reinforced their conviction that their perspective was valid. In a fundamental sense, the way they imagined the Berbers was consistent with their view of the world: demonstrably incorrect and flawed, but untroubled.

Reading Ibn Khaldūn, one is struck by just how modern his ideas seem. Even if he was firmly anchored in the ideas of his time, something about his project resonates with a modern reader's sensibility. At least this much his modern readers have repeated for the last two centuries. However, this recognition may have more to do with that modern sensibility than Ibn Khaldūn's ideas. In spite of everything that can be said about them, his ideas did not make sense only to him; they resonated with his contemporaries and many other "premoderns" after them, all of whom operated with remarkably nonmodern assumptions. Unless one wants to collapse the distinction between premodern and modern, what is at stake here is the act of claiming Ibn Khaldūn as a modern by moderns. In fact, modernizing Ibn Khaldūn was one of the most important events in the development and deployment of modern Berberization. Naturally, a statement like this requires elucidation, and the next chapters will try to do just that.

PART III

Modern Medieval Berbers

L'histoire du Maghreb pendant tout le moyen âge serait un fatras indéchiffrable, si nous la connaissions uniquement par des ouvrages comme le Qirtas. Sans Ibn-Khaldoun, on peut affirmer pratiquement que, sauf des noms tout secs et des dates, à peu près rien n'aurait surnagé de ce qui s'est passé entre Tunis et Tanger, depuis la venue des Arabes jusqu'aux temps modernes.

—Émile-Félix Gautier, *Le passé de l'Afrique du nord: Les siècles obscurs*

Chapter 5

Modern Origins

After the Berbers joined the ranks of known peoples, no medieval Arabic author thought that the category had come to be used at a specific time and for particular reasons, that its reach had expanded, or that its usage had evolved with time. No one believed that the Berbers were the original inhabitants of the Maghrib or that the Maghrib was their original homeland. No one did because the organization of societies, the character of dominant ideologies, and even language did not make that pertinent. These ideas did not occur to anyone not because of a moral or intellectual failure. Yet, there came a time when authors began to describe the Berbers as natives and the Maghrib as their country. That was a major event in the Berberization of the Maghrib and its inhabitants.

In a world in which European capitalists oversaw the integration of the world's regions and the universal rights of man became a revolutionary ideal, the Maghrib came under the control of Europeans who embarked on its discovery. Mobilizing the tools they had and those they invented in the process, Europeans domesticated the Maghrib. A colonized Maghrib emerged, one whose traditions and cultural heritage were no longer critical to the functioning of the entire society, downgraded to the rank of remnants and reminders of an old world, and restricted to the narrow confines of a subordinate native society. Stripped of their influence on politics and economy, the old learned classes, the ones that became native scholars, suffered through this *déclassement*. As a result, they lost the influence their class had had on Berberization. New personnel took over. With great confidence in their methods, the new brand of scholars proceeded to reinvent the Maghrib, using whichever bits of native knowledge fit their designs and worldview. In spite of the ambient sensitivity to history and historicity in European intellectual circles, academics who specialized in the colonial Maghrib did not consider the possibility of medieval origins of Berberization. As they proceeded to the fashioning of a new knowledge about those the colonial administration came to call natives (*indigènes*), they developed a number of blind spots. The latter came to distinguish this new form of Berberization, steeped in modern history and social science.

As the French colonized Algeria first and then only decades later set up protectorates in both Tunisia and Morocco, Algeria was at the center of the development of this modern form of Berberization. Moreover, since of all Europeans, the French came to have a near monopoly over the study of the Maghrib, modern Berberization came to have both French and Algerian

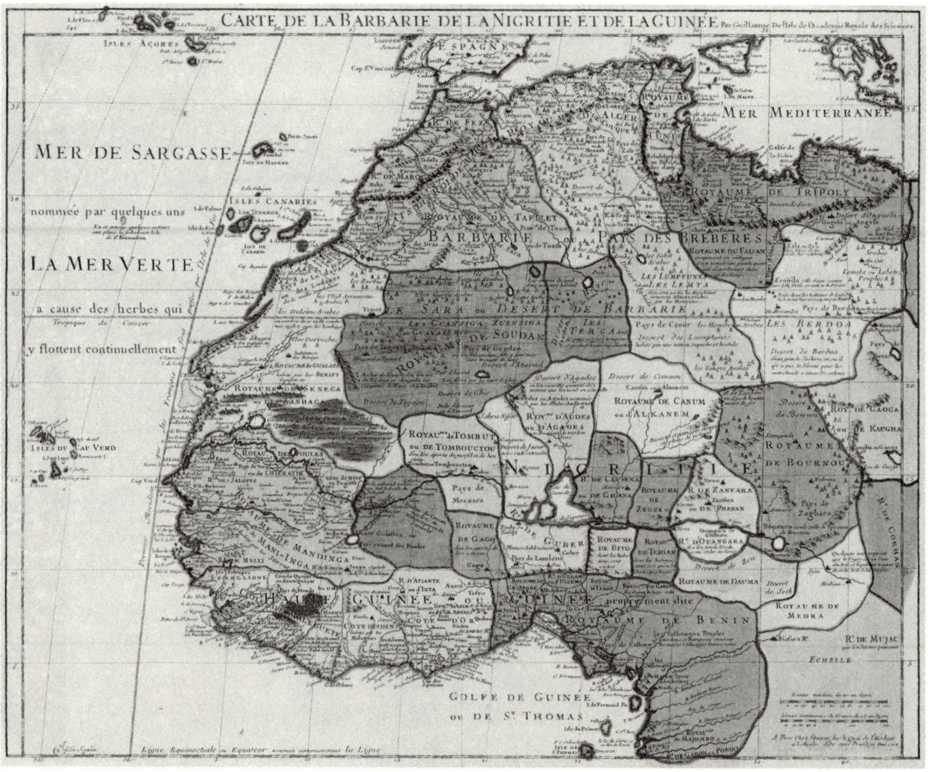

Figure 1. *Carte de la Barbarie, de la Nigritie, et de la Guinée*, by Guillaume De L'Isle and C. Inselin (A Paris: chez l'auteur sur le Quai de l'Horloge à l'Aigle d'Or, 1707 [i.e., 1718?]). Map. Library of Congress, Geography and Map Division, Washington, DC, 20540-4650 USA dcu.

foundations. This does not mean that Morocco and Tunisia were unimportant or that the contributions of non-French academics were less valuable. Chronologically speaking, however, the early steps of modern Berberization were grounded firmly in the realities of French colonialism in Algeria. This is so even if critical constituents such as the notion of Berberia had developed prior to and independently of French colonialism and later elements were entangled in specifically Moroccan realities.

Modern French colonial Berberization was implemented through a Khaldunization of the terms of knowledge on the Maghrib. Taking on a particular interpretation and adaptation of Ibn Khaldūn's ideas, scholars proceeded to set the foundations of French Maghribology according to Khaldunian blueprints. This Khaldunization of the medieval Maghrib distinguishes both the form and the content of modern Berberization, so much so that it would be difficult to confuse it with the medieval examples analyzed so far. Notably, even if they relied on Ibn Khaldūn, modern medievalists were immersed in intellectual traditions and historical circumstances of their own. Tracing the early phases of this process brings to light these aspects of modern Berberization.

Before Ibn Khaldūn

Until the French took over Algiers in 1830, Berberization continued on its course in Arabic from where Ibn Khaldūn had left it in the fifteenth century. The Ottomans did not rule over the entire Maghrib but rather over areas surrounding a network of cities on the Mediterranean coast and a few inland cities. While the privileges of those Turks associated with the empire were as clear as their gradual influence on the local urban culture, the discourse on Berbers under Ottoman rule did not alter the terms of learned knowledge about them, even if the Ottoman political order gradually gave rise to a set of new categories.[1] The Ottomans did not have the sort of control over intellectual production in the Maghrib that they had over the movement of people and commodities across the Mediterranean, for example. In addition to those western regions of the Maghrib that completely escaped their political control, vast regions inland, in the pre-Saharan and Saharan areas, and in the mountains resisted Ottoman rule and enjoyed varying degrees of autonomy. In general, those Maghribīs who were interested in history, political thought, and philosophy continued to read Ibn Khaldūn's work and engage with his ideas.[2] When Ottoman intellectuals and courtiers in the seventeenth century became interested in Ibn Khaldūn, it was not because they saw in him a good source of information about the medieval Maghrib—though some like the polymath Kâtip Çelebi (1609–57) did.[3]

On the other hand, Ottoman rule in the Maghrib seems to have had a negative effect on the quality of the information found in European writings. Exceptions to this general rule were very few and became authoritative rather quickly, retaining that weight for many centuries. Among these, Leo Africanus (d. ca. 1554) and Luis del Marmol de Carvajal (d. 1600) stand out for their acquaintance with Arabic sources and their travels in the region. At the same time, these authors' familiarity with medieval Arabic sources explains the appearance of artifacts of medieval Arabic Berberization in their writings. Marmol cites Ifrīqiyan writers (*escriptores Affricanos*) like Ibn al-Raqīq (11th c.) who attributed an Arabian origin to the Berbers of Ifrīqiyā, the "Zinhagia, Muçamuda, Zeneta, Haoara, and Gumera," and a postdiluvian genealogy for the Berber "Xilohes" who inhabited "Tingitania, Numidia, and Lybia."[4] Interestingly, Marmol uses the category Berber (Berέber, pl. Beréberes). Although it corresponds clearly to the geographic Berberia, which had appeared in Latin at least three centuries earlier, the ethnonym Beréber was new to the European scene. As he knew Arabic, Marmol found the category natural and did not feel the need to define it for his audience, other than by offering the genealogy of the Berbers as an introduction, in the manner of the Arabic authors he cited. However, where these Berbers (Beréberes) fit in relation to categories such as Moor, Numidian, and African was not immediately clear to everyone, at least not for many decades, not to say centuries.[5]

In his *Précis de la géographie universelle*, the famed Danish-French geographer Conrad Malte-Brun (1775–1826) offers an example of the effects that the intrusion of the category Berber had on preexisting knowledge:[6]

> The inhabitants of cities and cultivated plains are designated by the name Moors. Although they speak an Arabic dialect filled with idiotisms, their physical characteristics, whiter skin than that of the Arabs, a fuller face, a less protruding nose, and all the traits of a less energetic physiognomy, seem to prove that they are descendant from a mixture of ancient Mauritanians and Numidians with Phoenicians, Romans, and Arabs. Since Sallust states that the Numidians and Mauritanians are descendant from an Asian

> colony composed of Medes, Armenians, and Persians, it would be desirable to examine fully the idiotisms of the Moorish language.[7]

On the other hand,

> the nomad Arabs, who came from Asia since Mohametanism, kept their blood pure, which is recognizable for its more masculine physiognomy, brighter eyes, and a nearly olive complexion. Deprived of personal charms, their women enjoy great liberty. The tents of the Arabs, covered with thick fabrics, have conserved the form of an inverted ship, which Sallust attributes to the *mapalia* of the Numidians. They call this sort of shack a chaima; and a group of chaimas a *duar* or hamlet, often surrounded by a fence of thorns to prevent lions from entering.[8]

However, lest one be too eager to conclude that the Malte-Brun's Moors were simply the Berbers, the author adds a clarification that is telling of the state of knowledge in the eighteenth century:

> The race of the Berbers, which is entirely distinct from the Arabs and the Moors, seems indigenous to northern Africa. It comprises probably the remainders of the ancient Getulians in the west, and the Libyans in the east of Mount Atlas. Today, it makes four distinct nations: 1) the Amazirgh, called by the Moors Schilla or Schulla, in the Moroccan mountains; 2) the Kabyles or Cabailes, in the mountains of Algiers and Tunis; 3) the Tibbos, in the desert between Fezzan and Egypt; and 4) the Touaryks, in the great desert. . . . The Berber language, that the Amazirgh call Tamazeght, and the Kabyles Showia, presents, as it seems to us, a very original character, although close to Hebrew and Phoenician. The Berbers have a red and blackish complexion, and are tall and svelte, thin and skinny. Their religious fanaticism is greater than that of the Moors, and they satiate it, when the occasion presents itself, in the blood of Jews and Christians.[9]

References to religious fanaticism are almost de rigueur for a supporter of the French Revolution. And Malte-Brun could find a great deal about the fanaticism of the Moors in the captive narratives published in the preceding two centuries, which like that written by the Benedictine monk Diego de Haedo (fl. late 16th c.) made central the opposition between Christians and Muslims.[10] But unlike captive narratives, Malte-Brun's text is striking for its ethnographic interest and its reliance on ancient Greek and Roman authors, just like those very popular entertaining travelogues that kept Enlightenment gentlemen informed about the world.[11] Without Arabic sources to guide them, travelers from various parts of Europe combined whatever local knowledge they gathered from merchants, diplomats, and locals with an educated man's dose of ancient learning. When they encountered confusing or contradictory information, they felt free to exercise their natural intelligence to explain it away. The results were uneven: "The inhabitants of Barbary have many names. One calls Moors [Fr. Maures] those who inhabit the coasts; Arabs those deeper inland; Bedouin-Arabs or Berbers (*Bérébères*) those who lead a nomadic life, and who often live from thieving; finally, one calls Cabailes the hordes that cultivate the land and raise cattle."[12] As Greek and Latin sources replaced Arabic ones, European travelers and their readers found pleasure in "discovering" Barbary as an unfamiliar land, which they scoured with ancient maps and native guides. They looked for the cities mentioned by Herodotus, Strabo, and Sallust, but found only ruins, if that. Their tales of the discovery of unknown lands and often dangerous or disgusting peoples, coupled with a deep sense of loss for the world of the ancients, made travelogues reliable bestsellers. It also reinforced the perception that Arabs and their Islam (Mohamedanism) had been agents of violent destruction, by then a well-established conviction.

At the beginning of the nineteenth century, the British and French empires began to formalize their control over vast areas of the world. The process took them a few decades. As they built their world empires, they felt a serious need for reliable information about the peoples they began to rule. They needed information that could stand the test of actual relations with natives if only to defeat organized military resistance and prevent uprisings. As an information delivery system, the travelogue proved woefully inadequate. In 1837, Alexis de Tocqueville highlighted the effect that the conquest of Algiers had had on the state of knowledge:

> Even if the coast of Africa is separated from Provence by only 160 leagues approximately, [and even if] thousands of travelogues are published every year in Europe about every corner of the world, [and

> even if] in Europe [people] study ancient languages that are no longer spoken and living languages that one does not have occasion to speak, it is hard to convey the deep ignorance in which we were not even seven years ago about everything pertaining to Algeria. We had no clear idea of the different races that inhabit it, their customs, and not a single word of the languages these peoples spoke. . . . It is in this complete ignorance that we sailed there, which did not prevent us from winning, because in battle victory belongs to the stronger and braver, not to the more knowledgeable.[13]

Orientalism expanded organically to respond to this new historical situation—notably, as did anthropology, archaeology, and linguistics. Emerging out of the philological study of the Bible, Orientalism focused on understanding Islam through its foundational texts. Its development as a science and career saw a momentous shift in focus and method. Importantly, Orientalist philologists became self-authorized experts on the history of the medieval Maghrib, a development that accompanied the French conquest of Algiers and the gradual establishment of colonial rule over North Africa, the new name for Barbary. After centuries that had seen the gradual deliquescence of European knowledge on medieval Maghribī history, a key development that defines the new historical origins of Berberization, Orientalists still had important elements in hand, not least of which was the confusion about what categories to use. For many reasons, however, their interests, intellectual orientation, and methods led them elsewhere. So much is clear from the work of the first Orientalists.

Reconnoitering the Terrain

Although Arabic had been taught at the Collège Royal since the sixteenth century, it was truly with the French Revolution and foundation of the École spéciale des langues orientales in 1795 that Orientalist knowledge acquired a lasting institutional basis in the French educational system.[14] Before then, commerce, diplomacy, and church business had combined to produce those individuals with the language skills and interests who became specialists.[15] Napoleon's campaign in Egypt (1798–1801) spurred further curiosity about the Orient and raised the profile of Orientalists.[16] Whether these developments were part of an imperial vision that saw Orientalism as a tool is not fully clear. Since the focus here is simply on the study of the medieval Maghrib, it is enough to note that in the period preceding the French conquest, Orientalists had begun canvassing medieval works and publishing editions and translations. In spite of this preliminary work, however, one must agree with those like William McGuckin de Slane (1801–78), who noted that knowledge of the Maghrib, its geography, and toponymy greatly improved after the conquest of Algiers.[17]

But while it is difficult to disagree with de Slane, his comment points not to an absolute absence of knowledge about the Orient before 1830 but rather to its eastern orientation. For it is not just that the information improved with colonial rule, but that French Orientalists came to be more interested in the Maghrib. While one could find some information about the medieval Maghrib in the editions and translations of Mashriqī authors like Abū al-Fidā' (1273–1331) and al-Maqrīzī (1364–1442), that was not why those works were selected for publication and study. Even when Silvestre de Sacy (1758–1838) included excerpts from Ibn Khaldūn in his *Anthologie grammaticale arabe* (1829), he excerpted passages about the Arabic language, which he thought would help a student of Classical Arabic.[18] For this father of Orientalism, mastery of the language was a priority, and, much like medieval Arabic litterateurs, he believed that that expertise resided in the command of the language of *adab*, both prose and poetry. Given the prominent place he held in the French university, Silvestre de Sacy was able to expand the range of sources included in the Orientalist training toolbox well beyond the diplomatic, commercial, and religious texts of the previous generations. At the same time, his interest in literature led him eastward, where the exemplars of literary prowess were.

Silvestre de Sacy was the first Orientalist to include Ibn Khaldūn in the pantheon of great Arabic authors. Over the years, he introduced parts of the *Muqaddima*, whose complete Arabic text his student Étienne-Marc Quatremère (1782–1857) edited and published.[19] What stands out, therefore, is that when the French conquered Algiers, the development of the medieval historiography of the Maghrib was still in its infancy—to put it in the language of the time. Silvestre de Sacy's introduction of Ibn Khaldūn offers a concrete example of where knowledge of the medieval Maghrib stood in the early nineteenth century:

> The work of Ebn Khaldoun, from which this section is excerpted, enjoys great fame in the Levant, and truly deserves this reputa-

> tion. Hadj Khalfa [i.e., Kâtip Çelebi] mentions him in many places in his Bibliography.[20]
>
> Abou'lmahasen [al-Tighribirdī (d. 1470)] does not give any detail about the writings of this learned man, where he received the name of Ebn Khaldoun, or why he is given the nickname of Aschbili and Hadhrami. The first would have led us to believe that he settled for a while in Seville, the second that he was originally from the Hadhramaut.[21]

Silvestre de Sacy begins his note on Ibn Khaldūn by appealing to the opinion of an eastern author. He bases all his notes and comments on eastern writers, with the exception of a reference to the anonymous author of a history of Granada. The rudimentary character of the information he is able to ascertain about Ibn Khaldūn would be stunning if it were not a reasonable reflection of what was known at the time and how it was known. Taken together, these features allow us to measure the great leap forward accomplished between de Sacy's 1806 note (published again without corrections or additions in 1826) and William McGuckin de Slane's *Histoire des Berbères*.

Born in Belfast in 1801, the baron William McGuckin de Slane went to Paris to do formal work in Oriental languages. He studied with Silvestre de Sacy and was admitted to the Société Asiatique in 1828.[22] The Société hired the young de Slane to edit the *Taqwīm al-buldān*, the geographical summa written by Abū al-Fidā' al-Ḥamawī (d. 1331), and the *Wafāyāt al-a'yān*, the biographical dictionary written by Ibn Khallikān (d. 1282).[23] In the same journal, de Slane published translations of excerpts about the Maghrib from Ibn Ḥawqal (d. ca. 978), Ibn Baṭṭūṭa (d. 1369), and al-Nuwayrī (d. 1332). In 1844, he edited Ibn Khaldūn's "Autobiographie" (*Riḥla*).[24] Appointed in 1843 to assess the holdings of the libraries of Algiers and Constantine, as well as those of Malta and Istanbul, he became Chief Interpreter of the Army of Africa in 1846. Between 1847 and 1851 he edited parts of Ibn Khaldūn's *Kitāb al-'ibar* and then translated them under the title *Histoire des Berbères et des Arabes* (1852–56).[25] Between 1857 and 1859, he edited and then translated the sections of the geographical work of the Andalusī Abū 'Ubayd Allāh al-Bakrī (d. 1094) pertaining to North Africa (*Afrique septentrionale*).

Although his contributions were numerous and essential, de Slane was not alone in making rare manuscripts available to a broad public. In 1845, Edmond Pellissier de Raynaud and Jean-Pierre Abel de Rémusat translated *Al-mu'nis fī akhbār ifrīqiyā wa tūnis*, the seventeenth-century chronicle written by Ibn Abī Dinār (d. ca. 1698), and in 1852, the Abbé Bargès, a chronicle on the Zayānids (1236–1556) by Muḥammad b. ʿal-Jalīl al-Tanasī (d. 1493/4). In 1860, Auguste Beaumier translated Ibn Abī Zarʿ's *Rawḍ al-qirtās*, a fourteenth-century chronicle of the Maghrib focusing on the city of Fez.[26]

By the 1860s, the textual foundations for the historical study of the medieval Maghrib were basically set—at least in the sense that the major dynasties, the most significant events, and the names associated with them became known. While differences between authors, and even contradictions within the same texts, were noted, there was a strong sense that these were technical problems pertaining to the imperfect transfer of information from one source to another and the reliability of this or that author. But beyond these problems, there was no doubt that the chronicles were generally reliable and that it was possible on their basis to reconstruct a reasonable chronology, similar to that of Europeanists.

There is another chronology, however, which is brought to light by an examination of the date of these early contributions to the Orientalist archive. The early translations and editions were generally of later texts, written for the most part after the thirteenth century. Since they were not historical studies per se, their late date is not a priori a problem. But insofar as they informed the periodization that came to dominate the field, it is worth appreciating their late date, especially that their organization of time takes for granted a certain conception of the Berbers. Interestingly, in the course of translating Ibn Khaldūn, de Slane also translated parts of Ibn ʿAbd al-Ḥakam's ninth-century conquest narrative on the Maghrib, which he annotated with copious references to Ibn Khaldūn.[27] Before going any further in ascertaining the impact of the late date of the early (colonial) sources, it may be useful to take stock of de Slane's general approach.

In his translation of Ibn ʿAbd al-Ḥakam's reports on the large booty that ʿAbd Allāh b. Saʿd gathered from the raid he led on Ifrīqiyā, de Slane feels compelled to intervene:

> I consider the first part of this tradition to be false, although I accept that the infantryman in question took a thousand dinar booty. But I would say that this man had looted for his own benefit: a job that Arabs have always performed wonderfully; and I would add that the person who fabricated this tradition believed that this sum came in its entirety from the equal distribution of the booty between all individuals in the army. . . . Let us say that

> there were ten thousand cavalrymen and as many infantrymen, and let us suppose that the single gold piece [i.e., *dinār*] was worth ten Francs. The booty would have been four hundred million Francs, plus the fifth [for the treasury], which would make the total five hundred millions. The falseness of this information is patent (*saute aux yeux*).[28]

Some reports are acceptable, and others are not. One just has to be careful. What de Slane and his peers thought they were doing was establishing a factually correct narrative, in almost the very same language that Ibn Khaldūn (d. 1406) used to dismiss reports found in earlier books:

> The (writing of history) requires numerous sources and greatly varied knowledge. It also requires a good speculative mind and thoroughness. (Possession of these two qualities) leads the historian to the truth and keeps him from slips and errors. If he trusts historical information in its plain transmitted form and has no clear knowledge of the principles resulting from custom, the fundamental facts of politics, the nature of civilization, or the conditions governing human social organization, and if, furthermore, he does not evaluate remote or ancient material through comparison with near or contemporary material, he often cannot avoid stumbling and slipping and deviating from the highroad of truth.[29]

De Slane and his peers brought this sort of wisdom to bear on the sources. Whatever may be rightly said about the positivism of French Orientalists and their race to extract reliable facts, the rationality and modernity of Ibn Khaldūn that so attracted them resided also in a methodological meeting of the minds. In other words, the modernity of Ibn Khaldūn tended to mask a certain "medievality" of Orientalists. Without belaboring the point, it should be clear that in spite of their criticism of the sources, Orientalists did not consider that the difference between the perspectives of Ibn 'Abd al-Ḥakam and Ibn Khaldūn, for instance, may have had something to do with history. That is why, at least in part, a study of the early Arabic usage of categories like Berber and later ones did not occur to them—philologically trained and oriented as they were. Naturally, the idea could not occur to those who read only translations and did not have the opportunity to appreciate changes in Arabic usage. For them, modern French erased any sense of linguistic evolution in the original Arabic. It is striking that the early French translators on the whole do not seem to have been too sensitive or concerned about considerations of this sort. Based on the scholarship they produced, neither were the scholars who relied on their translations.

Anachronism was not de Slane's main concern, even when he knew that the natives had changed the way they used categories such as Berber. This much is clear from his definition of the word, found in his Arabic edition of sections from Ibn Khaldūn's *Kitāb al-ʿibar*: "The Berbers, the native (*autochtones*) people of Northern Africa, are the same race that one calls today by the name Kabiles. This word, which means "tribe" in Arabic, has been used to describe the Berbers only in the last three centuries or so. The introduction of this novel attribution must be attributed to the [Ottoman] Turks."[30] Whatever name one gives them, the Berbers are the natives of North Africa. This is a remarkable statement, and not just because it sets an equivalency between a new category and an older one, or that it does so very naturally, without the slightest hesitation. It is significant because it uses "native" and "race" to achieve this effect.[31] But unlike linguists and ethnographers who made similar statements based on field research in Algeria, de Slane did so as an Orientalist, steeped in medieval texts of great intellectual value. That gave Orientalists an aura of learnedness that the poorly educated Algerians whom the ethnographers interviewed could not deliver. As de Slane's translation of Ibn Khaldūn became required reading for anyone interested in the Maghrib—not just its medieval past—it became a privileged site for the authorized dissemination of an entire scaffolding of ideas, foremost among which were the notions of indigeneity and race. As students of the Maghrib sought out de Slane's translation, they encountered an apparatus that undermined the awareness of the historicity of collective categories. But de Slane was not alone in this. The active dehistoricizing that "race" and "native" unleashed was consistent with a broader vision of the world, with its habits of thought and sentiment.[32]

A Foundational New Text

De Slane's *Histoire des Berbères* introduced new ideas about the Berbers that went beyond the Arabic original, and it is therefore legitimate to think of it as a new text.[33] While the idea that a translation brings forth a new text is not extraordinary, in view of the impact this new book had on the historiography of the medieval Maghrib, doing so avoids confusing its particular way of conceiving the Berbers with that of the original. It also underlines the fact that de Slane did not translate the entire *Kitāb al-ʿibar* but only the part that pertained to the Berbers and the Arabs of the Maghrib, an act that is significant in itself.[34]

As the title he gave his translation declares, the *Histoire des Berbères* covers those parts of Ibn Khaldūn's history that he believed relevant, even if they belonged to different sections in the original: "The portion of the work that the Minister of War saw that they be published in Algiers, and of which we give a translation here, is composed of the fourth section of Book Two, which includes the history of the Barbarizing Arabs (*Arabes barbarisants*), and the two parts of Book Three, which is especially focused on the history of the Berbers. The fourth section introduces the history of the Arab tribes of northern Africa; Book Three includes the History of the Berbers, a people who, from the most remote antiquity, has lived in the same country."[35] This partial reconstitution of Ibn Khaldūn's work fits the interests of the monsieur Minister of War and is partial in that sense too. It also finds some validation in Ibn Khaldūn's personal interest in the Maghrib.[36] Even beyond the otherwise worthy examination of the implications that excerpting has, de Slane's focus on the Berbers supported a vision of history not found in the original. If he was particularly interested in Berber dynasties, Ibn Khaldūn situated their history in relation to the histories of the Arabs and others and as examples (*ʿibar*) that buttressed his theories about history. Whatever else can be said about him, Ibn Khaldūn was not a scholar working for a colonial state that ruled over peoples whose past it was discovering. Further distinguishing his history from Ibn Khaldūn's, de Slane gave his translation the title *Histoire des Berbères et des dynasties musulmanes de l'Afrique septentrionale*.[37] This juxtaposition of Berbers and Islamic dynasties is not found in Ibn Khaldūn's title, logic, or narrative. It has the benefit, however, of being a clear and powerful statement of the indigeneity of the Berbers and the external character of (dynastic) Islam.[38]

Another notion that is peculiar to de Slane is his translation of the category Maghrib. In addition to North Africa (*Afrique septentrionale*), he used the older category Barbarie. Needless to say, the original had no reference to these categories, as de Slane notes in his glossary, among other places:

> Maghreb, *or* more grammatically [correct], Maghrib, means the Sunset, the West. Among Arab historians, this word was first

> used to designate Northern Africa and Spain; but then they gave it a narrower sense by applying it to the country west of Ifrîkïa. Then they introduced the names of Central Maghreb and Far Maghreb, the first of which applies to the current provinces of Algiers and Oran . . . and the second to the Kingdom of Morocco. Ibn Khaldūn indicates that Asfi is the westernmost limit of this last region; but elsewhere he considers implicitly the limit to be the Atlas Chain until Agadir.[39]

By introducing North Africa and Barbary (Barbarie), de Slane reorganized Ibn Khaldūn's logic and way of thinking in another significant way.[40] While he does not use the category Berbérie, which became very popular later, he clearly sets the stage for the representation of the Maghrib as the land of the Berbers.[41]

In his effort to make Ibn Khaldūn's ideas palatable to specialists and non-specialists, de Slane innovated in yet another way, although this time by imposing a modern framework on Ibn Khaldūn's:

> Book Two includes the history of the dynasties of the Orient [i.e., Mashriq] and the four great Semitic (*semétiques*) races that successively inhabited the Arabian Peninsula, the last of which gave a considerable part of Northern Africa a large population. In order to distinguish between these races, the author uses a bizarre terminology that we give here. 1. El-Arab-el-Aréba, the arabizing (*arabisants*) Arabs, or pure Arabs; 2. El-Arab-el-Mostaréba, or arabized Arabs; 3. el-Arab-el-Tabéa-lil-arab, the Arabs successors of Arabs; and 4. El-arab-el-Mostadjema, barbarizing Arabs.[42]

Requiring some thought and perhaps a little patience, Ibn Khaldūn's terminology, which he did not invent, is certainly not bizarre, combining a linguistic element, as in the Greek and Roman "barbarian," with a genealogical frame. What is peculiar, however, is that this typology is converted into a racial frame. In addition to the introduction where he "explained" Ibn Khaldūn's thinking, de Slane deployed the notion of race in two ways. Sometimes he inserted the word "race" when the Arabic original had nothing. In other cases, he used it to translate notions that did not quite fit his own schema—though he did not notice that. Rather than examine where de Slane "failed" as a translator or simply as an intellectual (or human being), developing a sense of the multiplicity of meanings covered by "race" allows us to delineate the contours of this new form of Berberization, insofar as the Berbers were now a race too. A few examples drawn from the first few pages should suffice to illustrate this point:

> While the empire founded by their arms passed from race to race and from family to family (*ajyāl*, sing. *jīl*).[43]
>
> The warrior could only distinguish himself from the artisan by his lack of aptitude for work, and the individual of nomad race could only be distinguished from an urbanite by his clothing (*wa tashābaha al-jīl wa al-ḥaḍar*).[44]
>
> The Berber race (*umma*) occupied this country and prevented other peoples from settling in it.[45]
>
> These two people [i.e. Kutāma and Ṣanhāja] gradually became Berbers and mixed with this race (literally, "them," i.e. the Berbers) so that the authority of the Arabs completely disappeared from Ifrîkïa.[46]
>
> The Hilal and Soleim Tribes, Arabs of the Fourth Race (*ṭabaqa*), Enter Africa.[47]
>
> The Douaouida sought refuge in the Maghreb after the death of their chiefs, and entered the service of the kings of the Zenatienne race (*mulūk zanāta*).[48]
>
> Among the nomad populations of this race are the Agerma-Ibn-Abs, a sister tribe of the others.[49]

It is not necessary to be an Ibn Khaldūn expert or even to know Arabic to notice that de Slane's notion of race encompassed a wide range of clearly distinct meanings. The Berbers were a race, the Zanāta were a race, but then nomads and urbanites were also races. Likewise, the Arabs, only some of whom were pure, were at once a single race and many races—since they had a succession of at least four races. Ibn Khaldūn knew of no Semitic race, of course, just of the peoples who descended from Sem, son of Noah. Likewise, the notions of *ṭabaqa*, *umma*, *jīl*, and *jins,* which refer to known peoples like the Arabs and Berbers, a generation or a fraction of a people living at a particular time, and to distinctions within any of these, did not really correspond to a modern understanding of race. At least this much can be gathered from de Slane's notes, which did not deal with the complications inherent in Ibn Khaldūn's categories. For instance, de Slane thought that the Berber race was, if not outright white, at least not black: "We know that this [Senegal] river continued to separate for a long time the Berber race and the black race."[50] In another note, de Slane commented on the Arabic word *ghulām*, which he translated as "young slave" in the body of the text but felt the need to add to it: "The Arabic word *rolam* means *boy*, *domestic*, *young white slave*."[51] Inserting race and its associated set of allusions, suggestions, and indications made the text legible within the new historical context. De Slane did not invent the concept of "race," nor was he the only one applying it to the medieval Maghrib.[52] Nevertheless, because of his authorial interventions, de Slane's *Histoire des Berbères* was much richer than the original, with an impressive amount of new material. At the same time, it was much poorer because it reduced rich and complex meanings and folded them into new ones—thus displacing vital clues to the historicity of Berberization. Although it is not customary to consider de Slane's *Histoire des Berbères* a work of history, his 115-page introduction with its tables, glossary, and indexes definitely is. Even if he relied on Ibn Khaldūn, de Slane presented novel arguments, used concepts that did not exist in the original, and drew independent conclusions about the Maghrib, its peoples, and their pasts.[53]

These considerations apart, it is necessary to recognize that of the two men Ibn Khaldūn was by far the greater intellect and historian. Although this may appear to be unfair to de Slane, it is a reminder of the far greater familiarity that Ibn Khaldūn had with the country, the peoples, and even more glaringly, the texts. In comparison, and in spite of the great strides made by French Orientalists, de Slane barely scratched the surface, his understanding based mostly on the Qur'ān, a limited number of exegetical works, chronicles, and geographical works. In truth, de Slane could not really challenge Ibn Khaldūn's scheme, his views on the cycles of dynasties, civilization, tribal solidarity, or any of the ideas that he took from him—though he did maintain a rhetorical "critical distance" that gave the false sense that he was in charge.

In this vein, insisting on the distinctiveness of de Slane's translation should not distract from the fact that it instituted Ibn Khaldūn's ideas as a mode of interpretation. If specialists have debated the extent to which Ibn Khaldūn's history truly exemplified (*'ibar*) the theory he articulated in the *Muqaddima*, one thing is sure: Ibn Khaldūn thought it did, or at least, based on his continued rewriting of the work, he thought it should. In any case, whether Ibn Khaldūn succeeded in establishing a new science is different from whether his ideas had an influence on others. In the case of de Slane, there is no doubt that he borrowed Ibn Khaldūn's framework without fully understanding that he did—and that is true for many reasons. For instance, de Slane did not know the full title of Ibn Khaldūn's work because the manuscripts he consulted did not have it. But as has been ascertained since, the title included a very important precision at the end in the form of "and those contemporary with them from among the possessors of great authority" (*wa-man 'āṣarahum min dhawī al-sulṭān al-akbar*). What this means for the arguments about Berberization is that Ibn Khaldūn privileged "great" dynasties in his history. This particular vision of history the author implemented successfully, at least in the sense that his narrative centers on dynasties and powerful tribes. This is consistent with his ideas about the cycle of dynastic power. With this in mind, Ibn Khaldūn's history of the Maghrib reads as a succession of great dynasties that emerged from a Bedouin context, sometimes aided by religious fervor. Although there is much that it occults, Ibn Khaldūn's history presents itself as an account of the things that matter. With this in mind, de Slane's periodization is absolutely Khaldunian. Espousing a positivist outlook, he does not distance himself from it at all, thus accepting an important logical component of Ibn Khaldūn's thinking (see Figure 2). Moreover, Ibn Khaldūn organizes his great dynasties genealogically, which makes sense in his Bedouin-to-urban-dynasty cycle. A quick look at de Slane's reconstruction of these genealogies and at the glossary he prepared to guide his readers demonstrates, to be polite, a certain lack of critical distance. This is cut-and-paste historiography at its purest (see Figure 3).

It is in their relation to Ibn Khaldūn's overall schema, which represents the great dynasties as producers and depositors of civilization living under the threat of Bedouins, that events such as the Islamic conquests and the migration of the Banū Hilāl and Banū Sulaym to the Maghrib in the eleventh century gain significance. Even more precisely, they gain significance in relation to both great dynasties and the genealogical frame through which Ibn Khaldūn pegs them. Whether de Slane personally believed in the centrality of the state, its relation to civilization, and the genealogical character of states is not as important as his establishing these ideas as the natural way of organizing the medieval history of the Maghrib.

The centrality of genealogy in Ibn Khaldūn sheds light on the presence of "race" in de Slane's translation. However, a more fundamental problem with the *Histoire des Berbères* is its subscription to a dynastic view of history, which brought de Slane in line with many medieval historians, not just Ibn Khaldūn. The new Ibn Khaldūn effectively instituted dynasticism as history,

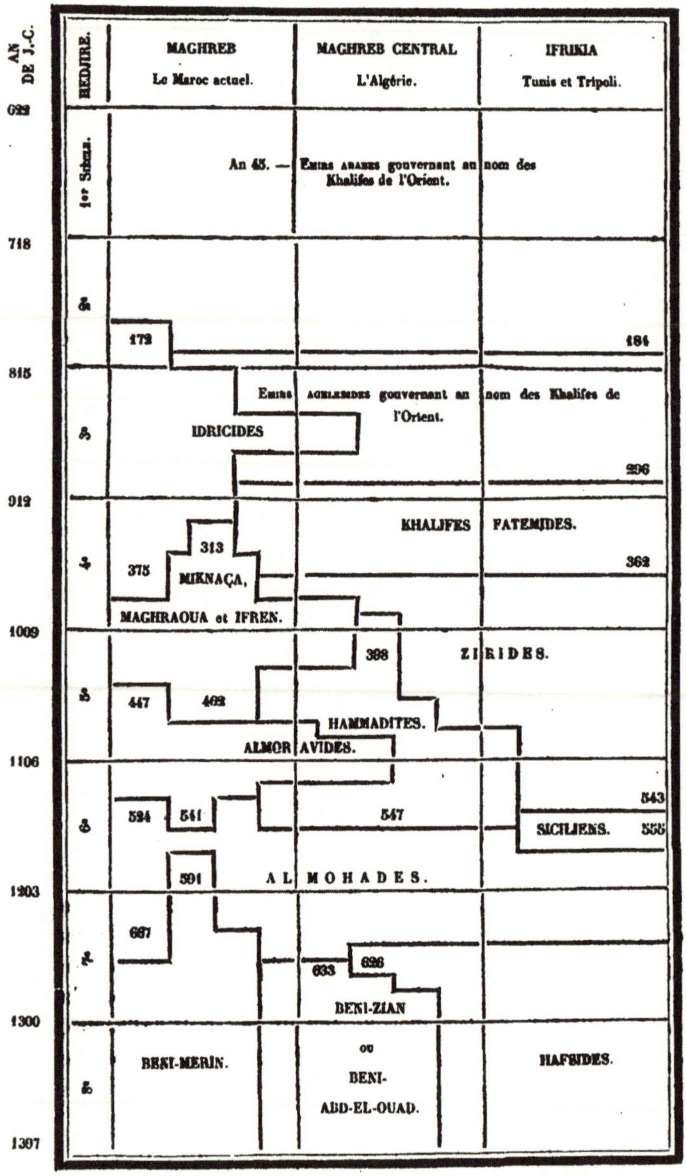

Figure 2. Table from William McGuckin de Slane, *Histoire des Berbères et des dynasties musulmanes de l'Afrique septentrionale* (Algiers: Imprimerie du gouvernement, 1852), 1:X.

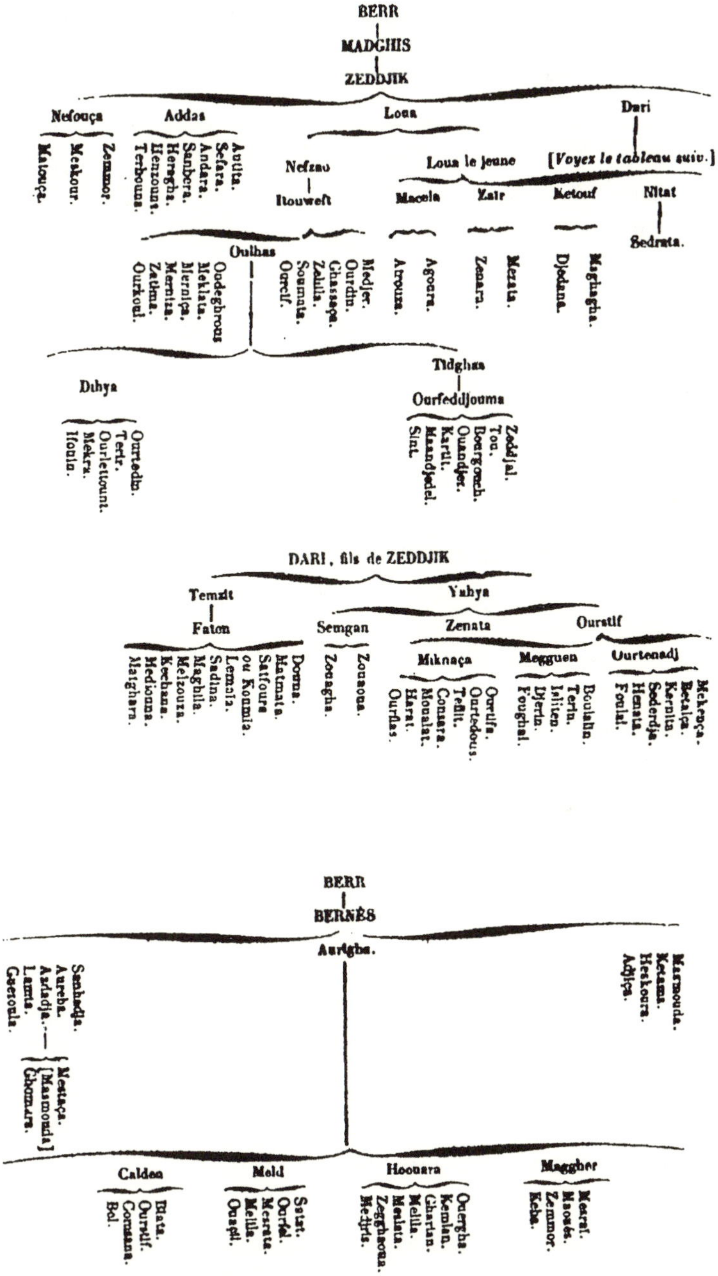

Figure 3. Genealogies from William McGuckin de Slane, *Histoire des Berbères et des dynasties musulmanes de l'Afrique septentrionale* (Algiers: Imprimerie du gouvernement, 1852), 1:XIV–XV.

setting the historical agenda and deciding the form of the division of labor in the field. Henceforth, a medievalist would specialize in the Idrīsids, the Aghlabids, or the Marīnids—de Slane's Ibn Khaldūn being a most convenient and intelligent reference. In retrospect, this privileged position explains why it has been so difficult to historicize Ibn Khaldūn's work. Of course, it also explains why Khaldunian Berberization was so successful—although that still remains to be shown.

Early Steps

The ink had not fully dried on de Slane's *Histoire des Berbères* when it became the principal reference for scholars working on the medieval Maghrib, especially those who did not know Arabic or felt that their command of it was not as good as de Slane's—and that meant almost everybody. Although some had recognized the importance of Ibn Khaldūn before de Slane's translation was published, it was truly with de Slane's translation that Ibn Khaldūn became standard.[54]

Foremost among the pioneers who made the medieval Maghrib a field was Count Louis de Mas Latrie (1815–97), a scholar-diplomat trained at the École des chartes who published in 1866 an impressive edition of documents found in European archives pertaining to the "relations between Christians and the Arabs of northern Africa."[55] According to the author, the emperor Napoleon III contributed his ideas about approach and organization, so that it might "enlighten public administration and the indigenous people themselves on the state and civilization of the country before Turkish domination."[56] Mas Latrie explained the usefulness of studying the history of the Maghrib:

> By faithfully depicting the past, it will become possible to see a future for the establishment of more honest relations between us and the Arabs, which would benefit both peoples. [Doing so will also] demonstrate by using the most certain evidence that the animosities and resentments that have for too long divided us are neither ingrained nor as powerful as one may think. [Rather, doing so will show that] they have less to do with differences in race and religion than the fanatical and greedy instincts of a nation [i.e., the Ottomans], thankfully changed today, that

> developed in the sixteenth century among the populations of the coast of Africa and associated them with [that nation's] devastations.[57]

In his long *Introduction historique*, a careful study of diplomatic and commercial relations between "Christian" powers and "Arab" ones, Mas Latrie relied on the few translations of Arabic chronicles that had been published up to that point. By any standard, Mas Latrie's introduction, which spans the period between the conquests of the seventh century and the coming of the Ottomans in the sixteenth, is a superior synthesis of the information available to him. While his avowed agenda of mutual understanding led him to reject the prevailing view of Islam (*Islamisme*) being imposed by force of arms, his understanding of the medieval Maghrib was shaped by the documents he himself edited and of course the few translated Arabic sources available to him. Among these, de Slane's Ibn Khaldūn was by far the most widely utilized, Mas Latrie relying on Ibn Khaldūn for a number of critical interpretations of primary documents, quoting copiously and often from him.[58]

Although interesting in many other respects, Mas Latrie's study is relevant here because it illustrates the emergence of the academic habit of referencing Ibn Khaldūn. In fact, in spite of his utilization of other translations, Mas Latrie would have had a very hard time setting up a basic chronology without Ibn Khaldūn's help. Of course, diplomatic and commercial documents allowed him to date a few treaties but contained no information about how Maghribī rulers came to power or the general conditions of the country. Although offering very useful information, other chronicles such as the *Rawd al-qirṭās* and the *Riḥla* of al-Tijānī (d. 1321/22) did not have the breadth of information that Ibn Khaldūn offered on the entirety of the Maghrib—not just one geographic and temporal slice of it. While it is clear that Mas Latrie's ideas about the natives were "softer" than de Slane's, at least given his lofty aspirations for a considerate mutual-aid colonial domination, his lack of access to the original Arabic texts put him at an unquestionable disadvantage, and reinforced the apparent probity of de Slane's views. In this vein, Mas Latrie's treatment of the migration of Hilālī tribes into the Maghrib in the eleventh century offers a concrete example of what the combination of European documentary evidence and translated Arabic texts amounted to in practice.

Mas Latrie noted that based solely on peace and commerce treaties and on European chronicles, the "considerable" event that was the Hilālī "invasion" had no measurable effects. But because the migration "deeply modified the relations and composition of tribes of the north of Africa," he felt the need to "speak of it."[59] Quoting from Ibn Khaldūn, he gave the story that explains the invasion as retribution that the Fāṭimid caliph in Egypt exacted on the Zīrid al-Muʿizz (r. 1016–62) who had betrayed him and declared independence. Mas Latrie accepts the conclusions of the mathematical geographer and historian Antoine Carrette (1808–90), who estimated the number of migrants to be around a million! Their large numbers and the fact that they were inveterate and miserable thieves explained the devastation that these Arabs caused in Ifrīqiyā.

From Ibn Khaldūn's narrative about the damage caused to urban life by the Bedouinization of Ifrīqiyā, a statement that neither de Slane or Carrette was in a position to contextualize, Mas Latrie moves on to discuss the effects of this migration on the region: "This second Arab migration was of great ethnographic importance. The descendants of the ancient conquerors had been nearly absorbed into the Berber population, far greater in number. The invasion of 1052 brought a new element to the Ismaelic blood that neared being extinguished, and what we have today of what remains purely Arab in the north of Africa comes from Hilālī tribes that the Caliph of Egypt threw like a plague on the country, in order take revenge after the defection of his vizier."[60] Nowhere in Ibn Khaldūn can one find a reference to Ismaelic blood, as Arabic genealogists had no use for "blood." But race does: "This race of invaders, Ibn Khaldūn said, never had a chief capable of directing and containing it. One moment, masters of the greatly fortified places of Kairouan, El-Mehadia, Constantine, they could not conserve any of them. Almost everywhere, they looked for alliances and accepted the suzerainty of the Berber emirs they had dispossessed. Chased out of the large cities, they settled in the countryside, where they were always feared for their insolence and thievery."[61] Dragged into Ibn Khaldūn's treatment of Bedouins, the construction of the migration of the Banū Hilāl and Banū Sulaym as a catastrophe, and de Slane's racialized language, Mas Latrie finds himself sounding not too kind toward the very Arabs he wanted to foster good relations with. Yet, because Ibn Khaldūn also adapts the Andalusī logic of the Taifa kings, his history casts Berber dynasties in the role of civilized urbanites threatened by Arab Bedouins.[62]

The assessment of the eleventh-century migrations continues to elicit scholarly interest.[63] Yet, even more than whether the Arab "catastrophe" was an invention, an exaggeration, or an accurate fact, when it comes to the Berberization of the medieval Maghrib, it functioned as a critical lever for the racialization of both Arabs and Berbers:

> In the medieval period, the Arabs called Magreb this large portion of the African continent, the only one known to the ancients, which faces Europe, and includes the entire Mediterranean coast from Tripoli to Morocco. Christian sailors and merchants gave this country its true name, Berberie, which means country of the Berbers (Berbères), its first indigenous [inhabitants] (*premiers indigènes*). In modern times, the political regime that the Turks established there led to the prevalence of Barbary (Barbarie), which justified this usage; these inhospitable lands became for civilized Europe the Barbary Coasts (*les côtes de Barbarie*) and the Barbary States (*États barbaresques*).[64]

Mas Latrie's evocation of European civilization, a notion with a prominent place in Enlightenment thought, found an echo, if not validation, in Ibn Khaldūn's cycle of dynasties. While Ibn Khaldūn's conception of civilization was not the same as that of nineteenth-century intellectuals, and Orientalists did not use it in as systematic a way as Ibn Khaldūn had, Mas Latrie found in de Slane's Ibn Khaldūn enough material to support his assertion that in the fifteenth century there was a "generalized decadence of Islamic civilization." In this regard, Ibn Khaldūn's take on the eleventh century is pertinent because it supports modern civilizational thinking, though Ibn Khaldūn did not envisage an Islamic civilization—civilization (*'umrān*) being a notion that distinguished settled urban dwellers from Bedouin nomads: "Earlier, the Sanhadja dynasty had made agriculture prosper, but the pastoral-nomadic Arabs brought devastation to it and succeeded in gradually narrowing, by their invasions and robbery, the limits of cultivated lands. All the arts, which supported human subsistence, ceased to be practiced; civilization was ruined and the country transformed into a desert."[65] It is as nomads and not as a genealogical, let alone racial, group that the Banū Hilāl and Banū Sulaym brought this devastation to the cities, the centers of settled civilization. A series of shifts in signification later, however, Islamic civilization itself is declining, mediated in Mas Latrie's case by his disdain for the Ottoman Turks, who put an end to the period of commercial and diplomatic exchanges dear to his heart. In a section entitled "1453. General Decadence of Islamic Civilization. Negative Effect of the Conquest of Constantinople by the Turk," Mas Latrie explains the decline:

> Diverse causes at the time led Arabs to multiply their incessant robberies that became the major fear of navigators. The main one was the general and perceptible decadence, from the end of the fourteenth century, of all that remained of what was intellectual and literate in Islamism. Everywhere, in the Orient, as in Africa and Spain, Mahométism, already well degraded, falls into a worse state of ignorance and barbarism. The lofty traditions of administration are lost; the use of force seems the only means to govern. In the Magreb, at the same time as the authority of the emirs weakens, the Arab and Berber populations become less hospitable and more fanatic; all recollection of the schools and libraries founded by the ancients is erased among them; crude instincts take over; they have less appreciation for relations with foreigners.[66]

Perhaps the civilization began its decline in the eleventh century, with the Banū Hilāl, but succumbed in the fifteenth because of the combined actions of Arabs and "the Turk." The chronology is not quite clear. While it is true that Ibn Khaldūn complained about the state of intellectual production in his lifetime, with a little contextualizing, his statement made sense. However, it became an important and recurring proof, validating a rather negative view of the Maghrib and its history. Most significantly, Ibn Khaldūn was everywhere.

The Contribution of Colonial Ethnography to the Medieval Maghrib

The medieval Maghrib continued to be the purview of Orientalists a long time after the publication of de Slane's *Histoire des Berbères*. In the half century after its publication, the main contributions to its historiography continued to be editions and translations of texts, the complete edition of Ibn Khaldūn's *Kitāb al-ʿibar* (1867), and, to a lesser extent, al-Ṭabarī's *Tārīkh al-rusul wa al-mulūk* (1879–1901). In fact, until the early years of the twentieth century, academic activity mainly focused on ethnographic studies of the native populations and on the native "legal systems," both of which were critical to the establishment and maintenance of a settler colonial system.[67] Those who ventured into the medieval period, like the Saint-Simonian engineer Henri Fournel (1799–1876), had a utilitarian approach to it, mostly seeking information about modern Berber tribes.[68]

Fournel was not a trained historian or Orientalist, even if he learned the Arabic alphabet and could make out personal names and place-names with inconsistent accuracy.[69] Hired by the military command in Algeria to do a survey of exploitable mineral resources, he came to know the country, and experience firsthand the "Arab" resistance of the 1840s. He developed the idea that the Arabs had victimized the Berbers, the true "autochthonous race."[70] Given his intellectual orientation and training, he saw this as a problem that needed to be corrected: "Since 1830, we were on the wrong path, by focusing too much on the Arabs, wrongly neglecting the true natives (*indigènes*), the Berbers, an eminently hard-working, non-fanatical race attached to the land by enclosed properties, where it lived in little houses covered with tiles, practicing, in a crude way, some industries, the improvement to which we could initiate them. In a word, [the Berbers had] all the rudiments of custom which made them closer to us than could the habits that make the life of the Arabs."[71] Fournel's two epigraphs to the book highlight his contribution to the field.[72] Taken from the Roman historian Livy (d. ca. 17), the first epigraph reads, "It is the sword of the Berbers that made Cannae a victory." The second, from the author himself, reads, "It is the plow of the Berbers that made Africa one of the breadbaskets of Rome." While it may not be immediately obvious, he had a special taste for those historical examples that demonstrated the productivity of the Berbers and the uselessness, if not destructiveness, of the Arabs, as he gathered from de Slane's Ibn Khaldūn—and from his own experience with the military efforts to pacify the Arabs.

It is difficult to take this work seriously as a work of medieval historiography, as the author does not have command of the sources. Yet, in spite of this, its naturalization of the anachronistic projection of the category Berber into the ancient past is an undeniable contribution to the field. As it focuses on the Arab conquests and Arab domination, Fournel's study encompasses the succession of foreigners (i.e., nonnatives) who ruled over the Berbers from the Carthaginians through the Arabs and up to the coming of the Turks. Whether he was following Ibn Khaldūn or not, his approach made it difficult for later students of the medieval Maghrib to imagine that Berber

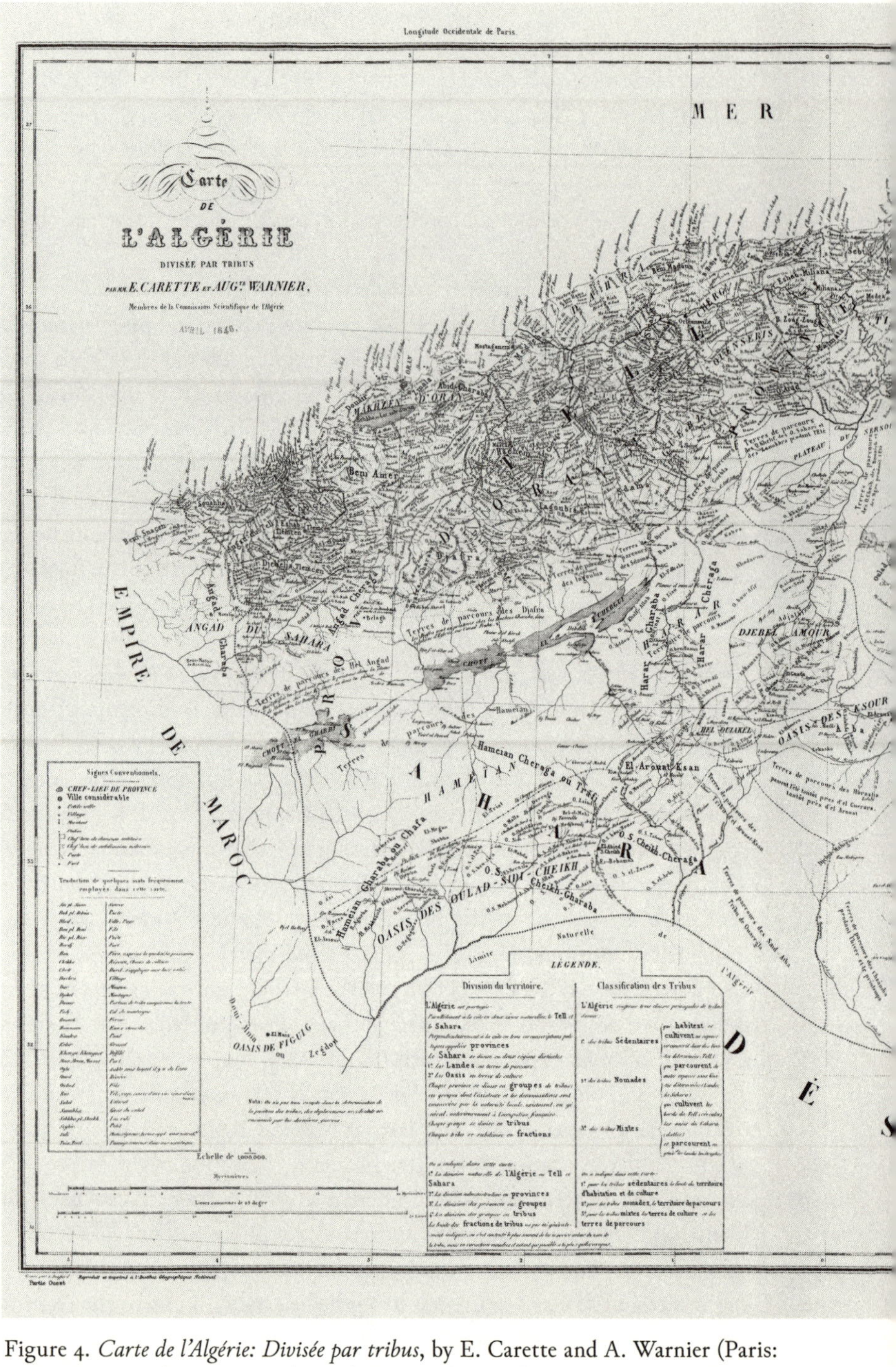

Figure 4. *Carte de l'Algérie: Divisée par tribus*, by E. Carette and A. Warnier (Paris: Institut géographique national, 1846). Map. Library of Congress, Geography and Map Division, Washington, DC, 20540-4650 USA dcu.

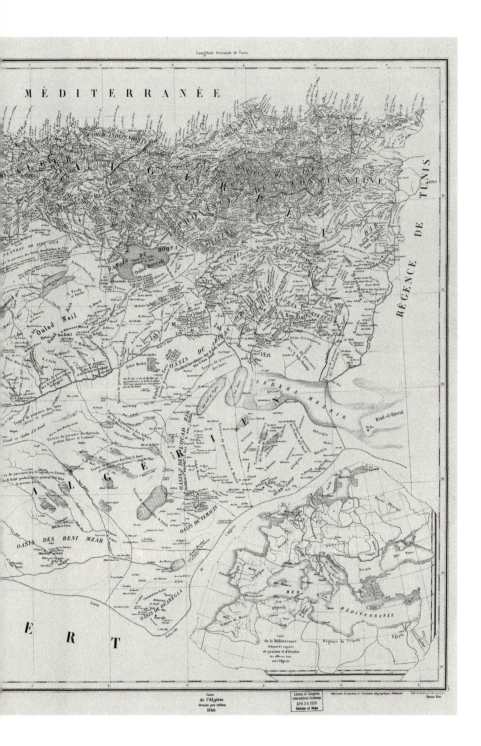

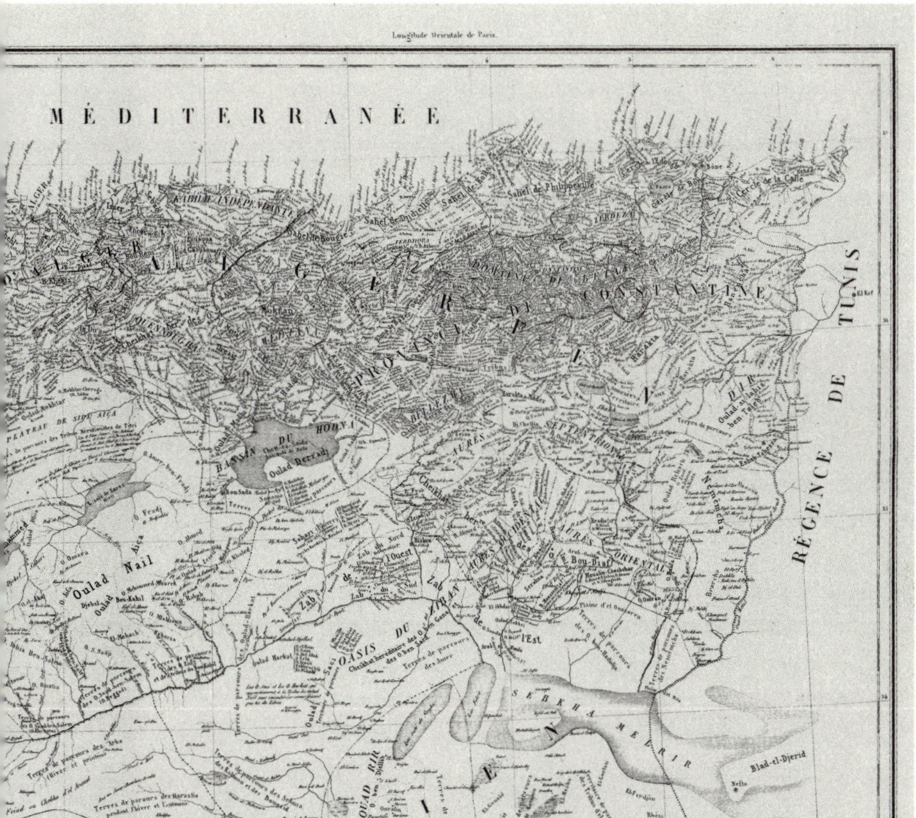

Carte
de l'Algérie
divisée par tribus
1846

Partie Est

was an Arabic category that emerged gradually. In the same vein, it is remarkable that although he believed that the Berbers were the true native population, Fournel did not call their country Berbérie but Maghreb and Afrique.[73]

It was Ernest Mercier (1840–1908), the first modern historian of the Maghrib, who sanctioned the use of Berbérie in historical writing.[74] His early study of the settlement of Arabs in North Africa (*Afrique septentrionale*) already employed the category, although not in the title.[75] In his 1888 general history of the region, *Berbérie* appears between parentheses in the title.[76] Noting that the region had been called a variety of names over time, Mercier expressed a preference for Berbérie over both Barbarie and Maghrib. As he explained it, Berbérie had the advantage of acknowledging the native inhabitants of the land, the Berbers.

> A single people (*un peuple unique*) seems to have inhabited northern Africa since the most remote antiquity. This autochthonous race can still be found intact on the western coast of the Red Sea, in Egypt, in the deserts of Nubia and the Sahara, on the banks of the Senegal River and the Atlantic coast, and finally in the mountains of Morocco, Algeria, and Tunisia. In these lands, [this race] bears the names of Berber, Tebou, Imouchar', Touareg, Chelouh, Kabile, Chaouïa, Maure, etc. We have kept the name Berber, an onomatopoeia that foreigners have doubtlessly applied first to its language then to its race, and from there, to a part of the country that it inhabits: Berbérie, improperly called by us Barbarie.[77]

It is difficult to distinguish Mercier's ideas as a scholar from those he articulated as a colonialist politician opposed to giving civil rights to the natives and to their assimilation into French society and culture. He was a first-generation settler whose family moved to Algeria when he was a teenager and lived off the revenues of a pharmacy and thirty acres of land they received from the colonial authorities. When he came of age, Mercier became a translator in the military and then in the courts. After that, he set up a private practice as a translator, which he kept all through his life. His knowledge of the law and his life as settler informed his later study *La propriété indigène au Maghreb* (1898)—a work that deserves more attention than it has garnered. His interest in matters of land, property, and settlement had been constant, although until that study it expressed itself indirectly. First drawn to the ethnography that dominated the intellectual scene in Algeria, Mercier published a few studies on Sufi orders. But his two major historical studies retained an ethnographic bent, with a consistent focus on population settlement. Methodologically, Mercier embraced the ambient positivism, his colonialist outlook standing for objectivity.

Mercier found intolerable the "contradictions" of Arab historians and labored to resolve them—he meant the discrepancy between dates, names, and numbers. As far as his framework is concerned, however, he adapted Ibn Khaldūn to his interests in population movement and racial composition. His analysis of the two waves of Arab settlement in northern Africa (Berbérie) followed the terms of Ibn Khaldūn's vision, although with new categories and new colonial concerns. Equipped with race, civilization, and indigeneity, Mercier reframed the history of the Maghrib from ancient times down to the French conquest. Interestingly, the medieval period occupied a central place, with Carthage and Rome being the main civilizations that preceded the Arabs. Given his focus on political events, Mercier linked civilization, political rule, and foreign invasions (of the Berbers) as Ibn Khaldūn would have had he had access to those texts and known ancient languages.

With Mercier, the Maghrib emerged as a Berbérie that had been Arabized. His project was to document this process. First through the Arab conquest of the Berbers, a notion that did not exist in Ibn Khaldūn or any Arabic source, and then through the onslaught that was the migration of the Banū Hilāl and Banū Sulaym in the eleventh century. After that, the Berbers had Berber dynasties for a while, but, under pressure from Arabs and the damages of Ottoman rule, the entire civilization declined. From a historiographic standpoint, Mercier made the medieval period critical to understanding the present.

Interestingly, Mercier followed ancient and medieval authors who believed in an eastern origin of the Berbers, or at least part of the native population. His views on race and his interest in settlement of foreign populations made him elaborate an explanation for what he saw as racial diversity:

> 1. Northern Africa must have been settled by a series of very ancient migrations of Asiatic peoples, coming from Palestine, northern Arabia, or the edges of the Euphrates; 2. These Asiatic groups assimilated or were driven back by populations of diverse origins,—blonds in the north, brown or black (*basanées ou nègres*)

> in the High Plateaus and the south,—found by them in the country; 3. The coming together (*réunion*) of these elements and their assimilation formed the Berber race; 4. Finally, this unification must have been completed at such a remote time that it is permissible to attribute the label autochthonous to the Berbers of Africa.[78]

His racial characterization of various groups in the Maghrib is well within the range of divagation of ethnographically oriented racialists. Yet, unlike them, he made the Berbers a "racially diverse" group that migrated to the region in prehistoric times, thus relativizing the notion of indigeneity itself—and bringing him closer to Ibn Khaldūn. Mercier replaced the ultimately unverifiable character of medieval genealogies with an explanation involving migrations and races, which, despite his methodological predilections, remains similarly impossible to document. While the homology may appear to be accidental, it is the consequence of Mercier's fundamentally Khaldunian vision.

Implementing his "Berber-by-any-other-name" approach to the past, Mercier succeeded in making the Berbers a prehistoric phenomenon that archaeologists, anthropologists, and linguists could study—not that they waited for his green light to do just that. His overall frame situates the contribution of the medieval period to the study of the Punicization, Romanization, and Arabization of the Berbers, especially the extension of Ibn Khaldūn's Arabized Berbers (*mostaréba*) to other civilizations, populations, and races.

Toward a Historiography of the Medieval Maghrib

There was a gap between the publication of de Slane's Ibn Khaldūn and the appearance of the first historical studies on the medieval Maghrib. For a few decades, specialists did little more than improve their knowledge of relevant medieval texts, edit and translate those that seemed significant, and build up expertise in language and methods. By the time studies began to emerge at the beginning of the twentieth century, the Khaldunization of the terms of knowledge on the Maghrib was well entrenched.

Importantly, the early specialists of the medieval Maghrib were not trained historians. They were individuals with an interest in languages whose training introduced them to medieval texts. The medieval was an area of knowledge that allowed them to hone and demonstrate their language skills. Their historical imagination was rather limited, and the quality of their work did not attract attention beyond their field. The best French historians of the time worked in other fields. The Maghribists were not necessarily the worst, but definitely not the best. Beyond the difficulties they had in learning languages and acquainting themselves with the texts, they worked in a small field and could not rely on the work of too many others. The first historians were pioneers in that alone-in-the-wilderness sense too. Perhaps this sheds light on a certain clannishness that developed in the field, although personal animosities kept it somewhat in check. Naturally, some of this could easily be said of the French university in general or, in fact, of a number of other university systems, but the small number of practitioners influenced both the significance of the scholarly consensus, the desire to break from it, and the form that departure could take. It is useful to keep in mind the scale of the scholarly enterprise compared to the monumentality of its consequences, especially when trying to analyze the operations of Berberization in medieval historiography.

Chapter 6

Beacons, Guides, and Marked Paths

The Khaldunization of the terms of historical research on the medieval Maghrib set the agenda of researchers and gave their work direction and justification. It also allowed historians to establish a recognizable map of the field with its stock of common references, inside jokes, and landmarks. But to be clear, if Ibn Khaldūn was a seminal text it was only because historians made it so. They were the ones who sought it to support their arguments and paraded it in front of outsiders as a source of pride. Even so, Ibn Khaldūn offered a generative framework not only for academics but also for politicians, journalists, and everyone in between. Although the focus here is on medievalists who should have recognized Berberization at work in their sources, omitting from our appreciation the extent to which Ibn Khaldūn constituted the structure of colonial sentiments toward the natives would be a mistake.

Colonial Ibn Khaldūn was also critical to the development of nationalist and anticolonial historiographies. Responding to what they felt was an inaccurate representation of their past, Maghribī historians were first to mobilize Ibn Khaldūn to shift the focus from the racial and religious bases of the decline of the civilization of the natives to identifying points of pride. As they did so, they gave renewed relevance to the representation of the Berbers as the original inhabitants of the Maghrib, their ancestral homeland. Given the influence of colonialism on the education of the natives, few knew Arabic well enough to approach the sources critically, and those who could tended not to do so. Besides, francophone native historians had to deal with the influence of French translations in academic publications and the framing of historical research. In time, however, and even more than their arabophone and bilingual counterparts, francophone natives uttered the most radical statements against French colonial historiography, in French.

There was a great deal of diversity in the approaches and emphases of medievalists. Any historiographic essay would be able to demonstrate that. In order to discern the operations of Berberization in the field, however, it is more prudent to limit our scope to a few historians who made significant and lasting contributions. Yes, there are others, and yes, I have mentioned many of them already, but the primary goal here is only to take note of the specificity of modern Berberization and its modalities in order to assess its reliance on medieval Berberization(s). Clearly, a fuller discussion of the dominant theoretical underpinnings of these works and the assumptions that undergird their methodological outlook would definitely improve our understanding of how Berberization has functioned. However, that is beyond the scope of this book, which seeks to establish Berberization as an object of study and delineate its most prominent features.

Arabs in Berbérie

In the years following Ernest Mercier's work, Berbérie became a standard way of referring to the Maghrib, with any misgivings and hesitation he might have had, forgotten. Helped by the naturalization of racial ideology, nationalism, ideas of progress, and a host of colonial policies toward the natives in Algeria, a rapid accumulation of firsthand and secondhand references and cross-references gave Berbérie currency among specialists. After all, the Berbers were the true natives, the autochthones, and original inhabitants of the land. Only a couple of decades of repetition, and no one even remembered just how recent the usage was. The currency of Berbérie at the beginning of the twentieth century illustrates well the rapidity of French colonial Berberization.[1] Its intellectual debt to de Slane's Ibn Khaldūn is undeniable, even if with the passing of time it became less common to recognize this contribution. With the publication of Georges Marçais' *Les Arabes en Berbérie du XIe au XIVe siècle* in 1913, the Khaldunization of the medieval period had its most wide-ranging and consistent effort to date.[2] Known for his "positive sentiments toward the natives," Georges Marçais (1876–1962) is credited with the foundation of the archaeology and art history of the Maghrib (*art musulman occidental*).[3] He held a number of positions in the colonial administration of native affairs, allowing him to improve his language skills and acquaintance with medieval Arabic sources. *Les Arabes en Berbérie* was the culmination of his studies.

Marçais articulated a colonialist vision in which history validated the separation between natives and settlers. The main difference for him was that the natives' history did not lead anywhere, whereas that of the European settlers exemplified the struggle for civilization and progress:

> Taken in its entirety, this history [of the Berbérie] lacks almost any unity. We will not discover here anything comparable to the unconscious and laborious effort, sometimes so hesitant about its goal and so often upset in its march, which seems to lead Europeans toward the realization of a social ideal or a greater state. The Berbérie does not seem capable of progressing by its own means; it must latch itself onto someone else. . . . In the grand duel between barbarism and civilization, how many times the latter was defeated? . . . Reservoir of resources without cohesion, [the Berbérie] needs to receive these directing influences from outside, from Phoenicia or Rome, or from the Islamic Orient or Spain [i.e., al-Andalus].[4]

Nothing in their history suggests that the Berbers worked collectively toward civilization. Because of their lack of cohesion, they lacked the ability to develop civilization, always requiring help from outside—Spain entering the scene as a source of civilization.

As an art historian, Marçais saw medieval art in the Maghrib as Islamic and therefore as alien to the Berbers, a banal idea by then. At the same time, the appearance of al-Andalus points to an idea dear to Ibn Khaldūn: civilization moved from the more urbanized Andalus to the more Bedouin Maghrib: "There are few cities and towns in Ifrīqiyā and the Maghrib. The reason for this is that these regions belonged to the Berbers for thousands of years before Islam. All (their) civilization was a Bedouin (civilization)."[5] Worse, the Maghrib experienced the plague of Bedouin depredations in the eleventh century, a migration that had negative effects on the cities: "The Debab, Auf, Zoghb and all the Hilalian families rushed onto Ifrīqiyā like a swarm of locust, damaging and destroying everything that was in their way."[6] Swarm of locust or not, Ibn Khaldūn thought that the Banū Hilāl were bearers of a form of civilization, which was Bedouin. In his cycle of dynasties, Bedouin cohesion (*'aṣabiya*) allows some of them to overpower urban dynasties, establish their own dynasties, and become new sponsors of urban civilization. As a form of civilization, Bedouin civilization had a number of characteristics that made urbanites like Ibn Khaldūn appreciate it, even if nostalgically, for practices and values that had disappeared in the cities. Even if one forgets that Ibn Khaldūn was of Andalusī origin and ignores the politics of his time, any comparison of the number of cities in al-Andalus and the Maghrib makes the latter appear less urbanized or more Bedouin. Ibn Khaldūn also thought that the disappearance of "tribal" politics in al-Andalus was an effect of the prevalence of cities.

As one reads Marçais, two things come to mind. On the one hand, like most of his contemporaries, Marçais conceived of civilization as the opposite of barbarism, which was an absence of civilization. On the other, Ibn Khaldūn's civilization (*'umrān*) was not the opposite of *waḥshiya* but of *badāwa* (*'umrān badawī*). Not only do Bedouins have a civilization; it has a number of positive qualities, not least the potential to form an urban dynasty. Once civilization becomes an organizing principle, however, deciding whether a "people" is a bearer of civilization or, as was the case for the Berbérie, a passive recipient of its lights is eminently relevant. The succession of conquering civilizers gains significance and comes to inform the historical question at the heart of the book: ascertaining whether the invasions of the Arab Banū Hilāl and Banū Sulaym in the eleventh century amounted to anything. That is how Marçais understands the intrusion of the foreign Arabs into the land of the Berbers, the Berbérie. For these "technical" reasons, Marçais, and like-minded others, included in their historical studies a discussion of the origins and essential characteristics of the "natives." Since the Arabs were an obviously Oriental Semitic people, and their Islam an Oriental religion, the question hinged on what the Maghrib was "originally"—and thus on who or what the Berbers were.[7] These considerations illuminate Marçais' choice of focusing on the period between the Arab migration of the eleventh century and Ibn Khaldūn's fourteenth century—the possibility that he projected Ibn Khaldūn's later perspective on an earlier period was not his main concern.

Setting out to establish a historical map of nomadic tribes in the Maghrib and to understand their social, economic, and political life builds on colonial ethnography and geography.[8] Although Marçais finds that the migration of Arab tribes was, in the last analysis, negative, his rich analysis of the functioning of tribes was grounded in textual evidence.[9] But even when he insisted on the importance of the relations between a tribe's character and what he called the material conditions in which it lived, Marçais remained well within Khaldunian parameters. For another way of understanding Ibn Khaldūn's focus on the great dynasties is through the Bedouin tribes from which they emerged, genealogically and historically. Marçais is Khaldunian too when he analyzes the settlement of the Arabs in Berbérie and their interaction with the local powers.[10] In fact, when he is not relying directly on Ibn Khaldūn, and he does that for all the major critical points, he culls information from texts that Ibn Khaldūn had studied and integrated into his vision.

Ultimately, the issue is not so much that Marçais adopted Ibn Khaldūn's vision and adapted it to modern social-scientific and historical language. It is more that his "additions" did not offer a radical improvement on Ibn Khaldūn. On the contrary, it may be argued that the introduction of race, for instance, confused matters. Yet, as a product of modern learning, *Les Arabes en Berbérie* set the scholarly agenda and oriented future research, making Ibn Khaldūn the foundational core of the field. Of course, it would be useful to examine more attentively the development of social-scientific thinking, especially those developments that pertain to tribes, to illuminate their apparent similarity to Ibn Khaldūn's notions of tribal solidarity, cohesion, savagery, and their relation to civilization, which is mediated through his particular brand of materialism. Without having to do so, however, it should be clear that the ethnicization and racialization of the medieval Maghrib was part of broader intellectual and ideological developments.

Interestingly, and importantly for the development of the field, Marçais' mapping of the effects of the Arab invasion showed him that it was mostly an eastern phenomenon. As he put it, the Banū Hilāl made no inroads into Morocco, a few in Algeria, but were deadly in Tunisia and Tripolitania.[11] From the point of view of Berberization, this map envisages a gradation that parallels differences between North African countries, ahead of policy enactments like the Berber Decree (*Le dahir Berbère, al-ẓahīr al-barbarī*) of 1930.[12] The extent to which this map is a projection of the concerns of elite Andalusīs in Ifrīqiyā like Ibn Khaldūn, and, by extension, whether there is an Ifrīqiyan perspective on the Maghrib that requires historicizing, are questions that the Khaldunization of the medieval Maghrib has tended to obfuscate.

Moreover, and importantly for medievalists, like those before him, Marçais believed that further ethnographic research would ameliorate the historians' understanding of medieval Maghribī tribes, thus establishing stagnation or at least the lack of change as a working assumption. Behind the political strife and the constant infighting so richly recorded in the sources, there lies a deeper reality, which resides in the general conditions of social organization (tribal), and which did not change much: "We are very fortunate to be dealing with a society that evolved very little over the centuries and that has kept rather intact its ancient organization."[13] In other words, the apparently dynamic elements failed to transform society, or they only reproduced it. Although civilizational decline was not his invention, Marçais made explaining this fact a task medievalists should undertake. From a study of change over time, history becomes the study of the reasons that prevented change from taking place—a "Berbérie: what went wrong?" that paralleled the more widely applicable "Islam: what went wrong?" of *islamologues.*

Berbers of *Islamologie*

Certain tendencies in Marçais' work find a more elaborate and articulate exposition in the work of *islamologues*, a brand of Orientalists who based their analyses of history on their understanding of Islamic institutions, the law being the one most widely regarded as having had a defining role in the evolution of societies understood as Islamic. Among specialists of the medieval Maghrib, Robert Brunschvig (1901–90) was the most accomplished *islamologue*, his study of Ifrīqiyā under the Ḥafṣids (1229–1574), a masterpiece that became the standard reference on both region and period.[14] Unlike many of his predecessors, Brunschvig had an extraordinary mastery of the sources, in Arabic and in European languages, which he canvassed meticulously and thoroughly—an impressive feat, since many of the texts were still manuscripts and catalogs were far from complete. Because of this, his study became a standard reference and remained so for decades.

Applying his critical mind to the sources, Brunschvig easily resisted received wisdom when it did not correspond to the evidence. No less positivistic than his colleagues, he always tried to bring a multiplicity of sources to bear on a question before he made a judgment about a particular matter of fact. When it comes to prejudices that influenced his perspective on the Berbers, it is clear that he struggled with the established discourse and departed from it in critical aspects. Overall, however, his view on the state may have influenced his analyses even more than his reliance on racialist notions and his views on Islam.[15]

Brunschvig's state-centric standpoint did not allow him to distance himself from the perspective of his sources, chief among whom was Ibn Khaldūn.[16] Preferring with Ibn Khaldūn strong dynastic rule to weak and fragmented power, Brunschvig tended to embrace and reproduce ideological elements that traversed Ibn Khaldūn's thought. Instead of a critique of the dynasticism found in pro-Ḥafṣid sources, Brunschvig delivers an "objective" description of the political map. Here is an example of how this loss of neutrality appears in his analysis: "The sultan only reached Gafsa after having eliminated the obstacle of the Arabs who tried to block his way: the Aulād Abī l-Lail, whom he weakened considerably by freeing from their guardianship the little Berber nomad Maranjīsa and then the Ḥakīm of the Sahel."[17] On the authority of Ibn Khaldūn, Brunschvig considers the Maranjīsa to be "little," even if their actions seem to have been critical. Why "little"? Ibn Khaldūn. Ibn Khaldūn's perspective imposes a hierarchy between tribes and dynasties. He is interested in the possessors of great royal power (*mulk al-akbar*). Why is this important? Because Ibn Khaldūn's thoughts about political decline in his time and the need for a strong ruler were the fodder on which the discourse on decline fed. As a pro-Ḥafṣid historian, Ibn Khaldūn thought that those who opposed the dynasty were illegitimate, and so little, by definition. Brunschvig agreed.

It is difficult to impute the prevalence of dynastic periodization in modern historiography solely to Ibn Khaldūn. The confluence of French intellectual currents influenced by the central position of the state, the tribalization of natives under French colonial rule, and the ideology that prevailed in Ibn Khaldūn's time raises a question that largely remains unexamined—certainly by medievalists. Nonetheless, in spite of the importance of these other elements, it is critical to recognize the contribution of Ibn Khaldūn in the institution of dynastic periodization, at least insofar as he identified those dynasties that mattered, and classified them as either Arab or Berber (book 2 and book 3). While Ibn Khaldūn stood at the end of a series of developments that illuminate his perspective, insisting on his contribution situates better the centrality of the perpetuation of dynasty/tribe as a mode of apprehending the past. In other words, the importance of colonial ethnographic knowledge in the eyes of medievalists does not derive purely from the place of that knowledge within the colonial edifice.[18] As an effect, however, the centrality of the state, and thus of a particular understanding of politics, precluded the identification of Berberization as a distinct process, and facilitated the Khaldunization of the medieval Maghrib. In this vein, the positivist orientation of medievalists cannot be underestimated. Concretely, acknowledging the centrality of this statism in Brunschvig's imagination sheds light on both his popularity and the peculiarity of his intellectual stance vis-à-vis the deployment of the Arab/Berber couple to analyze the medieval Maghrib:

> Let us explain first the terms "Arabs" and "Berbers" which have been used in the exposé above. What is their ethnic value? Within what geographic realities does one need to frame them? It is certain that even in our own time, in the eyes of the North African *indigènes*, this distinction (*discrimination*), always lively, results from a dual ethnic origin, and that it covers a racial difference that remained apparent through a long tradition. But it is no less certain, as has been established for a long while, that this alleged division of the North African population between "Berbers" and "Arabs" most often rests, in modern times, on no solid historical basis. . . . Over the centuries, thanks to the close contacts between "Arab" and Berber fractions, even when the Arab language won the day, Arab blood mixed with native blood (*le sang arabe s'est intimement mêlé au sang autochtone*). If we add to this natural and serious element of confusion that the pretended [claim that many natives make of having] Arab ancestry, considered superior, frequently distorts even traditional genealogies, we would conclude that, in most cases, it is fruitless to establish between the elements of the indigenous population other demarcations than those visible and indubitable, of language and religion. . . . But does the same apply to the Ḥafṣid period, and more specifically to the fourteenth century where, thanks to Ibn Khaldūn, we know less poorly the respective situation of the tribes? It does not seem to be fully the case.[19]

The Berber/Arab couple was not meaningful or useful for analyzing the modern Maghrib. It was, however, very useful for analyzing the (late) medieval period, thanks to Ibn Khaldūn. On the one hand, Brunschvig correctly identifies Berber/Arab as an ideological artifact, an insight drowned in race and blood. On the other, he genuinely agrees with Ibn Khaldūn's perspective, without taking stock of what that means. The question of the place of ethnographic knowledge in the historiography of the medieval Maghrib is, however, important enough to deserve repeating, if only to distinguish modern Khaldunization and shed light on the workings of Berberization:

> Another forced immigration was that of Blacks brought or, more accurately, imported from the Sudan as slaves by caravans. Even when Muslim and free, they continued most often to provide a nearly servile workforce; some were eunuchs, and as such, harem guards. Ethnically, they represented a far more distant element from the local population than did the Christians or former Christians who came from Europe; but even they were not protected from mixing. Black blood penetrated in many families, all the way to the cities of the north through the women, mainly, Black women (*négresses*) who were busy doing domestic work and who enjoyed the favors of the master or of one of the sons of the house. In the south, nearer its land of origin, it ran in the blood of a greater number of individuals. In any case, Islam does not teach nor does it practice any discrimination against mulattos (*mulâtres*) or people of color. What were the physiological and cultural consequences of this mixing (*métissage*), which was common in other Muslim countries? No one could answer this question with certainty. Yet, it is necessary to note, as a hypothesis and beyond any preconceived notion, the historical importance of this racial factor.[20]

The point here is not that Brunschvig was a racialist, but rather that his historical analysis was, to use his terminology, mixed between an analysis of politics in which the racial factor played no role whatsoever and an analysis of society in which these considerations mattered, at least discursively. Critically, for medievalists, the representation of medieval society did not emerge out of medieval texts but from modern ethnography. By linking Bedouin civilization and urban dynasties, Ibn Khaldūn offered a means of squaring that circle.

Islam offered another. While it is impossible here to review all the ways that Brunschvig's conception of Islam supported the discourse on decline without veering too far away from Khaldunization, a convenient way to approach this question is through his analysis of commerce. Where does Brunschvig begin? "One could not study commerce in the history of a Muslim country without taking into consideration the traditional views of Islam on the subject."[21] As it turns out the traditional views are rather permissive, but Brunschvig noted that they imposed "numerous and important limitations" on the conduct of business.[22] And even if individual merchants violated many of these rules and regulations in search of profit, "public opinion was very much attached to them; especially in the cities, which were more susceptible usually to receiving innovations, but [given] the religious spirit that imposed on the faithful its own economic conceptions of an intransigent conservatism."[23] However, since commercial practices did not always emanate from or follow Islamic precepts, Brunschvig explains the challenges jurists faced in imposing an Islamic legal framework:

> Customary practices [sing. *'urf*, pl. *a'rāf*], which ordered the details of commercial operations, had originally allowed a certain softening of the law, and its geographic diversification; but, integrated by [Muslim] jurists and in turn fixated, they quickly tended to become tyrannical, and come to constitute a serious obstacle to progress. One had to wait until the influence of Europe, in the last century, and the emergence of the awareness of an inevitable necessity, to break, little by little, in all Muslim countries the resistance of the public to the ideas and methods of the western world.[24]

Since "customary practices" were as much Berber as they were Arab, Brunschvig does not look for an ethnic or racial explanation for the failure of Ḥafṣid Ifrīqiyā to engender a commercial revolution comparable to that of the Italian city-states, which led to modern capitalism. Islamic law hindered progress and its positive effects. It also explains Islam's failure to launch and contributes to the sense of a society mired in political struggles that do not really bring about real change, the change that matters. The positive effects of modern European intervention overlay Brunschvig's analysis of medieval practices.

By shifting the analytical focus away from Arabs and Berbers, Brunschvig brought out Islam and its law as explanations for economic retardation and decline. The strong state of great rulers offered temporary relief from economic decline and stagnation, although these exceptional periods failed to be sustained.[25] At the heart of this stagnation-and-decline economy lies a lack of creativity and innovation that was also apparent in the intellectual sphere:

> Intellectual or artistic production under the Ḥafṣids did not shine, as a whole, with a new glow. The Berbérie orientale [i.e., Ifrīqiyā] delivers nothing, or almost nothing, remarkable of its own making. Influences from Morocco or Spain [brought] by immigrants or travelers, or from the Orient by the pilgrims upon their return, are insufficient to reinvigorate the old Ifrīqiyan stump to the point of provoking a flowering of original or high-priced values. Based on this, it is unsurprising to see that from the fourteenth century on Europe thought it had nothing to borrow from the inhabitants of Ifrīqiyā. . . . And yet, the second half of the fourteenth century was honored with the greatest name of Muslim Berbérie [i.e., Maghrib] in the intellectual domain: the Tunisan, of Arab Andalusi background, ʻAbd al-Raḥmān Ibn Khaldūn. . . . The modern accent of the method and conceptions of Ibn Khaldūn in his analysis of human society and its evolution explains the "discovery" that learned Europe made a hundred years ago, its admiration, and the favor that he has today among enlightened Muslims.[26]

Of course, the normative statements against the conservatism of the inhabitants make little sense without the idea of progress. In fact, Brunschvig enshrined the habit of comparing the medieval Maghrib with early modern and modern Europe and in using Islam as a way of explaining the various failures and absences. Looking back at the Ḥafṣid period, only a few great rulers and their strong states offered a respite from the otherwise drab existence of the masses. Ibn Khaldūn would have approved.

As a tool for inscribing local developments into broader ones, Islam allowed Brunschvig and others to bring texts written in faraway lands to bear on Maghribī ones. Fitting the Maghrib into the Islamic world contextualized its developments in relation to those of the Mashriq (Orient) imagined as *l'Islam classique*.[27] In this interpretative scheme, the Berbers come in to illuminate the deviation from the norm, the heresies, and the peculiarities of the local. In other words, in addition to imposing a distorting prism on local histories, Islam reinforced the peculiarity of the Maghrib, notably through its Berbers.

The decontextualizing and dehistoricizing effects of colonial Islam make historical sense in relation to the part it played in public discourse, as an alibi for the disenfranchisement of natives, officially *indigènes*, especially at a time of rising national sentiment among them. The Islam of the colonial natives served to explain away the wretchedness of their lives and diverted attention from the institutionalized discriminatory practices of those who benefited from colonialism. The conversion of the native to Christianity or republican *laïcité* was both longed for and impossible. Whether Islam became an unshakable atavism, an obstacle, or a construction site, it maintained the focus on the native, not colonial domination, reinforcing the confusion of cause and effect at the heart of colonial Islam's contribution to historiography.

Ultimately, Brunschvig's Islam prevented him from taking stock of the impact that Ibn Khaldūn had had on the historians' conception of the medieval Maghrib. If anything, a focus on Islam reinforced the notion that the conquests of the seventh century were to be understood in terms of the Islamization and Arabization of preexisting Berbers. Thanks to Ibn Khaldūn, the problem of the evidence gap during the critical decades of Berberization found a solution—the contribution of the notion of race and the anachronistic habit of projecting Berbers into the ancient past could not be underestimated. Brunschvig may have studied the Ḥafṣid period (1229–1574); his intellectual orientation kept him from conceiving of Khaldunization and Berberization and, worse, made him give fundamental Khaldunian ideas the guise of neutrality. Berberization continued to go unnoticed.

Beyond Orientalist Hermeticism

Émile-Félix Gautier (1864–1940) was a geographer, a colonial administrator, an explorer, an independent thinker, and a popularizer. Decried for his hurried theories and broad strokes by some, for his derogatory statements about the natives by others, Gautier was an outsider whose conception of geography as a link between history and geology reinvigorated historical research.[28] While specialists have refuted most of Gautier's hypotheses about the medieval Maghrib, their criticisms did not come with a critique of Khaldunization of the field and its questions.[29]

Framing his analysis of the conquests of the seventh century and the migrations of the eleventh in terms of differences and similarities in mode of life between conquerors and natives, Gautier forced a reinterpretation of literary sources and a reassessment of their perspectives. If this were not enough of a contribution, he also questioned the organization of academic disciplines and the lack of communication between them, and had rather negative, if generally correct, views about Orientalists: "Oriental Studies have a hermetic character. They operate in a vacuum, outside of public attention. If, however, a non-specialist or a semi-specialist were to venture into that field, he is not as lost as he would have been half a century ago. Among the Arab writers, who inform us on the Maghreb, many, today, have been translated."[30] Aware of the problems that can arise from a reliance on translations, Gautier thought that they are outweighed by the importance of reading original texts; besides, he quipped, one could always ask an Arabist if more precision were needed. Perhaps indecorous and even crude, his attitude pointed out the real chasm that had developed between those who studied North Africa before the Arabs (and their sources) and Orientalists. In distinctive Gautier style, he revealed the pitfalls of academic specialization in a comment on the presumed discontinuities between ancient and medieval periods, Classicists and Orientalists:

> The country has not changed, it is always there for our eyes to see, and it begins to be well known. The geography of the Maghreb has progressed much more than its history. Facts, which seem incoherent when one insists on considering them in isolation, will appear, I believe, logically connected when placed in their frame. Like the country, man has not changed. One of the main sources of obscurity is probably that his history is divided into two separate sections. It is obvious that Classical Studies and Oriental Studies do not communicate. The real man, however, the one who lived, the Berber who changed over the ages, crossed those impermeable borders. He took into the new period the full weight of his actions in the previous period. Life did not begin anew, it continued.[31]

Gautier thought that the original "Arab invasion" of the seventh century did not change the Maghrib, but that the eleventh-century one did, completely transforming livelihoods with effects that lasted all the way to the modern period. His project was to examine the dark centuries between these two moments in which documentation was sparse—and the influence of the Orientalists easier to keep in check.

> There is a great difficulty. It is that these glorious centuries [in which the Maghreb conquered Spain, Sicily, and Egypt] are at the

> same time dark centuries. Of all Maghribī history, it is the least well known period and the most difficult to know; a black hole of intractable opacity. Contemporary documents are completely absent. Conquering Islam did not care to narrate itself. The Arab (*l'Arabe*) was a barbarian, unconcerned about history. Intellectual curiosity in the Islamic world only emerges late, with the 'Abbāsids, when the decadence of the Arab element allowed the re-flowering of the seeds of the old Persian and Levantine civilizations, buried under the rubble of the conquest.[32]

Imagining the Maghrib as a "land of salt," focusing on nomads and settled agriculturalists, and subscribing to racialist ideas, Gautier could not possibly conceive of the emergence of the Berbers in Arabic sources. After all, the existence of the Berbers as a race preceded the Arab conquests by thousands of years:

> What are the Berbers, from a biological point of view, if not white Mediterranean men, very close to the others?[33]
>
> To explain the barbarism of the Maghreb, it does not seem necessary to use the hypothesis of original racial inferiority. That said, however, it is clear that *thousands of years* of barbarism could not but shape the race.[34]

Yet, and in spite of the space his legitimate criticisms of Orientalism opened up, his belief that the dark centuries were a total loss to historians, combined with his adaptation of Khaldunian terms, had a negative effect on the possibility of historicizing the emergence of the Berbers. As a result, his work further consolidated colonial Ibn Khaldūn's status as order giver, sense maker and chief agent of dehistoricizing.

Berbers and Early Nationalism

In 1931, Charles-André Julien (1891–1991) published a textbook that synthesized recent scholarship and presented it in a new, anticolonial, garb.[35] Julien's sympathy for the natives was noted. A reviewer commented that he tended to "always defend the Berber people against conquerors that victimized it over the centuries: Carthaginians, Romans, Vandals, Byzantines, Arabs, Turks, and French."[36]

With Julien, the representation of the Berbers as victims of a succession of foreign conquerors took center stage, his left-wing political views making him palatable to native intellectuals, and, later, to postcolonial historians who could not or would rather not read Arabic sources.[37] Instead of Berbérie, Julien chose North Africa, a category that had become the most widely used to describe French North Africa, that is, Tunisia, Algeria, and Morocco.[38] Interestingly, Julien thought that Berbérie was the best name to give North Africa because "if there are Berbers outside of its limits, its population is almost exclusively formed of Berbers."[39] Naturally, for him there were Berbers in pre-Islamic North Africa.

Relying on historical studies, Julien offered a synthesis of North African history that recapitulated Khaldunian terms: struggles between Bedouins and urbanites, cycles of dynasties, the effort to maintain civilization, Arab and Berber dynastic periodization, and even the impact of the natural environment on the culture. All this was in Ibn Khaldūn, and all of it was in the studies that Julien built on, criticized, and reframed.[40] However, and in spite of his popularity among later historians, Julien's contribution remains his rejection of the notion that the Berber lacked the ability to form a unified Pan-Berber state, his insistence that Berber resistance was constant, and that Berber attempts to constitute a unified political entity were defeated.[41] The Berbers' lack of political unity did not open up new lines of inquiry about the early act of naming them. In any case, it is worth insisting here that Julien's main contribution was to offer a synthesis of colonial knowledge that appealed to critics of colonialism, even if his ability to challenge that knowledge was limited.

Remarkably, Julien and other French-language "lefty" historians tended to ignore contemporary historiographic developments in Arabic. At the same time, historians writing in Arabic demonstrated an awareness of scholarship in French, often responding to particular claims, assumptions, and conclusions made in it. It is also true, however, that they did not imagine the Berbers in any way that challenged Berberization in either its Arabic or its French formulations. Here again, the political context illuminates certain choices, like the name of North African Star (*Étoile Nord-Africaine*), given to the nationalist organization created in 1926 as a way of organizing North African workers in France and on the African continent. In general, however, the political discourse did not invent ways of conceiving of North Africa or the

Berbers that veered too far off those articulated by academics. Although political mobilization did bring about change, it did so in terms that paralleled French colonial knowledge, even if it ran in an opposite direction.

It is difficult to convey the sense of superiority that French-language medievalists had toward their Arabic-language counterparts. In fact, so wide was the distance between them that they would never have thought of them as colleagues; and for all practical purposes, they were not. *Indigènes* who wrote about the medieval Maghrib attended different educational institutions, were part of distinct scholarly conversations, and published in their own magazines and newspapers. Most importantly, they were not professional historians, did not obtain regular academic positions in the colonial university system, and worked as translators, schoolteachers, and other such secondary positions. They were not even on the margins of colonial academic circles, as were the very few francophone natives who held "native" positions.

In 1928, Mubārak al-Mīlī (1889–1945) published the first volume of his *History of Algeria in Ancient and Modern Times* (*Tārīkh al-jazā'ir fī al-qadīm wa al-ḥadīth*), an important statement of the historical pedigree of Algeria and Algerians and, by extension, all North Africans.[42] Educated at the prestigious Zaytūna University in Tunis, in 1931, al-Mīlī was one of the founding members of the Association of Algerian Muslim 'Ulamā' (*jam'iyat al-'ulamā' al-muslimīn al-jazā'iriyīn*). He pursued his work of consciousness raising and cultural renaissance teaching *indigènes* youths. Al-Mīlī did not know French and relied on Aḥmad Tawfīq al-Madanī and 'Amr Dhīna to translate relevant sections from "modern" historical studies into Arabic. Writing a "modern" history in Arabic was a goal of his, a project grounded in an analysis of existing scholarship: "There is nothing more arduous for the Arab writer than writing history in the modern manner. There is no more obscure history for the Arab reader than the history of Algeria. There are no more distorted books than Arabic books written about it. And given the importance of Ibn Khaldūn's history, it enjoyed so much distortion that it is difficult for the reader to trust what is in it about the great intellectuals (*a'lām*) and cities."[43] The concept of "distortion" (*taḥrīf*) had a long and respectable pedigree, and al-Mīlī evoked it here as a negative effect of colonial rule, though mostly by implication. Having colonial knowledge in mind, it is unsurprising, if a bit repetitive at this point, to find a reference to Ibn Khaldūn. As he did not read French, al-Mīlī grumbled about the distortions within Arabic-language scholarship, a sentiment that fits his broader critique of colonial culture and its effects on natives.

Al-Mīlī begins his history with a thorough, if not exhaustive, review of Berber origin theories, distinguishing between those that rely on narrative sources, ancient and medieval, and those based on the parameters considered by French scholars: language, physical characteristics (*khalaqa*), and production techniques.[44] Offering criticisms and raising objections to many of these theories, al-Mīlī's conclusion ends up combining both approaches, selecting a version that, in retrospect, fits his nationalist conception of Algeria, its people, and their past:

> The Berbers are a nation (*umma*) with a unity of race (*waḥda jinsiya*) like other nations whose cohesion and greatness (*'aṣabiyatuhā wa 'aẓamatuhā*) history has recorded. Their homeland was in Syria (al-Shām) before they migrated to Libya. To this latter land, many groups from other nations migrated. There was a great deal of mixing between the inhabitants in the country under the umbrella of Berberness (*al-barbariya*). That is how the Berber nation acquired national unity, formed by varied and distinct elements in a Berber mold (*qālib barbarī*). The first Berber element is not the original inhabitant of Libya because there was a nation that preceded the Berber in the country. Ibn Khaldūn expressed this idea in Book Three of his history by calling the Berbers "the second nation (*umma*) among the people of the Maghrib."[45]

This definition and an appeal to Ibn Khaldūn allow al-Mīlī to call into question a pillar of colonial knowledge: the idea that the Berbers were the original inhabitants of North Africa. Al-Mīlī then goes on to discuss the great Berber tribes, Berber life, social organization, language, and beliefs before getting to the properly historical part. Interestingly, he casts the relations between the Carthaginians and the Berbers in a very positive light, which he attributes to their common eastern origins.[46] In contrast, the Roman "Europeans" used deceit to convince the Berbers to fight against Carthage, but then when it became apparent that the Romans wanted to rule the Berbers, they resisted.[47] Interestingly, his focus on great states and civilizations tends to confer on his narrative an eastern Maghrib focus—a recognized bias in the geographic distribution of the sources.

In this anachronistic national history of Algeria, neighboring regions appear as a means of contextualizing. So do the Berbers, who often end up being defined negatively as non-Romans living in Algeria, non-Vandals, and so on. But undeniably, there were Berbers in ancient times, and thus al-Mīlī imagines them predating the Arab and Muslim conquests (*ghazw al-ʿarab, al-fatḥ*). After the conquests, there was a great deal of mixing (*ikhtilāṭ, muṣāhara*) between Arab and Berber tribes, although Arabs maintained control of the government (*al-imāra*) "because of their experience in international affairs and because the Berbers had a tradition of disorder and were new to order. Even so, the Arabs confirmed some Berber leaders in their positions."[48]

In spite of his partially racialist definition of the Berbers, al-Mīlī makes no use of race in his narration. Instead, Ibn Khaldūn's claim of the closeness of lifestyles and livelihoods between Arabs and Berbers allows him to do away with the notion of intrinsic racial differences and opposition. Berber rebellion against Arab rule is explained, as in most medieval sources, by the unjust treatment that Berbers received from individual Arab governors.

Focusing on dynasties that ruled over Algeria or parts of it, al-Mīlī organizes the medieval period in terms of a succession of dynasties, including, after the eleventh, Berber dynasties. There is nothing in his presentation that separates it from the Khaldunian model, his focus on Algerian tribes falling well within its parameters. However, and unlike most French-language historians, al-Mīlī rejects Ibn Khaldūn's statement about the Banu Hilāl's destruction of the country, arguing that Ṣanhāja's failed politics toward the Arabs was behind much of the unrest, especially as the Ṣanhāja cousins (Zīrids and Ḥammādids) fought mercilessly to rule the country.[49]

Instead of a dichotomy between Arabs and Berbers, a product of French colonial knowledge, al-Mīlī emphasized the positive aspects of both, their collaboration, and their fraternity in Islam, the religion of true freedom and noble elevation (or progress).[50] All Algerians shared the Berber spirit of resistance, demonstrated repeatedly from ancient times to more recent ones. Even those who resisted the Arab conquests, like the Berber queen al-Kāhina, were national heroes. Rejecting the interpretations of colonial scholars like Gautier, whom he saw as smearing both Arabs and Berbers, al-Mīlī insisted on the great qualities of both: "Anyone who looks at history with truthful eyes will see that [al-Kāhina] was a great example of the history of woman and [will appreciate her for her] capable organizing, fierce fighting, steadfast defending of the country, and for standing for principle."[51] Al-Kāhina was not the only Algerian woman who exhibited great qualities; al-Mīlī's history is interspersed with their names, Arabs and Berbers. Even if it relies on colonial conceptions such as race, al-Mīlī's nationalist rapprochement in which Islam plays an important role was a strong statement against the colonial framing of Arabs and Berbers. His selective appropriation of colonial historiography allowed him to articulate an alternative vision of the medieval period, one, however, that remained resolutely Khaldunian.

The imprint of colonial knowledge is even more clearly visible in the work of ʿAbd al-Raḥmān al-Jīlālī (1908–2010), who did not think that reversing colonial prejudices was an exercise in subtlety. In his *General History of Algeria*, al-Jīlālī (1908–2010) often used the very same facts found in colonial studies to make the opposite point. For instance, in those instances when European merchants purchased a number of commodities from the Maghrib, he underlined their great quality, and noted examples of Europeans acquiring crafts and sciences (medicine, algebra, etc.) from the central Maghrib (i.e., Algeria).[52] Clearly, he wanted to establish that the light of civilization once flowed from the Maghrib to Europe, something colonial scholars acknowledged but did not emphasize. However, as he did so, he accepted the topos of Islamic decline, which validated his belief in revival and reform (*nahḍa*).

The appearance of modern racial categories in al-Jilālī's work, even more pronounced than in al-Mīlī's, sheds light on the dominant discourse at the time. In al-Jilālī's version, the Maghrib is the original home of the white race (*al-mahd al-awwal lil-jins al-abyaḍ*), and the prehistoric inhabitants of northern Africa belonged to the white race (*min sulālat al-jins al-abyaḍ*), which first founded civilization—again, long before the French (or westerners) had any civilization.[53] Racialist criteria allow him to distinguish Algerian Berbers from other Berbers.[54] At the same time, and in other passages, al-Jīlālī tends to articulate his ideas in less racialist terms: "In any case, whoever examines the history of the Berbers will see that they are a great nation (*umma ʿaẓīma*) with its own civilization and urbanity (*ḥaḍāratuhā wa madaniyatuhā*)."[55] Without the mediation of translation, al-Jīlālī accessed Ibn Khaldūn's ideas about urban civilization simply and naturally, especially that Arab intellectuals had made civilization a common modern word among the educated. But al-Jīlālī went further than that. In each chapter, he included a section on culture and civilization (*al-thaqāfa wa al-ḥaḍāra wa al-ʿumrān*). Armed with Ibn Khaldūn's framework, he cataloged notable historical developments and notable individuals, including women.[56] In so doing, he created a pantheon of hitherto little-known names of brilliant national minds and heroes. The French may have their heroes, but Algerians have theirs too.

As for the Muslim conquests, it was clear to him that Arabs may have led them, but they were not about imposing Arab rule:

> These conquering Arabs were not through these conquests trying to serve a race or a prophet of a specific people or a particular country they wanted to enrich. [They did not believe that they served a] country's interests above those of all others and that they were born to be rulers and that you were only born to be ruled by them. They did not leave their country to establish an Arab Empire from which they would benefit. They did not do it to replace the rule of the Romans and Persians with that of the Arabs but instead they rose up to lead people away from the worship of all types of idols to the worship of the one God.[57]

Just like al-Mīlī, al-Jīlālī did not think that a struggle between Arabs and Berbers was central to the medieval history of Algeria. Although he repeated the anecdote about the reasons for the migration of the Banū Hilāl and their defeat of the Ṣanhāja, he did so in a few sentences, preferring to focus on their political influence and their settlement in the central Maghrib.[58]

Decolonizing History?

When the Algerian philosopher, historian, and anticolonial activist Mohamed Chérif Sahli published *Décoloniser l'histoire* in 1965, the seamlessness of colonial historical knowledge was irretrievably shattered.[59] Pointing to fundamental assumptions and modes of apprehending the natives and their past, Sahli exposed the structure that kept history the hostage of colonial domination. Written in the style of the time, the book puts on the same plane colonialists and anticolonial sympathizers. As different as they were, Charles-André Julien, Georges Marçais, Stéphane Gsell, and Émile-Félix Gautier all contributed to the colonization of history, generous quotations from their work leaving no doubt about the extent of the damage and the seriousness of the challenge.[60] In Sahli's eyes, the hold that this colonial scaffolding had was such that a Copernican revolution was necessary. Importantly, he did not call for throwing colonial knowledge into the trash bin of history, or some such formulation: "Should one clear the table of all their works to imagine a history of Algeria on new bases? That would be unjust. These works, while flawed by their more or less pro-colonial postulates and their methods, constitute contestable constructions, but ones in which can be found valuable and useful elements."[61] What those elements were is difficult to judge solely based on his critique, although his appreciation of critical aspects of the Annales school offers a few clues. Moreover, since Sahli did not believe that the newly independent Maghribīs would be able to produce their own histories for at least a while, given the shortage of trained historians among them and the priorities of their societies, he outlined a program of intellectual collaboration to bring about change.[62] Whatever form it took, this change had to begin with an acknowledgment of those determinisms that had shaped and continued to shape historical research. Concretely, Sahli focused on the geographic, racial, and sociological determinisms that undermined historicity and disfigured history. He also pointed to the relation between "ideological conventions" and the colonial regime, the "myth of assimilation" being a recent colonial avatar.[63]

Interestingly, Sahli was impatient with the colonial historians' predilection for Ibn Khaldūn, even calling into question Ibn Khaldūn's views on the Banū Hilāl invasion.[64] Although Sahli was not the first to express misgivings about received wisdom, he tied the problem to Ibn Khaldūn and his reception among modern historians.[65] Probably because he was not a medievalist, Sahli did not appreciate the extent of the Khaldunization of the field. Even if he had, it is not clear, however, that medievalists would have paid attention. On the contrary, medievalists ignored Sahli, his critique, and his ideas about a Copernican revolution. As he did not and could not produce an example of what the new history would look like, Sahli was an easy target for learned head shaking and shoulder shrugging.

But change was in the air—at least as an idea. Sahli was not alone, and this became clear with the lively debate around the effects of the migration of the Banū Hilāl and Banū Sulaym. The medieval Maghrib, which had been the purview of positivists, received a strong dose of critique. In *L'histoire du Maghreb: Un essai de synthèse* (1970), Abdallah Laroui (b. 1933) reexamined colonial historiography, identifying problematic aspects of its assumptions, modes of interpretation, and conclusions. Unlike Sahli, he then rewrote the entire history of the Maghrib, or at least a sketch of it, from the ancient period to the modern, utilizing colonial historical scholarship and avoiding what he saw as its pitfalls.

Finding in materialist conceptions of history a way of articulating a vision of the historical past that departed from established frameworks, Laroui proposed a new periodization that centered not on the specificities of the archive or the succession of foreign conquerors and settlers but on an analysis of the relations between historical process and its representations: "It will also be necessary to make sure that the periods we distinguish are indeed periods, in the sense that they enable us to differentiate successive levels of economic and social development, of political organization, culture and psychology."[66] Laroui brought his methodological awareness to bear on Ibn Khaldūn and his ideas. His attempt to historicize Ibn Khaldūn's model, even if grounded in an understanding of History or the "course of history" rather than the historical context and its sources, signals the possibility of returning Ibn Khaldūn to his time. In spite of the scholarship it relied on, which was Khaldunian, Laroui's proposed periodization was not.

Taking a critical stance and distancing himself from Ibn Khaldūn, Laroui even finds fault with Ibn Khaldūn the historian:

> Ibn Khaldūn makes no attempt to explain history before the eleventh century, except by modeling the Zanāta of the first period on those of the second. And he offers no perspective on the future. Nowhere does he say that tribal structure and nomadism go hand in hand and that consequently the Hilālī nomads might resume on their own account the earlier efforts of the Berbers. He seems to have thought that the Arab race had long been exhausted and that consequently the weakening of the Berbers meant the end of all civilization, that there was no possibility of a renewal from within, and that the history of the Maghrib was at an end. Thus his work, far from being a rational interpretation of history, is a philosophy of history arising from an abstract analysis of a historical sequence.[67]

Were it not for his use of de Slane's translation, it might have been surprising to see the word "race" in Laroui's work, even if only as an analytically inert fossil.[68] Although he tended to fault modern historians for the use they made of Ibn Khaldūn, Laroui believes that a better contextualization of the work opens new and better prospects for a reevaluation of not just the medieval period but the entire history of the Maghrib:

> Perhaps the time has come to place the problems outside the Khaldunian framework, though at present there is little hope of

> arriving at solutions. Taking the general decadence as a working hypothesis, we can use Ibn Khaldūn's reflections as indications of the problems confronting Maghribi society at the time: essentially those of political organization and the army.[69]
>
> Despite his acute analysis of the situation, [Ibn Khaldūn] takes no account of the causes that produced it. His vision is static rather than genetic. Unless this is recognized, we cannot hope to understand the history of the Maghrib.[70]

In spite of the correctness of his insight, Laroui did not convince medievalists; the periodization he proposed and his very noticeable preference for "Maghribī" instead of Arab/Berber remains largely his own, though one can find echoes of some of his ideas in subsequent scholarship. In fact, taking the critique that Sahli, Laroui, and others like Hichem Djaït leveled against colonial knowledge as their own, medievalists moved toward a nationalization of medieval history that further lionized Ibn Khaldūn.[71] As it happens, continuities in personnel and institutional organization, pressing pedagogical needs, and political expediency prolonged the usefulness of the old scholarship and maintained its authority long after the sound of the first critical salvos of anticolonial critique had faded. Among Berber nationalists, those who could have brought their criticisms of official nationalist ideologies to bear on the medieval period did not—at least not beyond reinstating the discourse on the victimization of the Berbers.[72] Those whose rejection of Arabs and Arabic was most pronounced could not even read the sources in the original, continuing to rely on colonial French translations. Ultimately, postcolonial readjustments did not bring about a critique of Khaldunism, let alone Berberization.[73]

Until recently, the few historical studies conducted in the countries of the Maghrib did not confront the ambient Khaldunism directly. While national histories tended to retain the dynastic periodization and the discourse on Berber autochthones, they embraced the path of least antagonism between Arabs and Berbers and the historic fusion of the two to make the modern nations. If some Berber nationalists were critical of this move, their criticisms of the Berber policies of the nation-states, mostly Morocco and Algeria, did not elicit serious studies of the medieval period. At the same time, the rejection of the word Berber, a foreign name, kept alive the potential for the identification of Berberization as a process. Likewise, the tumultuous period of questioning "big models" did not produce great French historians of the medieval Maghrib. In the 1980s, scholarship began to emerge in France that combines an awareness of the theoretical and ideological stakes with a remarkable pragmaticism and a desire for more precision in characterizing social relations, intellectual movements, and the functioning of various institutions.[74] More recently, and in collaboration with historians of Spain and the Mediterranean, a number of French medievalists have begun to reevaluate both medieval representations and their own analytical categories. At the same time, it is also true that in view of the magnitude of the challenge, specialists of the medieval Maghrib are very few and represent a relatively small fraction of all Maghribists.

A Berber Encyclopedia

In 1984, Gabriel Camps (1927–2002) founded the *Encyclopédie Berbère*, a broad and ongoing project that has greatly contributed to the Berberization of the past. One of the most prominent Berberologists of the twentieth century, Camps set the terms of his project by responding to those who had poorly served the Berber cause—something the encyclopedia intends to remedy:

> The earliest references to populations that, since the Arab conquest, we call Berbers, go back to ancient Egypt.
>
> In fact, there is today no Berber language, in the sense that it would reflect a community aware of its unity, no Berber people, and even less so a Berber race. About these negative findings all specialists are in agreement . . . and yet, the Berbers do exist.
>
> [When it comes to Berber origins,] logically, we must give precedence to anthropology. But [anthropology] does not allow us today to delineate any "Berber" originality in the population of the southern Mediterranean. What allows us today to mention Berber groups in northwest Africa is [evidence] of another character, cultural rather than physical. Among these cultural elements, language remains the principal. We will thus examine successively the facts of anthropology and those of linguistics.[75]

Anachronistic, ideological, and a little too confident, Camps' statements exemplify the rhetoric of many of the entries in the encyclopedia. While the "and yet, they exist" seems to refer to Berbers, it actually points to the habits of francophone Berberists like Camps whose focus on prehistoric and ancient times has continued the practice of searching for origins in anthropology and linguistics—and biology—but not history. More than anything, the encyclopedia, whose entries on the medieval period stand out for their uneven familiarity with the sources, demonstrates the significance of the medieval Arabic archive to the identification and analysis of Berberization. While a scholarly assessment may again deliver negative findings, it should be clear that for as long as the conditions enable it, the encyclopedia does and will continue to exist.

From Berber to Amazigh?

In the early 1950s, a few specialists proposed to replace "Berber" with "Amazigh," the name some people in northern Morocco had. "Amazigh" was preferable because it was more authentically indigenous, in the sense that there were references in ancient (i.e., pre-Arabic) texts to a host of groups with that name or at least with names that sound like it (Mazices, Maxyes, Mazaces, Mazikes, etc.). Although it took a while for it to become widely accepted, the introduction of "Amazigh" was the culmination of a colonial idea that had simmered for a while in the minds of colonels, ethnographers, linguists, Orientalists, and missionaries. Nationalists put a native face on it.[76]

"Amazigh" could not fully conceal its colonial birthmark, however. Its rejection of Arab imperialism of centuries past, its search for an authentic indigenous category, and its reliance on the fruits of colonial historiography, epigraphy, and linguistics to do so are all telltale signs. Calling for name change could have led to the realization of the historicity of all names and from there to the historicity of Berberization.[77] It did not. Instead, the realities of Spanish and French colonial presence in Morocco fueled an autonomist project in the North (Rif) and focused the attention of the proponents of "Amazigh." They wanted to make a point in a specific context, and mobilized colonial indigeneity to perform the eviction of Arabness, a vital component of Maghribī nationalisms and of ʿAlawī royalist ideology. That was its most serious effect: fracturing native resistance to European colonialism. "Amazigh" (indigeneity) was the parting gift of a dying colonialism to the frail nationalisms it had never accepted. Pulling the rug from under "Algeria" and "Morocco," which as the *colons* repeated were new and artificial, "Amazigh" dealt a blow to anticolonial nationalism.

Until recently, medievalists continued to refer to Berbers. As their sources do too, this is reasonable. However, with the publication of a serious synthesis of the history of Morocco in 2011, "Amazigh" has made its entrance into medieval historiography as a demonym that replaces the derogatory "Berber," which appears seldom, in quotation marks, or preceded by "so-called."[78] In spite of these changes, the Amazigh are the Berbers. Instead of the Berbers being native indigenous autochthones, the Amazigh are. Their presence predates the Arab conquest, the Zanāta, Ṣanhāja, and others were Amazigh, and so the urban dynasties that ruled over the Maghrib were Amazigh, even if the Arabic sources call them Berber:

> For certain texts, Christianity may have existed [in antiquity] in Aghmāt and Nefīs (Nfis) and elsewhere inland. Likewise, there were, here and there, judaized Amazighs, whereas the inhabitants of the Near Souss who belong to the Tamesna tribes, may have remained pagan, according to some sources, and did not embrace any revealed religion before the coming of Islam.[79]
>
> Given the damages engendered in the course of this long struggle, both Arabs and Amazighs weakened. In these circumstances, the Byzantines tried to recover the supremacy they had had in Ifrīqiyā.[80]

This innovation apart, the *Histoire du Maroc* does not present a fundamental departure from nationalist ways of conceiving the Berbers or the history of the Maghrib. Perhaps, the multiple references to medieval "Morocco" are a clear-enough signal of the function of this official history.[81] In other words, the many anachronisms one finds alongside it are hardly accidental. However, it is precisely because an effect of Berberization is to evacuate historicity that this move is worthy of serious attention, although it is difficult today to predict the success this particular version will have among medievalists.[82]

Ultimately, "Amazigh" is just a calque of "Berber." The change of categories has had no bearing on linguistic analysis, archaeological finds, or computational genomics—although it is critical to the politicization of the knowledge these disciplines produce. The switch was, however, full of significance: it naturalized the inscription of (colonial) indigeneity into history and foreclosed the historicizing of the category Berber, which it transformed into a mere epithet, an insult, and the reminder of an unforgivable injury. In any case, if it was already difficult to imagine Berberization, when Maghribī historians began to replace Berber with Amazigh, it became almost impossible. While the category has an ancient pedigree, its historical function is new. It sets up a new mediation, an anachronistic one at that, which only misdirects historians and directs contemporary politics. It extends the shelf life of old ideologies and gives them pride of place in the prevailing modes of organizing the world. Since Amazigh delivers politically, for activists and governments (Maghribī and not), it is here to stay for now. However, because the category does not appear in the sources, medievalists will have no difficulty avoiding it, although . . .

Making Room for Historicity in History

Recognizing the historical specificity of the modern act of producing ancient and prehistoric "indigenous" Berbers draws attention to its implication in ideology—nothing less and not much more.[83] Likewise, the analysis of the medieval Maghrib as a field shows it to be too easily swayed by anachronisms created by classicists, archaeologists, and ethnographers. Rather than build on their awareness of the category's medieval origins, and develop a systematic rejection of anachronism, medievalists have tended to maintain the status quo. More than their individual motivations, however, their choices invite us to ponder the place that the ancient period occupied in the operations of the colonial civilizing mission, notably its function as a site for the production of a vision of North Africa closer to the West than to the Orient and its Islam. One needs only to compare the development of the archaeology of the ancient period to medieval archaeology to get a sense of this—a visit to colonial museums would be equally illustrative.

The instrumentalization of history has had deleterious effects on the task of historicizing. It has made a historical field a little too hospitable to ideology. This is particularly odd because these very medievalists have been generally sensitive to the ideological inclinations of medieval authors and their narratives. Of course, it is easier to declare Almohadism an ideology than to question one's subscription to racial, nationalist, or liberal ideology. For one thing, medievalists did not study the present with as much seriousness as they did the past. When it comes to their assessment of the present, medievalists have tended to be educated but no less partisan. The fact that Georges Marçais went along with Pétain can be only a first step in a serious analysis of the interplay between modern political ideologies and the production of a mutilated medieval past.

Physicians heal, engineers build. Historians historicize.

Conclusion

This book has sought to establish Berberization as an object of historical study. That was its overriding and primary goal. Although it has made other arguments along the way, and even called into question prevailing explanations and interpretations, it has done so mostly to identify those intellectual habits and inclinations that have been obstacles to historicizing. Separately, the character of the evidence, the difference between the chronology of sources and that of events, and the multiplicity of threads, historical and historiographic, all have made demands on presentation. Yet, even if they limited the scope of the book's arguments, they have done little to change its thesis: the invention of the Berbers is and has always been historical.

Everyone has known that there were no Berbers in northwest Africa before the Arabs, and everyone has known that projecting them back into the ancient past violates good historical sense. At the same time, too many have known these things and then envisaged among other things the Islamization of preexisting Berbers. In part, this explains the logical inconsistencies found in the field, which, as everyone also knows, are detrimental to the scholarly enterprise. In a sense, *Inventing the Berbers* has attempted to persuade historians of the soundness of their core mission. It has preached to the choir. And while it has made no secret of its marked preference for historicizing, this study has also documented the many hurdles that have stood in the way of the realization of the historian's charge. In this regard, the notion of Berberization presents a concrete way of overcoming this predicament through a return to the sources.

Identifying Berberization begins by recognizing that it has hidden in plain sight for a long time. Rather than heaping blame on those who fell for its charms, an altogether unproductive proposition, the book has offered an examination of the circumstances that illuminate their choices. Here, it highlighted the role of ideology in facilitating the occultation of the relation between the social conditions in which our medieval sources' authors lived and their contribution to Berberization. Insisting on this relation allows us to ground successive ideologies and thus to better gauge their operations. In the modern period, the analysis of various impediments to the manifestation of historical good sense has evinced the importance of race, religion, and nationalism. Under these ideological conditions, and the social inequalities they endorsed, the institution of the Islamization and Arabization of Berbers as dominant frameworks of historical inquiry appeared to be sensible. In this vein, the notion of Berberization allows us to reclaim good historical sense by refining and restating the question in a way that corresponds more closely to the historical record and to a sober understanding of history. The fact that doing so also sidesteps logical hazards inherent in current interpretative schemes is a bonus this book shares with all historicizing studies.

Berberization has been at work for centuries. Inevitably, it has been entangled in the myriad ideological processes that have accompanied the imposition of dynastic, colonial, and democratic rule both in the Maghrib and beyond it. The analysis of multiple sites of Berberization has shown this to be true. In the process of identifying some of these sites, it became clear that Ibn Khaldūn's work has played a critical function in mediating medieval and modern forms of Berberization. Naturally, this aspect has required special attention. Ultimately, however, it is clear that the Khaldunization of the field has enabled an unreasonable surrender to ideology. This requires further exploration. If the work of Berberization today seems to establish an indigeneity test on all things related to the Maghrib, it too draws attention to those sites that specialize in making it so.

A History of Berberization

In Part I, the main challenge was to reclaim the question of Berber origins for a historical perspective. Chapter 1 focused on the chronology of usage as it appears in the earliest extant Arabic sources. It documented the multiplicity of meanings and connected them to specific practices and institutions. Chapter 2 extended the logic to a multiplicity of sites of Berberization, from al-Andalus to Egypt, highlighting the role of political ideologies in the process of inventing the Berbers. In Part II, the focus was on the idea that medieval authors thought of the Berbers as a people (Chapter 3) and of the Maghrib as their exclusive homeland (Chapter 4). The examination of pertinent texts showed that instead of a unified coherent perspective, they present us with a multiplicity of largely unsystematic understandings, although some authors attempted to impose consistency. Doing so helped set Ibn Khaldūn's own ideas in relation to those developments that had left an imprint on them. It also laid the ground for an exploration of the Khaldunization of the terms of knowledge about the Maghrib in the modern period (Part III). Limiting themselves to the workings of Berberization in colonial Algeria, Chapters 5 and 6 demonstrate the centrality of the French translation of Ibn Khaldūn and explain why historians failed to see Berberization at work in medieval sources and in modern studies.

Because this book has focused primarily on establishing Berberization as an object of historical analysis, it has not drawn out the possible implications of its arguments. This is a shortcoming it accepts willingly, however, not only because of the disruption that pursuing other threads would certainly have caused, but, more importantly, because the implications are so many and in some cases so thorny that no single historian can address them with the degree of fluency and evenhandedness they deserve. A few related issues do stand out, however, and deserve to be acknowledged, if only to give a sense of what remains to be done.

Berberization After Colonialism

The demise of colonial rule and the mass departure of settlers from Algeria loosened the grip of colonial culture on the natives. To the wretched of the earth, anticolonial nationalists had delivered an end to the rule of "separate and unequal" and promoted them from natives (*indigènes*) to full citizens. They rushed to the cities, occupied abandoned farms and houses, and uprooted the outward signs of a system that had diminished them and their ancestors before them. In its brief duration and in its violence, the postvictory outburst contrasts with the process of making a new culture for the new political realities. Imbedded in the very fabric of social life, in the design of houses, towns, roads, schools, hospitals, farms, and factories, colonialism did not wither quickly, evenly, or silently. Neither did the culture that had blossomed under it. Nevertheless, irrespective of the choices nationalist leaders made or the challenges that confronted their plans to uplift their people, the end of colonial rule was an earth-shattering event.

Old habits die hard, and new ones take time to set in; and much stood in the way of the simple replacement of old with new that many fantasized. The end of colonial rule in the Maghrib (1956–62) coincided with the Cold War, a conflict on a world scale that weighed heavily on the prospects of the newly independent nations. For the Algerian leadership and later for Libyans too, socialism held the greatest appeal, whereas Moroccans and Tunisians opted for the other camp. In the first three decades after independence, Algeria experienced a large-scale emigration of European settlers (*pieds-noirs*), land reforms, a mass education drive, and intensive industrialization, which made the country's social structure look markedly different from that of neighboring Morocco. Three decades after independence, moreover, the Soviet Union collapsed, unleashing a wave of structural adjustment plans that exposed the postcolonial government to serious social upheavals. The struggle against "McJihadis"—as one scholar called armed groups with origins in anti-Soviet operations in Afghanistan—accompanied a large wave of privatizations in Algeria.[1] The drop in oil and gas prices gave proponents of neoliberal privatization the opportunity to weaken the already inefficient and bureaucratized social programs. In today's Maghrib of Berbers, in consequence, there are many similarities but also critical differences within and between countries, many of these differences resulting from decisions made outside the region. This recent history has naturally inflected the form and content of Berberization.

In a related register, the long history of Maghribīs in Europe and that of their European, mainly French, children, have contributed to Berberization in multiple ways. Whether transplanted Maghribīs echoed colonial motifs, reshaped them, or generated novel expressions, they did so in relation to the social conditions in which they lived. Although conditions prevailing among European Maghribīs differed markedly from those that prevailed in either the colonial or independent Maghrib, they were nonetheless tied to them in significant ways. For example, the colonial policy of recruiting Berbers from Kabylie to work in the mines and factories of France produced French-educated second-class citizens who then used wage differences between French and Algerian workers to acquire the symbols of social success, especially relative to "the Arabs."[2] Such symbols included labor organizing and politics, which were not as developed in less-industrialized Algeria. The investment in choice kernels of colonial ideology cast in racial and religious terms what are actually social and economic processes, an ideological sleight of hand that has produced tangible and lasting political consequences. The refitting of the colonial idea of a progressive civilized secular Berber victimized by reactionary religious Arabs has made those consequences palpable in the postcolonial period—especially in relation to the activities of McJihadism. Not all migrations were the same, of course, and Kabylie is not the Maghrib. For instance, the state's punishing policy of disinvestment in northern Morocco, which followed the rebellion of the Rif in the 1950s, molded distinct migration patterns, economic development, and thus Berberization, there too.[3] By cultivating ties to their original villages and towns, migrants inflected the evolution of local economies and political relations in the Maghrib, fostering imbalances between regions that, in turn, affected official development plans and lent new resonances to the old colonial tunes about Arabs and Berbers.

If this were not enough, the displacement of former colonial settlers and their relative *déclassement* in their new homes created its own set of associations with the colonial heritage. The French metropolitan culture, which had tried very hard to shield itself from the culture of its settlers, found itself confronted with unsightly reminders of a colonial reality it was accustomed to repressing. In the view of the *pieds-noirs*, the "Arab" was the primary cause of the failure of a civilizing effort he did little to deserve. The "Berber" was a friendlier native, despite the large role played by Berbers in the anticolonial struggle—the modest gains of Christian missionaries being the sort of sign proponents of this ideology have manipulated. Then there are the Jews of North Africa, as they are called, not all of whom migrated to Israel. Among those who "ascended" to Israel, the exilic French colonial culture found another "Arab" to dominate and another "white" (Ashkenazi) culture to cajole and win over. Whereas Algerians were an influential component of French Jewry, Moroccans formed the majority of Israel's North Africans, conferring on "Algeria" and its "Arabs" a special status. Since Israel has enjoyed friendlier relations with Morocco than with Algeria, anti-Algerian sentiment in Israel is rich and complex.[4] In any case, the involvement of Israel, among other governments, in supporting secessionist Berberist parties in Algeria, but not Morocco, illustrates the diversity of the sources of Berberization—to say nothing of the colonial lineages of the expertise that undergirds them.[5]

Academic matters are no less complicated. As by far the most important center for producing scholarly knowledge on the medieval Maghrib, the French university had to adjust to the end of colonial rule by finding employment for those academics "repatriated" from North Africa. In practice, that necessity underwrote the continued importance of the Islam of Orientalists as a context within which to frame the medieval Maghrib and kept the field relatively detached from the intellectual currents and lively debates that so dramatically shaped French historiography in the postwar period. That detachment has had a tremendous effect on the topography of the field. On the southern side of the Mediterranean, Maghribī academics faced the daunting task of adapting their university systems to new priorities. While the medieval period was not high on the governments' priorities, the decision to pursue mass education put a premium on textbooks at the expense of specialized historical studies.[6] With a very limited number of trained specialists, the nationalization of medieval history took the form of a nationalization of colonial medieval historiography, its main source of knowledge—Ibn Khaldūn's *Histoire des Berbères* continuing to dominate the historical imagination.

In light of the impact that these developments have had on the production of knowledge about the medieval Maghrib, it could be easy to forget the developments that followed the death of Francisco Franco in 1975.[7] Among its many benefits, the demise of *Franquismo* freed the study of al-Andalus from strict ideological oversight. It also put the Spanish university on a path of improving conditions, especially after Spain joined the European Union in 1977. As a result, Spanish scholarship on al-Andalus made qualitative leaps and bounds, and Spain has become an important center for the study of Berbers—although primarily, the Berbers of al-Andalus. Today, it is impossible to imagine a serious study of the Berbers that does not consider Spanish scholarship. For those interested in Berberization, this is a major event, although it is too early to discern its consequences.[8]

Much more can be said about the multiple sites of Berberization today and how the legacy of French colonialism plays out differently in each. This brief and condensed outline should serve as an indication that when it comes to analyzing a phenomenon like the workings of Berberization, an examination of institutional arrangements and the entanglements they create surpasses the bounds of conventional historiographic approaches.

Berberization After Today

Interviewed by the French daily *Le Monde* in 1985, the famed Algerian playwright Kateb Yacine stated, "I am neither Arab, nor Muslim. I am Algerian.

Let us first accept Algeria (*assumons d'abord l'Algérie*)." That same year, he reportedly summarized his vision of a truly independent Algeria with a double rejection of French cultural influence and an official Algerian policy that emphasized the Arab and Islamic heritage at the expense of the Berber (Amazigh) one. One of the solutions he proposed was to "unburden Ibn Khaldūn's *Histoire des Berbères* in order to make it a book of struggle."[9]

For the committed partisan of a popular revolution against colonialism and, as he often repeated, all forms of oppression, Kateb Yacine was keenly aware of the devastation that the colonial period had wrought on the culture of his people.[10] He could not imagine that the illiterate Bedouins, peasants, and workers would be able to stomach the full Ibn Khaldūn and its hundreds of pages.[11] Rather, good politics began by speaking the language of the common folk, even if that meant distilling Ibn Khaldūn's history down to its core teachings. Behind the arcane verbiage, Ibn Khaldūn's history contained a simple and vital message: Berbers have a history they can draw from to imagine a better future for themselves.[12] In fact, turning Ibn Khaldūn into a weapon to achieve cultural liberation seemed natural to Kateb Yacine, since in their struggle anticolonial activists had become experts at subverting the symbols of colonial domination. Instead of a call to go to the original *Kitāb al-ʿibar*, however, his call summons young Algerians to learn a lesson prepared for their colonized ancestors. Perhaps this is the song of a dying swan. It is hard to say. In any case, in today's Maghrib, when one hears "Ibn Khaldūn," it is most often in the mouth of a former colonial subject, young people having their own set of sources and references.

The Maghribī governments' implementation of new language policies, their active manipulation of public discourse about history, their actions on behalf of and against foreign interests, and their competition with one another all shape the form and content of Berberization today. So too do processes like the folklorization and commodification of culture, uneven geographical development and regionalist politics, the weaponization of anti-immigrant politics at home and abroad, and the transformation of university systems the world around. In any event, the implication of various forms of politics in the Maghrib in Berberization is undeniable, and, even if only in passing, it is necessary to recognize and acknowledge the fingerprints of colonial ideologies and postcolonial realities on attempts to configure a past for the region and its peoples.

And so, again, the invention of Berbers is and has always been historical.

Notes

ABBREVIATION

EI[2] *Encyclopaedia of Islam*. Ed. Peri J. Bearman, Thierry Bianquis, Clifford Edmund Bosworth, Emeri J. van Donzel, and W. P. Heinrichs. 2nd ed. Leiden: Brill, 2004.

INTRODUCTION

1. The impact of nationalism on historical research has been the subject of a great many studies. For a general introduction and for a sense of the variety of approaches, see Nadia Abu el Haj, *Facts on the Ground: Archaeological Practice and Territorial Self-Fashioning in Israeli Society* (Chicago: University of Chicago Press, 2001); Benedict Anderson, *Imagined Communities: Reflections on the Origin and Spread of Nationalism* (New York: Verso, 1991); Youssef M. Choueiri, *Modern Arab Historiography: Historical Discourse and the Nation-State* (New York: Routledge, 2003); Patrick J. Geary, *The Myth of Nations: The Medieval Origins of Europe* (Princeton: Princeton University Press, 2002); Eric J. Hobsbawm, *Nations and Nationalism Since 1780: Programme, Myth, Reality* (Cambridge: Cambridge University Press, 1990); Muḥammad ʿĀbid al-Jābirī, *Takwīn al-ʿaql al-ʿarabī* (Beirut, Dār al-Ṭalīʿa, 1984); Abdallah Laroui, *L'idéologie arabe contemporaine* (Paris: Maspero, 1982); Shlomo Sand, *The Invention of the Jewish People* (New York: Verso, 2010); Raouf Wafik, *Ishkāliyāt al-nuhūḍ al-ʿarabī min al-taraddī ilā al-taḥaddī* (Beirut: Markaz Dirāsāt al-Waḥda al-ʿArabiya, 2005).

2. For an introduction to anthropological literature and for an illustration of the variety of approaches, see, for example, David Crawford, *Moroccan Households in the World Economy: Labor and Inequality in a Berber Village* (Baton Rouge: Louisiana State University Press, 2008); A. José Farrujia de la Rosa, *An Archaeology of the Margins: Colonialism, Amazighity, and Heritage Management in the Canary Islands* (New York: Springer, [2014]); Jane E. Goodman, *Berber Culture on the World Stage: From Village to Video* (Bloomington: Indiana University Press, 2005); Katherine E. Hoffman, *We Share Walls: Language, Land, and Gender in Berber Morocco* (Malden, MA: Blackwell, 2008); Katherine E. Hoffman and Susan Gilson Miller, eds., *Berbers and Others: Beyond Tribe and Nation in the Maghrib* (Bloomington: Indiana University Press, 2010); Lawrence Rosen, *Two Arabs, a Berber, and a Jew: Entangled Lives in Morocco* (Chicago: University of Chicago Press, 2016); Susan Slyomovics, ed., *Clifford Geertz in Morocco* (London: Routledge, 2009); Si Belkacem Taieb, *Decolonizing Indigenous Education: An Amazigh/Berber Ethnographic Journey* (New York: Palgrave Macmillan, 2014).

3. David Hart, "Scratch a Moroccan, Find a Berber," *Journal of North African Studies* 4, no. 2 (1999): 23–26. Cf. Dominique Casajus, "Les noms de peuple ont un histoire," in *Léon l'Africain*, ed. François Pouillon, Alain Messaoudi, Dietrich Rauchenberger, and Oumelbanine Zhiri (Paris: Karthala, 2009), 105–17.

4. See, for example, Georges-Henri Bousquet, *Les Berbères: Histoire et institutions* (Paris: PUF, 1957); Gabriel Camps, *Berbères: Aux marges de l'histoire* (Paris: Éditions des Hespérides, 1980); Mouloud Gaïd, *Les Berbèr(e)s dans l'histoire*, 4 vols. (Algiers: Éditions Mimouni, 1990); Salem Chaker, *Berbères aujourd'hui* (Paris: L'Harmattan, 1989); Charles-André Julien, *Histoire de l'Afrique blanche des origines à 1945* (Paris: PUF, 1966); Jean Servier, *Les Berbères* (Paris: PUF, 1990).

5. Michael Brett and Elizabeth Fentress, *The Berbers* (Oxford and Cambridge, MA: Blackwell, 1996). In her review of the book, Julia Clancy-Smith concluded: "This is the most ambitious work on the Berbers and North Africa since the fourteenth century when the celebrated Tunisian-born scholar composed his massive *History of the Berbers*. Ibn Khaldun would approve." Julia Clancy-Smith, "Berber History: *The Berbers* by Michael Brett; Elizabeth Fentress," *Journal of African History* 38, no. 3 (1997): 498–99.

6. Brett and Fentress, *The Berbers*, 3–4.

7. Brett and Fentress, *The Berbers*, 4. For H. T. Norris, "the true Berbers are those who speak the Hamito-Semitic language known as Berber." H. T. Norris, *The Berbers in Arabic Literature* (London and New York: Longman; Beirut: Librairie du Liban, 1982), 1.

8. See, for example, Salem Chaker, "Le berbère," in Bernard Cerquiligni, ed., *Les langues de France* (Paris: PUF, 2003), 215–27; Lionel Galand, "La langue berbère existe-t-elle?," in *Mélanges linguistiques offerts à Maxime Rodinson par ses élèves, ses collègues, et ses amis*, ed. Christian Robin and Maxime Rodinson (Paris: Geuthner, 1985), 175–84; Lionel Galand, *Études de linguistique berbère* (Leuven: Peeters, 2002); Maarten Kossmann, *Essai sur la phonologie du proto-berbère* (Cologne: Rüdiger Köppe, 1999); Maarten Kossmann, *The Arabic Influence on Northern Berber* (Leiden: Brill, 2013); Terence F. Mitchell, *Zuaran Berber (Libya): Grammar and Texts* (Cologne: Rüdiger Köppe, 2009); Lameen Souag, *Berber and Arabic in Siwa (Egypt): A Study in Linguistic Contact* (Cologne: Rüdiger Köppe, 2013).

9. Brett and Fentress, *The Berbers*, 5.

10. For a discussion of the richness of medieval Berber texts, see Mohamed Meouak, *La langue berbère au Maghreb médiéval: Textes, contextes, analyses* (Leiden: Brill, 2016). Among other things, Meouak's study demonstrates that language was a specialized mode of Berberization. His extensive gathering of references on this subject has made it unnecessary to have a chapter on the subject here. Cf. Mehdi Ghouirgate, "Le berbère au Moyen Âge: Une culture linguistique en cours de reconstitutions," *Annales: Histoire, Sciences Sociales* 3 (2015): 577–606.

11. Brett and Fentress, *The Berbers*, 5.

12. The Saharan or pre-Saharan Atlas is the southernmost edge of the Atlas chain, which runs through Algeria in a southwest-to-northeast direction.

13. Malika Hachid, *Les premiers Berbères: Entre Méditerranée, Tassili et Nil* (Aix-en-Provence: Edisud, 2000), 19. Mechtoid refers to the site near Mechta el-Arbi, in eastern Algeria; Capsian to one near Gafsa, in southwestern Tunisia.

14. Hachid, *Les premiers Berbères*, 17. Cf. Gilles Boëtsch, "Égypte noire, Berbérie blanche: La rencontre manquée de la biologie et de la culture," *Cahiers d'Études Africaines* 33, no. 129 (1993): 73–98.

15. Even if some languages and dialects are not mutually understandable, that does not set Berbers apart from one another. Language sets Berbers apart from non-Berbers only.

16. "Both have been recently adopted throughout North Africa, although their first attestations are only known from Moroccan dialects and until 1945 did not spread outside them." Brett and Fentress, *The Berbers*, 5. Moreover, there is no clear evidence that "Imazighen" or any of its ancient predecessors (Mazices or MZC) was not originally an exonym.

17. Brett and Fentress, *The Berbers*, 5n5.

18. For a sense of the scholarship and the debates, see Kaoutar Bentayebi et al., "Genetic Ancestry of a Moroccan Population as Inferred from Autosomal STRs," *Meta Gene* 2 (2014): 427–38; Lotfi Cherni et al., "Female Gene Pools of Berber and Arab Neighboring Communities in Central Tunisia: Microstructure of mtDNA Variation in North Africa," *Human Biology* 77, no. 1 (2005): 61–70; Sarra Elkamel et al., "The Orientalisation of North Africa: New Hints from the Study of STRs in an Arab Population," *Annals of Human Biology* 44, no. 2 (2016): 180–90; Sabeh Frigi et al., "Ancient Local Evolution of African mtDNA Haplogroups in Tunisian Berber Populations," *Human Biology* 82, no. 4 (2010): 367–84; Natalie Gérard et al., "North African Berber and Arab Influences in the Western Mediterranean Revealed by Y-Chromosome DNA Haplotypes," *Human Biology* 78, no. 3 (2006): 307–16; Youssef Idaghdour et al., "Geographical Genomics of Human Leukocyte Gene Expression Variation in Southern Morocco," *Nature Genetics* 42, no. 1 (2010): 62–69; Shomarka O. Y. Keita, "Biocultural Emergence of the Amazigh (Berbers) in Africa: Comment on Frigi et al.," *Human Biology* 82, no. 4 (2010): 385–93; Houssein Khodjet-el-Khil et al., "Substructure of a Tunisian Population as Inferred from 15 Autosomal Short Tandem Repeat Loci," *Human Biology* 80, no. 4 (2008): 435–48.

19. Note that for the formation of an ethnos, many seem to prefer the male line. Biologists understand that the statistical notion of population is not the same as an ethnos. Yet, enough biologists believe that a particular ethnicity, often the one they identify with, has a biological foundation that it is legitimate to highlight the intellectual difficulties this position engenders. For issues associated with the search of ethnic origins in biology, see Nadia Abu el-Haj, *The Genealogical Science: The Search for Jewish Origins and the Politics of Epistemology* (Chicago: University of Chicago Press, 2012); Jonathan Marks, *Tales of the Ex-Apes: How We Think About Human Evolution* (Berkeley: University of California Press, 2015).

20. I use the term *medieval* without quotation marks, which would indicate that it is a modern construct with attached assumptions, implications, and effects on both historiography and public discourse. There is no need for them, since throughout this book the category has no analytical function whatsoever. But to the extent that it is not clear, the medieval begins here with the earliest reference to Berbers in Arabic sources and ends with Ibn Khaldūn (1332–1406). It is a period defined by the arguments of this book. In other words, there is nothing "medieval" about the period, and not simply because the focus is not on a European or Western region. If anything, my critical stance vis-à-vis established periodizations supports a reappraisal of such categories when they determine historical thinking in the slightest. Whenever possible, I will signal the importance of the category to the invention of the modern as the nonmedieval. At the same time, and because of the arguments I make, especially in Part III, Ibn Khaldūn has come to stand for and define the medieval.

CHAPTER 1

1. Our assumptions about literature and literariness as well as those about disciplines and sciences do not match the conceptual map assumed in the sources. To the extent that

the difference weighs on the arguments presented here, it is recognized and signaled. As will become clear in this book, the semantic fields associated with critical concepts such as "people" and "nation" require that we call into question the practice of imposing a modern frame through translation.

2. The English "Berber" is the common transliteration of the same Arabic word. I use the scholarly transliteration "Barbar" a few times to mean the East Africans and to highlight the habit of not connecting the two.

3. For varying approaches on the emergence of the Arabs, see, for example, Richard W. Bulliet, *The Camel and the Wheel* (Cambridge, MA: Harvard University Press, 1975); Robert Hoyland, *Arabia and the Arabs: From the Bronze Age to the Coming of Islam* (London and New York: Routledge, 2001); Jan Retsö, *The Arabs in Antiquity: Their History from the Assyrians to the Umayyads* (London and New York: RoutledgeCurzon, 2003).

4. Ibn Hishām (d. 834), *Das Leben Muhammed's nach Muhammed Ibn Ishāk (Kitāb sīrat rasūl Allah)*, ed. Ferdinand Wüstenfeld (Göttingen: Dieterichsche Universitäts-Buchhandlung, 1858), 45. In his translation of the work, Guillaume incorrectly translates *āl Barbar* as "barbarians." See Alfred Guillaume, *The Life of Muḥammad, a Translation of Isḥāq's Sīrat Rasūl Allāh* (Karachi, Oxford, and New York: Oxford University Press, 1967), 33.

5. Medieval authors made references to this fact. For example, see Ibn Sa'īd al-Maghribī (d. 1286), *Kitāb al-jughrāfiya*, ed. Ismā'īl al-'Arabī (Beirut: Manshūrāt al-Maktabal-Tijārī lil-Ṭibā'awa-al-Nashrwa-al-Tawzī', 1970), 81; Ibn Khaldūn (d. 1406), *The Muqaddimah: An Introduction to History*, trans. Franz Rosenthal (Princeton: Princeton University Press, 1967), 1:99.

6. *Periplus Maris Erythræi*, in *Geographi Graeci Minores*, ed. Karl Müller (Hildesheim: G. Olms, 1965), 1:258; *Ptolemaei Geographia,*ed. C.F.A. Nobbe (Hildesheim: G. Olms, 1966), 1.17.6; 4.7.28.

7. Marcianus Heracleensis ex Ponto, *Periplus Maris Exteri*, in *Geographi Graeci Minores*, ed. Karl Müller (Hildesheim: G. Olms, 1965), 1:523.

8. Cosmas Indicopleustes, *Topographie Chrétienne,* ed. Wanda Wolska-Conus (Paris: Éditions du Cerf, 1968–70), 2:26, 29, 30, 45, 48, 49, 50, 61, 64; Stephanus Byzantinus, *Ethnicorum quae supersunt*, ed. A. Meineke (Berlin: Reiner, 1849), 158. See "Barbaria" in Georg Wissowa, *Paulys Real-Encyclopädie der classischen Altertumswissenschaft* (Stuttgart: J. B. Metzler, 1896). In addition to the East African Barbar, one notes the existence of a Barbar in the Persian Gulf. See the suggestive article by Glen Warren Bowersock, "Tylos and Tyre: Bahrain in the Graeco-Roman World," in *Bahrain Through the Ages: The Archaeology*, ed. Shaikha Haya Ali Khalifa and Michael Rice (London: Kegan Paul International, 1986), 399–406.

9. Ibn 'Abd al-Ḥakam (d. 871), *The History of the Conquests of Egypt, North Africa, and Spain*, ed. Charles Torrey (New Haven: Yale University Press, 1922), 111, 115, 119; hereafter cited as *The Conquests*. The ancient Barbaria appears in later Arabic sources as *barbara* (modern Berbera) and as *jazīrat barbara*. See, for instance, al-Hamdānī (d. 945), *Ṣifat jazīrat al-'arab*, ed. David Heinrich Müller (Leiden: Brill, 1884), 52.

10. For more on the *futūḥ* genre, see Chapter 3.

11. Al-Wāqidī, *Futūḥ al-shām*, ed. 'Abd al-Laṭīf 'Abd al-Raḥmān (Beirut: Dār al-Kutub al-'Ilmiyya, 1997), 2:204.

12. Al-Wāqidī, *Futūḥ al-Shām*, 2:212. Cf. Abū 'Ubayd Allāh al-Bakrī (d. 1094), *Kitāb al-masālik wa al-mamālik*, ed. A.P. Van Leeuwen and A. Férré (Tunis: Al-Dār al-'Arabiyya lil-Kitāb, 1992), 1:88, 89 (*al-ḥabasha, al-qibṭ, wa* al-*barbar*). For a description of Buja in eastern Africa as belonging to the *bilād al-barbar* and not to the land of the Buja, see Abū al-Fidā'

(1273–1331), *Géographie d'Aboulféda: Texte arabe [Taqwīm al-buldān]*, ed. M. Reinaud and M. Le baron Mac Guckin de Slane (Paris: Imprimerie Royale, 1840), 163.

13. Al-Wāqidī, *Futūḥ al-Shām*, 2:214. It is possible that the reference recalls the Carthaginian Hanibal (a warrior in the West who used elephants in warfare) but that would raise too many additional questions and is ultimately implausible.

14. Al-Balādhurī, *Kitāb futūḥ al-buldān*, ed. Ṣalāḥ al-Dīn al-Munajjid (Cairo: Maktabat al-Nahḍa al-Miṣriya, 1956–58), 1:97–98.

15. Ibn Qutayba, *Al-ma'ārif*, ed. Tharwat 'Ukāsha (Cairo: Maṭba'at Dār al-Kutub, 1960), 26. Interestingly, the reference is to an indefinite *barbar* rather than *al-barbar*, as is the case for all the other groups.

16. Ibn Qutayba, *Al-ma'ārif*, 627–28. See also Ibn Daḥiya (d. 1235 or 1236), *Al-muṭrib min ash'ār ahl al-maghrib*, ed. Ibrāhīm al-Abyārī, Ḥamīd 'Abd al-Majīd, and Aḥmad Aḥmad Badawī (Cairo: al-Maṭba'a al-Amīriya, 1954), 60.

17. "All the way to Tangier" fits the description of the dominion of Jirjīr, the Byzantine governor who declared autonomy, struck his own currency, and ruled from Tripoli to Tangier. For example, see Ibn 'Abd al-Ḥakam, *The Conquests*, 183.

18. It is unlikely that Ibn Qutayba assembled this Frankenstein-like report himself but rather copied it from an earlier source whose projection of the presence of Yemenis in the Maghrib into a remote past served the political purposes of Yemeni settlers there.

19. Al-Balādhurī, *Kitāb futūḥ al-buldān*, 1:270. Al-Balādhurī does not include Ibn al-Kalbī's account of the settlement of the descendants of this enigmatic Qays b. Ṣayfī among the Ṣanhāja and Kutāma. See also al-Ṭabarī (d. 923), *Ta'rīkh al-rusul wa al-mulūk*, ed. Muḥammad Abū al-Faḍl Ibrāhīm (Cairo: Dār al-Ma'ārif, 1960), 1:442. The presence of Yemenis in the Maghrib in pre-Islamic times is worth noting again. Cf. Ibn Sa'īd (d. 1286), *Nashwat al-ṭarab fī tārīkh jāhiliyat al-'arab*, ed. Naṣrat 'Abd al-Raḥmān (Amman: Maktabat al-Aqṣā, 1982), 1:45.

20. The Islamic notion of *fatḥ* is projected back to a mythological past. See Fred Donner, "Arabic Fatḥ as 'Conquest' and Its Origin in Islamic Tradition," *Al-'Uṣūr al-Wusṭā* 24 (2016): 1–14. See also Alejandro García Sanjuán, *La conquista islámica de la peninsula ibérica y la tergiversación del pasado* (Madrid: Marcel Pons Historia, 2013), 56–62.

21. Ibn al-Kalbī, *Nasab ma'ad wa al-yaman al-kabīr*, ed. Nājī Ḥasan (Damascus: Dār al-Yaqaẓa al-'Arabiyya, 1988), 2:548.

22. See, for instance, Yāqūt al-Ḥamawī (d. 1229), *Mu'jam al-buldān* (Beirut: Dār Ṣādir, 1988), 1:369–70.

23. Gabriel Camps noted in a discussion following a paper by Paul-Albert Février that "en fait les Berbères des Arabes sont les Maures des Romains." Paul-Albert Février, *La Méditerranée de Paul-Albert Février* (Rome: École française de Rome; Aix-en-Provence: Université de Provence, 1996), 2:861. For a fuller discussion of the mobilization of the notion of native or original inhabitant and its effects on historicity, see my essay on the subject; Ramzi Rouighi, "The Berbers of the Arabs," *Studia Islamica*, n.s., 2011, 67–101.

24. Yves Modéran, *Les Maures et l'Afrique romaine (IVe-VIIe siècle)* (Rome: École Française de Rome, 2003), 811.

25. The term *autochtone* is analytically problematic here, especially since many "Romans" were born to people settled in the region for many generations. The category native may itself be anachronistic and ideologically ambiguous. Likewise, the idea of a "culturally complex" Moor does nothing to eliminate the idea of the "pure Berber."

26. Modéran, *Les Maures*, 11.

27. For a sense of the historical and historiographic stakes and for a helpful presentation of the events, see Jamil Abun-Nasr, *A History of the Maghrib in the Islamic Period* (Cambridge: Cambridge University Press, 1987); Allaoua Amara, "L'islamisation du Maghreb central (VIIe–XIe siècle)," in *Islamisation et arabisation de l'Occident musulman (VIIe-XIIe siècle)*, ed. Dominique Valérian (Paris: Publications de la Sorbonne, 2011), 103–30; Mohamed Benabbès, "L'Afrique byzantine face à la conquête arabe" (PhD diss., Université Paris X–Nanterre, 2004); Michael Brett and Elizabeth Fentress, *The Berbers* (Oxford and Cambridge, MA: Blackwell, 1996); Jonathan Conant, *Staying Roman: Conquest and Identity in Africa and the Mediterranean, 439-700* (Cambridge: Cambridge University Press, 2012); Walter Kaegi, *Muslim Expansion and Byzantine Collapse in North Africa* (Cambridge: Cambridge University Press, 2010); Philippe Sénac and Patrice Cressier, *Histoire du Maghreb médiéval VIIe–XIe siècle* (Paris: Armand Colin, 2012). See also Richard W. Bulliet, *Conversion to Islam in the Medieval Period: An Essay in Quantitative History* (Cambridge MA: Harvard University Press, 1979).

28. See, for example, Anon., *Fatḥ al-andalus*, ed. Luis Molina (Madrid: CSIC, 1994), 27.

29. The Maghrib had been under the purview of the governor of Egypt until then. The governor of Egypt continued to play a major role since soldiers from the East had to cross Egypt to reach the Maghrib. This Arab Ifrīqiyā extended beyond the Byzantine province of Africa Proconsularis.

30. Even if the control that Umayyad forces had was frail and did not extend to mountainous regions, the establishment of a province anchored the notion that the Maghrib (West) formed a unit. This explains why early authors often conflated Ifrīqiyā and the Maghrib. On the formation and organization of Ifrīqiyā, see Hichem Djaït, "L'Afrique arabe au VIIIe siècle (86–184 H/705–800)," *Annales: Économies, Sociétés, Civilisations* 28, no. 3 (1973): 601–21; Hichem Djaït, "La wilāya d'Ifrīqiya au IIe/VIIIe siècle: Étude institutionnelle," *Studia Islamica* 27 (1967): 77–121, and 28 (1968): 79–108. See also Paul-Louis Cambuzat, *L'évolution des cités du Tell en Ifrīḳiya du VIIe au XIe siècle* (Algiers: Office des Publications Universitaires, 1986); Corisande Fenwick, "From Africa to Ifrīqiya: Settlement and Society in Early Medieval North Africa (650–800)," *Al-Masāq* 25, no. 1 (2013): 9–33.

31. Ibn 'Abd al-Ḥakam, *The Conquests*, 204: "Twelve thousand Berbers and only sixteen Arab men." Cf. *Fatḥ al-Andalus*, 16: "Thirteen thousand men between Arabs and Berbers." Ibn al-Kardabūs (fl. 12th–13th c.), *Tārīkh al-andalus li-ibn al-kardabūs wa waṣfuhu li-ibn al-shabbāṭ, naṣṣān jadīdān*, ed. Aḥmad Mukhtār al-'Abbādī (Madrid: Instituto de Estudios Islámicos en Madrid, 1971), 134, 168: "Twelve thousand Berber fighters and only a few Arabs (*nafar yasīr*)"; "seven thousand Berbers and *mawālī* among whom were few Arabs (*illā qalīl*)." See also al-Raqīq al-Qayrawānī (fl. 11th c.), *Tārīkh ifrīqiyā wa al-maghrib*, ed. al-Munjī al-Ka'bī (Tunis: Maṭba'at al-Wasaṭ, 1968), 74.

32. The sources' distinction between northern and southern Arabs ('Adnānī v. Qaḥṭānī) is complicated by the pre-Islamic migration and settlement of Yemenis in Syria (al-Shām), and the migration of southern Arabians following the Muslim conquest.

33. The arrival in al-Andalus of the large and powerful Syrian contingent posed a threat to those Arabs who had been dominant in the previous decades. These are referred to as the *baladī* Andalusīs (also *baldī*). They are the "true" or "first" Arabs of al-Andalus.

34. For the significance of the dynastic change for the elaboration of learned knowledge in the East, see Antoine Borrut, *Entre mémoire et pouvoir: L'espace syrien sous les derniers Omeyyades et les premiers Abbasides (v. 72–193/692–809)* (Leiden: Brill, 2011).

35. For recent work on the Barghawāṭa and the Midrārids, see John Iskandar, "Devout Heretics: The Barghawata in Maghribi Historiography," *Journal of North African Studies* 12, no. 1 (2007): 37–53; Paul M. Love Jr., "The Sufris of Sijilmasa: Toward a History of the Midrarids," *Journal of North African Studies* 15, no. 2 (2010): 173–88. For a critical perspective, see Maribel Fierro, "Al-Aṣfar," *Studia Islamica* 77 (1993): 169–81. For a late reference to the Barghawāṭa as a tribe, see al-Tijānī (d. 1321/2), *Riḥlat al-tijānī*, ed. Ḥusnī 'Abd al-Wahhāb (Tripoli and Tunis: Al-Dār al-'Arabiya lil-Kitāb, 1981), 96. For other dynasties, see below.

36. See, for example, al-'Uṣfurī, *Tārīkh khalīfa b. khayyāṭ*, ed. Suhayl Zakkār (Damascus: Manshūrāt Wizārat al-Thaqāfa wa al-Syāḥa wa al-Irshād al-Qawmī, 1968), 1:359; Muḥammad b. al-'Ayyāshī al-Miknāsī (d. 1727), *Zahr al-bustān fī nasab akhwāl sayyidunā wa-mawlānā Zaydān*, ed. Aḥmad Qaddūr (Rabat: Maṭābi' al-Ribāṭ Nit, 2013), 53.

37. Most importantly, as an imperial genre par excellence, the *futūḥ* offered a genealogy of the empire's provinces.

38. Ibn 'Abd al-Ḥakam, *The Conquests*, 8. The Berbers and the Copts are described as the descendants of two different sons of Noah.

39. Ibn 'Abd al-Ḥakam, *The Conquests*, 170.

40. See "Marāqiya" in Yāqūt al-Ḥamawī, *Mu'jam*, 5:93.

41. It is also noteworthy that this genealogy presents these mostly eastern Maghribī Berbers (Zanāta, Maghīla, Luwāta, and Hawwāra) as having existed as such in Palestine. The association between the Berbers and mountains runs through the entire medieval archive. At the same time, the idea that like the Arabs, Berbers inhabited the deserts is also widespread. See, for example, *wa al-barbar mithl al-'arab fī suknā al-ṣaḥārī*, in Abū al-Fidā' (1273–1331), *Al-mukhtaṣar fī akhbār al-bashar* (Beirut: Dār al-Kitāb al-Lubnānī: Dār al-Baḥḥār, 1956–61), 1:97. Also *wakarihat al-barbar nuzūl al-madā'in fa nazalū al-jibāl wa al-rimāl*, in Ibn al-Faqīh al-Hamadhānī (fl. 902), *Mukhtaṣar kitāb al-buldān*, ed. M.J. de Goeje (Leiden: Brill, 1885), 83.

42. See "Barqa" in Yāqūt al-Ḥamawī, *Mu'jam*, 1:387–88.

43. See "al-Sūs" in Yāqūt al-Ḥamawī, *Mu'jam*, 3:281–82. The distinction between the *Sūs al-adnā* and the *Sūs al-aqṣā*, the former being the area near Ṭanja and the other a two-month journey south, is not always made.

44. Ibn 'Abd al-Ḥakam, *The Conquests,* 170.

45. Ibn 'Abd-al-Ḥakam, *The Conquests,* 198.

46. The epithet *al-barbarī* is used against an enemy.

47. Ibn 'Abd-al-Ḥakam, *The Conquest*, 198–99.

48. For Berber as enemy, see *ba'sa barbarā* in the poem by Sulaymān b. Ḥamīd al-Ghāfiqī cited by Ibn al-Abbār. Ibn al-Abbār (d. 1260), *Al-ḥulla al-sayrā'*, ed. Ḥusayn Mu'nis (Cairo: Al-Sharika al-'Arabiyya li al-Ṭibā'a wa al-Nashr, 1963), 1:83.

49. Ibn 'Abd-al-Ḥakam, *The Conquests*, 199.

50. Ibn 'Abd-al-Ḥakam, *The Conquests*, 199: *mala' al-barbar.*

51. Ibn 'Abd-al-Ḥakam, *The Conquests*, 200. Cf. al-Mālikī (d. 1061), *Riyāḍ al-nufūs fī ṭabaqāt 'ulamā'al-qayrawān wa-ifrīqīyā wa-zuhhādihim wa-nussākihim wa-siyar min akhbārihim wa-faḍā'ilihim wa-awṣāfihim*, ed. Bashīr al-Bakkūsh (Beirut: Dār al-Gharb al-Islāmī, 1994), 51: "The Kāhina became queen of all of Ifrīqiyā."

52. Ibn 'Abd-al-Ḥakam, *The Conquests*, 201.

53. Ibn al-Faqīh al-Hamadhānī (fl. 902) cites a *ḥadīth* in which the prophet Muḥammad says that "the women of the Berbers are better than their men. They were sent a prophet but they killed him and [it was] the women who buried him." Ibn al-Faqīh al-Hamadhānī,

Mukhtaṣar, 84. The Andalusī origin of the section in which this statement is found gives a sense of the broad circulation of Andalusī Berberization.

54. Ibn ʿAbd-al-Ḥakam, *The Conquests*, 201.

55. See the critical examination of this question in Yves Modéran, "Botr et Branès: Sur les origines du dualisme berbère médiéval," in *Mutations d'identités en Méditerranée: Moyen Âge et époque contemporaine*, ed. Henri Bresc and Christiane Veauvy (Saint Denis: Bouchène, 2000), 53–65; Modéran, *Les Maures*, 761–810.

56. Ibn ʿAbd-al-Ḥakam, *The Conquests*, 204. For the description of beautiful Berber slave girls, see Ibn ʿAbd-al-Ḥakam, *The Conquests*, 202: "Al-Layth [b. Saʿd] said: Nothing in [the history of] Islam compares to the number of captives made by Mūsā [b. Nuṣayr]." Ibn Ḥabīb, *Kitāb al-tārīkh*, ed. Sālim Musṭafā al-Badrī (Beirut: Dār al-Kutub al-ʿIlmiyya, 1999), 126. See also al-Raqīq al-Qayrawānī, *Tārīkh ifrīqiyā wa al-maghrib*, 67, 108.

57. For a more on this question, see Chapter 3.

58. The scholarship on the conquest of Iberia and its aftermath is vast and diverse. See, for example, Nicola Clarke, *The Muslim Conquest of Iberia: Medieval Arabic Narratives* (London: Routledge, 2011); García Sanjuán, *La conquista*; Pedro Chalmeta Gendrón, *Invasión e islamización: La sumisión de Hispania y la formación de al-Andalus* (Jaén: Universidad de Jaén, 2003); Eduardo Manzano Moreno, *Conquistadores, emires y califas: Los omeyas y la formación de al-Andalus* (Barcelona: Crítica, 2006); Joaquín Vallvé Bermejo, "Nuevas ideas sobre la conquista árabe de España: Toponimia y onomástica," *Al-Qanṭara* 10 (1989): 51–150.

59. Ibn ʿAbd-al-Ḥakam, *The Conquests*, 217–18. The notion that Ifrīqiyā encompassed the western Maghrib is consistent with the administrative realities of the time.

60. Ibn ʿAbd-al-Ḥakam, *The Conquests*, 218. Al-Fihrī was a relative of the general ʿUqba b. Nāfiʿ (d. 682).

61. Ibn ʿAbd-al-Ḥakam, *The Conquests*, 218–19.

62. One aspect of the Ṣufrīs that scares the Umayyad Arabs is the fact that they believed that the enslavement of Muslim Arabs was acceptable. Ibn ʿAbd-al-Ḥakam, *The Conquests*, 222.

63. Ibn ʿAbd-al-Ḥakam, *The Conquests*, 224.

64. Ibn ʿAbd-al-Ḥakam, *The Conquests*, 224–25.

65. It is perhaps worth repeating here that Ibn ʿAbd al-Ḥakam is only the earliest extant source and not the only one. However, if later authors offered more details about the conquests, it is not easy to judge the extent of their authorial intervention when they cite earlier sources. The point here is to see what "Berber" looked like in the earliest sources.

66. Historians have tended to approach all these dynasties as examples of Khārijite rule, a lumping that is problematic on many levels. For recent discussions of sources, different approaches, and greater detail, see Cyrille Aillet, "Introduction: L'ibâdisme, une minorité au sein de l'islam," *Revue des Mondes Musulmans et de la Méditerranée* 132 (2012): 13–36; ʿAwaḍ Sharqāwī, *Ibāḍīyat jabal nafūsa fī al-qarnayn al-thānī wa-al-thālith al-hijrīyayn: Dirāsa tārīkhīya* (Cairo: Dār al-ʿĀlam al-ʿArabī, 2017); Abdelkader El Ghali, *Les états kharidjites au Maghreb (IIe s.–IVe hég/VIIIe s.–Xe s. apr. J.-C.* (Tunis: Centre de Publications Universitaire, 2003); Virgine Prevost, *L'aventure ibāḍite dans le sud tunisien: Effervescence d'une région méconnue* (Helsinki: Academia Scientiarum Fennica, 2008); Virgine Prevost, "L'ibadisme berbère: La légitimation d'une doctrine venue d'Orient," in *La légitimation du pouvoir au Maghreb médiéval: De l'orientalisation à l'émancipation politique*, ed. Annliese Nef and Élise Voguet (Madrid: Casa de Velázquez, 2011), 55–71; Elizabeth Savage, *A Gateway to Hell, a Gateway*

to Paradise: The North African Response to the Arab Conquest (Princeton, NJ: Darwin Press, 1997).

67. Cyrille Aillet, "Tāhart et les origines de l'imamat rustumide: Matrice orientale et ancrage local," *Annales Islamologiques* 45 (2011): 47–78.

68. The concept of "tribe" has received great critical and theoretical attention. I translate the medieval Arabic concept of *qabīla* as "tribe" with the understanding that it was specific to the medieval Arabs' understanding of themselves and others. When used by medieval authors, the concept is especially problematic because it describes groups with stark differences in livelihood, size, and location (temporal and geographic). The same applies to my translation of the Latin *gens*. See discussion in Chapter 3.

69. Ibn al-Ṣaghīr, *Akhbār al-a'imma al-rustamiyīn*, ed. Muḥammad Nāṣir and Ibrāhīm Baḥāz (Beirut: Dār al-Gharb al-Islāmī, 1986), 52; and Ibn al-Ṣaghīr, "Chronique d'Ibn Saghir sur les imams Rostémides de Tahert," ed. Mohamed Talbi *Cahiers de Tunisie* 26 (1975): 331.

70. The political ferment around the Fāṭimids at the time may also have informed this gesture.

71. Assuming a very different audience, the great Mashriqī historian al-Ṭabarī distinguishes between the Ibāḍīs and the Berbers. See al-Ṭabarī, *Ta'rīkh*, 8:42.

72. Ibn Sallām al-Ibāḍī, *Kitāb Ibn Sallām: Eine ibaditisch-magribinische Geschichte des Islams aus dem 3./9/ Jahrhundert*, ed. Werner Schwartz and al-Shaykh Sālim Ibn Ya'qūb (Wiesbaden: Steiner, 1986).

73. Cyrille Aillet, "A Breviary of Faith and a Sectarian Memorial: A New Reading of Ibn Sallam's *Kitab* (3rd/9th century)," in *Ibadi Theology: Rereading Sources and Scholarly Works*, ed. Ersilia Francesca (Hildesheim, Zurich, and New York: Georg Olms, 2015), 67–82.

74. One also finds references to the Berbers as a military force opposed to the Arab armies. Ibn Sallām, *Kitāb*, 118–19, 127. See also also al-Raqīq al-Qayrawānī, *Tārīkh*, 148. Al-Raqīq al-Qayrawānī tends to describe Berbers and Romans as the antagonists of the Arabs with more emphasis on the religious background (Christian, non-Christian) of the groups—something that is consistent with the concerns of his own society. This source is critical to the construction of the modern narrative on the conversion of the Berbers.

75. Ibn Sallām, *Kitāb*, 122; see also 121–25. Cf. Ibn 'Abd al-Ḥakam, *The Conquests*, 287: "The prophet said that malice (*khubth*) comes in seventy parts. Sixty-nine of these parts belong to the Berbers and the remaining one is divided among the rest of humanity and the jinn."

76. Ibn Sallām, *Kitāb*, 124.

77. Ibn Sallām, *Kitāb*, 123.

78. Ibn Sallām, *Kitāb*, 84.

79. The Arabs' lack of knowledge about the Barbar is taken for granted. Both the prophet Muḥammad and his caliph 'Umar b. al-Khaṭṭāb are described as inquiring about them. Ibn Sallām, *Kitāb*, 122–23.

80. Ibn Sallām, *Kitāb*, 118.

81. The distinction and enmity between northern and southern Arabs, which was revived at the battle of Rāḥit (684), resurfaced in al-Andalus. Even after the imposition of Umayyad domination, it lingered for a long time, if only as the result of the memory of prominent Arab houses (genealogies). See Patricia Crone, "Were the Qays and Yemen of the Umayyad Period Political Parties?," *Der Islam* 71:1 (1994):1–57.

82. The distinction here is based on the usage that we can gather from early Arabic sources. See, for instance, Ibn Qutayba, *Al-ma'ārif*, 213. The political situation in Ifrīqiyā and Aghlabid Sicily suggests that they shared the Arab-centric imperial culture usually attributed to the Umayyads. In other words, and in spite of having pledged allegiance to the (anti-Umayyad) 'Abbāsids, the Aghlabids and their supporters sought to maintain the privileges of the Arabs in Ifrīqiyā. For example, al-Bakrī mentions that the armies of Ifrīqiyā the Aghlabids sent to Sicily were composed of "Quraysh, Arabs, Berbers, and others." Al-Bakrī (d. 1094), *Al-masālik*, 1:485. See also Ramzi Rouighi, "The Andalusi Origins of the Berbers?," *Journal of Medieval Iberian Studies* 2, no. 1 (2010): 93–108.

83. On the existence of a land of Berbers in al-Andalus, see Chapter 4.

84. *Crónica Mozárabe de 754*, ed. José Eduardo López Pereira (Zaragoza: Anubar Ediciones, 1980); Kenneth B. Wolf, *Conquerors and Chroniclers of Early Medieval Spain* (Liverpool: Liverpool University Press, 1990), 111–58.

85. For pre-Islamic Iberian examples of the use of Moor, see Wolf, *Conquerors*, 59–60. For a study of the evolution of the category over time, see Modéran, *Les Maures*. The anonymous Iberian author of the *Chronicle of 741* used the term Moor only once, when he described the fall of Byzantine rule in Africa in 698. He explained that "all the nobility of Africa, along with count Gregory, was destroyed to the point of extinction," after "the battle line of the Moors turned in flight." Juan Gil, *Corpus scriptores muzarabicorum* (Madrid: Instituto Antonio de Nebrija, 1973), 1:10. For an English translation, see Robert Hoyland, *Seeing Islam as Others Saw It* (Princeton, NJ: Darwin Press, 1997), 618. This usage, which is reminiscent of later Arabic usage, sees the Moors as a nondescript military force whose betrayal led to the fall of Carthage.

86. §75: Wolf, *Conquerors*, 140; López Pereira, *Crónica*,90.

87. §79: Wolf, *Conquerors*, 142; López Pereira, *Crónica*, 96. Naturally, Libya and Spain do not refer to the modern states.

88. §84: Wolf, *Conquerors*, 148; López Pereira, *Crónica*, 106. See also Anon., *Fatḥ al-andalus*, 54–55.

89. This passage seems to be based on an Arabic account with an eastern point of view. The Maghrib (western region) replaces Libya and is described as being "occupied more than any of the others by the Moors." Interestingly, the Maghrib is not "the land of the Moors" but only has the greatest concentration of them. See Chapter 4.

90. §84: Wolf, *Conquerors*, 148–49; López Pereira, *Crónica*, 106–8. Lineage was one of the most important arguments for legitimacy among the Arabs. See Franz Rosenthal, "Nasab," in *EI²*, 6:187–88. See also Chapter 3.

91. "When [in 741/2, 'Abd al-Malik] discovered that the third part of the army under Balj had arrived at the port, he denied them a crossing, withholding the ships. When the Moors of Spain realized this, they assembled for war, wanting to subject 'Abd al-Malik to themselves and, crossing over the sea in ships, offer his conquered kingdom to their allies on the other side of the sea." §85: Wolf, *Conquerors*, 148; López Pereira, *Crónica*, 109–10.

92. For unified Berber command, see Ibn al-Qūṭiya (d. 977), *Tārīkh iftitāḥ al-andalus*, ed. 'Abd Allāh Anīs al-Ṭabbā' (Beirut: Mu'assasat al-Ma'ārif, 1994), 79. Cf. Ibn al-Qūṭiya, *Tārīkh*, 157, 166: *wa kharaja min wujūh al-barbar mi'at rajul, fīhim banū kusayla, wa banū yaṣdur, wa banū mulūk al-barbar*; *adkhala 'alayhim mūsā mulūk al-barbar.*

93. Cyrille Aillet, *Les mozarabes: Christianisme, islamisation et arabisation en péninsule ibérique (IXᵉ-XIIᵉ siècle)* (Madrid: Casa de Velázquez, 2010); Pedro Chalmeta, "Muwallad," in *EI²*,7:806–8; Maribel Fierro, "Árabes, Beréberes, muladíes y mawālī: Algunas reflexiones so-

bre los datos de los diccionarios biográficos andalusíes," in *Estudios onomástico-biográficos de al-Andalus VII: homenaje a José Ma Fórneas*, ed. Manuela Marin and Helena de Felipe (Madrid: CSIC, 1995), 41–54.

CHAPTER 2

1. Michael Brett and Elizabeth Fentress, *The Berbers* (Oxford and Cambridge, MA: Blackwell, 1996), 8.

2. Brett and Fentress, *The Berbers*, 9.

3. Maya Shatzmiller, *The Berbers and the Islamic State: The Marīnid Experience in Pre-Protectorate Morocco* (Princeton, NJ: Markus Wiener, 2000), xvii. See also Brett and Fentress, *The Berbers*, 109. Cf. Abdallah Laroui, *The History of the Maghrib: An Interpretive Essay* (Princeton: Princeton University Press, 1977), 87: "The conquest, which consisted essentially in the imposition of Arab sovereignty, meant neither Islamization nor Arabization. Arabization required many centuries and Islamization was the work of the Berbers themselves." Although the difference between "Berber" and "Maghribi" in Laroui is not always clear, his approach contrasts sharply with Shatzmiller's.

4. For an early ethnographic statement on the imposition of despotic Islam on democratic Berbers, see Adolphe Hanoteau and Aristide Letourneux, *La Kabylie et les coutumes kabyles* (Paris: Imprimerie nationale, 1872–73), 1:2: "D'autres, tout en acceptant le code musulman et l'autorité de chefs nommés sans leur concours, ont conservé en partie les habitudes démocratiques particulières à leur races. Ces habitudes tempèrent, dans la pratique, ce que le pouvoir absolu peut avoir de trop arbitraire; mais leur action s'exerce sans règles fixes, et leur efficacité depend toujours de la force dont le gouvernement du pays dispose pour imposer ses volontés."

5. Anon. (14th c.), *Kitāb mafākhir al-barbar li-mu'allif majhūl*, ed. 'Abd al-Qādir Būbāya (Rabat: Dār Abī Raqrāq li-al-Ṭibā'a wa al-Nashr, 2005), 92. Cf. Al-Tijānī (d. 1321/2), *Riḥlat al-tijānī*, ed. Ḥusnī 'Abd al-Wahhāb (Tripoli and Tunis: Al-Dār al-'Arabiya lil-Kitāb, 1981), 96: "after the Shī'a ruled Egypt and the ruling dynasty in Ifrīqiyā changed from being Kutāmiya to Ṣanhājiya."

6. See Anon., *Kitāb mafākhir al-barbar*, 91.

7. Philip C. Naylor, *North Africa: A History from Antiquity to the Present* (Austin: University of Texas Press, 2009), 89.

8. One cannot expect that a textbook would do more than synthesize existing scholarship. However, this recent effort recapitulates the standard position in the field and is offered here only for illustration of its currency.

9. For critical and useful discussions of the period, see Pedro Chalmeta Gendrón, *Invasión e islamización: La sumisión de Hispania y la formación de al-Andalus* (Jaén: Universidad de Jaén, 2003); Alejandro García Sanjuán, *La conquista islámica y la tergiversación del pasado* (Madrid: Marcial Pons Historia, 2013); Eduardo Manzano Moreno, *Conquistadores, emires y califas: Los omeyas y la formación de al-Andalus* (Barcelona: Crítica, 2006). For a critical tour of Andalusī sources, see Gabriel Martinez-Gros, *Identité andalouse* (Paris: Sindbad, Actes Sud, 1997). For help with political chronology in English, see Leonard Patrick Harvey, *Islamic Spain, 1250–1500* (Chicago: University of Chicago Press, 1990); Hugh Kennedy, *Muslim Spain and Portugal: A Political History of al-Andalus* (London: Longman, 1996); Mahmoud Makki, "A Political History of al-Andalus (92/711–897/1492)," in *The Legacy of Muslim Spain*,

ed. Salma Khadra al-Jayyusi (Leiden: Brill, 1994), 3–87. See also Thomas F. Glick, *Islamic and Christian Spain in the Early Middle Ages* (Leiden: Brill, 2005); Mohammed Meouak, *Pouvoir souverain, administration centrale et élites politiques dans l'Espagne ummayade (IIe-IVe/VIIIe–Xe siècles)* (Helsinki: Academia Scientiarum Fennica, 1999). For the role of the Berbers of al-Andalus in the so-called Berber *fitna*, see 'Abd al-Qādir Būbāya, *Al-barbar fī al-andalus wa mawqifuhum min fitnat al-qarn al-khāmis al-hijrī, 422–92/711–1031* (Beirut: Dār al-Kutub al-'Ilmiyya, 2011); Eduardo Manzano Moreno, "Beréberes de al-Andalus: Los factores de un evolucion histórica," *Al-Qanṭara* 11 (1990): 397–428; Peter C. Scales, *The Fall of the Caliphate of Córdoba: Berbers and Andalusis in Conflict* (Leiden: Brill, 1994).

10. Many prominent men in the Mashriq had Berber slave mothers. The fact that 'Abd al-Raḥmān's mother remembered her tribal origins and that those origins were recognized by her relatives suggests that she was a concubine sent to the caliph. If that is the case, then she would not have been the descendant of a slave from a century early but relocated to Damascus more recently.

11. Būbāya, *Al-barbar*, 55.

12. Ibn al-Abbār (d. 1260), *Al-ḥulla al-sayrā'*, ed. Ḥusayn Mu'nis (Cairo: al-Sharika al-'Arabiyya li al-Ṭibā'a wa al-Nashr, 1963), 1:35–42; 2:341–42, 347–50; Ibn 'Idhārī (d. early 14th c.), *Al-bayān al-mughrib fī akhbār al-andalus wa al-maghrib*, ed. G.S. Colin and E. Levi-Provençal (Beirut: Dār al-Thaqāfa, 1967), 2:40–60; Būbāya, *Al-barbar*, 56.

13. Anon., *Fatḥ al-andalus*, ed. Luis Molina (Madrid: CSIC, 1994), 104. Noticeably, Berbers are Muslims and not slaves.

14. James L. Boone and Nancy L. Benco, "Islamic Settlement in North Africa and the Iberian Peninsula," *Annual Review of Anthropology* 28 (1999): 51–71.

15. Booty was the main form of payment for the Berbers. Ibn al-Khaṭīb, *al-iḥāṭa fī akhbār gharnāṭa*, ed. Muḥammad 'Abd Allāh 'Inān (Cairo: Maktabat al-Khānjī, 1973), 1:102–5. It was not until the rule of Muḥammad I (852–86) that land grants were extended to the Berbers on a large scale.

16. Helena de Felipe has contributed a great deal to our understanding of these issues. See Helena de Felipe, *Identidad y onomástica de los berebéres de al-Andalus* (Madrid: CSIC, 1997).

17. Al-Wansharīsī (d. 1508), *Al-mi'yār al-mu'rib wa-al-jāmi' al-mughrib 'an fatāwā ahl ifrīqīya wa-al-andalus wa-al-maghrib*, ed. Muḥammad Ḥajjī (Rabat: Wizārat al-Awqāf wa-al-Shu'ūn al-Islāmīya lil-Mamlaka al-Maghribiyya, 1981), 6:52.

18. For the tradition among the Berbers of al-Andalus of shaving their heads to distinguish themselves from the Arabs in battle, see Anon., *Fatḥ al-andalus*, 54. For the political tradition of breastfeeding adult men as a way of adopting them, see al-Raqīq al-Qayrawānī (fl. 11th c.), *Tārīkh ifrīqiyā wa al-maghrib.*, ed. al-Munjī al-Ka'bī (Tunis: Maṭba'at al-Wasaṭ, 1968), 58.

19. For the Berber tradition of drawing lots to divide up booty and territory, see Ibn Bulughīn (b. 1056), *Kitāb al-tibyān 'an al-ḥāditha al-kā'ina bi-dawlat banī zīrī fī gharnāṭa*, ed. 'Alī 'Umar (Riyadh: Maktabat al-Thaqāfa al-Dīniya, 2006), 34.

20. Dalāl Lawātī, *'Āmmat al-qayrawān fī 'aṣr al-aghāliba* (Cairo: Ru'ya lil-Nashrwa al-Tawzī', 2015); Hichem Djaït, "L'Afrique arabe au VIIIe siècle (86–184 H/705–800)," *Annales: Économies, Sociétés, Civilisations* 28, no. 3 (1973): 601–21; Hichem Djaït, "La wilāya d'Ifrīqiya au IIe/VIIIe siècle: Étude institutionnelle," *Studia Islamica* 27 (1967): 77–121, and 28 (1968): 79–108; Hichem Djaït, *Ta'sīs al-gharb al-islāmī: Al-qarn al-awwal wa-al-thānī H., al-sābi'wa-al-thāmin M.* (Beirut: Dār al-Ṭalī'a lil-Ṭibā'a wa-al-Nashr, 2004); Mohamed Talbi, *L'émirat*

Aghlabide 184–296/800–909 (Paris: Adrien-Maisonneuve, 1966); Fatḥī Zaghrūt, *Al-'alāqāt bayna al-umawiyīn wa-al-fāṭimiyīn fī al-andalus wa-al-shamāl al-ifrīqī, 300 H–350 H.* (Cairo: Dār al-Tawzī' wa-al-Nashr al-Islāmiyya, 2006).

21. For about a century, the Qarāmiṭa who ruled in eastern Arabia and Baḥrayn constituted a serious threat to the 'Abbāsids. They attacked caravans, raided cities, and even defeated 'Abbāsid armies. In 930, they sacked Mecca, plundered major sites, and took the Black Stone from the Ka'ba—the 'Abbāsids paid a hefty sum for its return in 952. A major defeat in 976 forced them to retreat, gradually losing influence until their complete defeat in the mid-eleventh century. Mixing Ismā'īlī Shī'ī ideas with a host of others, the Qarāmiṭa left an important imprint on intellectual production, if only negatively through those who argued against them. Although their ideas did circulate in the Maghrib and al-Andalus, they did not lead to the formation of major political forces capable of threatening the established order. See Farhad Daftary, *The Assassin Legends: Myths of the Isma'ilis* (London: I.B. Tauris, 1994); Muḥammad Fayyāḍ, *Qiyām al-dawla al-fāṭimīya: Ḥarakat al-tashayyu' al-ismā'īlī wa-atharuhā 'alá taṭawwur al-mashrū' al-shī'ī* (Cairo: Dār al-'Ālam al-'Arabī, 2014).

22. There is a tendency in the sources, especially Andalusī and pro-Aghlabid ones, to describe the supporters of Idrīs and his son Idrīs b. Idrīs as Berbers without qualification. See, for example, Ibn al-Abbār, *Al-ḥulla*, 1:98–101, 131–33. See also Chafik T. Benchekroun, "Les Idrissides: L'histoire contre son histoire," *Al-Masāq: Islam and the Mediterranean* 23, no. 3 (2011): 171–88.

23. This heightened interest in the genealogies of these groups. For an informed and helpful historical biography of 'Abd al-Raḥmān III and his times, see Maribel Fierro, *'Abd al-Raḥmān III: The First Cordoban Caliph* (Oxford: OneWorld, 2005).

24. In this political context, see the interesting distinction between the Berbers of al-Andalus and the "Maghāriba" in al-Ḍabbī (d. 1203), *Kitāb bughyat al-multamis fī tārīkh rijāl al-andalus*, ed. Franciscus Codera and Julianus Ribera (Madrid: Jose de Rojas, 1885), 21. For an example of those who migrated to al-Andalus, see the biographical note of Muḥammad b. al-Ḥusayn al-Ṭubnī al-Zabī (fl. 10th c.) in al-Ḥumaydī (d. 1095), *Jadhwat al-muqtabis fī dhikr wulāt al-andalus* (Cairo: al-Dār al-Maṣriya li al-Ta'līf wa al-Tarjama, 1966), 50. Maghribī *'ulamā'* may have Berber genealogies but are not called al-Barbarī. See al-Khushanī (d. 971?), *Ṭabaqāt 'ulamā' ifrīqiyā*, ed. As'ad Jum'a (Tunis: Dār Kīrānīs, 2014).

25. Al-Wansharīsī, *Al-mi'yār*, 6:182.

26. See Michael Brett, *The Rise of the Fatimids: The World of the Mediterranean and the Middle East in the Fourth Century of the Hijra, Tenth Century CE* (Leiden: Brill, 2001); Michael Brett, *The Fatimid Empire* (Edinburgh: Edinburgh University Press, 2017); Farhat Dachraoui, *Le Califat Fatimide au Maghreb (296–365 H./909–975 Jc.): Histoire politique et institutions* (Tunis: Société Tunisienne de Diffusion, 1981); Heinz Halm, *The Empire of the Mahdī: The Rise of the Fatimids* (Leiden: Brill, 1996).

27. For an illustration of the irrelevance of "Berber" in post-Fāṭimid Egypt and the preference for specificity, see Ibn al-Ṭuwayral-Qaysarānī (d. 1220), *Nuzhat al-muqlatayn fī akhbār al-dawlatayn*, ed. Ayman Fu'ād Sayyid (Stuttgart: Franz Steiner, 1992), 57, 165.

28. For an example of anti-Fāṭimid usage, see Ibn al-Abbār, *Al-ḥulla*, 1:198.

29. Al-Qāḍī al-Nu'mān (d. 974), *Iftitāḥ al-da'wā*, ed. Farḥāt al-Dachrāwī (Tunis: Al-Sharika al-Tūnisiya lil-Tawzī', 1975), 27.

30. Al-Qāḍī al-Nu'mān, *Iftitāḥ al-da'wā*, 104.

31. Al-Qāḍī al-Nu'mān, *Iftitāḥ al-da'wā*, 85. See also al-Nuwayrī (d. 1333), *Nihāyat al-arab fī funūn al-adab*, ed. Mustafa Abū Ḍayf Aḥmad (Rabat: Maṭba'at al-Najāḥ al-Jadīda, 1985),

30–31. Al-Nuwayrī relies on al-Raqīq al-Qayrawānī and very few Egyptian historians for his information.

32. Al-Qāḍī al-Nu'mān, *Iftitāḥ al-da'wā*, 48. Cf. al-Maqrīzī (d. 1442), *Itti'āẓ al-ḥunafā bi-akhbār al-a'imma al-fāṭimīyīn al-khulafā*, ed. Jamāl al-Dīn al-Shayyāl (Cairo: Lajnat Iḥyā' al-Turāth al-Islāmī, 1967), 1:55–59. In order to capture the political situation, al-Maqrīzī distinguished between the Kutāma and the Berbers: *ilā 'an taqātalat kutāma 'alayhi ma'a qabā'il al-barbar*; *wa tafarraqat al-barābir wa kutāma*; and *fa-ḥamala al-kutāmiyyūn 'alā al-barbar*. The Berbers were generally nondescript antagonists. In other instances, he described the Kutāma as Kutāma Berbers. Al-Maqrīzī, *Itti'āẓ*, 1:47.

33. Yaacov Lev, *State and Society in Fatimid Egypt* (Leiden: Brill, 1991), 89.

34. For a reference to a neighborhood in Cairo named after the Zawīla who followed Jawhar, the Fāṭimid general who conquered Egypt, see al-Maqrīzī, *Itti'āẓ*, 3:194.

35. Ibn 'Āmir never claimed to be ruler or caliph, making sure to acknowledge the precedence of the Umayyads, even as he made sure to weaken them. However, he did take on a royal name, and passed his title of *ḥājib* to his son. He also built a palace on the outskirts of the city and made it the center of government—thus marginalizing the Umayyad role in administration.

36. The Umayyads originally imported Ṣaqāliba slaves from central and eastern Europe but then from northern Iberia. They made them into a corps of soldiers and administrators whose loyalty lay with the ruler, much as the 'Abbāsid did with Turks.

37. Under Ibn 'Āmir, the title of *ḥājib* became that of the effective ruler. For an example of old Berbers (*baladiyūn*), see Ibn al-Qūṭiya, *Tārīkh*, 83.

38. See Pierre Guichard and Bruna Soravia, *Les royaumes de taifas: Apogée culturel et déclin politique des émirats andalolus du XIe siècle* (Paris: Geuthner, 2007); Göran Larsson, *Ibn García's Shu'ūbiyya Letter: Ethnic and Theological Tensions in Medieval al-Andalus* (Leiden: Brill, 2003); David J. Wasserstein, *The Rise and Fall of the Party Kings: Politics and Society in Islamic Spain, 1002–1086* (Princeton: Princeton University Press, 1986).

39. For Slavs defeating Berbers to establish an independent emirate, see Ibn al-Dalā'ī (1003–85), *Nuṣūṣ 'an al-andalus min kitāb tarṣī' al-akhbār wa-tanwī' al-athār, wa-al-bustān fī gharā'ib al-buldān wa-al-masālik 'ilā jamī' al-mamālik*, ed. 'Abd al-'Aziz al-Aḥwānī (Madrid: Maṭba'at Ma'had al-Dīrāsāt al-Islāmīyah, 1965), 16.

40. See 'Umar Amkāsū, *Al-mashrū' al-murābiṭī fī al-andalus: Bayna al-najāḥ wa-al-ikhfāq* (Casablanca: Ifrīqiyā al-Sharq, 2016); Muḥammad 'Amrānī, *Ḥawāḍir al-andalus bayna al-intifāḍa wal-thawra khilāl al-'aṣr al-murābiṭī fī al-qarn al-sādis al-hijrī, al-thānī 'ashar al-mīlādī* (Rabat: Dār Abī Raqrāq lil-Ṭibā'a wal-Nashr, 2006); Amira K. Bennison, *The Almoravid and Almohad Empires* (Edinburgh: Edinburgh University Press, 2016); Jacinto Bosch Vilá, *Historia de Marruecos: Los Almorávides* (Tetouan: Marroquí, 1956); Camilo Gómez-Rivas, *Law and the Islamization of Morocco under the Almoravids: The Fatwās of Ibn Rushd al-Jadd to the Far Maghrib* (Leiden: Brill, 2015); 'Alī Muḥammad Muḥammad Ṣallābī, *Dawlat al-murābiṭīn* (Beirut: Maktabat Ḥasan al-'Aṣriyya, 2012).

41. A number of dynasties took power in cities across the Maghrib, from Barqa to the Atlantic. Not all were Berber like the Maghrāwa Banū al-Rand of Qafṣa or the Banū Khazrūn of Tripoli; some like the Banū Qurra of Barqa were Arab (Hilālī). What is critical here is that the Banū Hilāl and Banū Sulaym were the most active "Arabs," a word that also means "Bedouin." The continued existence of Ibāḍī dynasties in the Sahara, like the Banū al-Khaṭṭāb of Zawīla (918-1172) and their role in trans-Saharan trade, ought not to be forgot-

ten even if they have tended to be understood more as Ibāḍī than Berber. Amar S. Baadj, *Saladin, the Almohads, and the Banū Ghāniya: The Contest for North Africa (12th and 13th centuries)* (Leiden: Brill, 2015), 117–18.

42. Al-Wansharīsī, *Al-mi'yār*, 3:399.

43. The word has often been "corrected" by editors of Andalusī texts. See, for example, Ibn al-Qūṭiya, *Tārīkh*, 145; Ibn al-Khaṭīb, *Al-iḥāṭa*, 1:103, 432, 516. What is noteworthy is that *barābir* refers to Berbers on the other side of al-Andalus and not all Berbers all over the Maghrib. In modern times, the term appears in northern Morocco, but without al-Andalus it appears as a local usage. Maghribī sources seem to have lagged behind Andalusī ones in using this word, but a closer look at the question may establish a more precise chronology. For an example of Andalusī *barābir*, see also Ibn al-Abbār, *Al-ḥulla*, 1:160, 257, 291; 2:5, 32, 38, 108; Ibn Ḥayyān (d. 1076), *Al-muqtabas min anbā'ahlal-Andalus*, ed. Maḥmūd 'Alī Makkī (Beirut: Dār al-Kitāb al-'Arabī, 1973), 84, 266; Ibn al-Khaṭīb, *Al-iḥāṭa*, 1:515; Ibn Sa'īd al-Maghribī (d. 1286), *Kitāb al-jughrāfiya*, ed. Ismā'īl al-'Arabī (Beirut: Manshūrāt al-Maktabal-Tijārī lil-Ṭibā'a wa-al-Nashr wa-al-Tawzī', 1970), 115. For an example from Ifrīqiyā about *barābir* in the West, see al-Raqīq al-Qayrawānī, *Tārīkh*, 70.

44. For Berber men in al-Andalus importing wives from the Maghrib, see al-Wansharīsī, *Al-mi'yār*, 3:84, 148.

45. Interestingly, the Almohad historian Ibn Ṣāḥib al-Ṣalāt does not seem to have liked the word Berber, using the names of specific groups throughout. See Ibn Ṣāḥib al-Ṣalāt (fl. 12th c.), *Tārīkh al-mann bi-al-imāma 'alā almustaḍ'afīn bi-an ja'alahum allāh a'imma wa-ja'alahum al-wārithīn*, ed. 'Abd al-Hādī al-Tāzī, 2 vols. (Beirut: Dār al-Andalus li al-Ṭibā'a wa al-Nashr, 1965).

46. See Baadj, *Saladin*, 154–67.

47. Hussein Fancy, *The Mercenary Mediterranean: Sovereignty, Violence, and Religion in the Medieval Crown of Aragon* (Chicago: University of Chicago Press, 2016).

48. Pascal Buresi and Hicham El Aallaoui, *Governing the Empire: Provincial Administration in the Almohad Caliphate (1224–1269); Critical Edition, Translation, and Study of Manuscript 4752 of the Hasaniyya Library in Rabat Containing 77 Taqādīm ("Appointments")*, trans. Travis Bruce (Leiden: Brill, 2013); Patrice Cressier, Maribel Fierro, and Luis Molina, eds., *Los almohades: Problemas y perspectivas* (Madrid: CSIC, 2005); Maribel Fierro, *The Almohad Revolution: Politics and Religion in the Islamic West During the Twelfth-Thirteenth Centuries* (Farnham: Ashgate, 2014); Mehdi Ghouirgate, *L'ordre almohade (1120–1269): Une nouvelle lecture anthropologique* (Toulouse: Presses Universitaires du Mirail, 2014); Mehdi Ghouirgate, "Le berbère au moyen âge: Une culture linguistique en cours de reconstitution," *Annales: Histoire, Sciences Sociales* 3 (2015): 577–605; Rachid El Hour, "Some Reflections about the Use of the Berber Language in the Medieval and Early Modern Maghrib: Data from Hagiographic Sources," *Al-Masāq: Journal of the Medieval Mediterranean* 26, no. 3 (2014): 288–98; Rachid El Hour, "Reflexiones acerca de las dinastías bereberes y lengua bereber en el magreb medieval," *Miscelánea de Estudios Árabes y Hebraicos: Sección Árabe-Islam* 64 (2015): 45–59; Mohamed Meouak, *La langue berbère au Maghreb médiéval: Textes, contextes, analyses* (Leiden: Brill, 2015), 157–68.

49. Abū al-Fidā' (1273–1331) noted that "Ibn Sa'īd (d. 1286) said that the languages of the Berbers had the same origin but that its branches are so different that they [speakers of any branch need] a translator to understand [speakers of another]." Abū al-Fidā', *Al-mukhtaṣar fī akhbār al-bashar* (Beirut: Dār al-Kitāb al-Lubnānī: Dār al-Baḥḥār, 1956–61), 1:97.

50. Ibn Rushd found himself in a difficult personal situation because of his translation of Aristotle's reference to the giraffe. The contentious sentence read: "I saw it in the hands of the king of the *barbar*," which was interpreted as an attack on his patrons. See 'Abd al-Wāḥid al-Marrākushī (b. 1185), *Al-mu'jib fī talkhīṣ akhbār al-maghrib, min ladun fatḥ al-Andalus ilā ākhir 'aṣr al-muwaḥḥidīn ma'a mā yattaṣilu bi-tārīkh hādhihi al-fatra min akhbār al-qurrā' wa-a'yān al-kuttāb*, ed. Muḥammad Sa'īd al-'Iryān (Cairo: al-Majlis al-A'lā li al-Shu'ūn al-Dīniya, 1963), 384–85.

51. The Marīnids landed a small army in Tarifa in 1271 but did not go any further.

52. The contribution of Ibāḍī written and oral traditions to the *mafākhir/faḍā'il* genre has its own lineages. See, for example, the section on the *faḍā'il al-barbar min al-'ajam* in Abū Zakariyā al-Warjalānī (d. ca. 1078), *Kitāb al-sīra wa akhbār al-a'imma*, ed. 'Abd al-Raḥmān Ayyūb (Tunis: Al-Dār al-Tūnusiyya lil-Nashr, 1985), 52–58; al-Darjīnī (fl. 13th c.), *Kitāb ṭabaqāt al-mashāyikh bi-al-maghrib*, ed. Ibrāhīm Ṭallāy (Qasanṭīna: Maṭba'at al-Ba'th, 1974), 1:15–19.

53. Brett and Fentress saw "profound changes affecting the Berbers even as Ibn Khaldūn was celebrating their grandeur as a great nation. With the disappearance of so many old identities and the formation of so many new, we are moving forward, out of the world of the *Kitāb al-'ibar* into the modern history of North Africa, in which the story of the Berbers is no longer the history of the great dynasties but of their retreat into relative isolation as they lost, in effect, their monopoly of tribal society in the Maghrib." Brett and Fentress, *The Berbers*, 152.

54. Al-Wansharīsī, *Al-mi'yār*, 3:279–80.

55. Nelly Amri, *Les saints en islam, les messagers de l'espérance: Sainteté et eschatologie au Maghreb aux XIVe et XVe siècles* (Paris: Les Éditions du Cerf, 2008); Vincent J. Cornell, *Realm of the Saint: Power and Authority in Moroccan Sufism* (Austin: University of Texas Press, 1998); Houari Touati, *Entre Dieu et les hommes: Lettrés, saints et sorciers au Maghreb, 17e siècle* (Paris: Éditions de l'École des hautes études en sciences sociales, 1994).

56. Al-Wansharīsī, *Al-mi'yār*, 3:84–85.

57. It is possible that the Qaysī in question belonged to the Banū Hilāl.

CHAPTER 3

1. The literature on religious difference (*al-milal wa al-niḥal*) left its imprint on Ibn Khaldūn's scheme. Yet, because he believed that "charismatic religious leadership" and "religious fervor" could exacerbate but never replace feelings of solidarity (*'aṣabiya*) among genealogically defined groups (tribes), Ibn Khaldūn privileged the "Bedouin" and "urban" as the two poles of civilization. This is just to say that in his fourteenth-century mind, the *milal* and *niḥal* genre was a source of information to be fitted within a primarily genealogical frame for history.

2. Jean Servier uses the same passage from Ibn Khaldūn as an epigraph to his own synthetic work. Jean Servier, *Que sais-je? Les Berbères* (Paris: PUF, 1990), 2. Although the English word *people* is the accepted translation for the French *peuple*, the two are not exactly the same.

3. Michael Brett and Elizabeth Fentress, *The Berbers* (Oxford and Cambridge, MA: Blackwell, 1996), 1.

4. Brett and Fentress, *The Berbers*, 7.

5. H. T. Norris, *The Berbers in Arabic Literature* (London and New York: Longman; Beirut: Librairie du Liban, 1982), 1. For Norris, the Berbers are a single people and many peoples. "By the Berbers I mean the family of North African peoples who share a common language of clearly distinguishable and frequently mutually unintelligible dialects. Arabic Literature in this context denotes the sources in Arabic which shed light on the life and ideas of these Berber peoples." "[This book] is a presentation of a people as revealed in written and oral literature." Norris, *The Berbers*, x.

6. "En aucun moment de leur longue histoire les Berbères ne semblent avoir eu conscience d'une unité ethnique ou linguistique." Gabriel Camps, *Berbères: Aux marges de l'histoire* (Paris: Éditions des Hespérides, 1980), 17.

7. Norris, *The Berbers*, 8.

8. Brett and Fentress, *The Berbers*, 8 (italics mine). Brett and Fentress express support for the so-called Berber Spring and take a political stand that explains why they believe doing so is "worth" it. Whether this commits them to particular interpretations of medieval texts is worth pondering.

9. Brett and Fentress, *The Berbers*, 282.

10. See, for example, Julia Bray, "Men, Women, and Slaves in Abbasid Society," in *Gender in the Early Medieval World: East and West, 300–900*, ed. Leslie Brubaker and Julia M. H. Smith (Cambridge: Cambridge University Press, 2004), 121–46; Matthew Gordon, "Preliminary Remarks on Slaves and Slave Labor in the Third/Ninth Century 'Abbasid Empire," in *Slaves and Households in the Near East*, ed. Laura Culbertson (Chicago: Oriental Institute, University of Chicago, 2011), 71–84; Craig Perry, "Historicizing Slavery in the Medieval Islamic World," *International Journal of Middle East Studies* 49 (2017): 133–38.

11. On *futūḥ*, see note 20 in Chapter 1.

12. Ibn 'Abd al-Ḥakam (d. 871), *The History of the Conquests of Egypt, North Africa, and Spain*, ed. Charles Torrey (New Haven: Yale University Press, 1922), 204; hereafter cited as *The Conquests*. For the description of beautiful Berber slave girls, see Ibn 'Abd-al-Ḥakam, *The Conquests*, 202. Ibn Ḥabīb (d. 852/3), *Kitāb al-tārīkh*, ed. Sālim Musṭafā al-Badrī (Beirut: Dār al-Kutub al-'Ilmiyya, 1999), 126: "Al-Layth [b. Sa'd] said: Nothing in [the history of] Islam compares to the number of captives made by Mūsā [b. Nuṣayr]." Also al-Mālikī (d. 1061), *Riyāḍ al-nufūs fī ṭabaqāt 'ulamā' al-qayrawān wa-ifrīqīya wa-zuhhādihim wa-nussākihim wa-siyar min akhbārihim wa-faḍā'ilihim wa-awṣāfihim*, ed. Bashīr al-Bakkūsh (Beirut: Dār al-Gharb al-Islāmī, 1994), 1:38, 57.

13. Egypt was an important site for the production of learned knowledge about the Maghrib and its inhabitants. The earliest narratives about the conquests of northwest Africa all have a clear Egyptian stamp on them.

14. Saḥnūn, *Al-mudawwana al-kubrā, riwāyat al-imām saḥnūn b. sa'īd al-tanūkhī 'an al-imām 'abd al-raḥmān b. al-qāsim al-'utakī* (Cairo: Maṭba'at al-Sa'āda, 1323 [1905]), 10:141. Interestingly, Saḥnūn included this quote from Mālik at a time when Khorasānian forces were an important component of the pro-'Abbāsid forces that had put the Aghlabids on the throne in Ifrīqiyā (800).

15. *Kātib*: a scribe and more generally someone who is able to write in Arabic, keep records, etc.

16. Saḥnūn, *Al-mudawwana*, 9:3–4.

17. Al-Mas'ūdī, *Murūj al-dhahab wa ma'ādin al-jawhar*, ed. Hishām al-Na'sān and 'Abd al-Majīd Ṭu'ma Ḥalabī (Beirut: Dār al-Ma'rifa, 1983), 1:60.

18. My examination of the use of *jins* and *ajnās* in early Arabic sources shows that they tend to be applied to non-Arabs rather than Arabs.

19. Ibn Sa'īd commented that the Berbers that were prized in the early period were not the Berbers of the Maghrib but rather those of East Africa and that they disappeared from the "Bilād al-Islām" after they converted to Islam. Ibn Sa'īd al-Maghribī (d. 1286), *Kitāb al-jughrāfiya*, ed. Ismā'īl al-'Arabī (Beirut: Manshūrāt al-Maktab al-Tijārī lil-Ṭibā'a wa-al-Nashr wa-al-Tawzī', 1970), 81.

20. Qur'ān 49:13. See also below.

21. Al-Ṭabarī, *Jāmi' al-bayān 'an ta'wīl al-qur'ān*, ed. Bashshār 'Awwād and 'Iṣām Fāris al-Ḥurristānī (Beirut, Mu'assasat al-Risāla, 1994), 7:86.

22. See also Mujāhid b. Jabr al-Makhzūmī (m. ca. 720), *Tafsīr mujāhid*, ed. 'Abd al-Raḥmān al-Ṭāhir b. Muḥammad al-Suwartī (Beirut: al-Manshūrāt al-'Ilmīya, [1977?]), 2:605–9.

23. Muqātil b. Sulaymān al-Balkhī (d. 767), *Tafsīr muqātil*, ed. 'Abd Allāh Maḥmūd Shiḥāta ([Cairo]: al-Hay'a al-Miṣrīya al-'Āmma lil-Kitāb, [1983–90]), 3:264.

24. Roy Mottahedeh, "The Shu'ūbiyah Controversy and the Social History of Early Islamic Iran," *International Journal of Middle East Studies* 7, no. 2 (1976): 165.

25. Al-Maḥallī (d. 1459) and al-Suyūṭī (d. 1505), *Tafsīr al-jalālayn: Taḥqīq wa-ikhrāj fī jadāwil 'aṣriya lil-imāmayn jalāl al-dīn al-maḥallī wa-jalāl al-dīn al-suyūṭī*, ed. Abū Fāris al-Daḥdāḥ (Beirut: Maktabat Lubnān Nāshirūn, 2000), 687.

26. Marmaduke Pickthall, *The Meaning of the Glorious Koran: An Explanatory Translation* (London: A.A. Knopf, 1930), 369.

27. Abdullah Yusuf Ali, *The Holy Qur'ān: Text, Translation, and Commentary* (New York: Hafner, 1946), 1407.

28. Arthur J. Arberry, *The Koran Interpreted* (London: Allen & Unwin; New York: Macmillan, 1955), 538.

29. Frederick Denny, "Umma," in *EI²*, 10:862.

30. See Fred Donner, *Muḥammad and the Believers: At the Origins of Islam* (Cambridge, MA: Belknap Press, 2010).

31. Ṣā'id al-Andalusī, *Ṭabaqāt al-umam*, ed. Louis Cheikho (Beirut: al-Maṭba'a al-Kāthūlikiya lil-Abā' al-Yasū'iyīn, 1912), 7–8. See also Ṣā'id al-Andalusī, *Science in the Medieval World: "Book of the Categories of Nations,"* trans. and ed. Sema'an I. Salem and Alok Kumar (Austin, University of Texas Press, 1991), 6.

32. Cf. al-Shahrastānī (d. 1153): "There are four great nations (*umam*): the Arabs, the Persians, the Romans, and the Indians." Ibn Ḥazm (d. 1064), *Kitāb al-fiṣal fī al-milal wa-al-ahwā' wa-al-niḥal li-abī muḥammad 'alī ibn aḥmad ibn ḥazm al-ẓāhirī; wa-bi-hāmishihi al-milal wa-al-niḥal li-abī al-fatḥ muḥammad ibn 'abd al-karīm al-shahrastānī* (Cairo: Al-Maṭba'a al-Adabiya, 1899–1903), 1:3. See also Ibn Qutayba (d. 889), *Faḍl al-'arab wa al-tanbīh 'alā 'ulūmiha*, ed. Walīd Maḥmūd Khāliṣ (Abu Dhabi: al-Majma' al-Thaqāfī, 1998).

33. Ṣā'id al-Andalusī, *Ṭabaqāt*, 9; *Science*, 8.

34. I follow the original insight by Maya Shatzmiller who was first to propose that these genealogies be analyzed in relation to the place and time of their appearance. Maya Shatzmiller, "Le mythe d'origine Berbère: Aspects historiographiques et sociaux," *Revue de l'Occident Musulman et de la Méditerranée* 35 (1983): 145–56. For a survey of scholarly approaches and useful bibliographic help, see *Genealogy and Knowledge in Muslim Societies: Understanding the Past*, ed. Sarah Bowen Savant and Helena de Felipe (Edinburgh: Edinburgh

University Press, 2014); Zoltán Szombathy, "Genealogy in Medieval Muslim Societies," *Studia Islamica* 95 (2002): 5–35.

35. Ibn al-Kalbī (d. 819/20), *Nasab maʿadd wa al-yaman*, ed. Nājī Ḥasan (Damascus: Dār al-Yaqaẓa al-ʿArabiyya, 1988), 2:548. Cf. Ibn Qutayba (d. 889), *Kitāb al-Maʿārif*, ed. Tharwat ʿUkkāsha (Cairo: Maṭbaʿat Dār al-Kutub, 1969), 627–28. It is possible that this is an older tradition pertaining to the Berbers of the Red Sea adapted to the new historical circumstances. See Daniela Amaldi, "La poesia yemenita dalla ǧāhiliyya al IX secolo: Stato degli studi in occidente," *Quaderni di Studi Arabi* 15 (1997): 119–30.

36. See the poem that ends "And from us in the lands of the west a *jund* who attached themselves to the Berbers until they reached the land of the Berbers (*arḍ barbar*)" in al-Hamdānī (d. 945), *Ṣifat jazīrat al-ʿarab*, ed. David Heinrich Müller (Leiden: Brill, 1884), 206.

37. For helpful guidance and relevant bibliographies, see Zayde Antrim, *Routes and Realms: The Power of Place in the Early Islamic World* (Oxford: Oxford University Press, 2012); Christophe Picard, *La mer des califes: Une histoire de la Méditerranée musulmane, VIIe–XIIe siècle* (Paris: Éditions du Seuil, 2015); Karen C. Pinto, *Medieval Islamic Maps: An Exploration* (Chicago: University of Chicago Press, 2016); Travis Zadeh, *Mapping Frontiers Across Medieval Islam: Geography, Translation, and the ʿAbbāsid Empire* (London: I.B. Tauris, 2011).

38. Al-Yaʿqūbī (d. 897/8), *Kitāb al-buldān*, ed. G.H.A. Juynboll (Leiden: Brill, 1861), 132.

39. For imperial politics of knowledge in the Mashriq, see Antoine Borrut, *Entre mémoire et pouvoir: L'espace syrien sous les derniers Omeyyades et les premiers Abbasides (v. 72–193/692–809)* (Leiden: Brill, 2011).

40. Ibn ʿAbd al-Ḥakam, *The Conquests*, 8.

41. See "Marāqiya" in Yāqūt al-Ḥamawī, *Muʿjam al-buldān* (Beirut: Dār Ṣādir, 1977), 5:93.

42. See "Barqa" in Yāqūt al-Ḥamawī, *Muʿjam al-buldān*, 1:388–89.

43. See "al-Sūs" in Yāqūt al-Ḥamawī, *Muʿjam al-buldān*, 3:280–81.

44. Ibn ʿAbd al-Ḥakam, *The Conquests*, 170.

45. Ibn ʿAbd al-Ḥakam, *The Conquest*, 200. Contrast this usage with Ibn al-Qūṭiya's who describes a multiplicity of kings of the Berbers, suggesting that al-Kāhina was the queen of those Berbers who fought Ibn al-Nuʿmān. Ibn al-Qūṭiya (d. 977), *Tārīkh iftitāḥ al-Andalus*, ed. ʿAbd Allāh Anīs al-Ṭabbāʿ (Beirut: Muʾassasat al-Maʿārif, 1994), 157, 166 (*wa kharaja min wujūh al-barbar miʾat rajul, fīhim banū kusayla, wa banū yaṣdur, wa banū mulūk al-barbar*; *adkhala ʿalayhim mūsā mulūk al-barbar*).

46. On the evolution of the legend of the Kāhina over the centuries, see Abdelmajid Hannoum, *Colonial Histories, Post-colonial Memories: The Legend of the Kahina, a North African Heroine* (Portsmouth: Heinemann, 2001).

47. Ibn Khaldūn, *The Muqaddimah: An Introduction to History*, trans. Franz Rosenthal (Princeton: Princeton University Press, 1967), 3:6.

48. For the state of the question, see Camilla Adang, Maribel Fierro, and Sabine Schmidtke,eds., *Ibn Ḥazm of Cordoba: The Life and Works of a Controversial Thinker* (Leiden: Brill, 2013).

49. Although it may seem surprising not to include Ibn Ḥazm's work on various schools of thought and groups (*al-Faṣl (or al-Fiṣal) fī al-milal wa al-ahwāʾ wa al-niḥal*), the argument here is that I am merely following Ibn Khaldūn's logic, which prioritizes genealogy as an organizing principle.

50. See his introductory notes in Ibn Ḥazm, *Jamharat ansāb al-ʿarab*, ed. Évariste Levi-Provençal (Cairo: Dār al-Maʿārif bi Miṣr, 1948). See also the articles by José Miguel Puerta

Vílchez, Bruna Soravia, Alejandro García Sanjuán, David J. Wasserstein, and Gabriel Martinez-Gros in Adang et al., *Ibn Ḥazm of Cordoba.*

51. See Anon., *Fatḥ al-Andalus*, ed. Luis Molina (Madrid: CSIC, 1994), 55: "[Ibn Ḥazm] said: the unbelievers of the Berbers were the worst unbelievers because they did not belong to the People of the Book and had no Law (*shar'*). The same goes for their Muslims who are the worst of Muslims and their most spiteful."

52. This reading of the outward meaning (*ẓāhir*) of the title may seem forced, but has the benefit of agreeing with Ibn Ḥazm's own intellectual stance. Even if he was criticized and shunned for his Ẓāhirī position, Ibn Ḥazm was not an uncritical proponent of that school, its founder, or its followers.

53. Ibn Ḥazm, *Jamhara*, 1.

54. Ibn Ḥazm, *Jamhara*, 1–6.

55. Ibn Ḥazm, *Jamhara*, 6.

56. Ibn Ḥazm, *Jamhara*, 430.

57. See also the case of the non-Berber African *'ajam*. Fathi Bahri, "Les 'Adjam al-balad: Une minorité sociale d'origine autochtone en Ifrīqiyā aghlabide (IIIe-IXe siècles)," in *Mutations d'identités en Méditerranée:Moyen Âge et époque contemporaine*, ed. Henri Bresc and Christiane Veauvy ([Saint-Denis]: Éditions Bouchène, 2000), 67–84.

58. See, for instance, Ibn Ḥazm, *Jamhara*, 89–91.

59. Ibn Ḥazm, *Jamhara*, 464.

60. Ibn 'Abd al-Halīm (fl. 14th c.), *Kitāb al-ansāb*, in *Tres textos árabes sobre beréberes en el occidente islámico*, ed. Muḥammad Ya'là (Madrid: CSIC, 1996), 46. For al-Bakrī, "all the Berbers claim to be [descendants of] Arabs" (*al-barbar kulluhum yaz'amnūn annahum min al-'arab*). Abū 'Ubayd Allāh al-Bakrī (d. 1094), *Kitāb al-masālik wa al-mamālik*, ed. A.P. Van Leeuwen and A. Férré (Tunis: al-Dār al-'Arabiyya lil-Kitāb, 1992), 1:91.

61. Pre-Islamic Arabs expressed similar sentiments about their tribes and the battles (*ayyām*) that recorded their honors.

62. *Faḍā'il al-andalus wa ahliha, li-ibn ḥazm wa ibn sa'īd wa al-shaqundī*, ed. Ṣalāḥ al-Dīn al-Munajjid (Beirut: Dār al-Kitāb al-Jadīd, 1968), 3. For an example of Berbers as distinct from the people of al-Andalus (*ahl al-balad*), see Ibn al-Qūṭiya, *Tārīkh*, 83 (*fa qāla ahl al-balad wa al-barbara sama'nā wa aṭa'nā*).

63. *Faḍā'il*, 3.

64. *Faḍā'il*, 8–9: "I do not recall reading about the history of al-Qayrawān, the country of our interlocutor, other than the *Mughrib 'an akhbār al-maghrib* and the writings of Muḥammad b. Yūsuf al-Warrāq [d. 963], who wrote a long time for al-Mustanṣir on the routes and kingdoms of Ifrīqiyā, and many books on its kings, their wars, and their courtiers. He also wrote on the history of Tāhart, Wahrān, Tunis, Sijilmāsa, Nakūr, and al-Baṣra, and other excellent works. This Muḥammad is of Andalusī origin (*al-aṣl wa al-far'*); even if he grew up for a few years (*nasha'a*) in al-Qayrawān, his ancestors were from Wādī al-Ḥijāra, and he was buried in Cordoba, the city to which he migrated."

65. *Faḍā'il*, 6.

66. For Ibn Ḥazm, al-Andalus has the honor of having produced seminal works that did not simply imitate others but blazed new trails—much like his own works. *Faḍā'il*, 12.

67. About his native Cordoba, Ibn Ḥazm boasts: "We have as much understanding and intelligence as fits our clime." *Faḍā'il*, 8.

68. *Faḍā'il*, 17.

69. *Faḍā'il*, 17.

70. Peter C. Scales, *The Fall of the Caliphate of Córdoba: Berbers and Andalusis in Conflict* (Leiden: Brill, 1994), 165.

71. See "*min andalusin wa barbarin*" in Ibn Bulughīn (b. 1056), *Kitāb al-tibyān 'an al-ḥāditha al-kā'ina bi-dawlat banī zīrī fī gharnāṭa*, ed. 'Alī 'Umar (Riyadh: Maktabat al-Thaqāfa al-Dīniya, 2006), 36. See also the use of "Andalusī" in al-Ḥumaydī (d. 1095), *Jadhwat al-muqtabis fī dhikr wulāt al-andalus*, ed. Ibrāhīm al-Ibyārī (Cairo: al-Dār al-Maṣriya li al-Ta'līf wa al-Tarjama, 1966).

72. On Ibn Khaldūn's chronology of nations, see Aziz al-Azmeh, *Ibn Khaldūn in Modern Scholarship: A Study in Orientalism* (London: Third World Centre for Research and Publishing, 1981), 140–49. For the most pertinent contributions to the arguments presented here, please see Aziz al-Azmeh, *Ibn Khaldūn: An Essay in Reinterpretation* (London and Totowa, NJ: Cass, 1982); Abdesselam Cheddadi, *Ibn Khaldūn: L'homme et le théoricien de la civilisation* (Paris: Gallimard, 2006); Gabriel Martinez-Gros, *Ibn Khaldūn et les sept vies de l'Islam* (Paris: Actes Sud, Sindbad, 2006). For a discussion of Ibn Khaldūn's work in light of European developments, see Krzysztof Pomian, *Ibn Khaldūn au prisme de l'Occident* (Paris: Éditions Gallimard, 2006).

73. *The Muqaddimah*, trans. Rosenthal, 1: 11–12 (italics mine). Rosenthal's original translation introduces the notion of race, which will be attended to in due time. I modified his translation slightly to avoid distraction, Ibn Khaldūn's logic being the primary concern here.

74. *The Muqaddimah*, trans. Rosenthal, 1:12–13.

75. Ibn Khaldūn, *Kitāb al-'ibar wa diwān al-mubtada' wa al-khabar fī tārīkh al-'arab wa al-barbar wa man 'āṣarahum min dhawī al-sha'n al-akbar*, ed. Khalīl Shahāda (Beirut: Dār al-Fikr, 2001), 2:5.

76. In his introduction to the history of the (Zanāta) Marīnids, Ibn Abī Zar' insists on the Arab origins of the Zanāta, whom he describes as having "many *umam* and many tribes (*qabā'il*)." Ibn Abi Zar' (d. 1340/1), *Al-dhakhīra al-saniya fī tārīkh al-dawla al-marīniya* (Rabat: Dār al-Manṣūr lil-Ṭibā'a wa al-Warāqa, 1972), 15.

77. *The Muqaddimah*, trans. Rosenthal, 1:52.

78. *The Muqaddimah*, trans. Rosenthal, 1:54.

79. Ibn Khaldūn, *Kitāb al-'ibar*, 2:3. For a plurality of Berber *umam*, see al-Bakrī, *Al-masālik*, 2:736: "Around [the city] there are many Berber *umam*" (*wa ḥawālīha min al-barbar umam kathīra*).

80. Ibn Khaldūn, *Kitāb al-'ibar*, 2:7: "Know that Adam is [called] Kyūmarth [by the Persians] and that King Afrīdūn is Noah."

81. See, for example, Ibn Khaldūn, *Kitāb al-'ibar*, 2:16 and 21.

82. *The Muqaddimah*, trans. Rosenthal, 1:128; Ibn Khaldūn, *Kitāb al-'ibar*, 1:75.

83. Ibn Khaldūn, *Kitāb al-'ibar*, 2:19.

84. Worth noting here is that *milla* refers to a religious group, and that in early modern Ottoman (and modern Turkish and Persian) it has the sense of nation. Insofar as modern Berberization is enabled by translation of terms like this one, it is important to be attentive to these changes. See M. O. H. Ursinus, "Millet," in *EI*², 7:61–64.

85. *The Muqaddimah*, trans. Rosenthal, 1:103.

86. *The Muqaddimah*, trans. Rosenthal, 1:64. An alternative translation could be "The Berber peoples (*ajyāl*, sing. *jīl*), [the] people [of the Maghrib] in ancient times, were replaced

by an influx of Arab peoples (*ajyāl*, sing. *jīl*) [into the region] in the eleventh century. [The Arabs] defeated [the Berbers], overpowered them, stripped them of most of the lands [they inhabited], and shared with them control of the lands (*awṭān*) that they retained." Ibn Khaldūn, *Kitāb al-ʿibar*, 1:42.

CHAPTER 4

1. For an example of how that knowledge found a place in early Arabic geographical, see Ibn Khordadhbeh (d. 912), *Kitāb al-masālik wa al-mamālik*, ed. M. J. de Goeje (Leiden: Brill, 1889), 83 (*wa kāna ahl al-maghrib wa al-qibṭ fī mulk al-rūm*).

2. H. T. Norris, *The Berbers in Arabic Literature* (London and New York: Longman; Beirut: Librairie du Liban, 1982), 1.

3. Maurice Vonderheyden, *La Berbérie orientale sous la dynasties des Benoû'l-Arlab 800–909*, (Paris: Librairie orientaliste Paul Geuthner, 1927), 2.

4. For a critical recapitulation of the scholarship on the question, see the articles in *Islamisation et arabisation de l'Occident musulman (VII*[e]*–XII*[e] *siècle)*, ed. Dominique Valérian (Paris: Publications de la Sorbonne, 2011), 7–99. Cf. Elizabeth Fentress, "Romanising the Berbers," *Past & Present* 190 (February 2006): 3–33; Robert Hoyland, *In God's Path: The Arab Conquests and the Creation of an Empire* (Oxford: Oxford University Press, 2015), 145; *Vandals, Romans, and Berbers: New Perspectives on Late Antique North Africa,* ed. A. H. Merrils (Aldershot: Ashgate, 2004); Mercedes García-Arenal, *Messianism and Puritanical Reform: Mahdīs of the Muslim West* (Leiden: Brill, 2006), 35–40. See also Mohamed Sadok Bel Ochi, *La conversion des berbères à l'Islam* (Tunis: Maison tunisienne de l'édition, 1981); Michael Brett, "The Islamisation of Morocco: From the Arabs to the Almoravids," *Morocco: The Journal of the Society for Moroccan Studies* 2 (1992): 57–71; *Les dynamiques de l'islamisation en Méditerranée centrale et en Sicile: Nouvelles propositions et découvertes récentes; Le dinamiche dell'islamizzazione nel Mediterraneo centrale e in Sicilia: Nuove proposte e scoperte recenti*, ed. Annliese Nef and Fabiola Ardizzone (Rome: École Française de Rome, 2014).

5. Louis de Mas Latrie, *Traités de paix et de commerce et documents divers concernant les relations des chrétiens avec les arabes de l'Afrique septentrionale au moyen âge: Recueillis par ordre de l'empereur et publiés avec une introduction historique* (Paris: Henri Plon Imprimeur-Éditeur, 1866), 1.

6. In some Andalusī writings, Cordoba was the capital of the Maghrib. See, for instance, al-Khushanī (d. 971?), *Quḍāt qurṭuba*, ed. Ibrāhīm al-Ibyārī (Cairo: Dār al-Kitāb al-Maṣrī, 1982), 24 (*bi-arḍ al-maghrib fī al-ḥāḍira al-ʿuẓmā qurṭuba dhāt al-fakhr al-aʿẓam*).

7. Abdallah Laroui, *The History of the Maghrib: An Interpretive Essay* (Princeton: Princeton University Press, 1977), 8. It was first published in French as *L'histoire du Maghreb: Un essai de synthèse* (Paris: François Maspero, 1970), 14. Cf. L. Carl Brown, "Maghrib Historiography: The Unit of Analysis Problem," in *The Maghrib in Question: Essays in History and Historiography*, ed. Michel Le Gall and Kenneth Perkins (Austin: University of Texas Press, 1997), 4–16; Edmund Burke III, "Towards a History of the Maghrib," *Middle Eastern Studies* 11, no. 3 (1975): 306–23.

8. See Fernand Braudel, "Nécrologie: Georges Yver (1890–1961)," *Annales: Économies, Sociétes, Civilisations* 18, no. 2 (1963): 407–8. Yver was a specialist of medieval Italy and, after his appointment at the University of Algiers in 1904, became an expert on the French conquest of Algeria. Braudel describes him as an early master of his.

9. Georges Yver, "Al-Maghrib," in *EI*[2], 5:1183. The idea that the Maghrib formed a single island (*jazīrat al-maghrib*) emerged after the constitution of Ifrīqiyā as an administrative unit. For the reasons discussed here, and unlike the *jazīrat al-'arab*, the Maghrib did not become exclusively the island of Berbers.

10. Yver, "al-Maghrib" (italics mine).

11. This is true of the early period in the Mashriq. See, for example, al-Iṣfahānī (d. 967), *Kitāb al-aghānī*, ed. Iḥsān 'Abbās, Ibrāhīm al-Sa'āfīn and Bakr 'Abbās (Beirut: Dār Ṣādir, 2008), 1:203; 2:171, 241; and the relatively late allusion to Berber slaves in al-Tijānī (d. 1321/2), *Riḥlat al-tijānī*, ed. Ḥusnī 'Abd al-Wahhāb (Tripoli; Tunis: al-Dār al-'Arabiya lil-Kitāb, 1981), 19. Later, we know of a few individuals called *al-barbarī*, like Abū Qurra al-Barbarī, who played an important role in Aghlabid politics.See Ibn al-Abbār (d. 1260), *Al-ḥulla al-sayrā'*, ed. Ḥusayn Mu'nis (Cairo: al-Sharika al-'Arabiyya li al-Ṭibā'a wa al-Nashr, 1963), 1:69.In general, however, this phenomenon is seen mostly in Aghlabid Ifrīqiyā, Sicily, and in al-Andalus, when tribal identity did not matter to the author. For the use of *al-barbarī* as an insult, see *ijlis yā barbarī* in Ibn al-Abbār, *Al-ḥulla*, 1:123. See also Anon. (11th c.), *Akhbār majmū'a*, ed. Ibrāhīm al-Ibyārī (Cairo: Dār al-Kitāb al-Maṣrī, 1981), 90. *Barbarī* is also added to the name of a person like 'Alyūn al-Ṣanhājī and Khazrūn to identify him socially and politically. Ibn al-Abbār, *Al-ḥulla*, 1:289; Ibn al-Abbār (d. 1260), *Tuḥfat al-qādim* (Beirut: Dār al-Gharb al-Islāmī, 1986), 52. See also the notice on the year 225 AH in Ibn Sa'īd, which describes Maḥmūd b. 'Abd al-Jabbār al-Barbarī as a famous hero. Ibn Sa'īd (d. 1286), *Al-mughrib fī ḥulā al-maghrib*, ed. Khalīl al-Manṣūr (Beirut: Dār al-Kutub al-'Ilmiya, 1997), 1:20. See also al-Ḥumaydī (d. 1095), *Jadhwat al-muqtabis fī dhikr wulāt al-andalus*, ed. Ibrāhīm al-Ibyārī (Cairo: al-Dār al-Maṣriya li al-Ta'līf wa al-Tarjama, 1966), 1:178. For the prevalence of urban *nisab* among Andalusī *'ulamā'* and the absence of *al-barbarī*, see al-Rušāṭī (d. 1147) and Ibn al-Jarrāṭ al-Išbīlī (d. 1186), *Al-Andalus en el Kitāb Iqtibās al-anwār y en el Ijtiṣār Iqtibās al-anwār*, ed. Emilio Molina López, Jacinto Bosch Vilá (Madrid: CSIC, ICMA, 1990).

12. Edward W. Lane, *The Arabic-English Lexicon* (London: Williams and Norgate, 1874), 1:247. Bold indicates what "former" and "latter" refer to. For a discussion that considers a different body of medieval texts, see François Clément, "À propos de balad/bilād et autres noms: Quelques observations sur la terminologie des grands territoires dans les sources arabes," *Cahiers de Recherches Médiévales et Humanistes* 21 (2011): 203–10. See also Zayde Antrim, *Routes and Realms: The Power of Place in the Early Islamic World* (Oxford: Oxford University Press, 2012), 11–29.

13. Lane, *Lexicon*, 1:247. For the sake of clarity, I omitted Lane's references to the sources. As is well known, Lane utilized a great selection of medieval and modern dictionaries.

14. Al-Ya'qūbī (d. 897), *Kitāb al-buldān*, ed. T.G.J. Juynboll (Leiden: Brill, 1861), 131. *Akhlāṭ* may also refer to groups of known mixed ancestry.

15. Qur'ān, 2:115. See also Qur'ān, 2:142,177, 258; 55:17 (*rabbu al-mashriqayn wa al-maghribayn*).

16. Al-Wāqidī (d. 823), *Futūḥ al-shām*, ed. 'Abd al-Laṭīf 'Abd al-Raḥmān (Beirut: Dār al-Kutub al-'ilmiyya, 1997), 1:280. In more literary or poetic usages, the plural (*maghārib*) is used in expressions like "from all the easts of the world to all the wests" (*min mashāriq al-arḍ ilā maghāribihā*).

17. Al-'Uṣfurī, *Tārīkh khalīfa b. khayyāṭ*, ed. Suhayl Zakkār (Damascus: Manshūrāt Wizārat al-Thaqāfa wa al-Syāḥa wa al-Irshād al-Qawmī, 1968), 1:381, 397; 2:471, 475, 517.

18. Al-Iṣṭakhrī (d. 957), *Kitāb masālik al-mamālik*, ed. M.J. de Goeje (Leiden: Brill, 1927), 9.

19. Al-Balādhurī (d. 892), *Futūḥ al-buldān*, ed. M.J. de Goeje (Leiden: Brill, 1866), 222. Cf. Ibn Qutayba (d. 889), *Kitāb al-ma'ārif*, ed. Tharwat 'Ukkāsha (Cairo: Dār al-Ma'ārif bi-Miṣr, 1969), 570.

20. Al-Iṣṭakhrī, *Kitāb masālik al-mamālik*, 4.

21. Ibn 'Abd al-Ḥakam, *The History of the Conquests of Egypt, North Africa, and Spain*, ed. Charles Torrey (New Haven: Yale University Press, 1922), 110.

22. Ibn Ḥabīb (d. 852/ 3), *Kitāb al-tārīkh*, ed. Sālim Musṭafā al-Badrī (Beirut: Dār al-Kutub al-'Ilmiyya, 1999), 124.

23. Al-Iṣṭakhrī, *Kitāb masālik al-mamālik*, 39-40.

24. Al-Iṣṭakhrī, *Kitāb masālik al-mamālik*, 38.

25. See Mohamed Talbi, "Ifrīqiyā," in *EI*², 3:1047–50. See also al-Ḥumaydī, *Jadhwat al-muqtabis*, 1:3. "Ṭanja: A city among the cities connected with the country (*barr*) of al-Qayrawān [located] in the extreme west (*fī aqṣā al-maghrib*)." Interestingly, al-Ḥumaydī does not refer to Berbers in his narration of the events of the conquest of al-Andalus. See al-Ḥumaydī, *Jadhwat al-muqtabis*, 1:2–7.

26. Ibn 'Abd al-Ḥakam, *The Conquests*, 183; al-Balādhurī, *Futūḥ*, 227.

27. Ibn 'Abd al-Ḥakam, *The Conquests*, 170. See also Ibn Khordadhbeh, *Kitāb al-masālik wa al-mamālik*, 91.

28. Ibn Khoradadbeh, *Kitāb al-masālik wa al-mamālik*, 91–92. See Al-Bakrī: "As for the Berbers, their homes (*diyāruhum*) were in Palestine which belongs to Syria (*bilād al-shām*)." Abū 'Ubayd Allāh al-Bakrī (d. 1094), *Kitāb al-masālik wa al-mamālik*, ed. A.P. Van Leeuwen and A. Férré (Tunis: al-Dār al-'Arabiyya lil-Kitāb, 1992), 1: 328–29. See also Al-Idrīsī (d. 1065/6), *Nuzhat al-Mushtāq fī ikhtirāq al-āfāq, Description de l'Afrique et de l'Espagne*, ed. R. Dozy and M.J. de Goeje (Leiden: Brill, 1866), 42. Al-Idrīsī describes a Jabal Jālūt *al-Barbarī* in Egypt and provides a story about Goliath running with his horsemen there after his defeat. This suggests that this genealogy may have been an explanation of a toponym.

29. See also al-Bakrī, *Kitāb al-masālik wa al-mamālik*, 125–26.

30. Ibn Rosteh (d. early 10th c.), *Al-a'lāq al-nafīsa*, ed. M.J. de Goeje (Leiden: Brill, 1892), 96. See also al-Hamdānī (d. 945), *Ṣifat jazīrat al-'arab*, ed. David Heinrich Müller (Leiden: Brill, 1884), 7, 8. A more precise study of the question is necessary, but it seems that usage of *arḍ* is associated with geographical works. For its presence in a chronicle but in reference to the name and location of a river, see al-Raqīq al-Qayrawānī (fl. 11th century), *Tārīkh ifrīqiyā wa al-maghrib*, ed. al-Munjī al-Ka'bī (Tunis: Maṭba'at al-Wasaṭ, 1968), 110.

31. Al-Ya'qūbī, *Kitāb al-buldān*, 132. In the eleventh century, al-Mālikī describes a city whose name is unclear in the manuscript as "the city of the Berbers" in Ifrīqiyā—i.e., their capital. Al-Mālikī (d. 1061), *Riyāḍ al-nufūs fī ṭabaqāt 'ulamā' al-qayrawān wa-ifrīqīya wa-zuhhādihim wa-nussākihim wa-siyar min akhbārihim wa-faḍā'ilihim wa-awṣāfihim*, ed. Bashīr al-Bakkūsh (Beirut: Dār al-Gharb al-Islāmī, 1994), 1:32.

32. For *al-bilād al-barbariya*, in reference to the East African Berbera, see Ibn Sa'īd al-Maghribī (d. 1286), *Kitāb al-jughrāfiyā*, ed. Ismā'īl al-'Arabī (Beirut: Manshūrāt al-Maktab al-Tijārī lil-Ṭibā'a wa-al-Nashr wa-al-Tawzī', 1970), 82.

33. Ibn Ḥazm, *Jamharat ansāb al-'arab*, ed. Évariste Levi-Provençal (Cairo: Dār al-Ma'ārif bi Miṣr, 1948), 91. See also Ibn al-Qūṭiya (d. 977), *Tārīkh iftitāḥ al-andalus*, ed. 'Abd Allāh Anīs al-Ṭabbā' (Beirut: Mu'assasat al-Ma'ārif, 1994), 85.

34. Ibn Ḥazm, *Jamhara*, 89. See also Abū al-Fidā' (1273–1331), *Géographie d'Aboulféda: Texte arabe [Taqwīm al-buldān]*, ed. M. Reinaud and M. Le baron Mac Guckin de Slane (Paris: Imprimerie Royale, 1840), 163. For the use of Barbaria in Iranian sources, see, for

example, Vladimir Minorsky, "Vīs u Rāmīn, a Partian Romance (continued)," *Bulletin of the School of African and Oriental Studies* 11, no. 4 (1946): 741–63.

35. Yāqūt al-Ḥamawī, *Mu'jam al-buldān* (Beirut: Dār Ṣādir, 1977), 5:161.

36. Yāqūt al-Ḥamawī, *Mu'jam al-buldān*, 1: 368–69.

37. *Ḥadīth* refers here to the corpus of references to the sayings and deeds of the Prophet. *Adab* is usually translated as "belles lettres."

38. See, for example, al-Bakrī, *Kitāb al-masālik wa al-mamālik*, 2:800, 883.

39. Al-Bakrī, *Kitāb al-masālik wa al-mamālik*, 2:895. See also Ibn al-Qūṭiya, *Tārīkh*, 74 and 75 (*inḥidārihi ilā al-andalus 'alā qarbin min bilād al-barbar* and *kāna yakhtalifu min al-andalus ilā bilād al-barbar wa kānat ṭanja . . .'alayhā*); Anon., *Fatḥ al-andalus (La conquista de al-Andalus)*, ed. Luis Molina (Madrid: CSIC, 1994), 55.

40. See Dominique Valérian, "La diaspora andalouse et le commerce des ports maghrébins (XIe-XVe siècle)," *Les Cahiers de Framespa* 16 (2014), https://doi.org/10.4000/framespa.2939.

41. Al-Idrīsī, *Nuzhat al-mushtāq*, 84. See also Anon., *Fatḥ al-andalus*, 55.

42. Ibn al-Qūṭiya, *Tārīkh*, 102. This characterization contrasts with the one found in reports about the early conquests in which the Romans (Byzantines) occupied the coasts and the Berbers the country. It seems that this statement, repeated by many authors, applied to Ṭanja and its backcountry. See for example, Anon., *Fatḥ al-andalus*, 12, 21, 22; Ibn al-Kardabūs (fl. 12th–13th c.), *Tārīkh al-andalus li-ibn al-kardabūs wa waṣfuhu li-ibn al-shabbāṭ, naṣṣān jadīdān*, ed. Aḥmad Mukhtār al-'Abbādī (Madrid: Instituto de Estudios Islámicos en Madrid, 1971), 42, 131, and 152: "Al-Andalus and the Maghrib-Across-the-Sea were in the hands of the Romans and the Berbers. The entire sea coast [belonged to] the Romans and the country (*al-barriya*) to the Berbers"; "Mūsā appointed his *mawlā* Ṭāriq b. Ziyād [governor of] Ṭanja and *bilād al-barbar*'"; and "the cities of the Berbers and their forts."

43. Al-Bakrī, *Kitāb al-masālik wa al-mamālik*, 1:178.

44. Ibn al-Abbār, *Al-ḥulla al-sayrā'*, 1:45. See also Anon., *Akhbār majmū'a*, 15, 62: "Until he reached Ṭanja which is the fortress of the *bilād al-barbar*" (*ḥattā balagha ṭanja wa hiya qaṣabatu bilād al-barbar*); "The people of al-Andalus went out to Ṭanjā, Aṣīla, and the *rīfal-barbar*." The Rīf became a region later and not as Rīf of the Berbers.

45. Cf. Guy Turbet-Delof, *L'Afrique barbaresque dans la littérature française aux XVIe et XVIIe siècles* (Paris and Geneva: Libraire Droz, 1973), 3–48.

46. Giulio Ferrario, *Il costume antico e moderno, o, storia del governo, della milizia, della religione, delle arti, scienze ed usanze di tutti i popoli antichi e moderni, provata coi monumenti dell'antichità e rappresentata cogli analoghi disegni dal dottor Giulio Ferrario: Africa, Tomo I* (Milan: Dalla tipografia dell'editore, 1827), 363. Ambrogio Levanti offered his own take on the origin of the word: "More reasonable is the opinion that Barbaria comes from Berbes or Berberi, which means people who live next to a strait." Ambrogio Levati, *Storia della Barbaria* (Milan: Stella, Antonio Fortunato e figli, 1826), 22.

47. Sebastián Fernández de Medrano, *Breve descripcion del mundo, y sus partes, ò, Guia geographica, y hydrographica: Dividida en tres libros* (Brussels: En casa de los herederos de Francisco Foppens, 1686), 216: "La Berberia, nombrada assi despues que hizieron la barbaridad de dexar la fee de Christo, y leyes Romanas, abrazando la de los Arabes, y maldita feta de Mahoma."

48. Mas Latrie, *Traités de paix*, 2:7 (1076) VII.

49. Mas Latrie, *Traités de paix*, 2:15 (1246) XVI. See also 2:17–18 (1290) XVIII.

50. Mas Latrie, *Traités de paix*, 2:32, 33 (1234 or 1229). The Pisans were aware of differences in prices, customs taxes, etc. and recognized them in these documents. See, for instance, Mas Latrie, *Traités de paix*, 2:43–47, XI, 2:55–65 (1353) XV.

51. See Dominique Valérian, *Bougie: Port Maghrébin, 1067–1510* (Rome: École Française de Rome, 2006).

52. Mas Latrie, *Traités de paix*, 2:66 (1358) XVI. For a discussion of the various errors associated with document, see Michele Amari, *I diplomi arabi del R. archivio fiorentino: testo originale con la traduzione letterale e illustrazioni di Michele Amari* (Florence: Le Monnier, 1863), 476–77. At the time of this document, the Ḥafṣids had regained Ifrīqiyā and the Marinid ruler had to run back to his western territories before being strangled to death by his vizier.

53. A 1228 document from Marseille cites a number of African cities where Marsilian merchants conduct their wine business (Sabta, Bijāya, Tunis, and Wahrān) and then adds "other Saracen territories." Mas Latrie, *Traités de paix*, 2:80 (1228) II.

54. Mas Latrie, *Traités de paix*, 2:70.

55. See, for example, Francesco Balducci Pegolotti, *La pratica della mercatura*, ed. Allan Evans (Cambridge, MA: The Medieval Academy of America, 1936). The document offers a multiplicity of spellings when Barbaria is attached to the name of a city: Buggiea di Barbaria and Barberia, Buona di Barbaria, Gerbi di Barberia, Sarabese di Barberia, Tripoli of Barberia, and Tunisi di Barbaria and Barberia.

56. Mas Latrie, *Traités de paix*, 2:102 (1390) X. The same formula appears in the treaty between Genoa and Abū Fāris in 1433. Mas Latrie, *Traités de paix*, 2:134 (1433), XVI.

57. For "le voiage d'aler en Barbarie" and "le voyage de Barbarie," see Mas Latrie, *Traités de paix*, 2:102 (1390), X.

58. Addressing members of minor orders, who were probably doing missionary work in Africa, a letter from Pope Honorius III describes local Africans as Barbarians. Mas Latrie, *Traités de paix*, 2:9 (1226) IX. A few years later, another letter, sent by Gregory IX to the "king of Tunis," describes the order itself as Minorum de Barbaria. Mas-Latrie, *Traités de paix*, 2:11 (1235) XI.

59. References to the "cantare barbaresco" of Majorca in the Pratica della mercatura suggests that the island's weights and measures were clearly associated with the previous rulers. James I of Aragon conquered the island in 1229/30. Since there were differences between barbaresque measures in Barbaria, the epithet was not technically relevant—other than indicating that the measures differed from those of Catalan cities on the Continent.

60. See Pegolotti, *La practica*, 178.

61. See for example, Mas Latrie, *Traités de paix*, 2:164 (1393) XIII.

62. Leo Africanus (Ioannis Leonis Africani), *Africa descriptio* (Lugdunum, Batavia: Apud Elzevir, 1632); *A Geographical Historie of Africa Written in Arabick and Italian by John Leo a More, Born in Granada and Brought up in Barbarie* (London: [Printed by Eliot's Court Press] Impensis Georg. Bishop, 1600). For a translation of Barbaria into Arabic (*barbariyya*) probably from Spanish, see *Letters from Barbary: Arabic Documents in the Public Record Office*, ed. and trans. J.F.P. Hopkins (Oxford: Oxford University Press, 1982), 68.

63. Leo Africanus, *Africa descriptio*, 4–5.

64. Ibn Khaldūn, *Kitāb al-ʿibar wa diwān al-mubtada' wa al-khabar fī tārīkh al-ʿarab wa al-barbar wa man ʿāṣarahum min dhawī al-sha'n al-akbar*, ed. Khalīl Shahāda (Beirut: Dār al-Fikr, 2001), 1:63. "Our main concern is with the Maghrib, the home of the Berbers, and the Arab home countries in the East." Ibn Khaldūn, *The Muqaddimah: An Introduction to History*, trans. Franz Rosenthal (Princeton: Princeton University Press, 1967), 1:103. Ibn Khaldūn considers the migration of South Arabians to the north and the Arabization of that region before the Muslim conquests. For him, there are Yemenis in Syria, a meaning that Rosenthal's translation does not make explicit.

65. Edward Lane gives this definition for *waṭan*: "the place of abode or residence of a man: a man's settled place of abode, a country; his place of constant residence; his dwelling; his home." Lane, *Lexicon*, 8:3056. At issue here is the modern difference between resident (alien), citizen, non-national citizen, and national citizen. The *waṭan* of Bedouin nomads is wherever they settled.

66. *The Muqaddimah*, trans. Rosenthal, 2:266.

67. Ibn Khaldūn, *Kitāb al-ʿibar*, 1:8–9. "I based the work on the history of the two races that constitute the population of the Maghrib at this time and people its various regions and cities, and on that of their ruling houses, both long- and short-lived, including the rulers and allies they had in the past. These two races are the Arabs and the Berbers. They are the two races known to have resided in the Maghrib for such a long time that one can hardly imagine they ever lived elsewhere, for its inhabitants know no other human races." *The Muqaddimah*, trans. Rosenthal, 1:11.

68. Al-Bakrī and other geographers did not limit themselves to purely "geographic" material and relayed historical information. In those cases, Ibn Khaldūn tended to report it as is. "His son Mālīq b. Nadārus ruled after him. He rejected the Ṣābi'a and embraced monotheism. He invaded the *bilād al-barbar* and al-Andalus and fought the Ifranj (Franks)." Ibn Khaldūn, *Kitāb al-ʿibar*, 2:85. See al-Bakrī, *Kitāb al-masālik wa al-mamālik*, 2:578, 586–87.

69. Ibn Khaldūn, *Kitāb al-ʿibar*, 6:131.

70. Ibn Khaldūn, *Kitāb al-ʿibar*, 6:241.

71. Ibn Khaldūn, *Kitāb al-ʿibar*, 6:263. See also Anon., *Kitāb mafākhir al-barbar li-mu'allif majhūl*, ed. ʿAbd al-Qādir Būbāya (Rabat: Dār Abī Raqrāq lil-Ṭibāʿa wa al-Nashr, 2005), 185: "The borders of the Maghrib from the West [begin from] the Ocean—the Maghrib being like an island in which enters Egypt and al-Qayrawān, the Central Maghrib, the Zāb, and the Sūs al-Aqṣā. The borders of the homes (*masākin*) of the Berbers [begin from] the end of the districts of Egypt north of Alexandria to the Ocean and the Land of the Blacks (*bilād al-sūdān*)." The very fact of giving a description for each (Maghrib and *masākin al-barbar*) illustrates their difference in the minds of late medieval authors, including those writing about the points of pride/honor (*mafākhir*) of the Berbers.

72. Ibn Khaldūn, *The Muqaddimah*, trans. Rosenthal, 1:178. Cf. Ibn al-Khaṭīb, *Al-iḥāṭa fī akhbār gharnāṭa*, ed. Muḥammad ʿAbd Allāh ʿInān (Cairo: Maktabat al-Khānjī, 1973), 4:348 (*fīhim ashyākh lamtūna wa qabā'il al-barābira wa al-maṣāmida*).

73. "[These Black nations] neighbor the *bilād al-barbar* of the Maghrib and Ifrīqiyā, the Yemen, the Ḥijāz in the center, and Baṣra and after that to the east India." Ibn Khaldūn, *Kitāb al-ʿibar*, 6:244.

74. *The Muqaddimah*, trans. Rosenthal, 2:38.

75. Ibn Khaldūn, *Kitāb al-ʿibar*, 7:719. "When the Ifranja [i.e. Romans] ruled [the coastal areas], the [Zanāta and the Berbers] in the surrounding *bilād al-barbar* obeyed them, paid them taxes on a regular schedule, participated in their wars, but refused to collaborate with them in all other matters." Ibn Khaldūn, *Kitāb al-ʿibar*, 7:11.

76. *The Muqaddimah*, trans. Rosenthal, 2:279.

77. Ibn Khaldūn, *Kitāb al-ʿibar*, 4:237. "The ruler [of the Goths] was at that time Ludhrīq which is a common name for their kings, the way Jirjīr is common among the rulers of Sicily. The genealogy and the history of their dynasty have been already mentioned. [Ludhrīq] had influence (*ḥuẓwa*) on the other side of the sea on the southern shores with those who controlled [the sea] passage in Ṭanja, and from the strait to the *bilād al-barbar*, and they (?) enslaved them. The ruler of the Berbers (*barābira*) in that country (*al-quṭr*), which

is called today Jibāl Ghumāra, was Lulyān and was their servant and coreligionist." Ibn Khaldūn, *Kitāb al-ʿibar*, 4:149. On an anti-Almohad rebellion by the Ghumāra that gained them a bad reputation as "ignorant Berbers" among pro-Almohad authors, see Ibn Ṣāḥib al-Ṣalāt (fl. 12th c.), *Tārīkh al-mann bi-al-imāma ʿalā al-mustaḍʿafīn bi-an jaʿalahum allāh aʾimma wa-jaʿalahum al-wārithīn*, ed. ʿAbd al-Hādī al-Tāzī (Beirut: Dār al-Andalus li al-Ṭibāʿa wa al-Nashr, 1965), 2:308. Although this author has no use for the word Berber, it comes again in the form of *barābir* rebels (*qawm min al-barābir al-murtaddīn*). Ibn Ṣāḥib al-Ṣalāt, *Tārīkh*, 360.

78. "[Ibn Ḥazm] said in the *Kitāb al-jamhara*: Some factions (*ṭawāʾif*) among the Berbers claimed that they were from the Yemen and Ḥimyar, some claiming to descend from Barbar b. Qays. This is all false without any doubt. Genealogists [of the Arabs] never recorded that Qays b. ʿAylān had a son named Barr and there was no way for Ḥimyar to reach the *bilād al-barbar* other than in the lies of the historians of the Yemen." Ibn Khaldūn, *Kitāb al-ʿibar*, 6:127. "As for the opinion of the genealogists of Zanāta who hold that they are from Ḥimyar, it was rejected as untrue by the two compilers of historical traditions Abū ʿUmar b. ʿAbd al-Barr and Abū Muḥammad b. Ḥazm who said that there was no way for Ḥimyar to reach the *bilād al-barbar* other than in the lies of the historians of the Yemen." Ibn Khaldūn, *Kitāb al-ʿibar*, 7:6.

79. Ibn Khaldūn, *Kitāb al-ʿibar*, 7:11.

CHAPTER 5

1. The emergence of the category Qabāʾil (tribes) in reference to the tribes the Ottomans deal with in the region east of Algiers was a new development. The idea that Qabāʾil (Fr. Kabylie) was the name of the region east of Algiers did not emerge instantly. Until the late eighteenth century, Arabic sources do not imagine it as such. See, for example, Ibn Abī Dīnār (d. ca. 1698), *Al-muʾnis fī akhbār ifrīqiyā wa tūnis*, ed. Muḥammad Shammām (Tunis: al-Maktaba al-ʿAtīqa, 1967). See Yassin Temlali, *La genèse de la Kabylie: Aux origines de l'affirmation berbère en Algérie (1830-1962)* (Algiers: Éditions Barzakh, [2015]). For other categories, see Pierre Boyer, "Le problème kouloughli dans la régence d'Alger," *Revue de l'Occident Musulman et de la Méditerranée* 8, no. 1 (1970): 79–94; Sami Bargaoui, "Des Turcs aux Hanafiyya: La construction d'une catégorie 'métisse' à Tunis aux XVIIe et XVIIIe siècles," *Annales: Histoire, Sciences Sociales* 1 (2005): 209–28. For further guidance, see François Pouillon, "Simplification ethnique en Afrique du nord: Maures, Arabes, Berbères (XIIIe–XXe siècles)," *Cahiers d'Études Africaines* 33, no. 129 (1993): 37–49.

2. Ahmed Abdesselem, *Ibn Khaldūn et ses lecteurs* (Paris: Presses Universitaires de France, 1983).

3. Cornell Fleischer, "Royal Authority, Dynastic Cyclism, and "Ibn Khaldûnism" in Sixteenth-Century Ottoman Letters," *Journal of Asian and African Studies* 18, no. 3 (1983): 198–220; Ejder Okumuş, "İbn Haldun ve Osmanlı'da çöküş tartışmaları," *Dîvân: Disiplinlerası Çalişmalar Dergisi* 1 (1999): 183–209.

4. "Como lo dize Ybny Alraquiq en el libro deel Arbol de la generacion Affricana." Luis del Marmol Carvajal, *Primera parte de la descripcion general de Africa, con todos los successos de guerras que a auido entre los infieles y el pueblo Christiano, y entre ellos mesmos desde que Mahoma inuẽto su secta, hasta el aña de seẽnor 1571* (Granada: Casa del Rene Rabut, 1573), capit. xxiiii, fol. 31.

5. It is useful to think of these works in relation to intellectual movements such as humanism and processes such as the so-called age of discovery. See Fernando Rodríguez Mediano, "Luis de Mármol y el humanismo: Comentarios sobre una fuente de la *Historia de la*

rebelión y castigo de los moriscos del Reyno de Granada," *Bulletin Hispanique* 105, no. 2 (2003): 371–404.

6. Malte-Brun's work shaped the emergence of geography as a science. For a fuller appreciation of his approach, see Anne Godlewska, "L'influence d'un homme sur la géographie française: Conrad Malte-Brun (1775–1826)," *Annales de Géographie* 558 (1991): 190–206; Laura Péaud, "Relire la géographie de Conrad Malte-Brun," *Annales de Géographie* 701 (2015): 99–122.

7. Conrad Malte-Brun, *Précis de la géographie universelle, ou description de toutes les parties du monde, sur un plan nouveau, d'après les grandes divisions naturelles du globe, tome quatrième: Description de l'inde, de l'océanique et de l'Afrique septentrionale* (Paris: Fr. Buisson Libraire-Éditeur, 1813), 562–63.

8. Malte-Brun, *Précis*, 564.

9. Malte-Brun, *Précis*, 564–65.

10. Diego de Haedo, *Topografía e historia general de Argel por Fray Diego de Haedo* (Valladolid: Diego Fernandez de Cordoua y Oviedo Impressor de libros, 1612); Nicolas Perrot, *L'Afrique de Marmol, de la traduction de Nicolas Perrot sieur d'Ablancourt. Divisée en trois volumes, et enrichie des cartes géographiques de M. Sanson, géographe ordinaire du roy. Avec l'Histoire des chérifs, traduite de l'espagnol de Diego Torrés, par le duc d'Angoulesme le père. Reveuë et retouchée par P. R. A.* (Paris: Thomas Iolly, 1667). For a discussion of the Inquisition in relation to the work of Marmol and others, see Vincent Parello, "La visite du licencié Diego de Haedo dans le district inquisitorial de Saragosse (1575)," *Bulletin Hispanique* 109, no. 1 (2007): 67–95.

11. See, for example, Thomas Shaw, *Travels: or Observations Relating to Several Parts of Barbary and the Levant* (London: Printed for A. Millar in the Strand, and W. Sandby in Fleet-Street, 1757).

12. Jean Luis Marie Poiret, *Voyage en Barbarie, ou lettres écrites de l'ancienne Numidie pendant les années 1785 & 1786, sur la religion, les coutumes & les mœurs des Maures et des Arabes-Bédouins; avec un essai sur l'histoire naturelle de ce pays. Première Partie* (Paris: Chez J.B.F. Née de la Rochelle, 1789), 5. For a critical bibliography of French writings on the Maghrib in the sixteenth and seventeenth centuries, see Guy Turbet-Delof, *Bibliographie critique du Maghreb dans la littérature française, 1532–1715* (Algiers: SNED, 1976).

13. Alexis de Tocqueville, *De la colonie en Algérie*, ed. Tzvetan Todorov (Brussels: Éditions Complexe, 1988), 38. Cf. Jean Michel Venture de Paradis (1739–99), *Alger au XVIII*[e] *siècle, 1788–1790: Mémoires, notes et observations d'un diplomate-espion*, ed. Abderrahmane Rebahi (Algiers: Éditions Grand-Alger Livres, 2006). This travelogue was first edited by Edmond Fagnan in 1898. Note the absence of "Berber" in this travelogue and the use instead of categories like Cabaïli and Zevawa.

14. Orientalism has become a field of study in its own right. In addition to Edward W. Said, *Orientalism* (New York: Pantheon Books, 1978), see the very helpful bibliography and discussion in Alain Messaoudi, *Les arabisants et la France coloniale: Savants, conseillers, médiateurs (1780–1930)* (Paris: ENS Éditions, 2015). For a general overview with an American orientation, see Zachary Lockman, *Contending Visions of the Middle East: The History and Politics of Orientalism* (Cambridge: Cambridge University Press, 2009). See also Irini Apostolou, *L'orientalisme des voyageurs français au xviii*[e] *siècle: Une iconographie de l'Orient méditerranéen* (Paris: Presses de l'Université Paris-Sorbonne, 2009); Henry Laurens, *L'orientalisme français: Un parcours historique*, in *Penser l'Orient: Traditions et actualité des orientalismes français et allemand* (Beirut: Presses de l'Ifpo, 2004), http://books.openedition.org/ifpo/206; Raymond Schwab, *La renaissance orientale* (Paris: Payot, 1950).

15. The study of Ibn Khaldūn followed many paths, some leading nowhere, others becoming important. My discussion here should not be confused with an exhaustive study of all references to Ibn Khaldūn in France or Europe. Cf. Eric Chaumont, "L'ego-histoire d'Ibn Khaldûn, historien et soufi," *Comptes Rendus des Séances de l'Académie des Inscriptions et Belles-Lettres* 3 (1996): 1042: "En Occident, les études khaldûnienne débutent à la fin du XVIIe siècle avec la Bibliothèque orientale de d'Heberlot publiée en 1697."

16. Juan Cole, *Napoleon's Egypt: Invading the Middle East* (New York: Palgrave Macmillan, 2007); Messaoudi, *Les arabisants*, 55–91.

17. Wiliam McGuckin de Slane, ed., *Description de l'Afrique septentrionale par Abou-Oubeid-El-Bekri* (Algiers: Imprimerie du gouvernement, 1857), 18: "L'occupation de l'Algérie par la France, les travaux des officiers de l'état-major, et les cartes publiées par le Dépôt de la guerre venaient, depuis quelques années, de fournir aux géographes une foule d'excellentes notions sur la topographie de l'Afrique."

18. Antoine-Issac Silvestre de Sacy, *Anthologie grammaticale arabe: ou, Morceaux choisis de divers grammairiens et scholiastes arabes, avec une traduction française et des notes; pouvant faire suite à la Chrestomathie arabe* (Paris: Imprimerie Royale, 1829). For a more detailed examination of the personnel and the production, see Messaoudi, *Les arabisants*, 93–132. On Silvestre de Sacy, see the relevant essays in Michel Espagne, Nora Lafi, and Pascale Rabault-Feuerhahn, *Silvestre de Sacy: Le projet européen d'une science orientaliste* (Paris: Les éditions du Cerf, 2014).

19. De Slane published a translation of the *Muqaddima* (*Prolégomènes*) based on Quatermère's Arabic text and notes. William McGuckin de Slane, *Les prolégomènes d'Ibn Khaldoun: Traduits en français et commentés par M. de Slane* (Paris: Imprimerie Impériale, 1858). Illustrating the state of knowledge at the time, Quatremère had used European travelogues to illuminate the information he found in Ibn Khaldūn.

20. Silvestre de Sacy, *Chrestomathie arabe, ou extraits de divers écrivains arabes tant en prose qu'en vers, à l'usage des élèves de l'École spéciale des langues orientales vivantes* (Paris: Imprimerie Royale, 1806), 1:390.

21. Silvestre de Sacy, *Chrestomathie*, 1:393.

22. The Société Asiatique was founded in 1822 and has published its influential *Journal Asiatique* from that date on. Silvestre de Sacy was its first president.

23. Joseph-Toussaint Reinaud (1795–1867) coedited Abū al-Fidā''s geography with de Slane.

24. See Alain Messaoudi, "Slane, William McGuckin baron de," in *Dictionnaire des orientalistes de langue française, nouvelle édition revue et augmentée*, ed. François Pouillon (Paris: IISMM and Karthala, 2012), 959.

25. De Slane expected Quatremère to translate the full text, but the latter died before he completed it.

26. Ibn Abī Dinār (d. ca. 1698), *Exploration scientifique de l'Algérie: 7, Histoire de l'Afrique / de Moh'hammed-ben-Abi-el-Raïni-K'aïrouāni; trad. de l'arabe par MM. E. Pellissier et Rémusat* (Paris: Imprimerie Royale, 1845); al-Tanasī (d. 1493/4), *Histoire des Beni-Zeiyan, rois de Tlemcen, par l'iman Cidi Abou-Abd'-Allah-Mohammed Jbn-Abd'el Djelyl el-Tenessy*, trans. Jean-Joseph-Léandre Bargès (Paris: Duprat, 1852); Ibn Abī Zar' al-Fāsī (d. 1340/41), *Roudh el-Kartas: Histoire des souverains du Maghreb (Espagne et Maroc) et annales de la ville de Fès, traduit de l'arabe par A. Beaumier* (Paris: Impr. impériale, 1860).

27. William McGuckin de Slane, trans., *Histoire des Berbères et des dynasties musulmanes de l'Afrique septentrionale par Ibn Khaldoun* (Algiers: Imprimerie du gouvernement, 1852), 1:301–12.

28. De Slane, *Histoire des Berbères*, 1:305–6.

29. Ibn Khaldūn, *The Muqaddimah: An Introduction to History*, trans. Franz Rosenthal (Princeton: Princeton University Press, 1967), 15–16.

30. Ibn Khaldūn, *Histoire des Berbères et des dynasties musulmanes: Texte arabe*, ed. William MacGuckin de Slane (Algiers: Imprimerie du gouvernement, 1847), 1:v.

31. For Bargès, "Les habitants appartenaient à deux races principales: la race arabe et la race berbère." Al-Tanasī, *Histoire*, trans. Bargès, xlii.

32. No less remarkable, de Slane's reference to the Kabiles suggests that his *Histoire des Berbères* was steeped in the French conquest. Without having to exaggerate his political ties to Thomas Robert Bugeaud (1784–1849), the famed general and governor of Algeria (gouverneur général), it is enough that he seemed to find pleasure in using the expression "our Algeria" (*notre Algérie*), even when he was describing the political situation in the eleventh century. De Slane, *Description*, 7.

33. Abdelmajid Hannoum, "Translation and the Colonial Imaginary: Ibn Khaldūn Orientalist," *History and Theory* 42, no. 1 (2003): 61–81.

34. As de Slane explains, Quatremère was supposed to translate the entire book. De Slane, *Histoire des Berbères*, 1:iv.

35. De Slane, *Histoire des Berbères*, 1:viii. *Barbarisant* is de Slane's translation of *musta'jam*, which refers to Arabs who speak a non-Arabic language.

36. De Slane, *Histoire des Berbères*, 1:vii.

37. In his Arabic edition, he chose "History of the Islamic Dynasties in the Maghrib" with no mention of the Berbers.

38. Cf. Maya Shatzmiller, *The Berbers and the Islamic State: The Marīnid Experience in Pre-Protectorate Morocco* (Princeton, NJ: Markus Wiener, 2000).

39. De Slane, *Histoire des Berbères*, 1:xci.

40. For de Slane's introduction of words that do not exist in the original, see Mohamed Meouak, *La langue berbère au Maghreb médiéval: Textes, contextes, analyses* (Leiden: Brill, 2015), 72.

41. See Chapter 4. For an intelligent discussion of French colonial mapping of Algeria, see Helène Blais, *Mirages de la carte: L'invention de l'Algérie coloniale XIXe–XXe siècle* (Paris: Fayard, 2014).

42. De Slane, *Histoire des Berbères*, 1:iii.

43. De Slane, *Histoire des Berbères*, 1:2.

44. De Slane, *Histoire des Berbères*, 1:2.

45. De Slane, *Histoire des Berbères*, 1:27.

46. De Slane, *Histoire des Berbères*, 1:28 (*fa istaḥālat ṭabī'atuhum ilā al-barbar wa indarajū fī a'dādihim*).

47. De Slane, *Histoire des Berbères*, 1:28.

48. De Slane, *Histoire des Berbères*, 1:74.

49. De Slane, *Histoire des Berbères*, 1:89. There is no reference in the original to nomads (Bedouins) or to race.

50. De Slane, *Histoire des Berbères*, 2:69. For the Negro race (*race nègre*), see de Slane, *Description*, 43.

51. De Slane, *Histoire des Berbères*, 1:342(italics in the original).

52. Beaumier, Bargès, Pellissier, and Rémusat all used the word "race" in their translations. Interestingly, and much like de Slane, they used it to describe a host of meanings, not always consistent with racial ideology as articulated in later works.

53. De Slane identified Deguignes' *General History of the Huns* as having a similar organization with a combination of genealogical logic and linear chronology for each genealogy. The possibility that these similarities were connected to the rise of nationalism, racial ideology, or anything of that order did not occur to de Slane. As a reminder, Gobineau's *Essai sur l'inégalité des races* was published in 1853, half a century after Herder (1744–1803) and Rousseau (1712–78). Joseph Deguignes, *Histoire générale des Huns, des turcs, des mogols et des autres tartares occidentaux . . . : par M. Deguignes, . . . Suite des Mémoires de l'Académie Royale des Inscriptions et Belles-Lettres* (Paris: Chez Desaint et Saillant, 1756); Arthur de Gobineau, *Essai sur l'inégalité des races humaines par M.A. de Gobineau*, 2 vols. (Paris: Fermin-Didot Frères, 1853–55).

54. References to Silvestre de Sacy's translation practically ceased after the publication of de Slane's.

55. Louis de Mas Latrie, *Traités de paix et de commerce et documents divers concernant les relations des chrétiens avec les Arabes de l'Afrique septentrionale au moyen âge: Recueillis par ordre de l'empereur et publiés avec une introduction historique* (Paris: Henri Plon, 1866). For a helpful overview of Mas Latrie's text and context, see Dominique Valérian, "Louis de Mas Latrie, historien du Maghreb: L'usage des documents d'archives européens dans la construction de l'histoire du Maghreb médiéval," in *La naissance de la médiévistique: les historiens et leurs sources en Europe (XIXe-début du XXe siècle): actes du colloque de Nancy, 8–10 novembre 2012*, Isabelle Guyot-Bachy and Jean-Marie Moeglin, ed. (Genève : Librairie Droz, 2015), 473–89.

56. Mas Latrie, *Traités*, i. In other words, the title refers to "Arab States" because "Barbary States" was stained by centuries of Ottoman rule.

57. Mas Latrie, *Traités*, ii.

58. See, for instance, Mas Latrie, *Traités*, 152–53.

59. Mas Latrie, *Traités*, 13.

60. Mas Latrie, *Traités*, 13–14.

61. Mas Latrie, *Traités*, 14.

62. See Chapter 2.

63. For a recent contribution, see Matt King, "The Sword and the Sun: The Old World Drought Atlas as a Source for Medieval Mediterranean History," *Al-masāq* 29, no. 3 (2017): 1–14.

64. Mas Latrie, *Traités*, 1.

65. De Slane, *Histoire des Berbères*, 1:164.

66. Mas Latrie, *Traités*, 313.

67. The goal here is simply to gauge the impact that ethnography had on medieval history and not to discuss the emergence and evolution of colonial ethnography. For an introduction to that topic in English, see Abdelmajid Hannoum, "Colonialism and Knowledge in Algeria: The Archives of the Arab Bureau," *History and Anthropology* 12, no. 4 (2010): 343–79.

68. Henri Fournel, *Étude sur la conquête de l'Afrique par les arabes, et recherches sur les tribus berbères qui ont occupé le Maghreb central* (Paris: Imprimerie Impériale, 1857). The second volume has a slightly different title: *Les Berbers: Étude sur la conquête de l'Afrique par les arabes, d'après les textes arabes imprimés* (Paris: Imprimerie nationale, 1881). Perhaps even more important than Fournel's study was the ethnography conducted by Hanoteau and Letourneux on the Kabyles. Adolphe Hanoteau and Aristide Letourneux, *La Kabylie et les coutumes kabyles*, 3 vols. (Paris: Imprimerie nationale, 1872–73). Their contribution to the Kabylization of "Berber," especially in Algeria, shaped ethnographic Berberization to a great degree. In order not to make matters too complicated, however, I have chosen to focus on Fournel, and

a few others, with the understanding that the extension of the argument to Hanoteau and Letourneux will require careful analysis of their work. On Saint-Simonians in Algeria, see Osama W. Abi-Mershed, *Apostles of Modernity: Saint-Simonians and the Civilizing Mission in Algeria* (Stanford: Stanford University Press, 2010).

69. Fournel, *Étude*, iii.

70. Fournel, *Étude*, 2. Fournel used the notion of race in such a way that allowed for racial hostility (*hostilité de race*) between the (Berber) Zanāta and the Ṣanhāja (Berbers). Fournel, *Les Berbers*, 207.

71. Henri Fournel, *Les Berbers*, ii. Volume 2 was published posthumously by Fournel's son-in-law, a military officer and baron who wanted to be faithful to Fournel's ideas.

72. Fournel relied on *The History of the Saracens* (1708–18) written by the British Orientalist Simon Ockley (1678–1720). Fournel had access to the French translation of the work (1748). He also made good use of the "history of Arab domination in Spain" written by the Spanish Orientalist José Antonio Conde y García (1766–1820). José Antonio Conde, *Historia de la dominación de los árabes en España* (Madrid: García, 1820); Simon Ockley, *The conquest of Syria, Persia, and Ægypt, by the Saracens: containing the lives of Abubeker, Omar and Othman . . . illustrating the religion, rites, customs and manner of living of that . . . people . . . By Simon Ockley . . .* (London: Printed for R. Knaplock, J. Sprint, R. Smith [et al.], 1708–18).

73. See, for example, Fournel, *Étude*, 2. The notion of barbarian contrasts with civilization. The latter is undoubtedly positive for Fournel and in Fournel's understanding of de Slane's Ibn Khaldūn.

74. Although Berbérie appeared earlier, it was mostly the old early Barbary and did not conceive of the region as the original home of the Berbers. See Omar Carlier, "Mercier, Ernest," in Pouillon, *Dictionnaire des orientalistes*, 716–17; Jacques Zeiller, "Un historien de l'Afrique du nord; Ernest Mercier," *Journal des Savants* 3, no. 1 (1945): 166–70.

75. Ernest Mercier, *Histoire de l'établissement des Arabes en Afrique septentrionale* (Constantine: Imprimerie de L. Marle, 1875), 361.

76. Ernest Mercier, *Histoire de l'Afrique septentrionale (Berbérie) depuis les temps les plus reculés jusqu'à la conquête française*, 3 vols. (Paris: Ernest Leroux Éditeur, 1888–91). "Cette vaste contrée est désignée généralement sous le nom d'Afrique septentrionale, sans y comprendre l'Égypte, qui a, pour ainsi dire, une situation à part. Les Grecs l'ont appelée Libye; les Romains ont donné le nom d'Afrique à la Tunisie actuelle, et ce vocable s'est étendu à tout le continent. Les Arabes ont appliqué à cette région la dénomination de Mag'reb, c'est-à-dire Occident, par rapport à leur pays. Nous emploierons successivement ces appellations, auxquelles nous ajouterons celle de Berbérie, ou pays des Berbères." Mercier, *Histoire de l'Afrique*, ix. While the expression "land of Berbers" exists in medieval Arabic (*bilād al-barbar*), de Slane preferred *pays des Berbères* to Berbérie. De Slane, *Histoire des Berbères*, 1:190.

77. Mercier, *Histoire de l'établissement*, 361.

78. Mercier, *Histoire de l'établissement*, 375–76.

CHAPTER 6

1. Cf. Gabriel Camps, "Comment la Berbérie est devenue le Maghreb arabe," *Revue de l'Occident Musulman et de la Méditerranée* 35 (1983): 7–24.

2. Before Marçais, the General de Beylié (1849–1910) published a study of the Ḥammādid capital that presented a similar, if less thoroughly researched, thesis. Léon Marie Eugène de

Beylié, *La Kalaa des Beni Hammad: Une capitale berbère de l'Afrique du nord au XI*^e^ *siècle* (Paris: Éditions Leroux, 1909).

3. Alain Messaoudi, "Marçais, Georges," in *Dictionnaire des orientalistes de langue française, nouvelle édition revue et augmentée*, ed. François Pouillon(Paris: IISMM and Karthala, 2012), 681.

4. Georges Marçais, *Les arabes en Berbérie du XI*^e^ *au XIV*^e^ *siècle* (Paris: E. Leroux, 1913), 1–2.

5. Ibn Khaldūn, *The Muqaddimah: An Introduction to History*, trans. Franz Rosenthal (Princeton: Princeton University Press, 1967), 2:266.

6. William McGuckin de Slane, trans., *Histoire des Berbères et des dynasties musulmanes de l'Afrique septentrionale par Ibn Khaldoun* (Algiers: Imprimerie du gouvernement, 1852), 1:34.

7. Marçais recognized the difficulty of ascertaining who was a Berber and who an Arab in the Maghrib. For him, ethnographers and linguists would eventually settle this question. Marçais, *Les arabes*, 19.

8. On the uses of native knowledge (*savoirs vernaculaires*), see Helène Blais, *Mirages de la carte: L'invention de l'Algérie coloniale XIX*^e^*-XX*^e^ *siècle* (Paris: Fayard, 2014), 153–92.

9. Marçais, *Les arabes*, 701.

10. Throughout the book, Marçais distinguished between indigenous (i.e., Berber) nomads and Arab nomads.

11. Marçais, *Les arabes*, 702.

12. The efforts to Christianize the Berbers undertaken by French missionaries were behind the development of strategies to distance them from the Arabs and their Islam and bring them back into the fold of Christianity. Although it is not always clear, secular progress-minded missionaries may have sought to achieve different outcomes, but when it comes to the terms of their knowledge of the natives, they relied on the same scholarship.

13. Marçais, *Les arabes*, 702–3.

14. Robert Brunschvig, *La Berbérie orientale sous les Ḥafṣides: Des origines à la fin du XV*^e^ *siècle*, 2 vols. (Paris: Adrien-Maisonneuve, 1940–47).

15. Grabriel Martinez-Gros, "Brunschvig, Robert," in Pouillon, *Dictionnaire des orientalistes*, 167–68.

16. On Brunschvig's analysis of the political history, see Ramzi Rouighi, *The Making of a Mediterranean Emirate: Ifrīqiyā and Its Andalusis* (Philadelphia: University of Pennsylvania Press, 2011).

17. Brunschvig, *La Berbérie*, 1:189.

18. "Jusqu'à une époque relativement récente, le Maghreb [occidental] est resté purement berbère. Au contraire, la partie orientale de la Berbérie, a toujours été plus mélangée. La civilisation y a été plus cosmopolite, a davantage reçu la marque des dominations successives." Maurice Vonderheyden, *La Berbérie orientale sous la dynasties des Benoû'l-Aṛlab 800–909* (Paris: Librairie orientaliste Paul Geuthner, 1927), 2.

19. Brunschvig, *La Berbérie*, 1:325–26.

20. Brunschvig, *La Berbérie*, 2:158.

21. Brunschvig, *La Berbérie*, 2:243.

22. Brunschvig, *La Berbérie*, 2:243.

23. Brunschvig, *La Berbérie*, 2:244.

24. Brunschvig, *La Berbérie*, 2:244.

25. Brunschvig, *La Berbérie*, 2:441–42.

26. Brunschvig, *La Berbérie*, 2:442–43.

27. The idea of a classical Islam affected the study of the Mashriq too. It is important to highlight the chronological vagueness that surrounds its supposed emergence and the methodological laissez-faire that has characterized its mobilization in arguments about widely distant (geographically and temporally) contexts.

28. See Florence Deprest, "Gautier, Émile-Félix," in Pouillon, *Dictionnaire des orientalistes*, 456–57. For the place of geography in colonial knowledge, see Florence Deprest, *Géographes en Algérie* (Paris: Belin, 2009).

29. See Yves Modéran, "Botr et Branès: Sur les origines du dualisme berbère médiéval," in *Mutations d'identités en Méditerranée: Moyen Âge et époque contemporaine*, ed. Henri Bresc and Christiane Veauvy ([Saint-Denis]: Éditions Bouchène, 2000), 53–65. Modéran correctly identified Ibn Khaldūn's influence in reintroducing the Butr/Barānis dichotomy and its important effects on modern historiography. He later expanded his original argument in his excellent work on the Mauri. Yves Modéran, *Les Maures en Afrique romaine (IVe–VIIe siècle)* (Rome: École Française de Rome, 2003), 685–810.

30. Émile-Félix Gautier, *Le passé de l'Afrique du nord: Les siècles obscurs* (Paris: Payot, 1937), 63.

31. Gautier, *Le passé*, 61–62.

32. Gautier, *Le passé*, 60.

33. Gautier, *Le passé*, 23.

34. Gautier, *Le passé*, 24 (italics mine). "This race, which has an irreducible vitality, has no positive individuality." Gautier, *Le passé*, 25.

35. Charles-André Julien, *Histoire de l'Afrique du Nord: Tunisie, Algérie, Maroc*(Paris: Payot, 1931).

36. Jean-Remy Palanque, "Charles-André Julien, *Histoire de l'Afrique du Nord: Tunisie, Algérie, Maroc*," *Revue d'Histoire de l'Église de France* 17, no.77 (1931): 488–89.

37. "Aussi loin que l'on remonte dans l'histoire de l'Afrique du Nord, on constate que tout ce passe comme si elle était frappée d'une inaptitude congénitale à l'indépendance." Charles-André Julien, *Histoire de l'Afrique du Nord: Tunisie, Algérie, Maroc*, ed. Christian Courtois (Paris: Payot, 1951–52), 1:49. The impact of Julien's work on anglophone historians requires further examination.

38. While chronologically his North Africa led to Tunisia, Algeria, and Morocco in this book, it is useful to note that in 1966, and so after the independence of these countries, he published a condensed synthesis in the *Que sais-je* series with a very telling title and updated racial classification. See Charles-André Julien, *Histoire de l'Afrique blanche des origines à 1945* (Paris: Presses Universitaires de France, 1966), 17–20.

39. Julien, *Histoire de l'Afrique du Nord*, 1:9.

40. Although he raised questions about Gautier's judgments, Julien followed many of his insights.

41. While Julien looked for the past possibilities of a Berber state, he also thought that Morocco presented historians with a more coherent unit than Algeria and Tunisia, whose histories were too difficult to disentangle. Geography was the main obstacle here, especially the absence of mountainous chains able to make conquests difficult. Julien, *Histoire de l'Afrique du Nord*, 1:25. On the "incapacité historique de l'Afrique du Nord à réaliser son unité," see Gabriel Camps, *Monuments et rites funéraires protohistoriques, aux origines de la Berbérie* (Paris: Arts et métiers graphiques, 1961), 7.

42. The second volume was published in 1932.

43. Mubārak al-Mīlī, *Tārīkh al-jazā'ir fī al-qadīm wa al-ḥadīth*, ed. Muḥammad al-Mīlī (Algiers: Maktabat al-Nahḍa al-Jazā'iriya, 2004), 1:13.

44. Al-Mīlī, *Tārīkh al-jazā'ir*, 1:81.

45. Al-Mīlī, *Tārīkh al-jazā'ir*, 1:91–92.

46. Al-Mīlī, *Tārīkh al-jazā'ir*, 1:80. See also Aomar Hannouz, "Mémoires et patrimonialisation d'un passé antéislamique: Mubârak al-Mîlî et l'ethnogenèse du peuple algérien," *L'Année du Maghreb* 10 (2014): 115–41.

47. Al-Mīlī, *Tārīkh al-jazā'ir*, 1:80, 128–327.

48. Al-Mīlī, *Tārīkh al-jazā'ir*, 2:43–44.

49. Al-Mīlī, *Tārīkh al-jazā'ir*, 2:186.

50. Abdelmajid Hannoum, *Colonial Histories, Post-colonial Memories: The Legend of the Kahina, a North African Heroine* (Portsmouth: Heinemann, 2001), 116.

51. Al-Mīlī, *Tārīkh al-jazā'ir*, 2:33.

52. For example, see 'Abd al-Raḥmān al-Jīlālī, *Tārīkh al-jazā'ir al-'āmm*, 7th ed., 4 vols., (Algiers: Diwān al-Maṭbū'āt al-jāmi'iyya, 1994), 1:292.

53. Al-Jīlālī, *Tārīkh*, 1:33, 34, 36. Al-Jilālī rejected the claim made by Pascal Duprat, who thought the Berbers belonged to the Aryan race and preferred to think that the earliest civilization in the Maghrib was influenced by the Aegean civilization that preceded that of the Greeks. This prehistoric civilization was not, however, that of the Berbers who migrated from southern Palestine ca. 1300 BC, a thesis supported by references to medieval Arabic genealogies. Aḥmad b. Khālid al-Nāṣirī al-Salawī (1835–97) first published his *Kitāb al-istiqṣā* in Cairo in 1894. The work has recently been reedited and awaits further critical study as a modern work of medieval historiography. Aḥmad b. Khālid al-Nāṣirī al-Salawī, *Kitāb al-Istiqṣā li akhbār duwal al-maghrib al-aqṣā*, ed. Aḥmadal-Nāṣirī, 9 vols. (Casablanca: Manshūrāt Wizārat al-Thaqāfa wa al-Ittiṣāl, 2001–5). See also 'Abd al-Hādī al-Tāzī, *Al-Wasīṭ fī tārīkh al-duwalī lil-maghrib* (Rabat: Dār Nashr al-Ma'rifa, 2001), 1:50. Al-Tāzī (1921–2015) rejects the idea that the Berbers constitute a single pure race. Rather, the Berbers are a mix, as the study of crania and blood types demonstrates. For mixes between Semites and Aryans, see Mūsā Laqbāl, *Tārikh al-maghrib al-islāmī* (Algiers: al-Sharika al-Waṭaniya lil-Nashr wa al-Tawzī', 1984), 14.

54. Al-Jīlālī, *Tārīkh*, 1:37.

55. Al-Jīlālī, *Tārīkh*, 1:36.

56. Al-Jīlālī, *Tārīkh*, 1:37, 148–49.

57. Al-Jīlālī, *Tārīkh*, 1:119–20.

58. Al-Jīlālī, *Tārīkh*, 1:257–59.

59. Mohamed Sahli, *Décoloniser l'histoire: Introduction à l'histoire du Maghreb* (Paris: François Maspero, 1965). Although it has "Maghreb" in the title, the book focuses on Algeria. See also Thomas Brisson, "Pourquoi Said? Une relecture socio-historique de la genèse de l'*Orientalisme*,"in *Après l'orientalisme: L'Orient créé par l'Orient [Colloque"L'orientalisme et après? Médiations, appropriations, contestations," Paris, ÉHESS, Institut du monde arabe, 15–17 juin 2011]*, ed. François Pouillon, Jean-Claude Vatin, Guy Barthèlemy, Mercedes Volait, and François Zabbal (Paris: Karthala, 2011), 105–25.

60. Stéphane Gsell (1864–1932) was easily the most important ancient historian, epigraphist, and archaeologist of his time. His multivolume *Histoire ancienne de l'Afrique du Nord* is a masterpiece that remained unequaled for decades. Insofar as it produced Berbers in pre-Islamic times, it contributed greatly to the Berberization of knowledge. For biographical notes

and a helpful bibliography, see Clémentine Gutron, "Gsell, Stéphane," in Pouillon, *Dictionnaire des orientalistes*, 490–91.

61. Sahli, *Décoloniser l'histoire*, 140.

62. Sahli, *Décoloniser l'histoire*, 141.

63. See Thomas Brisson, "Décoloniser l'orientalisme? Les études arabes françaises face aux décolonisations," *Revue d'Histoire des Sciences Humaines* 2, no. 24 (2011): 105–30.

64. Sahli, *Décoloniser l'histoire*, 78–86.

65. Assessing the effects of the Banū Hilāl was one of the most hotly debated issues in the new postcolonial context. See Jean Poncet, "Le mythe de la 'catastrophe' hilalienne [H. R. Idris, *La Berbérie orientale sous les Zîrides, X^e–XIIIe siècles*]," *Annales: Économies, Sociétés, Civilisations* 22, no. 5 (1967): 1099–1120; Roger Idris, "De la réalité de la catastrophe hilâlienne," *Annales: Économies, Sociétés, Civilisations* 23, no. 2 (1968): 390–96.

66. Abdallah Laroui, *The History of the Maghrib: An Interpretive Essay*, trans. Ralph Manheim (Princeton: Princeton University Press, 1977), 11.

67. Laroui, *The History of the Maghrib*, 219.

68. "From Ibn Khaldūn the colonial historians borrow only what he has to say about the role of the Bedouins, into which they inject their own racial prejudices by playing on the ambiguity of his Arabic vocabulary." Laroui, *The History of the Maghrib*, 220.

69. Laroui, *The History of the Maghrib*, 221.

70. Laroui, *The History of the Maghrib*, 223.

71. Hichem Djaït, *L'Europe et l'Islam* (Paris: Le Seuil, 1978).

72. See, for example, Mouloud Gaid, *Les Berbèr(e)s dans l'histoire*, 4 vols. (Algiers, Éditions Mimouni, 1990).

73. For the intellectual and institutional colonial heritage of the postcolonial university in the Maghrib and in France, see Mounira Chapoutot-Remadi, "Thirty Years of Research on the History of the Medieval Maghrib (Seventh to Sixteenth Centuries)," in *The Maghrib in Question: Essays in History and Historiography*, ed. Michel le Gall and Kenneth Perkins (Austin: University of Texas Press, 1997), 35–61; Pierre Vermeren, *Misère de l'historiographie du "Maghreb" post-colonial, 1962–2012* (Paris: Publications de la Sorbonne, 2012).

74. See, for example, Jean-Claude Vatin et al., *Connaissances du Maghreb: Sciences sociales et colonisation* (Paris: Éditions du CNRS, 1984).

75. Gabriel Camps,"Avertissement," in *Encyclopédie Berbère*, vol. 1,*Abadir—Acridophagie* (Aix-en-Provence: Edisud, 1984), 6–48.

76. See Gilles Lafuente, *La politique berbère de la France et le nationalisme marocain* (Paris: L'Harmattan, 1999); Ali Guenoun, *Chronologie du mouvement berbère, 1945–1990: Un combat et des hommes* (Algiers: Casbah, 1999); Muḥammad Mūnīb, *Al-ẓahīr al-barbarī: Akbar ukdhūba siyāsīya fī al-maghrib al-mu'āṣir* (Rabat: Dār Abī Riqrāq lil-Ṭibā'a wa-al-Nashr, 2002); Gabriele Kratochwil, *Die Berberbewegung in Marokko: zur Geschichte der Konstruktion einer ethnischen Identität (1912–1997)*, (Berlin: K. Schwarz, 2002). For a reasoned discussion of various positions within Berberism, see Salem Chaker, *Berbères aujourd'hui* (Paris: L'Harmattan, 1989); Mohand Tilmatine, "Du Berbère à l'Amazigh: De l'objet au sujet historique," *Al-Andalus-Maghreb* 14 (2007): 225–47.

77. "Berber" was clearly an Arabic exonym, and thus tied to the victimization of the true natives by the Arabs. Interestingly, the Berber etymology of "Amazigh" is not as certain as many seem to assume. See Salem Chaker, "Amazigh," in *Encyclopédie Berbère IV* (1987), 562–68.

78. *Histoire du Maroc: Réactualisation et synthèse*, ed. Mohamed Kably (Rabat: Edition de l'Institut Royal pour la Recherche sur l'Histoire du Maroc, 2011). For a mix of "Berber" and "Amazigh," see 'Abd al-Karīm Ghallāb, *Qirā'a jadīda fī tārīkh al-maghrib al-'arabī*, 3 vols. (Beirut: Dār al-Gharb al-Islāmī, 2005).

79. Kably, *Histoire du Maroc*, 142.

80. Kably, *Histoire du Maroc*, 144. See also Kably, *Histoire du Maroc*, 145, 147, 214, 215 (amazighophones), 220, 248, 261 (tamazight), 264 (genealogies), 264 (*mafākhir al-barbar* as rehabilitation of Amazighs), 312.

81. See also Mahfoud Kaddache, *L'Algérie médiévale* (Algiers: ENAL, 1992); Hicham Djait, Mohamed Talbi, Farhat Dachraoui, Abdelmajid Douib, and M'hamed Alì M'rabet, *Histoire de la Tunisie: Le moyen âge* (Tunis: Société Tunisienne de Diffusion, [1970?]).

82. The more "Amazigh" becomes the word of choice of governments and the official histories they finance, the more it runs the risk of losing some of its original political edge as a carrier of the oppositional discourse about a threatened Berber identity.

83. Cf. "Quelle que soit l'importance que l'on veuille accorder à ces "pesanteurs" idéologiques, on doit reconnaître que les berbérisants de l'époque coloniale ont été de bons descriptivistes. . . . Il faut leur rendre cette justice, que, globalement ils n'ont été ni les inspirateurs, ni les conseillers d'une quelconque politique 'berbère', a fortiori 'berbériste' . . . ce qui ramène à peu de chose la mythique 'politique berbère' de la France." Salem Chaker, "Réflexions sur les études Berbères pendant la periode coloniale (Algérie)," *Revue de l'Occident Musulman et de la Méditerranée* 34 (1982): 81–89.

CONCLUSION

1. Timothy Mitchell, "McJihad: Islam in the U.S. Global Order," *Social Text* 20, no. 4 (2002): 1–18.

2. Colonial policies were never coherent or consistent, and it would be a mistake to imagine a single colonial policy toward the Berbers or even the Kabyles.

3. Emigration from northern Morocco to Spain, Belgium, Germany, and the Netherlands has affected the weight of France and French-specific concerns.

4. Compared to those Algerian Jews who relocated to France, those who went to Israel came from relatively low social backgrounds and educational attainment, a circumstance that illuminates their relative attachment to the most virulent antinative expressions of colonial culture. That their status in Israel was for a long time lower than that of everyone except the "Arabs" (i.e., Palestinians) explains the spectacular fierceness of their communal politics there and the spectacular pronouncements of their leadership. See 'Abd al-Ḥamīd al-'Awnī, *Al-ta'thīr al-isrā'īlī 'alā maghrib muḥammad al-sādis: Li-awwal marra tunsharu 'alāqāt al-būlīsāryū wa-isrā'īl* (Fez: Manshūrāt 'Arabiya, 2004); Jeremy Allouche, *The Oriental Communities in Israel, 1948–2003: The Social and Cultural Creation of an Ethnic Political Group* (Geneva: Institut Universitaire de Hautes Études Internationales, 2003); *The Jews of Modern France: Images and Identities*, ed. Zvi Jonathan Kaplan and Nadia Malinovich (Leiden: Brill, 2016); Ella Shohat, *On the Arab-Jew, Palestine, and Other Displacements: Selected Writings of Ella Shohat* (London: Pluto Press, 2017).

5. The same applies to the support that the governments of Algeria and Morocco give to each other's Berberists. See Bruce Maddy-Weitzman, *The Berber Identity Movement and the Challenge to North African States* (Austin: University of Texas Press, 2011).

6. A numerical minority, arabophone Berberists (more numerous in Morocco) have a more direct access to the sources, but their handling of medieval ideologies embedded in them remains an issue. See, for example, Muḥammad al-Mukhtār al-ʻArbāwī, *Al-barbar, mashāriqa fī al-maghrib* (Marrakesh: Ittiṣālāt Sabwa, 2012); Muḥammad Bin Laḥsan, *Al-amāzīgh: Aḍwā' jadīda ʻalā al-masīra al-ḥaḍārīyaʻabra al-tārīkh* (Rabat: Maṭābiʻ al-Rabāṭ Nit, 2015); Saʻid ibn ʻAbd Allāh al-Dārūdī, *Ḥawlaʻurūbat al-barbar: Madkhal ilā ʻurūbat al-amāzīghiyīn min khilāl al-lisān* (Rabat: Manshūrāt al-Fikr, 2012); ʻAbd al-Laṭīf Hassūf, *Al-amāzīgh: qiṣṣat shʻab* (Beirut: Dāral-Sāqī, 2016); ʻUthmān Saʻdī, *Al-barbar al-amāzīgh ʻarab ʻāriba, wa-ʻurūbat al-shamāl al-Ifrīqī ʻabra al-tārīkh* (Beirut: Dār al-Multaqā, 1998).

7. For a helpful discussion of the main currents and the stakes, see Helena de Felipe, "Los estudios sobre bereberes en la historiografía española: Arabismo y africanismo," in Manuela Marín, *Al-Andalus/España: historiografías en contraste, siglos XVII–XXI* (Madrid: Casa de Velazquez, 2009), 105–17.

8. Although my references could not always show it, this book has greatly benefited from the critical work of my Spanish colleagues and from that of historians working on medieval Iberia more generally.

9. Cited in *Algérie arabe: En finir avec l'imposture*, ed. Rabah Ait Messaoud, Hand Mairi, and Hend Sadi (Algiers: Koukou, 2016), 7: "Alléger l'*Histoire des Berbères* d'Ibn Khaldoun pour en faire un livre de combat." See also Mehana Amrani, *La poétique de Kateb Yacine: L'autobiographie au service de l'histoire* (Paris: L'Harmattan, 2012); *Kateb Yacine, un intellectuel dans la révolution algérienne*, ed. Jacques Girault and Bernard Lecherbonnier (Paris: L'Harmattan, 2002); Benamar Médiène, *Kateb Yacine: Le coeur entre les dents; Biographie hétérodoxe* (Paris: R. Laffont, 2006).

10. The scholarship on the postcolonial Maghrib is both dense and diverse. See, for example, *Penser le national au Maghreb et ailleurs: Actes du colloque diraset-études maghrébines 22, 23 et 24 septembre 2011, Tunis*, ed. Fatma Ben Slimane and Hichem Abdessamad (Tunis: Arabesques, 2013); Réda Bensmaïa, *Experimental Nations, or, The Invention of the Maghreb*, trans. Alyson Waters (Princeton: Princeton University Press, 2003); Mounira Charrad, *States and Women's Rights: The Making of Postcolonial Tunisia, Algeria, and Morocco* (Berkeley: University of California Press, 2001); Abdelmajid Hannoum, *Violent Modernity: France in Algeria* (Cambridge, MA: Center for Middle Eastern Studies of Harvard University Press, 2010); Olivia Harrison, *Transcolonial Maghreb: Imagining Palestine in the Era of Decolonization* (Stanford: Stanford University Press, 2016); Jane Hiddleston, *Decolonising the Intellectual: Politics, Culture, and Humanism at the End of the French Empire* (Liverpool: Liverpool University Press, 2014); Edwige Tamalet Talbayev, *The Transcontinental Maghreb: Francophone Literature Across the Mediterranean* (New York: Fordham University Press, 2017). See also Fatima Ahnouch, *Littérature francophone du Maghreb: Imaginaire et représentations socioculturelles* (Paris: L'Harmattan, 2014); Taïeb Berrada, *La figure de l'intrus: Représentations postcoloniales maghrébines* (Paris: L'Harmattan, 2016); Hanan Elsayed, *L'histoire sacrée de l'Islam dans la fiction maghrébine* (Paris: Éditions Karthala, 2016).

11. Cf. Kateb Yacine's preface in Amar Ouerdane, *La question berbère dans le mouvement national algérien, 1926–1980* (Algiers: Épigraphe, 1993).

12. Kateb Yacine's dream remains unfulfilled: Ibn Khaldūn's history never formed the basis of a people's history of the Maghrib.

Bibliography

Abdesselem, Ahmed. *Ibn Khaldūn et ses lecteurs*. Paris: Presses Universitaires de France, 1983.

Abi-Mershed, Osama W. *Apostles of Modernity: Saint-Simonians and the Civilizing Mission in Algeria*. Stanford: Stanford University Press, 2010.

Abū al-Fidā' (1273–1331). *Géographie d'Aboulféda: Texte arabe [Taqwīm al-buldān]*. Ed. M. Reinaud and M. Le baron Mac Guckin de Slane. Paris: Imprimerie Royale, 1840.

———. *Al-mukhtaṣar fī akhbār al-bashar*. 2 vols. Beirut: Dār al-Kitāb al-Lubnānī: Dār al-Baḥḥār, 1956–61.

Abu el Haj, Nadia. *Facts on the Ground: Archaeological Practice and Territorial Self-Fashioning in Israeli Society*. Chicago: University of Chicago Press, 2001.

———. *The Genealogical Science: The Search for Jewish Origins and the Politics of Epistemology*. Chicago: University of Chicago Press, 2012.

Abulafia, David. *The Great Sea: A Human History of the Mediterranean*. Oxford: Oxford University Press, 2011.

Abun-Nasr, Jamil. *A History of the Maghrib in the Islamic Period*. Cambridge: Cambridge University Press, 1987.

Abū Zakariyā al-Warjalānī (d. ca. 1078). *Kitāb al-sīra wa akhbār al-a'imma*. Ed. 'Abd al-Raḥmān Ayyūb. Tunis: Al-Dār al-Tūnusiyya lil-Nashr, 1985.

Adang, Camilla, Maribel Fierro, and Sabine Schmidtke, eds. *Ibn Ḥazm of Cordoba: The Life and Works of a Controversial Thinker*. Leiden: Brill, 2013.

Ahnouch, Fatima. *Littérature francophone du Maghreb: Imaginaire et représentations socioculturelles*. Paris: L'Harmattan, 2014.

Aillet, Cyrille. *Les mozarabes: Christianisme, islamisation et arabisation en péninsule ibérique (IXe–XIIe siècle)*. Madrid: Casa de Velázquez, 2010.

———. "Tāhart et les origines de l'imamat rustumide: Matrice orientale et ancrage local." *Annales Islamologiques* 45 (2011): 47–78.

———. "Islamisation et arabisation dans le monde musulman médiéval: Une introduction au cas de l'Occident musulman (VIIe–XIIe siècle)." In *Islamisation et arabisation de l'Occident musulman (VIIe–XIIe siècle)*, ed. Dominique Valérian. Paris: Publications de la Sorbonne, 2011. 7–34.

———. "Introduction: L'ibâdisme, une minorité au sein de l'islam." *Revue des Mondes Musulmans et de la Méditerranée* 132 (2012): 13–36.

———. "A Breviary of Faith and a Sectarian Memorial: A New Reading of Ibn Sallam's Kitab (3rd/9th century)." In *Ibadi Theology: Rereading Sources and Scholarly Works*, ed. Ersilia Francesca. Hildesheim, Zurich, and New York: Georg Olms, 2015. 67–82.

Ait Messaoud, Rabah Hand Mairi, and Hend Sadi, eds. *Algérie arabe: En finir avec l'imposture.* Algiers: Koukou, 2016.

Allouche, Jeremy. *The Oriental Communities in Israel, 1948–2003: The Social and Cultural Creation of an Ethnic Political Group.* Geneva: Institut Universitaire de Hautes Études Internationales, 2003.

Amaldi, Daniela. "La poesia yemenita dalla ǧāhiliyya al IX secolo: Stato degli studi in occidente." *Quaderni di Studi Arabi* 15 (1997): 119–30.

Amara, Allaoua. "L'islamisation du Maghreb central (VIIe-XIe siècle)." In *Islamisation et arabisation de l'Occident musulman (VIIe-XIIe siècle)*, ed. Dominique Valérian. Paris: Publications de la Sorbonne, 2011. 103–30.

Amari, Michele. *I diplomi arabi del R. archivio fiorentino: testo originale con la traduzione letterale e illustrazioni di Michele Amari.* Florence: Le Monnier, 1863.

Amkāsū, 'Umar. *Al-mashrū' al-murābiṭī fī al-andalus: Bayna al-najāḥ wa-al-ikhfāq.* Casablanca: Ifrīqiyā al-Sharq, 2016.

Amrani, Mehana. *La poétique de Kateb Yacine: L'autobiographie au service de l'histoire.* Paris: L'Harmattan, 2012.

'Amrānī, Muḥammad. *Ḥawāḍir al-andalus bayna al-intifāḍa wal-thawra khilāl al-'aṣr al-murābiṭī fī al-qarn al-sādis al-hijrī, al-thānī 'ashar al-mīlādī.* Rabat: Dār Abī Raqrāq lil-Ṭibā'a wal-Nashr, 2006.

Amri, Nelly. *Les saints en islam, les messagers de l'espérance: Sainteté et eschatologie au Maghreb aux XIVe et XVe siècles.* Paris: Les Éditions du Cerf, 2008.

Anderson, Benedict. *Imagined Communities: Reflections on the Origin and Spread of Nationalism.* New York: Verso, 1991.

Anonymous (11th c.). *Akhbār majmū'a.* Ed. Ibrāhīm al-Ibyārī. Cairo: Dār al-Kitāb al-Maṣrī, 1981.

———. *Crónica Mozárabe de 754.* Ed. José Eduardo López Pereira. Zaragoza: Anubar Ediciones, 1980.

———. *Fatḥ al-Andalus (La conquista de al-Andalus).* Ed. Luis Molina. Madrid: CSIC, 1994.

———(14th c.). *Kitāb mafākhir al-barbar li-mu'allif majhūl.* Ed. 'Abd al-Qādir Būbāya. Rabat: Dār Abī Raqrāq lil-Ṭibā'a wal-Nashr, 2005.

———. *Periplus Maris Erythræi.* In *Geographi Graeci Minores*, ed. Karl Müller. Hildesheim: G. Olms, 1965. 1: 257–305.

Antrim, Zayde. *Routes and Realms: The Power of Place in the Early Islamic World.* Oxford: Oxford University Press, 2012.

Apostolou, Irini. *L'orientalisme des voyageurs français au XVIIIe siècle: Une iconographie de l'Orient méditerranéen.* Paris: Presses de l'Université Paris-Sorbonne, 2009.

Al-'Arbāwī, Muḥammad al-Mukhtār. *Al-barbar, mashāriqa fī al-maghrib.* Marrakesh: Ittiṣālāt Sabwa, 2012.

Arberry, Arthur J. *The Koran Interpreted.* London: Allen & Unwin; New York: Macmillan, 1955.

Al-'Awnī, 'Abd al-Ḥamīd. *Al-ta'thīr al-isrā'īlī 'alā maghrib muḥammad al-sādis: Li-awwal marra tunsharu 'alāqāt al-būlīsāryū wa-isrā'īl.* Fez: Manshūrāt 'Arabiya, 2004.

Al-Azmeh, Aziz. *Ibn Khaldūn in Modern Scholarship: A Study in Orientalism.* London: Third World Centre for Research and Publishing, 1981.

———. *Ibn Khaldūn: An Essay in Reinterpretation.* London and Totowa, NJ: Cass, 1982.

Baadj, Amar Salem. *Saladin, the Almohads, and the Banū Ghāniya: The Contest for North Africa (12th and 13th Centuries).* Leiden: Brill, 2015.

Bahri, Fathi. "Les 'Adjam al-balad: Une minorité sociale d'origine autochtone en Ifrīqiyā aghlabide (IIIe-IXe siècles)." In *Mutations d'identités en Méditerranée: Moyen Âge et époque contemporaine*, ed. Henri Bresc and Christiane Veauvy. [Saint-Denis]: Éditions Bouchène, 2000. 67–84.

Al-Bakrī, Abū 'Ubayd Allāh (d. 1094). *Kitāb al-masālik wa al-mamālik*. Ed. A.P. Van Leeuwen and A. Férré. 2 vols. Tunis: Al-Dār al-'Arabiyya lil-Kitāb, 1992.

Al-Balādhurī (d. 892). *Futūḥ al-buldān*. Ed. M.J. de Goeje. Leiden: Brill, 1866.

———. *Kitāb futūḥ al-buldān*. Ed. Ṣalāḥ al-Dīn al-Munajjid. 3 vols. Cairo: Maktabat al-Nahḍa al-Miṣriya, 1956–58.

Bargaoui, Sami. "Des Turcs aux Hanafiyya: La construction d'une catégorie 'métisse' à Tunis aux XVIIe et XVIIIe siècles." *Annales: Histoire, Sciences Sociales* 1 (2005): 209–28.

Bearman, Peri J., Thierry Bianquis, Clifford Edmund Bosworth, Emeri J. van Donzel, and W. P. Heinrichs, eds. *Encyclopaedia of Islam (EI²)*. 2nd ed. Leiden: Brill, 2004.

Bel Ochi, Mohamed Sadok. *La conversion des berbères à l'Islam*. Tunis: Maison tunisienne de l'édition, 1981.

Benabbès, Mohamed. "L'Afrique byzantine face à la conquête arabe." PhD diss., Université Paris X–Nanterre, 2004.

Benchekroun, Chafik T. "Les Idrissides: L'histoire contre son histoire." *Al-Masāq: Islam and the Mediterranean* 23, no. 3 (2011): 171–88.

Bennison, Amira K. *The Almoravid and Almohad Empires*. Edinburgh: Edinburgh University Press, 2016.

Ben Slimane, Fatma, and Hichem Abdessamad, eds. *Penser le national au Maghreb et ailleurs: Actes du colloque diraset-études maghrébines 22, 23 et 24 septembre 2011*. Tunis: Tunis Arabesques, 2013.

Bensmaïa, Réda. *Experimental Nations, or, The Invention of the Maghreb*. Trans. Alyson Waters. Princeton: Princeton University Press, 2003.

Bentayebi, Kaoutar, et al. "Genetic Ancestry of a Moroccan Population as Inferred from Autosomal STRs." *Meta Gene* 2 (2014): 427–38.

Berrada, Taïeb. *La figure de l'intrus: Représentations postcoloniales maghrébines*. Paris: L'Harmattan, 2016.

Beylié, Léon Marie Eugène de. *La Kalaa des Beni Hammad: Une capitale berbère de l'Afrique du nord au XIe siècle*. Paris: Éditions Leroux, 1909.

Bin Laḥsan (Ben Lahcen), Muḥammad. *Al-amāzīgh: Aḍwā' jadīda 'alā al-masīra al-ḥaḍārīya 'abra al-tārīkh*. Rabat: Maṭābi' al-Ribāṭ Nit, 2015.

Blais, Helène. *Mirages de la carte: L'invention de l'Algérie coloniale XIXe–XXe siècle*. Paris: Fayard, 2014.

Bloch, Marc. *Apologie pour l'histoire, ou, Métier d'historien*. Paris: Armand Colin, 1949.

Boëtsch, Gilles. "Égypte noire, Berbérie blanche: La rencontre manquée de la biologie et de la culture." *Cahiers d'Études Africaines* 33, no. 129 (1993): 73–98.

Boone, James L., and Nancy L. Benco. "Islamic Settlement in North Africa and the Iberian Peninsula." *Annual Review of Anthropology* 28 (1999): 51–71.

Borrut, Antoine. *Entre mémoire et pouvoir: L'espace syrien sous les derniers Omeyyades et les premiers Abbasides (v. 72–193/692–809)*. Leiden: Brill, 2011.

Bosch Vilá, Jacinto. *Historia de Marruecos: Los Almorávides*. Tetouan: Marroquí, 1956.

Bousquet, Georges-Henri. *Les Berbères: Histoire et institutions*. Paris: Presses Universitaires de France, 1957.

Bowen Savant, Sarah, and Helena de Felipe, eds. *Genealogy and Knowledge in Muslim Societies: Understanding the Past*. Edinburgh: Edinburgh University Press, 2014.

Bowersock, Glen Warren. "Tylos and Tyre: Bahrain in the Graeco-Roman World." *Bahrain Through the Ages: The Archaeology*, ed. Shaikha Haya Ali Khalifa and Michael Rice. London: Kegan Paul International, 1986. 399–406.

Boyer, Pierre. "Le problème kouloughli dans la régence d'Alger." *Revue de l'Occident Musulman et de la Méditerranée* 8, no. 1 (1970): 79–94.

Braudel, Fernand. "Nécrologie: Georges Yver (1890-1961)." *Annales: Économies, Sociétés, Civilisations* 18, no. 2 (1963): 407–8.

Bray, Julia. "Men, Women, and Slaves in Abbasid Society." In *Gender in the Early Medieval World: East and West, 300–900*, ed. Leslie Brubaker and Julia M. H. Smith Cambridge: Cambridge University Press, 2004. 121–46.

Brett, Michael. "The Islamisation of Morocco: From the Arabs to the Almoravids." *Morocco: The Journal of the Society for Moroccan Studies* 2 (1992): 57–71.

———. *The Rise of the Fatimids: The World of the Mediterranean and the Middle East in the Fourth Century of the Hijra, Tenth Century CE*. Leiden: Brill, 2001.

———. *The Fatimid Empire*. Edinburgh: Edinburgh University Press, 2017.

Brett, Michael, and Elizabeth Fentress. *The Berbers*. Oxford and Cambridge, MA: Blackwell, 1996.

Brisson, Thomas. "Décoloniser l'orientalisme? Les études arabes françaises face aux décolonisations." *Revue d'Histoire des Sciences Humaines* 2, no. 24 (2011): 105–30.

———. "Pourquoi Said? Une relecture socio-historique de la genèse de l'*Orientalisme*." In *Après l'orientalisme: L'Orient créé par l'Orient (Colloque "L'orientalisme et après? Médiations, appropriations, contestations," Paris, ÉHESS, Institut du monde arabe, 15–17 juin 2011)*, ed. François Pouillon, Jean-Claude Vatin, Guy Barthèlemy, Mercedes Volait, and François Zabbal.Paris: Karthala, 2011. 105–25.

Brown, L. Carl. "Maghrib Historiography: The Unit of Analysis Problem." In *The Maghrib in Question: Essays in History and Historiography*, ed. Michel Le Gall and Kenneth Perkins. Austin: University of Texas Press, 1997. 4–16.

Brunschvig, Robert. *La Berbérie orientale sous les Ḥafṣides: Des origines à la fin du XVe siècle*. 2 vols. Paris: Adrien-Maisonneuve, 1940–47.

Būbāya, ʿAbd al-Qādir. *Al-barbar fī al-andalus wa mawqifuhum min fitnat al-qarn al-khāmis al-hijrī,422–92/711–1031*. Beirut: Dār al-Kutub al-ʿIlmiyya, 2011.

Bulliet, Richard W. *The Camel and the Wheel*. Cambridge, MA: Harvard University Press, 1975.

———. *Conversion to Islam in the Medieval Period: An Essay in Quantitative History*. Cambridge, MA: Harvard University Press, 1979.

Buresi, Pascal, and Hicham El Aallaoui. *Governing the Empire: Provincial Administration in the Almohad Caliphate (1224–1269); Critical Edition, Translation, and Study of Manuscript 4752 of the Hasaniyya Library in Rabat Containing 77 Taqādīm ("Appointments")*. Trans. Travis Bruce. Leiden: Brill, 2013.

Burke, Edmund III. "Towards a History of the Maghrib." *Middle Eastern Studies* 11, no. 3 (1975): 306–23.

Cambuzat, Paul-Louis. *L'évolution des cités du Tell en Ifrīḳiya du VIIe au XIe siècle*. Algiers: Office des Publications Universitaires, 1986.

Camps, Gabriel. *Monuments et rites funéraires protohistoriques, aux origines de la Berbérie*. Paris: Arts et métiers graphiques, 1961.

———. *Berbères: Aux marges de l'histoire*. Paris: Éditions des Hespérides, 1980.

———. "Comment la Berbérie est devenue le Maghreb arabe." *Revue de l'Occident musulman et de la Méditerranée* 35 (1983): 7–24.

Carlier, Omar. "Mercier, Ernest." In *Dictionnaire des orientalistes de langue française: Nouvelle édition revue et augmentée*, ed. François Pouillon. Paris: IISMM and Karthala, 2012. 716–18.

Casajus, Dominique. "Les noms de peuple ont un histoire." In *Léon l'Africain*, ed. François Pouillon, Alain Messaoudi, Dietrich Rauchenberger, and Oumelbanine Zhiri. Paris: Karthala, 2009. 105–17.

Chaker, Salem. "Amazigh." *Encyclopédie Berbère* 4 (1987): 562–68.

———. *Berbères aujourd'hui*. Paris: L'Harmattan, 1989.

———. "Le berbère." In *Les langues de France*, ed. Bernard Cerquiligni. Paris: Presses Universitaires de France, 2003. 215–27.

Chalmeta Gendrón Pedro. *Invasión e islamización: La sumisión de Hispania y la formación de al-Andalus*. Jaén: Universidad de Jaén, 2003.

———. "Muwallad." In *EI²*, 7:806–8.

Chapoutot-Remadi, Mounira. "Thirty Years of Research on the History of the Medieval Maghrib (Seventh to Sixteenth Centuries)." In *The Maghrib in Question: Essays in History and Historiography*, ed. Michel le Gall and Kenneth Perkins. Austin: University of Texas Press, 1997. 35–61.

Charrad, Mounira. *States and Women's Rights: The Making of Postcolonial Tunisia, Algeria, and Morocco*. Berkeley: University of California Press, 2001.

Chaumont, Eric. "L'Ego-histoire d'Ibn Khaldûn, historien et soufi." *Comptes Rendus des Séances de l'Académie des Inscriptions et Belles-Lettres* 3 (1996): 1041–57.

Cheddadi, Abdesselam. *Ibn Khaldūn: L'homme et le théoricien de la civilisation*. Paris: Gallimard, 2006.

Cherni, Lotfi, et al. "Female Gene Pools of Berber and Arab Neighboring Communities in Central Tunisia: Microstructure of mtDNA Variation in North Africa." *Human Biology* 77, no. 1 (2005): 61–70.

Choueiri, Youssef M. *Modern Arab Historiography: Historical Discourse and the Nation-State*. New York: Routledge, 2003.

Clancy-Smith, Julia. "Berber History: *The Berbers* by Michael Brett; Elizabeth Fentress." *Journal of African History* 38, no. 3 (1997): 498–99.

Clarke, Nicola. *The Muslim Conquest of Iberia: Medieval Arabic Narratives*. London: Routledge, 2011.

Clément, François. "À propos de balad/bilād et autres noms: Quelques observations sur la terminologie des grands territoires dans les sources arabes." *Cahiers de Recherches Médiévales et Humanistes* 21 (2011): 203–10.

Cole, Juan. *Napoleon's Egypt: Invading the Middle East*. New York: Palgrave Macmillan, 2007.

Collingwood, R. G. *The Idea of History*. Oxford: Oxford University Press, 2005.

Conde, José Antonio. *Historia de la dominación de los árabes en España*. Madrid: García, 1820.

Cornell, Vincent J. *Realm of the Saint: Power and Authority in Moroccan Sufism*. Austin: University of Texas Press, 1998.

Cosmas Indicopleustes. *Topographie chrétienne*. Ed. Wanda Wolska-Conus. 2 vols. Paris: Les Éditions du Cerf, 1968–70.

Crawford, David. *Moroccan Households in the World Economy: Labor and Inequality in a Berber Village*. Baton Rouge: Louisiana State University Press, 2008.

Cressier, Patrice, Maribel Fierro, and Luis Molina, eds. *Los almohades: Problemas y perspectivas*. 2 vols. Madrid: CSIC, 2005.

Crone, Patricia. "Were the Qays and Yemen of the Umayyad Period Political Parties?" *Der Islam* 71, no. 1 (1994): 1–57.

Al-Ḍabbī (d. 1203). *Kitāb bughyat al-multamis fī tārīkh rijāl al-andalus*. Ed. Franciscus Codera and Julianus Ribera. Madrid: Jose de Rojas, 1885.

Dachraoui, Farhat. *Le califat Fatimide au Maghreb (296–365 H./909–975 Jc.): Histoire politique et institutions*. Tunis: Société Tunisienne de Diffusion, 1981.

Daftary, Farhad. *The Assassin Legends: Myths of the Isma'ilis*. London: I.B. Tauris, 1994.

Al-Darjīnī (fl. 13th c.). *Kitāb ṭabaqāt al-mashāyikh bi-al-maghrib*. Ed. IbrāhīmṬallāy. 2 vols. Qasanṭīna: Maṭba'at al-Ba'th, 1974.

Al-Dārūdī, Sa'id ibn 'Abd Allāh. *Ḥawla 'urūbat al-barbar: Madkhal ilā 'urūbat al-amāzīghiyīn min khilāl al-lisān*. Rabat: Manshūrāt al-Fikr, 2012.

Deguignes, Joseph. *Histoire générale des Huns, des turcs, des mogols et des autres tartares occidentaux . . . : par M. Deguignes, . . . Suite des Mémoires de l'Académie Royale des Inscriptions et Belles-Lettres*. Paris: Chez Desaint et Saillant, 1756.

Denny, Frederick. "Umma." In *EI*², 10:862.

Deprest, Florence. *Géographes en Algérie*. Paris: Belin, 2009.

———. "Gautier, Émile-Félix." In *Dictionnaire des orientalistes de langue française, nouvelle édition revue et augmentée*, ed. François Pouillon. Paris: IISMM and Karthala, 2012. 456–57.

de Slane, William McGuckin, trans. *Histoire des Berbères et des dynasties musulmanes de l'Afrique septentrionale par Ibn Khaldoun*. 4 vols. Algiers: Imprimerie du gouvernement, 1852–56.

———, ed. *Description de l'Afrique septentrionale par Abou-Oubeid-El-Bekri*. Algiers: Imprimerie du gouvernement, 1857.

———. *Les prolégomènes d'Ibn Khaldoun: Traduits en français et commentés par M. de Slane*. Paris: Imprimerie Impériale, 1858.

Djaït, Hichem. "La wilāya d'Ifrīqiya au IIᵉ/VIIIᵉ siècle: Étude institutionnelle." *Studia Islamica* 27 (1967): 77–121 and 28 (1968): 79–108.

———. "L'Afrique arabe au VIIIe siècle (86-184 H/705-800)." *Annales: Économies, Sociétés, Civilisations* 28, no. 3 (1973): 601–21.

———. *L'Europe et l'Islam*. Paris: Le Seuil, 1978.

———. *Ta'sīs al-gharb al-islāmī: Al-qarn al-awwal wa-al-thānī H., al-sābi' wa-al-thāmin M.* Beirut: Dār al-Ṭalī'a lil-Ṭibā'a wa-al-Nashr, 2004.

Djaït, Hichem, Mohamed Talbi, Farhat Dachraoui, Abdelmajid Douib, and M'hamed Alì M'rabet. *Histoire de la Tunisie: Le moyen âge*. Tunis: Société Tunisienne de Diffusion, [1970?].

Donner, Fred. *Muḥammad and the Believers: At the Origins of Islam*. Cambridge, MA: Belknap Press, 2010.

———. "Arabic Fatḥ as 'Conquest' and Its Origin in Islamic Tradition." *Al-'Uṣūr al-Wusṭā* 24 (2016): 1–14.

El Ghali, Abdelkader. *Les états kharidjites au Maghreb (IIᵉ s.–IVᵉ hég/VIIIᵉ s.–Xᵉ s. apr. J.-C.)*. Tunis: Centre de Publications Universitaire, 2003.

El Hour, Rachid. "Some Reflections about the Use of the Berber Language in the Medieval and Early Modern Maghrib: Data from Hagiographic Sources." *Al-Masāq: Journal of the Medieval Mediterranean* 26, no. 3 (2014): 288–98.

———. "Reflexiones acerca de las dinastías bereberes y lengua bereber en el magreb medieval." *Miscelánea de Estudios Árabes y Hebraicos: Sección Árabe-Islam* 64 (2015): 45–59.

Elkamel, Sarra, et al. "The Orientalisation of North Africa: New Hints from the Study of STRs in an Arab Population." *Annals of Human Biology* 44, no. 2 (2016): 180–90.

Elsayed, Hanan. *L'histoire sacrée de l'Islam dans la fiction maghrébine*. Paris: Éditions Karthala, 2016.

Espagne, Michel, Nora Lafi, and Pascale Rabault-Feuerhahn. *Silvestre de Sacy: Le projet européen d'une science orientaliste*. Paris: Les Éditions du Cerf, 2014.

Fancy, Hussein. *The Mercenary Mediterranean: Sovereignty, Violence, and Religion in the Medieval Crown of Aragon*. Chicago: University of Chicago Press, 2016.

Farrujia de la Rosa, A. José. *An Archaeology of the Margins: Colonialism, Amazighity, and Heritage Management in the Canary Islands*. New York: Springer, [2014].

Fayyāḍ, Muḥammad. *Qiyām al-dawla al-fāṭimīya: Ḥarakat al-tashayyuʿ al-ismāʿīlī wa-atharuhā ʿalá taṭawwur al-mashrūʿ al-shīʿī*. Cairo: Dār al-ʿĀlam al-ʿArabī, 2014.

Felipe, Helena de. *Identidad y onomástica de los berebéres de al-Andalus*. Madrid: CSIC, 1997.

———. "Los estudios sobre bereberes en la historiografía española: Arabismo y africanismo." In *Al-Andalus/España: Historiografías en contraste, siglos XVII-XXI*, ed. Manuela Marín. Madrid: Casa de Velazquez, 2009. 105–17.

Fentress, Elizabeth. "Romanising the Berbers." *Past & Present* 190 (2006): 3–33.

Fenwick, Corisande. "From Africa to Ifrīqiya: Settlement and Society in Early Medieval North Africa (650–800)." *Al-Masāq: Islam and the Medieval Mediterranean* 25, no. 1 (2013): 9–33.

Ferrario, Giulio. *Il costume antico e moderno, o, storia del governo, della milizia, della religione, delle arti, scienze ed usanze di tutti i popoli antichi e moderni, provata coi monumenti dell'antichità e rappresentata cogli analoghi disegni dal dottor Giulio Ferrario: Africa, Tomo I*. Milan: Dalla tipografia dell'editore, 1827.

Février, Paul-Albert. *La Méditerranée de Paul-Albert Février*. 2 vols. Rome: École française de Rome; Aix-en-Provence: Université de Provence, 1996.

Fierro, Maribel. "Árabes, Beréberes, muladíes y mawālī: Algunas reflexiones sobre los datos de los diccionarios biográficos andalusíes." In *Estudios onomástico-biográficos de al-Andalus VII: homenaje a José Ma Fórneas*, ed. Manuela Marin and Helena de Felipe. Madrid: CSIC, 1995. 41–54.

———. *ʿAbd al-Raḥmān III: The First Cordoban Caliph*. Oxford: Oneworld, 2005.

———. *The Almohad Revolution: Politics and Religion in the Islamic West During the Twelfth-Thirteenth Centuries*. Farnham: Ashgate, 2014.

Fleischer, Cornell. "Royal Authority, Dynastic Cyclism, and 'Ibn Khaldûnism' in Sixteenth-Century Ottoman Letters." *Journal of Asian and African Studies* 18, no. 3 (1983): 198–220.

Fournel, Henri. *Étude sur la conquête de l'Afrique par les Arabes, et recherches sur les tribus berbères qui ont occupé le Maghreb central*. Paris: Imprimerie Impériale, 1857.

———. *Les Berbers: Étude sur la conquête de l'Afrique par les Arabes, d'après les textes arabes imprimés*. Paris: Imprimerie nationale, 1881.

Frigi, Sabeh, et al. "Ancient Local Evolution of African mtDNA Haplogroups in Tunisian Berber Populations." *Human Biology* 82, no. 4 (2010): 367–84.

Gaïd, Mouloud. *Les Berbèr(e)s dans l'histoire*. 4 vols. Algiers: Éditions Mimouni, 1990.

Galand, Lionel. "La langue berbère existe-t-elle?" In *Mélanges linguistiques offerts à Maxime Rodinson par ses élèves, ses collègues, et ses amis*, ed. Christian Robin and Maxime Rodinson. Paris: Geuthner, 1985. 175–84.

———. *Études de linguistique berbère*. Leuven: Peeters, 2002.

García-Arenal, Mercedes. *Messianism and Puritanical Reform: Mahdīs of the Muslim West*. Leiden: Brill, 2006.

García Sanjuán, Alejandro. *La conquista islámica y la tergiversación del pasado*. Madrid: Marcial Pons Historia, 2013.

Gautier, Émile-Félix. *Le passé de l'Afrique du nord: Les siècles obscurs*. Paris: Payot, 1937.

Geary, Patrick J. *The Myth of Nations: The Medieval Origins of Europe*. Princeton: Princeton University Press, 2002.

Gérard, Natalie, et al. "North African Berber and Arab Influences in the Western Mediterranean Revealed by Y-Chromosome DNA Haplotypes." *Human Biology* 78, no. 3 (2006): 307–16.

Ghallāb, 'Abd al-Karīm. *Qirā'a jadīda fī tārīkh al-maghrib al-'arabī*. 3 vols. Beirut: Dār al-Gharb al-Islāmī, 2005.

Ghouirgate, Mehdi. *L'ordre almohade (1120–1269): Une nouvelle lecture anthropologique*. Toulouse: Presses Universitaires du Mirail, 2014.

———. "Le berbère au Moyen Âge: Une culture linguistique en cours de reconstitutions." *Annales: Histoire, Sciences Sociales* 3 (2015): 577–606.

Gil, Juan. *Corpus scriptores muzarabicorum*. 2 vols. Madrid: Instituto Antonio de Nebrija, 1973.

Gilotte, Sophie, and Annliese Nef. "L'apport de l'archéologie, de la numismatique et de la sigillographie à l'histoire de l'islamisation de l'Occident musulman: En guise d'introduction." In *Islamisation et arabisation de l'Occident musulman (VIIe-XIIe siècle)*, ed. Dominique Valérian. Paris: Publications de la Sorbonne, 2011. 63–99.

Girault, Jacques, and Bernard Lecherbonnier, eds. *Kateb Yacine, un intellectuel dans la révolution algérienne*. Paris: L'Harmattan, 2002.

Glick, Thomas F. *Islamic and Christian Spain in the Early Middle Ages*. Leiden: Brill, 2005.

Gobineau, Arthur de. *Essai sur l'inégalité des races humaines par M.A. de Gobineau*. 2 vols. Paris: Fermin-Didot Frères, 1853–55.

Godlewska, Anne. "L'influence d'un homme sur la géographie française: Conrad Malte-Brun (1775-1826)." *Annales de Géographie* 558 (1991): 190–206.

Gómez-Rivas, Camilo. *Law and the Islamization of Morocco Under the Almoravids: The Fatwās of Ibn Rushd al-Jadd to the Far Maghrib*. Leiden: Brill, 2015.

Goodman, Jane E. *Berber Culture on the World Stage: From Village to Video*. Bloomington: Indiana University Press, 2005.

Gordon, Matthew. "Preliminary Remarks on Slaves and Slave Labor in the Third/Ninth Century 'Abbasid Empire." In *Slaves and Households in the Near East*, ed. Laura Culbertson. Chicago: Oriental Institute, University of Chicago, 2011. 71–84.

Guenoun, Ali. *Chronologie du mouvement berbère, 1945–1990: Un combat et des hommes*. Algiers: Casbah, 1999.

Guichard, Pierre, and Bruna Soravia. *Les royaumes de taifas: Apogée culturel et déclin politique des émirats andalolus du XIe siècle*. Paris: Geuthner, 2007.

Guillaume, Alfred. *The Life of Muḥammad, a Translation of Isḥāq's Sīrat Rasūl Allāh*. Karachi, Oxford, and New York: Oxford University Press, 1967.

Gutron, Clémentine. "Gsell, Stéphane." In *Dictionnaire des orientalistes de langue française, nouvelle édition revue et augmentée*, ed. François Pouillon. Paris: IISMM and Karthala, 2012.490–91.

Guyot-Bachy, Isabelle and Jean-Marie Moeglin, ed. *La naissance de la médiévistique: les historiens et leurs sources en Europe (XIXe-début du XXe siècle): actes du colloque de Nancy, 8–10 novembre 2012*. Geneva: Librairie Droz, 2015.

Hachid, Malika. *Les premiers Berbères: Entre Méditerranée, Tassili et Nil*. Aix-en-Provence: Edisud, 2000.
Haedo, Diego de. *Topografía e historia general de Argel por Fray Diego de Haedo*. Valladolid: Diego Fernandez de Cordoua y Oviedo Impressor de libros, 1612.
Halm, Heinz. *The Empire of the Mahdī: The Rise of the Fatimids*. Trans. Michael Bonner. Leiden: Brill, 1996.
Al-Hamdānī (d. 945). *Ṣifat jazīrat al-ʿarab*. Ed. David Heinrich Müller. Leiden: Brill, 1884.
Hannoum, Abdelmajid. *Colonial Histories, Post-colonial Memories: The Legend of the Kahina, a North African Heroine*. Portsmouth: Heinemann, 2001.
———. "Translation and the Colonial Imaginary: Ibn Khaldūn Orientalist." *History and Theory* 42, no. 1 (2003): 61–81.
———. "Colonialism and Knowledge in Algeria: The Archives of the Arab Bureau." *History and Anthropology* 12, no. 4 (2010): 343–79.
———. *Violent Modernity: France in Algeria*. Cambridge, MA: Center for Middle Eastern Studies of Harvard University Press, 2010.
Hannouz, Aomar. "Mémoires et patrimonialisation d'un passé antéislamique: Mubârak al-Mîlî et l'ethnogenèse du peuple algérien." *L'année du Maghreb* 10 (2014): 115–41.
Hanoteau, Adolphe, and Aristide Letourneux. *La Kabylie et les coutumes kabyles*. 3 vols. Paris: Imprimerie nationale, 1872–73.
Harrison, Olivia. *Transcolonial Maghreb: Imagining Palestine in the Era of Decolonization*. Stanford: Stanford University Press, 2016.
Hart, David. "Scratch a Moroccan, Find a Berber." *Journal of North African Studies* 4, no. 2 (1999): 23–26.
Harvey, Leonard Patrick. *Islamic Spain, 1250–1500*. Chicago: University of Chicago Press, 1990.
Hassūf, ʿAbd al-Laṭīf. *Al-amāzīgh: Qiṣṣat shʿab*. Beirut: Dār al-Sāqī, 2016.
Hiddleston, Jane. *Decolonising the Intellectual: Politics, Culture, and Humanism at the End of the French Empire*. Liverpool: Liverpool University Press, 2014.
Hobsbawm, Eric J. *Nations and Nationalism Since 1780: Programme, Myth, Reality*. Cambridge: Cambridge University Press, 1990.
Hoffman, Katherine E. *We Share Walls: Language, Land, and Gender in Berber Morocco*. Malden, MA: Blackwell, 2008.
Hoffman, Katherine E., and Susan Gilson Miller, eds. *Berbers and Others: Beyond Tribe and Nation in the Maghrib*. Bloomington: Indiana University Press, 2010.
Hopkins, J.F.P., ed. and trans. *Letters from Barbary: Arabic Documents in the Public Record Office*. Oxford: Oxford University Press, 1982.
Hoyland, Robert. *Seeing Islam as Others Saw It*. Princeton, NJ: Darwin Press, 1997.
———. *Arabia and the Arabs: From the Bronze Age to the Coming of Islam*. London and New York: Routledge, 2001.
———. *In God's Path: The Arab Conquests and the Creation of an Empire*. Oxford: Oxford University Press, 2015.
Al-Ḥumaydī (d. 1095). *Jadhwat al-muqtabis fī dhikr wulāt al-andalus*. Ed. Ibrāhīm al-Ibyārī. 2 vols. Cairo: Al-Dār al-Maṣriya li al-Ta'līf wa al-Tarjama, 1966.
Ibn al-Abbār (d. 1260). *Al-ḥulla al-sayrā'*. Ed. Ḥusayn Mu'nis. 2 vols. Cairo: al-Sharika al-ʿArabiyya lil-Ṭibāʿa wa al-Nashr, 1963.
———. *Tuḥfat al-qādim*. Beirut: Dār al-Gharb al-Islāmī, 1986.
Ibn ʿAbd al-Ḥakam (d. 871). *The History of the Conquest of Egypt, North Africa, and Spain*. Ed. Charles Torrey. New Haven: Yale University Press, 1922.

Ibn 'Abd al-Halīm (fl. 14th c.). *Kitāb al-ansāb: Tres textos árabes sobre beréberes en el occidente islámico*. Ed. Muḥammad Ya'là. Madrid: CSIC, 1996. 15–121.

Ibn Abī Dīnār (d. ca. 1698). *Exploration scientifique de l'Algérie: 7, Histoire de l'Afrique / de Moh'hammed-ben-Abi-el-Raïni-K'aïrouâni; trad. de l'arabe par MM. E. Pellissier et Rémusat*. Paris: Imprimerie Royale, 1845.

———. *Al-mu'nis fī akhbār ifrīqiyā wa tūnis*. Ed. Muḥammad Shammām. Tunis: al-Maktaba al-'Atīqa, 1967.

Ibn Abi Zar' al-Fāsī (d. 1340/1). *Al-dhakhīra al-saniya fī tārīkh al-dawla al-marīniya*. Rabat: Dār al-Manṣūr lil-Ṭibā'a wa al-Warāqa, 1972.

———. *Roudh el-Kartas: Histoire des souverains du Maghreb (Espagne et Maroc) et annales de la ville de Fès, traduit de l'arabe par A. Beaumier*. Paris: Impr. impériale, 1860.

Ibn al-'Ayyāshī al-Miknāsī (d. 1727). *Zahr al-bustān fī nasab akhwāl sayyidunā wa-mawlānā zaydān*. Ed. Aḥmad Qaddūr. Rabat: Maṭābi' al-Ribāṭ Nit, 2013.

Ibn Bulughīn (b. 1056). *Kitāb al-tibyān 'an al-ḥāditha al-kā'ina bi-dawlat banī zīrī fī gharnāṭa*. Ed. 'Alī 'Umar. Riyadh: Maktabat al-Thaqāfa al-Dīniya, 2006.

Ibn Daḥiya al-Kalbī (d. 1235 or 1236). *Al-muṭrib min ash'ār ahl al-maghrib*. Ed. Ibrāhīm al-Abyārī, Ḥamīd 'Abd al-Majīd, and Aḥmad Aḥmad Badawī. Cairo: Al-Maṭba'a al-Amīriya, 1954.

Ibn al-Dalā'ī (1003–85). *Nuṣūṣ 'an al-andalus min kitāb tarṣī' al-akhbār wa-tanwī' al-athār, wa-al-bustān fī gharā'ib al-buldān wa-al-masālik 'ilā jamī' al-mamālik*. Ed. 'Abd al-'Aziz al-Aḥwānī. Madrid: Maṭba'at Ma'had al-Dīrāsāt al-Islāmīyah, 1965.

Ibn al-Faqīh al-Hamadhānī (fl. 902). *Mukhtaṣar kitāb al-buldān*. Ed. M.J. de Goeje. Leiden: Brill, 1885.

Ibn Ḥabīb (d. 852/3). *Kitāb al-tārīkh*. Ed. Sālim Musṭafā al-Badrī. Beirut: Dār al-Kutub al-'Ilmiyya, 1999.

Ibn Ḥayyān (d. 1076). *Al-Muqtabas min anbā' ahl al-andalus*. Ed. Maḥmūd 'Alī Makkī. Beirut: Dār al-Kitāb al-'Arabī, 1973.

Ibn Ḥazm (d. 1064). *Jamharat ansāb al-'arab*. Ed. Évariste Levi-Provençal. Cairo: Dār al-Ma'ārif bi Miṣr, 1948.

———. *Faḍā'il al-Andalus wa ahliha, li-ibn ḥazm wa ibn sa'īd wa al-shaqundī*. Ed. Ṣalāḥ al-Dīn al-Munajjid. Beirut: Dār al-Kitāb al-Jadīd, 1968.

Ibn Ḥazm (d. 1064) and al-Shahrastānī (d. 1053). *Kitāb al-fiṣal fī al-milal wa-al-ahwā' wa-al-niḥal li-abī muḥammad 'alī ibn aḥmad ibn ḥazm al-ẓāhirī; wa-bi-hāmishihi al-milal wa-al-niḥal li-abī al-fatḥ muḥammad ibn 'abd al-karīm al-shahrastānī*. 5 vols. Cairo: Al-Maṭba'a al-Adabiya, 1899–1903.

Ibn Hishām (d. 834). *Das Leben Muhammed's nach Muhammed Ibn Ishâk (Kitāb sīrat rasūl Allah)*. Ed. Ferdinand Wüstenfeld. Göttingen: Dieterichsche Universitäts-Buchhandlung, 1858.

Ibn 'Idhārī (d. early 14th c.). *Al-bayān al-mughrib fī akhbār al-andalus wal-maghrib*. Ed. G.S. Colin and E. Levi-Provençal. 4 vols. Beirut: Dār al-Thaqāfa, 1967.

Ibn al-Kalbī (d. 819/20). *Nasab ma'add wa al-yaman*. Ed. Ḥasan Nājī. 3 vols. Damascus: Dār al-Yaqaẓa al-'Arabiyya, 1988.

Ibn al-Kardabūs (fl. 12th–13th c.). *Tārīkh al-andalus li-ibn al-kardabūs wa waṣfuhu li-ibn al-shabbāṭ, naṣṣān jadīdān*. Ed. Aḥmad Mukhtār al-'Abbādī. Madrid: Instituto de Estudios Islámicos en Madrid, 1971.

Ibn Khaldūn (d. 1406). *Histoire des Berbères et des dynasties musulmanes: Texte arabe*. Ed. William MacGuckin de Slane. Algiers: Imprimerie du gouvernement, 1847.

———. *The Muqaddimah: An Introduction to History*. Trans. Franz Rosenthal. 3 vols. Princeton: Princeton University Press, 1967.

———. *Kitāb al-ʿibar wa diwān al-mubtada' wa al-khabar fī tārīkh al-ʿarab wa al-barbar wa man ʿāṣarahum min dhawī al-sha'n al-akbar*. Ed. Khalīl Shahāda. 8 vols. Beirut: Dār al-Fikr, 2001.

Ibn al-Khaṭīb (d. 1374). *Al-iḥāṭa fī akhbār gharnāṭa*. Ed. Muḥammad ʿAbd Allāh ʿInān. 4 vols. Cairo: Maktabat al-Khānjī, 1973.

Ibn Khordadhbeh (d. 912). *Kitāb al-masālik wa al-mamālik*. Ed. M.J. de Goeje. Leiden: Brill, 1889.

Ibn Qutayba (d. 889). *Al-maʿārif*. Ed. Tharwat ʿUkāsha. Cairo: Dār al-Maʿārif bi-Miṣr, 1969.

———. *Faḍl al-ʿarab wa al-tanbīh ʿalā ʿulūmiha*. Ed. Walīd Maḥmūd Khāliṣ. Abu Dhabi: Al-Majmaʿ al-Thaqāfī, 1998.

Ibn al-Qūṭiya (d. 977). *Tārīkh iftitāḥ al-andalus*. Ed. ʿAbd Allāh Anīs al-Ṭabbāʿ. Beirut: Mu'assasat al-Maʿārif, 1994.

Ibn Rosteh (d. early 10th c.). *Al-aʿlāq al-nafīsa*. Ed. M.J. de Goeje. Leiden: Brill, 1892.

Ibn al-Ṣaghīr (fl. early 10th c.). "Chronique d'Ibn Saghir sur les imams Rostémides de Tahert." Ed. Mohamed Talbi. *Cahiers de Tunisie* 26 (1975): 315–68.

———. *Akhbār al-a'imma al-rustamiyīn*. Ed. Muḥammad Nāṣir and Ibrāhīm Baḥāz. Beirut: Dār al-Gharb al-Islāmī, 1986.

Ibn Ṣāḥib al-Ṣalāt (fl. 12th c.). *Tārīkh al-mann bi-al-imāma ʿalā al-mustaḍʿafīn bi-an jaʿalahum allāh aʿimma wa-jaʿalahum al-wārithīn*. Ed. ʿAbd al-Hādī al-Tāzī. 2 vols. Beirut: Dār al-Andalus li al-Ṭibāʿa wa al-Nashr, 1965.

Ibn Saʿīd (d. 1286). *Kitāb al-jughrāfiyā*. Ed. Ismāʿīl al-ʿArabī. Beirut: Manshūrāt al-Maktab al-Tijārī lil-Ṭibāʿa wa-al-Nashr wa-al-Tawzīʿ, 1970.

———. *Nashwat al-ṭarab fī tārīkh jāhiliyat al-ʿarab*. Ed. Naṣrat ʿAbd al-Raḥmān. 2 vols. Amman: Maktabat al-Aqṣā, 1982.

———. *Al-mughrib fī ḥulā al-maghrib*. Ed. Khalīl al-Manṣūr. 2 vols. Beirut: Dār al-Kutub al-ʿIlmiya, 1997.

Ibn Sallām (d. after 887). *Kitāb Ibn Sallām, Eine Ibaditisch-Magribinische Geschichte des Islams aus dem 3./9/ Jahrhundert*. Ed. Werner Schwartz and al-Shaykh Sālim Ibn Yaʿqūb. Wiesbaden: Steiner, 1986.

Ibn al-Ṭuwayr al-Qaysarānī (d. 1220). *Nuzhat al-muqlatayn fī akhbār al-dawlatayn*. Ed. Ayman Fu'ād Sayyid. Stuttgart: Franz Steiner, 1992.

Idaghdour, Youssef, et al. "Geographical Genomics of Human Leukocyte Gene Expression Variation in Southern Morocco." *Nature Genetics* 42, no. 1 (2010): 62–69.

Idris, Roger. "De la réalité de la catastrophe hilâlienne." *Annales: Économies, Sociétés, Civilisations* 23, no. 2 (1968): 390–96.

Al-Idrīsī (d. 1065/6). *Nuzhat al-Mushtāq fī ikhtirāq al-āfāq, Description de l'Afrique et de l'Espagne*. Ed. R. Dozy and M.J. de Goeje. Leiden: Brill, 1866.

Iskandar, John. "Devout Heretics: The Barghawata in Maghribi Historiography." *Journal of North African Studies* 12, no. 1 (2007): 37–53.

Al-Iṣṭakhrī (d. 957). *Kitāb masālik al-mamālik*. Ed. M.J. de Goeje. Leiden: Brill, 1927.

Al-Iṣfahānī (d. 967). *Kitāb al-aghānī*. Ed. Iḥsān ʿAbbās, Ibrāhīm al-Saʿāfīn, and Bakr ʿAbbās. 24 vols. Beirut: Dār Ṣādir, 2008.

Al-Jābirī, Muḥammad ʿĀbid. *Takwīn al-ʿaql al-ʿarabī*. Beirut, Dār al-Ṭalīʿa, 1984.

Al-Jīlālī, ʿAbd al-Raḥmān. *Tārīkh al-jazā'ir al-ʿāmm*. 7th ed. 4 vols. Algiers: Diwān al-Maṭbūʿāt al-Jāmiʿiyya, 1994.

Julien, Charles-André. *Histoire de l'Afrique du Nord: Tunisie, Algérie, Maroc*. Paris: Payot, 1931.

———. *Histoire de l'Afrique du Nord: Tunisie, Algérie, Maroc*. 2 vols. Paris: Payot, 1951–52.

———. *Histoire de l'Afrique blanche des origines à 1945*. Paris: Presses Universitaires de France, 1966.

Kably, Mohamed, ed. *Histoire du Maroc: Réactualisation et synthèse*. Rabat: Édition de l'Institut Royal pour la Recherche sur l'Histoire du Maroc, 2011.

Kaddache, Mahfoud. *L'Algérie médiévale*. Algiers: ENAL, 1992.

Kaplan, Zvi Jonathan, and Nadia Malinovich, eds. *The Jews of Modern France: Images and Identities*. Leiden: Brill, 2016.

Keita, Shomarka O. Y. "Biocultural Emergence of the Amazigh (Berbers) in Africa: Comment on Frigi et al." *Human Biology* 82, no. 4 (2010): 385–93.

Kennedy, Hugh. *Muslim Spain and Portugal: A Political History of al-Andalus*. New York: Longman, 1996.

Khodjet-el-Khil, Houssein, et al. "Substructure of a Tunisian Population as Inferred from 15 Autosomal Short Tandem Repeat Loci." *Human Biology* 80, no. 4 (2008): 435–48.

Al-Khushanī (d. 971?). *Quḍāt qurṭuba*. Ed. Ibrāhīm al-Ibyārī. Cairo: Dār al-Kitāb al-Maṣrī, 1982.

———. *Ṭabaqāt ʿulamāʾ ifrīqiyā*. Ed. Asʿad Jumʿa. Tunis: Dār Kīrānīs, 2014.

King, Matt. "The Sword and the Sun: The Old World Drought Atlas as a Source for Medieval Mediterranean History." *Al-Masāq: Journal of the Medieval Mediterranean* 29, no. 3 (2017): 1–14.

Kossmann, Maarten. *Essai sur la phonologie du proto-berbère*. Cologne: Rüdiger Köppe, 1999.

———. *The Arabic Influence on Northern Berber*. Leiden: Brill, 2013.

Kratochwil, Gabriele. *Die Berberbewegung in Marokko: zur Geschichte der Konstruktion einer ethnischen Identität (1912–1997)*. Berlin: K. Schwarz, 2002.

Lafuente, Gilles. *La politique berbère de la France et le nationalisme marocain*. Paris: L'Harmattan, 1999.

Lane, Edward W. *The Arabic-English Lexicon*. 8 vols. London: Williams and Norgate, 1874.

Laqbāl, Mūsā. *Tārikh al-maghrib al-islāmī*. Algiers: Al-Sharika al-Waṭaniya lil-Nashr wa al-Tawzīʿ, 1984.

Laroui, Abdallah. *L'histoire du Maghreb: Un essai de synthèse*. Paris: François Maspero, 1970.

———. *The History of the Maghrib: An Interpretive Essay*. Trans. Ralph Manheim. Princeton: Princeton University Press, 1977.

———. *L'idéologie arabe contemporaine*. Paris: Maspero, 1982.

Larsson, Göran. *Ibn García's Shuʿūbiyya Letter: Ethnic and Theological Tensions in Medieval al-Andalus*. Leiden: Brill, 2003.

Laurens, Henry. "L'orientalisme français: Un parcours historique." In *Penser l'Orient: Traditions et actualité des orientalismes français et allemande*, ed. Youssef Courbage and Manfred Kropp. Beirut: Presses de l'Ifpo, 2004. 103–128.

Lawātī, Dalāl. *ʿĀmmat al-qayrawān fī ʿaṣr al-aghāliba*. Cairo: Ruʾya lil-Nashr wa al-Tawzīʿ, 2015

Leo Africanus. *A Geographical Historie of Africa Written in Arabick and Italian by John Leo a More, Born in Granada and Brought up in Barbarie*. London: [Printed by Eliot's Court Press] Impensis Georg. Bishop, 1600.

———. *Africa descriptio*. Lyon, Batavia: Elzevir, 1632.

Lev, Yaacov. *State and Society in Fatimid Egypt*. Leiden: Brill, 1991.

Levati, Ambrogio. *Storia della Barbaria*. Milan: Stella, Antonio Fortunato e figli, 1826.

Love, Paul M. Jr. "The Sufris of Sijilmasa: Toward a History of the Midrarids." *Journal of North African Studies* 15, no. 2 (2010): 173–88.

Maddy-Weitzman, Bruce. *The Berber Identity Movement and the Challenge to North African States.* Austin: University of Texas Press, 2011.

Al-Maḥallī (d. 1459) and al-Suyūṭī (d. 1505). *Tafsīr al-jalālayn: Taḥqīq wa-ikhrāj fī jadāwil ʿaṣriya lil-imāmayn jalāl al-dīn al-maḥallī wa-jalāl al-dīn al-suyūṭī.* Ed. Abū Fāris al-Daḥdāḥ. Beirut: Maktabat Lubnān Nāshirūn, 2000.

Makki, Mahmoud. "A Political History of al-Andalus (92/711–897/1492)." In *The Legacy of Muslim Spain,* ed. Salma Khadra al-Jayyusi. Leiden: Brill, 1994. 3–87.

Al-Mālikī (d. 1061). *Riyāḍ al-nufūs fī ṭabaqāt ʿulamāʾ al-qayrawān wa-ifrīqīya wa-zuhhādihim wa-nussākihim wa-siyar min akhbārihim wa-faḍāʾilihim wa-awṣāfihim.* Ed. Bashīr al-Bakkūsh. 2 vols. Beirut: Dār al-Gharb al-Islāmī, 1994.

Malte-Brun, Conrad. *Précis de la géographie universelle, ou description de toutes les parties du monde, sur un plan nouveau, d'après les grandes divisions naturelles du globe, tome quatrième: Description de l'inde, de l'océanique et de l'Afrique septentrionale.* Paris: Fr. Buisson Libraire-Éditeur, 1813.

Manzano Moreno, Eduardo. "Beréberes de al-Andalus: Los factores de un evolucion histórica." *Al-Qanṭara* 11 (1990): 397–428.

———. *Conquistadores, emires y califas: Los omeyas y la formación de al-Andalus.* Barcelona: Crítica, 2006.

Al-Maqrīzī (d. 1442). *Ittiʿāẓ al-ḥunafā bi-akhbār al-aʾimma al-fāṭimīyīn al-khulafā.* Ed. Jamāl al-Dīn al-Shayyāl. 3 vols. Cairo: Lajnat Iḥyāʾ al-Turāth al-Islāmī, 1967.

Marçais, Georges. *Les Arabes en Berbérie du XIe au XIVe siècle.* Paris: E. Leroux, 1913.

Marcianus Heracleensis ex Ponto. *Periplus Maris Exteri.* In *Geographi Graeci Minores,* ed. Karl Müller. Hildesheim: G. Olms, 1965. 1:515–62.

Marks, Jonathan. *Tales of the Ex-Apes: How We Think About Human Evolution.* Berkeley: University of California Press, 2015.

Marmol Carvajal, Luis del. *Primera parte de la descripcion general de Africa, con todos los successos de guerras que a auido entre los infieles y el pueblo Christiano, y entre ellos mesmos desde que Mahoma inuẽto su secta, hasta el aña de seẽnor 1571.* Granada: Casa del Rene Rabut, 1573.

Al-Marrākushī ʿAbd al-Wāḥid (b. 1185). *Al-muʿjib fī talkhīṣ akhbār al-maghrib, min ladun fatḥ al-Andalus ilā ākhir ʿaṣr al-muwaḥḥidīn maʿa mā yattaṣilu bi-tārīkh hādhihi al-fatra min akhbār al-qurrāʾ wa-aʿyān al-kuttāb.* Ed. Muḥammad Saʿīd al-ʿIryān. Cairo: Al-Majlis al-Aʿlā li al-Shuʾūn al-Dīniya, 1963.

Martinez-Gros, Gabriel. *Identité andalouse.* Paris: Sindbad, Actes Sud, 1997.

———. *Ibn Khaldūn et les sept vies de l'Islam.* Paris: Sindbad, Actes Sud, 2006.

———. "Brunschvig, Robert." In *Dictionnaire des orientalistes de langue française, nouvelle édition revue et augmentée,* ed. François Pouillon. Paris: IISMM and Karthala, 2012. 167–68.

Mas Latrie, Louis de. *Traités de paix et de commerce et documents divers concernant les relations des chrétiens avec les arabes de l'Afrique septentrionale au moyen âge: Recueillis par ordre de l'empereur et publiés avec une introduction historique.* Paris: Henri Plon Imprimeur-Éditeur, 1866.

Al-Masʿūdī (d. 956). *Murūj al-dhahab wa maʿādin al-jawhar.* Ed. Hishām al-Naʿsān and ʿAbd al-Majīd Ṭuʿma Ḥalabī. 2 vols. Beirut: Dār al-Maʿrifa, 1983.

Mediano Rodríguez, Fernando. "Luis de Mármol y el humanismo: Comentarios sobre una fuente de la *Historia de la rebelión y castigo de los moriscos del Reyno de Granada*." *Bulletin Hispanique* 105, no. 2 (2003): 371–404.

Médiène, Benamar. *Kateb Yacine: Le coeur entre les dents; biographie hétérodoxe*. Paris: R. Laffont, 2006.

Medrano, Sebastián Fernández de. *Breve descripcion del mundo, y sus partes, ò, Guia geographica, y hydrographica: Dividida en tres libros*. Brussels: En casa de los herederos de Francisco Foppens, 1686.

Meouak, Mohammed. *Pouvoir souverain, administration centrale et élites politiques dans l'Espagne ummayade (IIe-IVe/VIIIe–Xe siècles)*. Helsinki: Academia Scientiarum Fennica, 1999.

———. *La langue berbère au Maghreb médiéval: Textes, contextes, analyses*. Leiden: Brill, 2015.

Mercier, Ernest. *Histoire de l'établissement des Arabes en Afrique septentrionale*. Constantine: Imprimerie de L. Marle, 1875.

———. *Histoire de l'Afrique septentrionale (Berbérie) depuis les temps les plus reculés jusqu'à la conquête française*. 3 vols. Paris: Ernest Leroux Éditeur, 1888–91.

Merrils, A.H., ed. *Vandals, Romans, and Berbers: New Perspectives on Late Antique North Africa*. Aldershot: Ashgate, 2004.

Messaoudi, Alain. "Marçais, Georges." In *Dictionnaire des orientalistes de langue française, nouvelle édition revue et augmentée*, ed. François Pouillon. Paris: IISMM and Karthala, 2012. 681–82.

———. *Les arabisants et la France coloniale: Savants, conseillers, médiateurs (1780–1930)*. Paris: ENS Éditions, 2015.

Al-Mīlī, Mubārak. *Tārīkh al-jazā'ir fī al-qadīm wa al-ḥadīth*, Ed. Muḥammad al-Mīlī. 2 vols. Algiers: Maktabat al-Nahḍa al-Jazā'iriya, 2004.

Mitchell, Terence F. *Zuaran Berber (Libya): Grammar and Texts*. Cologne: Rüdiger Köppe, 2009.

Mitchell, Timothy. "McJihad: Islam in the U.S. Global Order." *Social Text* 20, no. 4 (2002): 1–18.

Modéran, Yves. "Botr et Branès: Sur les origines du dualisme berbère médiéval." In *Mutations d'identités en Méditerranée: Moyen Âge et époque contemporaine*, ed. Henri Bresc and Christiane Veauvy. Saint Denis: Bouchène, 2000. 53–65.

———. *Les Maures et l'Afrique Romaine (IVe–VIIe siècle)*. Rome: École Française de Rome, 2003.

Mottahedeh, Roy. "The Shu'ūbiyah Controversy and the Social History of Early Islamic Iran." *International Journal of Middle East Studies* 7, no. 2 (1976): 161–82.

Mujāhid b. Jabr al-Makhzūmī (m. ca. 720). *Tafsīr mujāhid*. Ed. 'Abd al-Raḥmān al-Ṭāhir b. Muḥammad al-Suwartī. 2 vols. Beirut: Al-Manshūrāt al-'Ilmīya, [1977?].

Al-Munajjid, Ṣalāḥ al-Dīn, ed. *Faḍā'il al-andalus wa ahliha, li-ibn ḥazm wa ibn sa'īd wa al-shaqundī*. Beirut: Dār al-Kitāb al-Jadīd, 1968.

Mūnīb, Muḥammad. *Al-ẓahīr al-barbarī: Akbar ukdhūba siyāsīya fī al-maghrib al-mu'āṣir*. Rabat: Dār Abī Riqrāq lil-Ṭibā'a wa-al-Nashr, 2002.

Muqātil b. Sulaymān al-Balkhī (d. 767). *Tafsīr muqātil*. Ed. 'Abd Allāh Maḥmūd Shiḥāta. 5 vols. [Cairo]: al-Hay'a al-Miṣrīya al-'Āmma lil-Kitāb, 1983–90.

Al-Nāṣirī al-Salawī, Aḥmad b. Khālid (1835–97). *Kitāb al-istiqṣā li akhbār duwal al-maghrib al-aqṣā*. Ed. Aḥmad al-Nāṣirī. 9 vols. Casablanca: Manshūrāt Wizārat al-Thaqāfa wa al-Ittiṣāl, 2001-2005.

Al-Nawawī (d. 1333). *Nihāyat al-arab fī funūn al-adab*. Rabat: Maṭba'at al-Najāh al-Jadīda, 1988.

Naylor, Philip C. *North Africa: A History from Antiquity to the Present.* Austin: Texas University Press, 2009.

Nef, Annliese, and Fabiola Ardizzone, eds. *Les dynamiques de l'islamisation en Méditerranée centrale et en Sicile: Nouvelles propositions et découvertes récentes; Le dinamiche dell'islamizzazione nel Mediterraneo centrale e in Sicilia: nuove proposte e scoperte recenti.* Rome: École Française de Rome, 2014.

Norris, Harry T. *The Berbers in Arabic Literature.* London: Longman; Beirut: Librairie du Liban, 1982.

Al-Nuʿmān b. Muḥammad, al-Qāḍī (d. 974). *Iftitāḥ al-daʿwā.* Ed. Farḥāt al-Dachrāwī. Tunis: Al-Sharika al-Tūnisiya lil-Tawzīʿ, 1975.

Ockley, Simon. *The conquest of Syria, Persia, and Ægypt, by the Saracens: containing the lives of Abubeker, Omar and Othman . . . illustrating the religion, rites, customs and manner of living of that . . . people . . . By Simon Ockley . . .* London: Printed for R. Knaplock, J. Sprint, R. Smith [et al.], 1708–18.

Okumuş, Ejder. "İbn Haldun ve Osmanlı'da çöküş tartışmaları." *Dîvân: Disiplinlerası Çalişmalar Dergisi* 1 (1999): 183–209.

Ouerdane, Amar. *La question berbère dans le mouvement national algérien, 1926–1980, Préface de Kateb Yacine.* Algiers: Épigraphe, 1993.

Parello, Vincent. "La visite du licencié Diego de Haedo dans le district inquisitorial de Saragosse (1575)." *Bulletin Hispanique* 109, no. 1 (2007): 67–95.

Péaud, Laura. "Relire la géographie de Conrad Malte-Brun." *Annales de Géographie* 701 (2015): 99–122.

Pegolotti, Francesco Balducci. *La pratica della mercatura.* Ed. Allan Evans. Cambridge, MA: The Medieval Academy of America, 1936.

Perrot, Nicolas. *L'Afrique de Marmol, de la traduction de Nicolas Perrot sieur d'Ablancourt. Divisée en trois volumes, et enrichie des cartes géographiques de M. Sanson, géographe ordinaire du roy. Avec l'Histoire des chérifs, traduite de l'espagnol de Diego Torrés, par le duc d'Angoulesme le père. Reveuë et retouchée par P. R. A.* Paris: Thomas Iolly, 1667.

Perry, Craig. "Historicizing Slavery in the Medieval Islamic World." *International Journal of Middle East Studies* 49 (2017): 133–38.

Picard, Christophe. "Islamisation et arabisation de l'Occident musulman médiéval (VIIe–XIIe siècle): Le contexte documentaire." In *Islamisation et arabisation de l'Occident musulman (VIIe–XIIe siècle)*, ed. Dominique Valérian. Paris: Publications de la Sorbonne, 2011. 35–61.

———. *La mer des califes: Une histoire de la Méditerranée musulmane, VIIe–XIIe siècle.* Paris: Éditions du Seuil, 2015.

Pickthall, Marmaduke. *The Meaning of the Glorious Koran: An Explanatory Translation.* London: A. A. Knopf, 1930.

Pinto, Karen C. *Medieval Islamic Maps: An Exploration.* Chicago: University of Chicago Press, 2016.

Poiret, Jean Luis Marie. *Voyage en Barbarie, ou lettres écrites de l'ancienne Numidie pendant les années 1785 & 1786, sur la religion, les coutumes & les mœurs des Maures et des Arabes-Bédouins ; avec un essai sur l'histoire naturelle de ce pays. Première Partie.* Paris: Chez J.B.F. Née de la Rochelle, 1789.

Pomian, Krzysztof. *Ibn Khaldūn au prisme de l'Occident.* Paris: Éditions Gallimard, 2006.

Poncet, Jean. "Le mythe de la 'catastrophe' hilalienne [H. R. Idris, *La Berbérie orientale sous les Zîrides, Xe–XIIIe siècles.*]" *Annales: Économies, Sociétés, Civilisations* 22, no. 5 (1967): 1099–1120.

Pouillon, François. "Simplification ethnique en Afrique du nord: Maures, Arabes, Berbères (XIIIe–XXe siècles)." *Cahiers d'Études Africaines* 33, no. 129 (1993): 37–49.

———, ed. *Dictionnaire des orientalistes de langue française, nouvelle édition revue et augmentée.* Paris: IISMM and Karthala, 2012.

Prescott Barrow, David. *Berbers and Blacks: Impressions of Morocco, Timbuktu, and the Western Sudan.* New York and London: The Century Co., 1927.

Prevost, Virgine. *L'aventure ibāḍite dans le sud tunisien: Effervescence d'une région méconnue.* Helsinki: Academia Scientiarum Fennica, 2008.

———. "L'ibadisme berbère: La légitimation d'une doctrine venue d'Orient." In *La légitimation du pouvoir au Maghreb médiéval: De l'orientalisation à l'émancipation politique*, ed. Annliese Nef and Élise Voguet. Madrid: Casa de Velázquez, 2011. 55–71.

Ptolemaeus, Claudius. *Ptolemaei Geographia.* Ed. C.F.A. Nobbe. Hildesheim: G. Olms, 1966.

Al-Raqīq al-Qayrawānī (fl. 11th c.). *Tārīkh ifrīqiyā wa al-maghrib.* Ed. al-Munjī al-Ka'bī. Tunis: Maṭba'at al-Wasaṭ, 1968.

Retsö, Jan. *The Arabs in Antiquity: Their History from the Assyrians to the Umayyads.* London and New York: RoutledgeCurzon, 2003.

Rodríguez Mediano, Fernando. "Luis de Mármol y el humanismo: Comentarios sobre una fuente de la *Historia de la rebelión y castigo de los moriscos del Reyno de Granada.*" *Bulletin Hispanique* 105, no. 2 (2003): 371–404.

Rosen, Lawrence. *Two Arabs, a Berber, and a Jew: Entangled Lives in Morocco.* Chicago: University of Chicago Press, 2016.

Rosenthal, Franz. "Nasab." In *EI²*, 6: 187–88.

Rouighi, Ramzi. "The Andalusi Origins of the Berbers?" *Journal of Medieval Iberian Studies* 2, no. 1 (2010): 93–108.

———. "The Berbers of the Arabs." *Studia Islamica,* n.s., 2011, 67–101.

———. *The Making of a Mediterranean Emirate: Ifrīqiyā and Its Andalusis.* Philadelphia: University of Pennsylvania Press, 2011.

Al-Rušāṭī Abū Muḥammad (d. 1147) and Ibn al-Jarrāṭ al-Išbīlī (d. 1186). *Al-Andalus en el Kitāb Iqtibās al-anwār y en el Ijtiṣār Iqtibās al-anwār.* Ed. Emilio Molina López and Jacinto Bosch Vilá. Madrid: CSIC, ICMA, 1990.

Sa'dī, 'Uthmān. *Al-barbar al-amāzīgh 'arab 'āriba, wa-'urūbat al-shamāl al-ifrīqī 'abra al-tārīkh.* Beirut: Dār al-Multaqā, 1998.

Safran, Janina. *The Second Umayyad Caliphate: The Articulation of Caliphal Legitimacy in al-Andalus.* Cambridge, MA: Harvard University Press, 2000.

Sahli, Mohamed. *Décoloniser l'histoire: Introduction à l'histoire du Maghreb.* Paris: François Maspero, 1965.

Saḥnūn (d. 854). *Al-mudawwana al-kubrā, riwāyat al-imām saḥnūn b. sa'īd al-tanūkhī 'an al-imām 'abd al-raḥmān b. al-qāsim al-'utakī.* 16 vols. Cairo: Maṭba'at al-Sa'āda, 1323 [1905].

Ṣā'id al-Andalusī (d. 1070). *Ṭabaqāt al-umam.* Ed. Louis Cheikho. Beirut: Al-Maṭba'a al-Kāthūlikiya lil-Abā' al-Yasū'iyīn, 1912.

———. *Science in the Medieval World: "Book of the Categories of Nations."* Ed. and trans. Sema'an I. Salem and Alok Kumar. Austin: University of Texas Press, 1991.

Said, Edward W. *Orientalism.* New York: Pantheon Books, 1978.

Sand, Shlomo. *The Invention of the Jewish People.* New York: Verso, 2010.

Ṣallābī, 'Alī Muḥammad Muḥammad. *Dawlat al-murābiṭīn.* Beirut: Maktabat Ḥasan al-'Aṣriyya, 2012.

Savage, Elizabeth. *A Gateway to Hell, a Gateway to Paradise: The North African Response to the Arab Conquest.* Princeton, NJ: Darwin Press, 1997.

Scales, Peter C. *The Fall of the Caliphate of Córdoba: Berbers and Andalusis in Conflict.* Leiden: Brill, 1994.

Schwab, Raymond. *La renaissance orientale.* Paris: Payot, 1950.

Servier, Jean. *Les Berbères.* Paris: Presses Universitaires de France, 1990.

Sharqāwī, ʻAwaḍ. *Ibāḍīyat jabal nafūsa fī al-qarnayn al-thānī wa-al-thālith al-hijrīyayn: Dirāsa tārīkhīya.* Cairo: Dār al-ʻĀlam al-ʻArabī, 2017.

Shatzmiller, Maya. "Le mythe d'origine Berbère: Aspects historiographiques et sociaux." *Revue de l'Occident Musulman et de la Méditerranée* 35 (1983): 145–56.

———. *The Berbers and the Islamic State: The Marīnid Experience in Pre-Protectorate Morocco.* Princeton, NJ: Markus Wiener, 2000.

Shaw, Thomas. *Travels: or Observations Relating to Several Parts of Barbary and the Levant.* London: Printed for A. Millar in the Strand, and W. Sandby in Fleet-Street, 1757.

Shohat, Ella. *On the Arab-Jew, Palestine, and Other Displacements: Selected Writings of Ella Shohat.* London: Pluto Press, 2017.

Silvestre de Sacy, Antoine-Issac. *Chrestomathie arabe, ou extraits de divers écrivains arabes tant en prose qu'en vers, à l'usage des élèves de l'École spéciale des langues orientales vivantes.* 3 vols. Paris: Imprimerie Royale, 1806.

———. *Anthologie grammaticale arabe: ou, Morceaux choisis de divers grammairiens et scholiastes arabes, avec une traduction française et des notes; pouvant faire suite à la Chrestomathie arabe.* Paris: Imprimerie Royale, 1829.

Slyomovics, Susan, ed. *Clifford Geertz in Morocco.* London: Routledge, 2009.

Souag, Lameen. *Berber and Arabic in Siwa (Egypt): A Study in Linguistic Contact.* Cologne: Rüdiger Köppe, 2013.

Stephanus Byzantinus. *Ethnicorum quae supersunt.* Ed. A. Meineke. Berlin: Reiner, 1849.

Szombathy, Zoltán. "Genealogy in Medieval Muslim Societies." *Studia Islamica* 95 (2002): 5–35.

Al-Ṭabarī (d. 923). *Ta'rīkh al-rusul wa al-mulūk.* Ed. Muḥammad Abū al-Faḍl Ibrāhīm. 11 vols. Cairo: Dār al-Maʻārif, 1960.

———. *Jāmiʻ al-bayān ʻan ta'wīl al-qur'ān.* Ed. Bashshār ʻAwwād and ʻIṣām Fāris al-Ḥurristānī. 7 vols. Beirut, Mu'assasat al-Risāla, 1994.

Taieb, Si Belkacem. *Decolonizing Indigenous Education: An Amazigh/Berber Ethnographic Journey.* New York: Palgrave Macmillan, 2014.

Talbayev, Edwige Tamalet. *The Transcontinental Maghreb: Francophone Literature Across the Mediterranean.* New York: Fordham University Press, 2017.

Talbi, Mohamed. *L'émirat Aghlabide 184–296/800–909.* Paris: Adrien-Maisonneuve, 1966.

———. "Ifrīqiyā." In *EI*[2], 3:1047–50.

Al-Tanasī (d. 1493/4). *Histoire des Beni-Zeiyan, rois de Tlemcen, par l'iman Cidi Abou-Abd'-Allah-Mohammed Jbn-Abd'el Djelyl el-Tenessy.* Trans. Jean-Joseph-Léandre Bargès. Paris: Duprat, 1852.

Al-Tāzī, ʻAbd al-Hādī. *Al-wasīṭ fī tārīkh al-duwalī lil-maghrib.* 3 vols. Rabat: Dār Nashr al-Maʻrifa, 2001.

Temlali, Yassin. *La genèse de la Kabylie: Aux origines de l'affirmation berbère en Algérie (1830–1962).* Algiers: Éditions Barzakh, 2015.

Al-Tijānī (d. 1321/2). *Riḥlat al-tijānī.* Ed. Ḥusnī ʻAbd al-Wahhāb. Tripoli and Tunis: Al-Dār al-ʻArabiya lil-Kitāb, 1981.

Tilmatine, Mohand. "Du Berbère à l'Amazigh: De l'objet au sujet historique." *Al-Andalus-Maghreb* 14 (2007): 225–47.

Tocqueville, Alexis de. *De la colonie en Algérie*. Ed. Tzvetan Todorov. Brussels: Éditions Complexe, 1988.

Touati, Houari. *Entre Dieu et les hommes: Lettrés, saints et sorciers au Maghreb, 17e siècle*. Paris: Éditions de l'École des hautes études en sciences sociales, 1994.

Turbet-Delof, Guy. *L'Afrique barbaresque dans la littérature française aux XVIe et XVIIe siècles*. Paris and Geneva: Libraire Droz, 1973.

———. *Bibliographie critique du Maghreb dans la littérature française, 1532–1715*. Algiers: SNED, 1976.

Ursinus, M.O.H. "Millet." In *EI²*, 7:61–64.

Al-'Uṣfurī (d. 854). *Tārīkh khalīfa b. khayyāṭ*. Ed. Suhayl Zakkār. 2 vols. Damascus: Manshūrāt Wizārat al-Thaqāfa wa al-Siyāḥa wa al-Irshād al-Qawmī, 1968.

Valérian, Dominique. *Bougie: Port Maghrébin, 1067–1510*. Rome: École Française de Rome, 2006.

———, ed. *Islamisation et arabisation de l'Occident musulman (VIIe–XIIe siècle)*. Paris: Publications de la Sorbonne, 2011.

———. "La diaspora andalouse et le commerce des ports maghrébins (XIe–XVe siècle)." *Les Cahiers de Framespa* 16 (2014). https://doi.org/10.4000/framespa.2939.

Vallvé Bermejo, Joaquín. "Nuevas ideas sobre la conquista árabe de España: Toponimia y onomástica." *Al-Qanṭara* 10 (1989): 51–150.

Vatin, Jean-Claude, et al. *Connaissances du Maghreb: Sciences sociales et colonisation*. Paris: Éditions du CNRS, 1984.

Venture de Paradis, Jean Michel (1739–99). *Alger au XVIIIe siècle, 1788–1790: Mémoires, notes et observations d'un diplomate-espion*. Ed. Abderrahmane Rebahi. Algiers: Éditions Grand-Alger Livres, 2006.

Vermeren, Pierre. *Misère de l'historiographie du "Maghreb" post-colonial, 1962–2012*. Paris: Publications de la Sorbonne, 2012.

Vonderheyden, Maurice. *La Berbérie orientale sous la dynasties des Benoû'l-Arlab 800–909*. Paris: Librairie orientaliste Paul Geuthner, 1927.

Wafik, Raouf. *Ishkāliyāt al-nuhūḍ al-'arabī min al-taraddī ilā al-taḥaddī*. Beirut: Markaz Dirāsāt al-Waḥda al-'Arabiya, 2005.

Al-Wansharīsī (d. 1508). *Al-mi'yār al-mu'rib wa-al-jāmi' al-mughrib 'an fatāwā ahl ifrīqīya wa-al-andalus wa-al-maghrib*. Ed. Muḥammad Ḥajjī. 13 vols. Rabat: Wizārat al-Awqāf wa-al-Shu'ūn al-Islāmīya lil-Mamlaka al-Maghribiyya, 1981.

Al-Wāqidī (d. 823). *Futūḥ al-shām*. Ed. 'Abd al-Laṭīf 'Abd al-Raḥmān. 2 vols. Beirut: Dār al-Kutub al-'Ilmiyya, 1997.

Wasserstein, David J. *The Rise and Fall of the Party Kings: Politics and Society in Islamic Spain, 1002–1086*. Princeton: Princeton University Press, 1986.

Wissowa, Georg. *Paulys Real-Encyclopädie der classischen Altertumswissenschaft*. Stuttgart: J. B. Metzler, 1896.

Wolf, Kenneth B. *Conquerors and Chroniclers of Early Medieval Spain*. Liverpool: Liverpool University Press, 1990.

Al-Ya'qūbī (d. 897). *Kitāb al-Buldān (Kitābo'l-Boldān)*. Ed. T.G.J. Juynboll. Leiden: Brill, 1861.

Yāqūt al-Ḥamawī (d. 1229). *Mu'jam al-buldān*. 5 vols. Beirut: Dār Ṣādir, 1977.

Yusuf, Abdullah Ali. *The Holy Qur'ān: Text, Translation, and Commentary*. New York: Hafner, 1946.

Yver, Georges. "Al-Maghrib." In *EI*², 5:1183.
Zadeh, Travis. *Mapping Frontiers Across Medieval Islam: Geography, Translation, and the 'Abbāsid Empire*. London: I.B. Tauris, 2011.
Zaghrūt, Fatḥī. *Al-'alāqāt bayna al-umawiyīn wa-al-fāṭimiyīn fī al-andalus wa-al-shamāl al-ifrīqī, 300 H–350 H*. Cairo: Dār al-Tawzī' wa-al-Nashr al-Islāmiyya, 2006.
Zeiller, Jacques. "Un historien de l'Afrique du nord; Ernest Mercier." *Journal des Savants* 3, no. 1 (1945): 166–70.

Index